HAVANA

BEYOND THE RUINS

HAVANA

BEYOND THE RUINS

Cultural Mappings after 1989

ANKE BIRKENMAIER AND

ESTHER WHITFIELD, EDITORS

Duke University Press
Durham and London
2011

© 2011 DUKE UNIVERSITY PRESS

All rights reserved. Printed in the United

States of America on acid-free paper ∞

Designed by Amy Ruth Buchanan

Typeset in Minion by Keystone Typesetting, Inc.

Library of Congress Cataloging-in-Publication Data

appear on the last printed page of this book.

CONTENTS

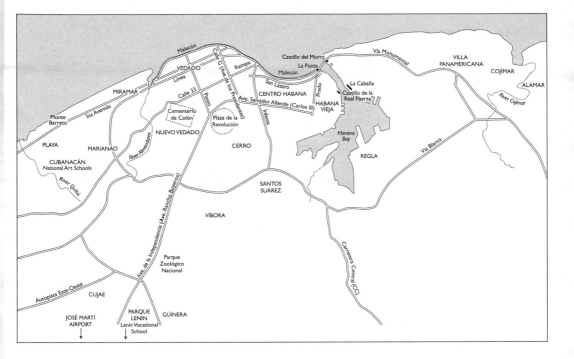

Map of Havana.

DESIGNED BY BILL NELSON.

PREFACE

This collection had its origin in a double panel at the Latin American Studies Association Conference in Montreal in September 2007. We would like to thank the panelists and those who attended the two sessions for engaging in a productive discussion and giving us the impetus for this book in the first place. Since then, we have received assistance from many individuals and institutions. Our thanks go to the two reviewers of this book, Isabel Álvarez-Borland and César Salgado, for their support and helpful suggestions; to Reynolds Smith and Valerie Millholland, our editors at Duke University Press; and to Sharon Torian, Rebecca Fowler, and Gisela Fosado, also at Duke.

We are grateful for a translation grant from Columbia University's Institute of Latin American Studies, under the leadership of Pablo Piccato and Tom Trebat, that paid for Elisabeth Enenbach's and Eric Barkin's wonderful translation work. Many thanks go to Pedro Valero Puente for crafting and researching the glossary, as well as to Bill Nelson for the map of Havana.

For encouragement at crucial moments, Anke Birkenmaier wishes to thank Laura Redruello, Rafael Rojas, Gustavo Pérez Firmat, and Viviane Mahieux.

Esther Whitfield would like to thank Rey Chow, Adrián López Dénis, and Caridad Tamayo for their advice and conversation.

The following contributions were published originally in Spanish, and we gratefully acknowledge the authors' permission to translate and publish them here: Emma Álvarez-Tabío Albo's chapter was published in Spanish as "La ciudad en el aire" in Iván de la Nuez's anthology *Cuba y el día después: Doce ensayistas nacidos con la revolución imaginan el futuro* (Barcelona: Mondadori, Reservoir Books, 2001). A first, abridged version of Mario Coyula's "El trinquenio amargo" appeared in *Diseño y Sociedad* (Universidad Autónoma Metropolitana–Xochimilco) 21 (otoño 2006): 26–35. The entire lecture was originally published in the anthology *La política cultural de la Revolución: memoria y reflexión. Primera parte*, edited by Eduardo Heras León and Desiderio Navarro (Havana: Centro Teórico-Cultural Criterios, 2007), 47–68. Margarita Zamora and Francisco Scarano also published Coyula's lecture in Spanish in their anthology *CUBA: Contrapuntos de cultura y sociedad* (San Juan: Ediciones Callejón, 2007). Parts of Rafael Rojas's chapter for this volume were originally published in *El estante vacío: Literatura y política en Cuba* (Barcelona: Anagrama, 2009). Antonio José Ponte's chapter was published online in Spanish as "La Habana: Ciudad y archivo" at the Cuban Research Institute's CubaInfo website, http://cubainfo.fiu.edu. Finally, José Quiroga's "Daiquirís amargos (crónica de cristal)" was previously pulished in *La Habana Elegante* 21 (Fall 2000), http://www.habanaelegante.com.

This book is divided into three parts. Chapters in the first part, "Mapping Havana: Citizenship and the City," explore different historical and theoretical perspectives on the city, how it has evolved as a symbolic site, how new groups of actors have emerged, and what kind of future they envision.

Cecilia Bobes's "Visits to a Non-Place: Havana and Its Representation(s)" analyzes the city as a place where the divisions between the private and the public, inside and outside, before and after, have been reconfigured repeatedly since 1959. According to Bobes, all major events in Cuban history since the revolution have been echoed by a change in attitude toward the capital: after 1959 rural development was emphasized over that of the capital, increasingly so after 1971; in the 1980s, the city was retaken by the younger generation of students and professionals; and finally, in the 1990s, it turned into a virtual city, a "non-place" or a "memory city" without a civic public space, where tourism and the advertising industry have become dominant.

Mario Coyula's "The Bitter Trinquennium and the Dystopic City: Autopsy of a Utopia" critically revisits the "gray" period of the 1970s, when Cuba became entrenched in conspiracy theories and bureaucratic maneuvering that led to the deposition and silencing of many writers and artists. Coyula draws the institutional history of architecture as a discipline that suffered a climate of intolerance for at least fifteen years and shows Cuban architecture of the revolution as a history of failures due in part to moral issues. He views the globalizing trends in the architecture of the 1980s and 1990s as a chance to develop a stronger sense of place, yet also notes a deterioration of civic culture. According to Coyula, without revisiting the "bitter" years of 1968–1983, more recent renovations and local initiatives to foment citizen participation cannot be understood.

Patricio del Real and Joseph Scarpaci's chapter analyzes the informal constructions in Havana's colonial houses known as *barbacoas,* or mezzanine platforms, as spaces where citizens participate in the transformation of the city. According to the authors, these barbacoas testify to the population's initiative and a creative use of inherited structures. They argue that barbacoas are a phenomenon that should not be condemned as such but that the government could channel better, in order to avoid putting entire buildings at risk. Even though the building of barbacoas increased in the 1990s, the authors tell of a much longer history of barbacoas and social housing in Havana. They end by associating the vertical growth within Havana housing with the "new frontier" theory in the nineteenth-century United States, where it was the initiative of individuals settling in new terrains in the West that helped create what came to be a characteristic culture of independent small-scale enterprises.

Jill Hamberg's chapter, "The 'Slums' of Havana," asks how Havana's present-day slum dwellings compare to Havana's shantytowns before 1959 and also to those of other Latin American cities. Based on her extensive research into recent definitions of slums and into statistics and publications on living conditions in different areas of Havana, Hamberg demonstrates that there is indeed much substandard housing in Havana, and that there is, at least since the 1990s, a modest trend toward racial resegregation. However, she argues that the percentage of slum dwellers in Havana is considerably lower than in the rest of Latin America, and that in newly renovated areas like Old Havana, gentrification has been avoided. Hamberg speaks of a race against time to save crumbling inner-city slums and hopes for continued citizen participation in the efforts.

In his chapter, the late Nicolás Quintana, a Cuban architect who lived and taught in Venezuela, Puerto Rico, and Miami, develops a large-scale vision for Havana that summarizes his project developed at Florida International University, "Havana and Its Landscapes." Like Coyula, Quintana notes the necessity of developing the city so that it continues to express Cuban culture. He insists on an urban plan for developing the city once greater investments are possible. The "paradigmatic city" conceived by Quintana and his team relies on the traditional grid system and on the notion that Havana needs to be better articulated around the bay. The main problems faced by Havana—overcrowding, decrepit infrastructure and public transport, isolated foreign developments—can be solved only using "internal and external experience" and avoiding nostalgic replications of the past as well as futuristic abstraction.

Rafael Rojas's contribution, "The Illegible City: Havana after the Messiah" situates its literary readings on the cusp of three transitions—from the colony to the republic, the republic to the revolution, and the revolution to whatever now lies ahead—to ask, via Giorgio Agamben, how and whether a notion of historical time might return in the aftermath of the Cuban Revolution. Rojas believes that the protagonist role of the city in the literature of the 1990s is due to the unresolved tension between the desire to move on and the fiction of a continuing socialist society. For Rojas, the weakening of the socialist model of citizenship has manifested itself most recently in the new "urban tribes"— youths identifying with the gothic, rasta, or other global movements, gathering in certain areas of El Vedado and on the Malecón. Rojas argues that their lifestyle preferences are the result of the cultural impact of globalization as well as of the will to form alternative communities in Cuba.

Between the first two parts of this edited volume is a photo-essay that records a range of moments, places, and paradoxes in today's Havana. Some images mark details of the city's rich but precarious architectural stock, tracing its curves, patterns, reflections, and scaffolds. Others photographs note an uneven culture of monument making that can move between Che Guevara, John Lennon, and a Russian Orthodox church. Another image catches a skateboarder in midflight and a photographer in the middle of capturing an image. The photo-essay is the work of Orlando Luis Pardo Lazo, a writer and blogger whose "Boring Home Utopics" project, where Cubans abroad request shots of the city that Pardo Lazo then photographs and posts on a blog, has expanded the scope of the photographed city as well as the notion of exile.

The second part is entitled "Havana's Shifting Margins" and addresses how changing political, racial, and socioeconomic circumstances have affected urban planning in Havana.

In her chapter "The City in Midair," Emma Álvarez-Tabío Albo offers a poignant firsthand account of the architectural movement of the 1980s in Cuba, whose products she characterizes as an "architecture of paper," beautiful in its presentation and the craftsmanship of its drawings but condemned to inaction. The ongoing renovation of Old Havana and these architecture initiatives of the 1980s marked a departure from the previous inaction with respect to Havana and contributed significantly to the sense of a "citizen decade," fostered by different types of creative public interventions in the urban space. In the 1990s, according to Álvarez-Tabío Albo, this coherent urban vision lost its contours as new urban policies began to be implemented and new investors appeared, due to the crisis. For Álvarez-Tabío Albo, the city ceased to be legible; it is now "in midair," a phenomenon illustrated in the dark fiction of Pedro Juan Gutiérrez.

Sujatha Fernandes's "Made in Havana City" offers us a window into the complex relationship between racial identity, urban public space, and cultural politics. Fernandes places the rap movement of the 1980s and 1990s in the context of the Special Period and its rising racial inequalities, called by some a "tourist apartheid"—a period when *jineterismo* (hustling) becomes a strategy to raise oneself up. For the 1990s Fernandes sees new transnational spaces for rappers, some tour abroad or receive foreign artists and many finally choose exile to pursue their careers, with mixed success. As Fernandes points out, the spaces of the city have continued to provide cohesion for an increasingly dispersed movement as well as a means of entry into a competitive music industry.

Cecelia Lawless's chapter "Urban Performance Pieces in Fragmented Form" presents a reading of the interiors of Havana, as seen through her personal experience as a visitor and through the fictions of two prominent writers of the 1990s in Cuba, Pedro Juan Gutiérrez and Antonio José Ponte. Lawless uses Giuliana Bruno's notion of architexture, as the sensuous fabric of intimate space, to analyze the ruinous buildings of Old Havana and Centro Havana. Lawless shows how both Ponte and Gutiérrez emphasize the lesser-known or invisible places of Havana, the private dwellings of its residents, and the life behind crumbling façades. In her reading, these lives are performances of the everyday liminal period in which habaneros live during the 1990s, constantly threatened by the ongoing decay of their homes. She shows thus an architexture in motion and the challenge implied by it for peoples' sense of home.

Jacqueline Loss's contribution addresses the phenomenon of Ostalgie, of nostalgia for Cuba's past association with the Soviet Union, by discussing the distorted memory of important moments in Cuba's relation with the Soviet Union. A recent exhibit in Centro Havana, *Vostok*, and the documentary film *Existen* demonstrate how young artists in Havana use the public spaces of the city and its most marginalized citizens, a number of deranged people living on the streets there, to reconstruct a phantasmagorical topography of Cuba's experience during its close association with the Soviet Union. These artists visualize a Soviet Havana plagued by schizophrenia, suggesting a new imaginary topography of the city. They critically reread the past and deserve to be included in the ongoing discussion of the so-called gray period of the 1970s, as presented by Mario Coyula.

Laura Redruello in "Touring Havana in the Work of Ronaldo Menéndez" compares the Aristotelian notion of the polis as the art of community life to Cuban writer Ronaldo Menéndez's assessments of urban life in several novels. Three of Menéndez's novels depict three important moments in Havana that roughly coincide with the decades of the 1980s, the 1990s, and the 2000s. For

Redruello, like for Bobes, there is a sea change between the 1980s and the 1990s, when the city turns from a space of artistic and political intervention into a marketplace. While in the 1980s performance artists appropriate urban spaces to express the sometimes disenchanted experience of their generation, in the 1990s public spaces become commercialized. In the 2000s, finally, the mercantile city disappears, leaving barbarism in its wake, where the word itself has lost its currency.

Our Coda, finally, presents Antonio José Ponte's chapter, "La Habana: City and Archive." Ponte takes Cicero's parable on Scopas's dinner, where a poet restores the memory of a collapsed house and its illustrious dinner guests by associating visual and discursive recollections, as a metaphor of the Cuban "house of memory." Ponte worries about the philosophy of the restoration of Old Havana, in particular about what he calls "false monuments" that are not representative of Havana's culture. He also denounces what he considers the clearing out of the old city for possible future inhabitants and argues that the greatest task ahead will be the reconstruction not only of the city but of a community of citizens divided by years of vigilance and secret archives.

José Quiroga's "Bitter Daiquiris—A Crystal Chronicle" tells of his first visit to Havana in 2000 as a Cuban born in Havana and raised in Puerto Rico, but with memories of the city only from hearsay or pictures. He chronicles a sense of unreality where his own divided feelings about being a Cuban and a foreigner are steeped in the atmosphere of a city selling nostalgia, returning to a middle-class aesthetic of lovable kitsch, and he evokes the gap between the grandeur of the past and the squalor of the objects to which it is tied. In a fitting conclusion to this edited volume on Havana's present and future, Quiroga turns his attention not to how the city is lived but to how it is imagined. Forgetting, he insists, is as constitutive of the experience of Havana as is memory: both allow for the invention of not one but many Havanas.

Beyond the Ruins

ANKE BIRKENMAIER AND ESTHER WHITFIELD

Havana, the twenty-first-century city that is home to over two million people and has captured the imagination of countless others, seems to stand at the brink of a new era. The impulse to read a city of rich and varied physical spaces from a temporal perspective is perhaps inevitable in the once utopian context of the Cuban Revolution, where history—as a past to be undone and a future to be built—weighs heavily. It is certainly through its relationship to time that many of the contributions in this edited volume read Havana; and in doing so they prise open what José Quiroga has called a palimpsestic city, one whose different temporal, structural, and social layers allow one city to live as many.

Havana's architecture corresponds broadly to the three political orders that have governed Cuba: the Spanish colonial order, from the city's founding in the sixteenth century to the end of the nineteenth; the Republican period of 1902–1958, a relatively short period but responsible for most of the city's buildings and public spaces; and the revolutionary period, 1959 to the present. Rafael Rojas, in this edited volume, reads not from the heyday of these periods but from their moments of crisis—their transition from political utopia to urban heterotopia, in the terms of Manuel Cruz—to position Havana, its spaces, and its inhabitants as always subject to spectacular change. In choosing to focus on Havana after 1989, we are foregrounding an accumulation of crises and transitions; an accumulation, that is, of pasts to be interrogated and futures open to question. Indeed, the legacy of many pasts makes itself felt in these chapters: through the restored colonial spaces of Old Havana that for Emma Álvarez-Tabío Albo are to be mined for their meaning to the present and that Antonio José Ponte critiques eloquently; and through the achievements and excesses of the republican city that was for decades subdued but is now reemerging, as Velia Cecilia Bobes says, not only in reinvigorated hotels but also in cultural practices and the ornamentation of private dwellings.

Havana's most recent past, or its most recently closed chapter, is one that bears particular importance for this collection. The period of close Cuban and Soviet relations and particularly the decade of the 1980s linger in subsequent decades in various ways. Laura Redruello reads in the fiction of Ronaldo Menéndez a decade of contention where art occupied public spaces and artists openly renegotiated their relationship to the state. Sujatha Fernandes sees in this same decade of public art the beginnings of a discourse of exclusion, social and spatial, articulated by a now transnational hip-hop movement. But to read post-Soviet Cubans' recollection of the 1980s as nostalgic would be to simplify the intricate ways in which people relate to a political past, as Jacqueline Loss and Emma Álvarez-Tabío Albo explore.

It was as an architect practicing in Havana during the 1980s that Álvarez-Tabío Albo, now a resident of Spain, recognized the importance of understanding and living the past of the city's homes and buildings. Only through such understanding, she wrote in *Vida, mansión y muerte de la burguesía cubana*, will Havana cease to be a museum piece and instead become "an authentic meeting space for different generations," leading to a modern architecture suited to its inhabitants' lives and needs (Álvarez-Tabío Albo 1989, 31). After decades of neglecting the capital city, a new generation of architects and urban planners practicing in the 1980s sought to define the potential social importance of a housing stock inherited from the colonial and republican eras. While Cuban writers such as Alejo Carpentier, José Lezama Lima, or Guillermo Cabrera Infante had glorified a Havana associated with a neoclassical grandeur and glamour that reached into their own present time, in the 1980s, architects, writers, and artists took note of the gap that had arisen between a city that had aged but fundamentally remained the same and a society that defined itself as revolutionary. Socialist housing in Havana had not produced great changes in the city, as most efforts had been concentrated on developing new projects in the countryside and in Havana's suburbs.[1] Also, in 1982 the historic center of Havana, La Habana Vieja or Old Havana, had been declared a UNESCO World Heritage Site, and the Office of the City Historian of Havana, Eusebio Leal Spengler, designed a vast plan of renovations that were well under way by the end of the 1980s. Old Havana came alive again with festivals that celebrated the founding date of the city, street activities of artists, and new bars and restaurants. In 1984, the Ley General de la Vivienda (General Housing Law) allowed longtime residents of an apartment to become homeowners, even though they could not sell it. It produced incentives to better maintain apartments and created a new sense of belonging.

The end of the decade then took on several meanings. On the one hand, the fall of the Berlin Wall in 1989 brought hope to many that in Cuba, and specifically in Havana, the trend toward reforms and renovations was going to continue. On the other hand, however, the political and economic crisis that set in with the severing of Soviet ties to Cuba had as a consequence the premature termination of many innovative projects and the limiting of renovation efforts to Old Havana. In 1990 the Cuban government announced a series of austerity measures, termed the Special Period in Times of Peace. As one way of rebuilding the economy, tourism was encouraged, hotels were renovated, and privately owned rentals and restaurants were permitted. Havana was the city that profited most from the ensuing boom in foreign visitors to the country, drawing tourists from Europe, the Americas, and beyond. With the exception of Old Havana and the Malecón, however, the city continued to decay, a situation that was aggravated by the influx of Cubans from the provinces who came in the hopes of finding work in Havana's tourist sector. As Jill Hamberg shows in her chapter, the overpopulation of Havana became a nagging concern of urban planners in the 1990s, a trend that led to a new migration law in 1997.

Nevertheless, Álvarez-Tabío Albo recalls the 1980s as Havana's "citizen decade," a time in which the city took center stage as a character rather than a backdrop, and its inhabitants—particularly its architects and artists—began to participate in new ways in urban life. Today, as the question of citizenship is at the forefront of contexts both theoretical and very real, we might ask what it means for Cuba's "citizen decade" to have come to a close. The question is an urgent one for the future of Havana and for many of the contributions to this edited volume. Some writers, like Ronaldo Menéndez, whose twenty-first-century city Laura Redruello sees as "bestial" and "Hobbesian," imagine Havana's future as the disintegration of social, as well as physical, structures; an image perpetuated in Antonio José Ponte's explorations, in this book and elsewhere, of a city abandoned to its last ghostly survivor. Other contributors, particularly those from the fields of architecture and urbanism, think concretely about how to rebuild Havana in the aftermath of its current experience, with visions that are nevertheless not too distant from the inventive readings of authors like Ponte. Nicolás Quintana and participants in his "Havana and Its Landscapes" project hope for a future city that preserves the best of its past, combining the old and the new in ways enriched by the experience of Cubans on the island and in exile; while Patricio del Real and Joseph Scarpaci present city dwellers' construction of *barbacoas*, mezzanine-like structures that create new space within already existing homes, as an important way in which Havana's inhabitants continue to play an active role in creating their city.

Between the legacy of its layered pasts and the expansive possibilities for its future, the city of Havana seems at present suspended in time. This is certainly how a booming tourist industry portrays it; and, indeed, what Havana is, or what it is becoming, is open to question for its inhabitants and its observers. The post-Soviet present continues to be a time of dramatic change and intense uncertainty. For writers and artists who have produced a myriad of films, short stories, books, and artwork about the city, it is Havana that best symbolizes this uncertainty. The boom in literary, visual, and musical representations of Cuba and particularly of Havana's ruins has a variety of causes (Whitfield 2008, 127–55). The complexity of the imaginary topographies of Havana represented in those works has been ever growing.

As travelers flowed into the city and admired its newly renovated colonial center, they could not be blind to the dilapidation of surrounding areas. Armchair visitors to the city, too, were drawn to this vision of decay, and were encouraged by popular circulating images of the city—the film *Buena Vista Social Club* (1999) being just the most successful example—to read Havana's ruins allegorically: architectural decay signaled the inevitable decline of Cuba's socialist project. This aesthetic and ideological representation has been challenged from different sides. On behalf of the Cuban government, city planners have worked to extend the renovations to some affected areas such as the Malecón sea front, although these areas do not fall within the boundaries of the UNESCO-protected city. Ruined buildings have been torn down to make space for new hotels, public squares, or museums. For their part, several essayists, filmmakers, and writers have moved literally inside the ruins to show some of the very concrete problems that the inhabitants of Havana are facing when living in buildings that have become hazardous; to contest, that is, representations that fail to look beyond the city's façades. A few state-level initiatives have helped inhabitants remedy the problems that they experience within their apartments and houses, although most financing for repairs relies on the black market and on materials collected from irreversibly ruined houses to better those that are still standing. Through informal constructions such as barbacoas, Havana has grown to accommodate constant migration from rural areas of Cuba and, as del Real, Scarpaci, and Coyula explore, new actors and new investors have begun to work on changing the interior of the city. But they have not always done so without putting at further risk buildings that stood in need of renovation long before and exacerbating what Ponte, in his well-known short story "A Knack for Making Ruins," casts as a battle between "tugurization," or overpopulation, and the "miraculous statics" of buildings that remain standing in defiance of what is structurally possible (Ponte 2002, 21–44). That themes from this fantastic story— overcrowding, illegal construction, community, spaces more imagined than real—repeat themselves in the chapters of this edited volume is a testament to the creativity inherent in writing, reading, and rebuilding as complex a city as Havana.

This book surveys contemporary discussions about Havana and its urban development considering the Cuban capital's symbolic significance in and outside the country. Through its individual contributions, the book explores how the city has been experienced and read by its inhabitants, all the while taking stock of how intricate, subjective, and volatile a process reading is. Indeed, it is Havana's illegibility that both Rojas and Álvarez-Tabío Albo highlight, confronting the difficulty of tracing a single or coherent narrative for the many Havanas that have manifested themselves historically, socially, economically, and culturally.

In spite of a growing list of publications on Havana's recent and not so recent past, there is a lack of discussion about the 1990s and the time after, when the worst economic crisis was over. Several publications have surveyed the cultural history of the capital city, but they end usually with the Special Period of the 1990s (see Scarpaci, Segre, and Coyula 2002; Kapcia 2005; Estrada 2007; Cluster and Hernández 2006). Also, books generally focus on Havana's housing and infrastructure, but they do not really account for the way in which it is creatively used. A number of photographic and architectural guides on Havana published since the early 1990s present many aspects of Havana's architectural patrimony, renovated or in ruins (see Noval 2004; Fagiuoli 2003; Moore 2002; Polidori 2001; Rodríguez 1998 and 2000), yet these factual accounts cannot account for the contradicting visions of Havana that have been formulated by architects, artists, film directors, and writers alike. New Cuba "readers" have surveyed Havana from an area studies perspective where economics, politics, literature, and the arts are juxtaposed (Ryan 1997; Smorkaloff 2003; Brenner, Jiménez, Kirk, and Leo Grande 2008; Henken 2008). We have found that in important aspects those who write about Havana do not agree on the history, the priorities, and the new actors of the city, and we aim to draw attention to the difficulties inherent in understanding the challenges facing the Cuban capital and its inhabitants.

We take 1989 as our departure point because the breathtaking events in the Soviet Union and Eastern Europe mark not only the beginning of Cuba's reinsertion into the world economy—the opening up to tourism and an ever increasing flow of remittances to the country—but also an ideological redrawing of boundaries. As frontiers were being undone in Eastern Europe, and the European Union extended its domain considerably, in Cuba the limits of *cubanía* were being rethought and the idea of a common culture of "Greater Cuba," with hubs not only in Havana and Miami but also in other European, Latin American, and U.S. cities, was being articulated. In the arts, the Havana biennials had begun in the late 1980s to become forums of exchange for Cuban artists and art dealers from all over the world. Jesús Díaz founded the literary journal *Encuentro de la cultura cubana* in Madrid in 1996 to create a platform, away from the politicized hotspots of Havana and Miami, for Cubans everywhere to share a sense of common history and identity. Such efforts did not fully alleviate Cubans' sense of isolation and despair, however, and the large-scale emigration that had begun with the boat lift of Mariel in 1980 continued in renewed waves through the 1990s, including the emigration of the young architects, writers, and artists who had initiated much discussion on the modernization of the Cuban Revolution. But despite the tightening of government control after 2000 (the year of the Elián González affair and the beginning of the so-called Battle of Ideas) there persisted, thanks also to a burgeoning e-mail and blogosphere, a sense of a transnational Cuban community that continued to interact beyond governmental decision making. Havana was the city most visibly affected by migration and the increased influx of tourists. Our focus on the capital city intends to offer a model of how Cubans are negotiating the dramatic changes that have affected them and their dwellings. To read Havana in this sense means to measure the complexity of the web of social relations and common "lieux de mémoire," in the words of Pierre Nora, that exceed the domain of institutions and public discourses, yet define Cubans today as a civic community, if only by virtue of their creative imagination.

Havana beyond the Ruins introduces, from various perspectives, some of the principal questions about Havana that have been raised in and outside the city since 1989. Given the city's debated legibility, we do not offer conclusions about its future, nor about that of Cuba as a nation. Rather, we invite our readers to consider how Havana might be understood as an urban space that embodies some of the major economic, political, and ideological challenges to Cuba's hesitant renegotiation of its place in the world.

Two lines of thought have guided our selection of contributions. Not unlike other Latin American cities, Havana has been made in the 1990s into the image of a modern cosmopolitan city, a trading place for international visitors and joint ventures and a city with problems similar to those of other growing world capitals, such as poor housing and increasing social and racial inequalities. In spite of these similarities, however, we believe that the mechanisms of cultural memory, as they have been put in place in Havana, have particularities that need to be taken into account. In contrast to Latin American cities such as São Paulo, Mexico City, Buenos Aires, or Lima, which grew exponentially in the second half of the twentieth century, Havana's population has since the revolution of 1959 slightly decreased, and even in the 1990s the city did not grow or change substantially, apart from the new hotel constructions and service areas that were added in Old Havana and to the west of the city. It is thus the same "text" that architects, writers, and artists alike are debating in the 1950s through the 2000s, and the ways in which they choose to inhabit the city's squares, parks, streets, and dwellings are related by necessity to earlier or different public and private uses of Havana. We have encouraged comparative approaches that further analyze the degree to which Havana presents a historically unique challenge, and how, if at all, the comparison with other modern capitals can further a productive approach to resolving the city's most urgent problems.

We also have encouraged social scientists to look at literary representations of Havana, and literary and film scholars to consider the significance of their analyses for the current discussion on urban development in Havana. This interdisciplinary approach allows us to offer an urban semiotics of Havana, showing in a series of analyses the ways in which Havana's social and urban plight has been inscribed in the texts of its artists, writers, musicians, and film directors just as much as in the existing statistics, laws, and master plans. It also allows us to establish a forum for urbanists, architects, historians, and cultural critics alike to assess the ideologies and fantasies implicit in urban planning and renovation efforts in Havana on the part of its citizens and its city agencies. Precisely because many architectural projects—from the National Art Schools of the early 1960s to the plans of the 1980s generation of architects—could not be realized or finished in Cuba, the connections between fiction and urban planning have grown especially close since 1989. In the visual arts, Carlos Garaicoa's projections and manipulations of Havana's buildings and also the drawings of architect Francisco Bedoya, beautiful and extremely detailed pictures of the historic buildings and squares of Havana, are impressive testimonies to the imagination and reconstruction of spaces in

Havana.[2] As our contributors show, the literature, films, and popular music of Havana in the 1990s and later are replete with references to the reconstruction of the city. We believe that the study of urban planning alongside the texts, film, and other cultural manifestations in and about Havana can inspire new insights into the workings of Cuban culture today.

This edited volume has its origins in our realization that the changing shape and urban future of Havana have raised interest among scholars in the humanities and the social sciences, as well as architects and urbanists, but, at the same time, there have been few forums for dialogue between these different groups. We have therefore invited some of the most distinguished scholars and architects working on Cuba to present how they perceive the capital city and the ways in which it has changed since 1989. Many prominent figures involved in the debate on Havana of recent years are assembled in this edited volume: Emma Álvarez-Tabío Albo, the architect who initiated discussion about the contemporary creative use of Havana's prerevolutionary structures, synthesizes her view of Havana in the 1980s;[3] Mario Coyula, the architectural director of Havana's Group for Integral Development who has been a central participant in the city's restoration, revisits the architectural movement in Havana in an important chapter published here for the first time in English;[4] Antonio José Ponte, the writer and essayist who became recognized as the "ruinologist" of Havana and whose short stories and essays have provoked much debate, has developed his thoughts on memory and the city in his chapter;[5] José Quiroga, whose *Cuban Palimpsests* has inspired our own perspective on the city as text, offers a chronicle of his first visit to Havana in the 1990s; Cecilia Bobes, Rafael Rojas, Nicolás Quintana, Joseph Scarpaci, and Jill Hamberg are among the most highly regarded analysts of Cuban culture and architecture in the present, and all have made important contributions to the field; Laura Redruello, Jacqueline Loss, Cecelia Lawless, Sujatha Fernandes, and Patricio del Real represent new currents in the study of Cuban popular culture and informal architecture.

We have attempted to equally represent authors favorable to the current urban renovation efforts in Havana and authors who are critical of them, and we have included Cuban scholars from the island and from outside, as well as scholars from the United States. Consequently, there is at times a polemical relationship between the contributions. The renovation of Old Havana, the city's colonial core, is a principal focus of disagreement. Ponte, for example, criticizes the renovations for turning Havana into a "theme park" that privileges museums and monuments over preserving residential housing, whereas Scarpaci and del Real focus on the initiatives of the area's individual residents who, while the public spaces around them are meticulously rehabilitated, draw from minimal budgets to creatively adapt and enlarge their private homes. Similarly, several Cubans now living outside the country—Quintana, Ponte, and Álvarez-Tabío Albo—criticize the marketing of Havana's dilapidated buildings to foreigners and propose strategies for a careful restructuring and rebuilding more appropriate to the needs of the city's present and future inhabitants. Coyula, on the other hand, locates the problems with current renovation projects in deregulation and a building boom financed with money from foreign investors or through remittances. As is evident from these examples, we consider these divergences complementary rather than contradictory, even if their tone is a contentious one at times.

Our authors also share many concerns. Several, in particular the architects Quintana and Coyula, fear that in the probably imminent frenzy of new construction little concern will be left for architecture that is meaningful to its residents but of negligible economic value, and they insist that there be a comprehensive and farsighted urban plan to steer and check innovation. Several architectural critics have called attention to the need to maintain the modernist constructions that make up the bulk of Vedado, Nuevo Vedado, Marianao, La Víbora and Cerro neighborhoods, just as much as Havana's colonial housing stock.[6] Construction from the period after 1959 is cause for concern, partly because little advance thought seems to have been given to how recent, foreign-financed buildings, new hotels in particular, would be integrated with the city more broadly and partly because the revolutionary regime's early architectural endeavors, in the years following the abandonment of the National Art Schools, have come to demarcate the city economically and racially, as well as physically.[7] Relative to the previous fifty years, little was built in the post-1959 period, but what construction did occur tended to emulate Soviet architectural models. As Fernandes's chapter shows, the Soviet-style Alamar housing complex, built in the 1970s and located at the geographic margins of the city, was the birthplace of a hip-hop movement that asked urgent questions about racial and economic marginality. A further division between the capital city and the rest of Cuba has been implied, as Bobes outlines, since the early political discourse of the revolution, in which the capital was cast as the seat of bourgeois injustice and the countryside as authentically revolutionary—terms that are less relevant today, as Havana becomes the motor of a new state-driven market economy. Similarly, Hamberg explores areas of Havana that can be described as slums and the initiatives that have originated there in the 1980s and the 1990s that are specific to the capital city.

Rather than its opposite, Havana's onetime "other," Miami, is now regarded by several of our contributors as its twin. In Bobes's words, for example, Miami is Havana's "mirror city." Movement between Cuba and the United States during the post-Soviet period, most markedly during the rafter exodus of August and September 1994 when over thirty thousand Cubans took to the sea on makeshift vessels, has been constant and two-way, to the extent allowed by the stringent migration laws of both countries. While permanent migration has been almost exclusively from Cuba to the United States, with Southern Florida as the destination of most Cubans, family members and their money have been able to travel in the opposite direction; indeed, for much of this period, remittances have been one of Cuba's most important sources of hard currency. As a result of this fraught proximity between the two cities—divided, as many have noted, by only ninety miles of sea but vast ideological difference—Havana's fashions, both cultural and architectural, draw increasingly from Miami. Álvarez-Tabío Albo and Coyula comment on the new culture of adornment that has been imported from Miami to Havana's homes, and Bobes regards the revival of 1950s practices, like the elaborate celebration of girls' fifteenth birthdays (*quinceañeras*), as directly influenced by Miami.

The transition of Cuba toward a new society and a new political system has been widely expected after the handing over of government from Fidel Castro to his brother Raúl in July 2006 and even more importantly, after Fidel Castro ceded his seat as Cuba's president to his brother in February 2008. It remains unclear where this transition is headed, who will be its protagonists, and how long it will take. It is the thesis of this book that the capital city itself and its new architects and citizens, in the broadest sense, will play a central role in Cuba's future. Many decisive economic and social transformations occurred during the 1990s, but in order to understand Cuba's future course it will be crucial to better understand the ways in which citizens living in and outside of Cuba have attempted to negotiate their participation in those processes. The years since 1989, even though they were marked at first by the economic crisis and then by an increasing sense of political and economic stagnation, have also been years of intensified contacts and solidarity among resident and nonresident Cubans and of the growing acceptance of diasporic identities and international cooperation.[8] The chapters of this book give an appreciation of the potential inherent in these changes that have affected the way in which the city was viewed with new eyes by foreign tourists and spectators and also how Havana's citizens themselves began to reflect on the meanings of place in a transnational context.

Notes

1. For a comprehensive account of socialist housing in Havana, see Scarpaci, Segre, and Coyula (2002, 196–234).

2. Garaicoa's work has appeared in many single and collective exhibits. See, most notably, his catalogue *Carlos Garaicoa: La ruina, la utopía* (2000), edited by José Ignacio Roca, and his contribution to *Inside/Outside: Contemporary Cuban Art* (2003). Francisco Bedoya's drawings were published recently in *La Habana desaparecida* (2009), edited by Emma Álvarez-Tabío Albo.

3. In addition to her essay "La ciudad en el aire" (Álvarez-Tabío Albo 2001), translated here for the first time into English, Álvarez-Tabío Albo's book *Invención de La Habana* (2000) presents an analysis of the literary imagination of Havana by major Cuban writers.

4. Coyula has published numerous essays and books about the ongoing renovation efforts and discussions on Havana (see Scarpaci, Segre, and Coyula 2002), and in 2009 he coordinated a special issue on Havana for *Revista Temas* (volume 58).

5. Ponte's book on Havana, *La fiesta vigilada,* was published in 2007, and before that he published two controversial articles: "Una catedral rusa en La Habana" (2006) and "La Habana está por inventarse" (2007) that provoked responses both anonymous and from participants in the ongoing renovation of Old Havana. The ensuing exchange was published in *Encuentro en la red*, and a reply by Ponte appeared in the summer 2007 issue of the online journal *La Habana Elegante*.

6. Eduardo Luis Rodríguez (2000) in his *The Havana Guide: Modern Architecture, 1925–1965* surveys modern architecture in Havana. His Spanish-language publication *La Habana: Arquitectura del siglo XX* (1998) includes an annex titled "Saving the Legacy of the Twentieth Century," where he details the premises for maintaining Havana's modern architecture.

7. For an account of the conception and eventual abandonment, on ideological grounds, of Havana's National Art Schools, see John Loomis (1999).

8. Several collaborative art shows have attested to these intensified contacts, especially in the art world, between Cuba and the United States. See, for example, the 2007 exhibit in New York *Killing Time*, a show of Cuban art of the 1980s and 1990s, co-curated by Elvis Fuentes, Yuneikys Villalonga, and Glexis Novoa, and analyzed by Anke Birkenmaier (2009). The exhibit in Montreal *¡Cuba! Art and History from 1868–Today* (2008) featured for the first time art from the Cuban Museo Nacional de Bellas Artes as well as from museums and collectors in the United States. Finally, the exhibit *Cuban Artists' Books and Prints / Libros y grabados de artistas cubanos 1985–2008* (2009), curated by Linda S. Howe, also presented artists' books and drawings from Cuba in the United States. The three exhibits have produced important catalogues (Fuentes, Villalonga, Novoa 2007; Bondil 2008; Howe, 2009).

PART I

MAPPING HAVANA:

CITIZENSHIP AND

THE CITY

Visits to a Non-Place:
Havana and Its Representation(s)

VELIA CECILIA BOBES

Translated by Elisabeth Enenbach

If the notion of a city first implies the idea of the citizen and cohabitation in a physically delimited space, no less important is its reference to a civic imaginary and the symbolic construction of the city itself. The representations of the city, along with the memories and dreams that are produced in and by it, constitute the city itself and are expressed as the familiar, everyday narratives of its inhabitants. Such narratives are fostered by symbolic representations of life in the city, as well as of political, economic, and physical and spatial relationships that constitute the everyday goings-on of the urban citizen. All of this appears in the writings, speeches, and the specific imaginary of every moment in every city.

Practices and their symbolic representations interact in a continuous process of feedback that contributes to the configuration of social meanings associated with the city. At the same time, the city is represented as an object and as a place of action, integrating—together with a sense of spatiality—a vision of temporality (past, present, future). This temporality, inasmuch as it incorporates the expectations of its subjects and future projects, relates the representation of the city with models of (social and political) action.

The city, then, as it can be seen here, is more than a physical space inhabited by people and groups who selectively appropriate its places; it is also a setting for language, evocation, and writing, a representation of the topographical and the human, of the space and its inhabitants: "the real part of a city is not just its economy, urban planning, or social conflicts, but also the *imagined images* that are constructed from these phenomena, as well as what is imagined outside of them, as a narrative exercise, as representations of its spaces and writings" (Silva 1992, 135). From this perspective, it is possible to see Havana as a "memory-city" (Augé 1995), a space (physical and symbolic at the same time) that is built upon collective memory and representations of its history. Such representations are simultaneously given on two levels: on the one hand, in the appropriation and modifications of its physical space; and, on the other, in the speech and narratives of its inhabitants. Thus, since the Havana that is shown today in literature, film, the visual arts, and the speech of its residents constitutes a "non-place" of civic and public space, the first question that presents itself to the researcher is how did this representation come about.

The answer to this question is not easy and entails a long genealogy that involves political rhetoric and decisions as well as its residents' practices and imaginaries. The current image of the city can be said to be constructed upon a landmark moment of (re)foundation that radically modifies the previous representation; that representation, in turn, constitutes the minimum base for understanding the present.

The city and the perception of it reflect social intentions that are projected in the speech of its protagonists: in the case of Havana, the production of a particular sense of what today is urban or habanero comes from a lengthy process of selection and legitimation that originates, for the most part, in political discourse. The territorial self-representation reveals political strategies and perspectives about social life, also implying deep ties between these spheres (Silva 1992).

The social construction of an imaginary around the production of an urban sensibility, of a feeling of the city, is constantly updated through the different axes of mental maps representing the city's space: inside and outside, public and private, center and periphery, interior and exterior, before and after (Silva 1992). Of all of these axes, none determines the makeup of Havana's imaginary as much as the narrative and visual order of before and after; the rest of its dimensions are reshaped based upon these. Just as in other cities, self-representation endures some natural disaster (the earthquake of 1985 in Mexico City), some fatal accident (the Great Chicago Fire), or the implantation of urban models (Haussman in Paris)—for Havana, the parting of the waters occurred with the revolution in 1959. This moment defines a before and after in Havana. As we will see, this (before and after) axis leads to the transformation of representation on the rest of the city's planes of meaning.

Political discourse and the practice of power are at the center of this reconfiguration of the urban imaginary. As I have argued in previous works (Bobes 2000), no speech has been of greater influence, nor more monopolizing of the social imaginary, in post-1959 Cuba than political rhetoric. Havana, as an imagined and real city, has been the center of many texts produced for and by it, texts of the most diverse natures (literary and artistic, colloquial speech, and urban legends), but if any discourse has been central for the representation of the revolutionary city, it would be the political discourse emanating from power—so much so that it can be said that it has managed to modulate, upon occasion, the rest of the city's discourses and representations.

It is well known that the new revolutionary power declared from the beginning that the revolution's objective transcended the defeat of Batista's dictatorship and proposed to transform Cuban society to build a "better society"—one that was defined at the beginning in a rather abstract way. It entailed "overcoming the ills of the past" to guarantee a "greater happiness" for citizens. The Moncada program outlined a proposal for social change in terms of eliminating large plantations, unemployment, and the backwardness of the economy and, similarly, within the general framework of a program of industrialization, the defense of national products, the improvement of public administration, and an increase in technology. The first measures the government took were salary increases, the First Agrarian Reform of 1959, Law 135, which lowered rents by 50 percent and then led to the Urban Reform Law.

The justification of these nationalist plans for social justice was presented in the rhetoric as a fight to clean up the past and achieve a better society. In one of his speeches in the early years, Fidel Castro asked, "how are we as a people going to resign ourselves to that past of horror, that past of crime, that past of immorality, that past of abuse, that past of theft, that past of hunger, that past without hope, that past of submission?" (Castro 1960, 18). Within this panorama, the city of Havana appeared as the principal embodiment of the vices and problems that formed an obstacle for the desired society. In this new discourse, the city was represented as an environment of inequality, vice (gambling, prostitution), frivolity, and the reign of political and social corruption. The chosen discursive strategy depended upon showing the sharp contrast between the capital city, where all the modernity, political power, entertainment, glamour, prosperity, and development was concentrated (as is the case in the majority of Latin American capital cities), and the misery, underdevelopment, and helplessness of its rural countrymen. This begins to legitimate an investment strategy for development outside of the city.

The revolutionary government had to concentrate its efforts on making productive investments and on the development of the countryside. To support this decision, Fidel Castro said: "And it is not logical that the revolution would invest its resources, especially the resources it has in the midst of the embargo, to build small palaces, that it would invest them to bring in luxury cars, to maintain that whole bourgeois façade that is still maintained in our country and especially in the capital" (Castro 1960, 27). Affirmations such as this one decisively influenced the transformation of the city's representation. A city that had been the pride of the nation during most of its history—for its architecture, its layout, its works of engineering, its modern technology, and its nightlife—will begin to be the living image of injustice, no more than a "bourgeois façade" to cover up the exploitation and backwardness of the rest of the country:

> The revolution was not going to buy perfumes from Paris with the foreign exchange it needs to buy materials to fix the teeth of our nation's peasants! No, the façade of the country had to change, the façade of luxury, the façade that revealed the life of that minority that always looked elegant, always gave parties, always went for trips inside and outside of the country in luxury cars, that façade had to change so that our country could acquire the appearance of a nation of workers, of a country of workers, of a nation without parasites, of a nation without exploiters nor the exploited. (Castro 1960, 27)

Now that the new society should be based on the responsibility and commitment of its members, the archetype of the urban subject is radically modified. As such, the city's inhabitants suddenly saw themselves obligated to reformulate their place in history and, consequently, their own representation of the city. Against the frivolous, ludic, and elegant subject that had prevailed as the archetype of the habanero in the imaginary of the 1950s, the revolution would impose a proletarian Havana inhabited by the *hombre nuevo* (new man).

The glamorous Havana of the 1950s with its high-end shops, mansions, cabarets, and all of its great tourist attractions—the city portrayed in Guillermo Cabrera Infante's novel *Tres tristes tigres* (*Three Trapped Tigers*)—would become the antithesis of the better society; what is more, it is presented as a hindrance to development and social justice, as a remnant of the past. This is a starting point for a double symbolic and material process. On the one hand, the city is symbolically identified as the epitome of the worst aspects of the past, and on the other, its old splendor, far from making one proud, makes one ashamed and requires decisive action to be transformed.

Diverse actions are taken with the objective of getting rid of all of that, of ending the protagonism and centrality of the capital city. On the symbolic plane, images of change are disseminated: the people destroying the parking meters installed by the Batista government, or the gambling machines at the casinos; the *guajiros* invading the city to participate in the first big revolutionary gathering. On this occasion, for the first celebration of the twenty-sixth of July, one million farmers were invited to a massive event in Havana; messages, announcements, and posters appeared everywhere to welcome these "ambassadors of the authentic Cuba," who momentarily populated the city (Guerra 2007). With this event, the inside and outside borders are changed, and the image of a *guajira* Havana multiplies, entering Cubans' visual memory (for example, in Alberto Korda's beautiful photo *El Quijote de la farola* [The streetlamp Quijote]).

At the same time, the old symbols of republican power are resemanticized. If before presidents had chosen public works in the city as their monumental objects, seeking to leave their imprimatur as the promoters of modernity and progress, then the new government takes recourse to the opposite strategy: it does not build palaces or buildings for its institutions; rather, it recycles those that already exist, erecting radical symbolic transformations instead of monumental works. At first barracks were transformed into schools (the most emblematic cases being the Oscar Lucero School City in the Fortress of Holguín and Ciudad Libertad in Columbia); the National Capitol, seat of the old legislative power, goes on to house the Cuban Academy of Sciences; the Presidential Palace is turned into the Museum of the Revolution; and the Civic Plaza built by Batista is transformed into the Plaza de la Revolución. Thus, the old physical space of politics is symbolically transmuted into the space of the revolution.

This strategy continues with the demolition of the statues on the Avenue of Presidents (which, years later, would exhibit at the top of Third Street the surprising image of a pair of bronze shoes, the only remains of what had been the statue dedicated to Tomás Estrada Palma), and the monument to the Maine loses its imperial eagle to symbolize the end of submission to the United States, the rejection of the old imagery of the relationship with our neighbor to the north.

Revolutionary Havana also transforms the boundaries between the public and the private; many of the great mansions abandoned by those who went into exile are turned into offices, schools, or lodgings for students from the countryside who are on scholarship; the old private clubs are opened to the public and become Workers' Social Circles, with the most exclusive of all, the Country Club, turned into an area that houses the new National Schools of Art—open to the children of workers and farmers.

The process of the mass exodus of the upper and middle classes, produced in the early years of the revolution, also contributes to modifying the imaginary borders of the city in terms of interior and exterior relationships. Although the process involves the entire country, for Havana the emigration of a good part of its former inhabitants also signified the beginning of a relationship with its "mirror city," Miami, where, ninety miles from the coast, those who left began to re-create and re-found the "lost city."[1] With that—and in a context of isolation, the end of tourism, prohibitions on temporarily leaving the country, and so on—imaginary relationships with the exterior are radically changed.

In the midst of this atmosphere, and with the escalation of the conflict with the United States, the National Revolutionary Militias are founded. The population is incorporated into them en masse, and constant military mobilizations surround events like the invasion of Playa Girón, the Missile Crisis, and other threats. Havana dresses in uniform, and traditional commercial propaganda is traded in for posters and slogans defending and reaffirming the nation and the revolution.

Finally, toward the end of the 1960s, Havana becomes ruralized. Extrapolating for the city what Fagen (1969) observed for the country, it can be said that after 1959 the hierarchies of social relations, habits, and manners of habaneros are reversed, and the new man liquidates the elegant bourgeois paradigm.[2] Hence, while the use of private automobiles is anathema and use of the bus is encouraged, the city becomes a productive agricultural space with the Plan del Cordón de La Habana (Greenbelt Plan of Havana).[3] Through large agricultural mobilizations and volunteer work on weekends, city dwellers also turn into producers and farmers.

Beginning in 1968, two other phenomena occur that transfigure the city: the Revolutionary Offensive in 1968 and The Ten Million Ton Sugar Harvest.[4] The first brings about the disappearance of the network of small commercial businesses, services, and so forth that were still in private hands. This is the culmination of the process of nationalization of the country's economy, and with it the physical aspect of the city and the relationships of its inhabitants are changed (the neon lights of commercial advertisements are turned off, and neighborhood corners languish). In the meantime, with the objective of using the effort of the entire nation to reach ten million tons of sugar in the

1970 harvest, nightlife centers and restaurants are closed throughout 1968, 1969, and 1970, and the majority of "superfluous" activities are canceled to mobilize the majority of the capital's students and workers for the agricultural labor of the harvest.

Thus, the city gradually fades away, in terms of its physical space—with blackouts, the deterioration of its physical foundations, the gradual reduction in the number of vehicles, the closure of entertainment spaces, and the relocation of thousands of its residents to the countryside—becoming phantasmagoric and unreal. In terms of its imaginary and its self-representation, the modern city of luxury and diversion disappears, yielding its place to a city ethic of sacrifice, political engagement, and dedication. Havana politicizes itself and takes on a type of guilt complex about the countryside. The ethic of the new man is also the new imaginary of the city, which implies its negation.[5] The new image of austerity and equality is supposed to replace the extravagance and splendor; and, at the same time, proletarian enthusiasm replaces parties, joy, and fun. With bitter lucidity, Sergio, a character in *Memorias del subdesarrollo* (*Inconsolable Memories*) by Edmundo Desnoes, thinks:

> I can't be, I no longer am the same. My possibilities have been reduced to a minimum. I can't travel, choose the car I want to buy or the magazine I want to read. There's no longer bourgeois variety for the happy few, only flat socialist equality for all. There's no future for me: the future is worked out by the State. The future of a bourgeois—that's what I am, because it's true, I'm living in the "First Socialist Country of the Americas"—has been reduced to zero. (Desnoes 1990, 145)

The image of the city projected onto its discourse takes on materiality through the foundation of a group of policies on planning and development that put priority on shortening the distance between the country and the city, which should translate into a narrowing of the gap (of size, population, services, and quality of life) between the rural and urban zones (particularly the capital city). The policy that was designed insisted upon placing greater importance on rural development (at the same time reducing that of Havana) through the creation of medium-sized cities and small rural communities to replace the traditional dwellings spread out through the countryside. These were all given sanitary services, electricity, schools, health services, and access to cultural resources.

To this end, toward the 1970s the Community Development Group was founded. It was made up of architects, designers, psychologists, and social workers to promote and execute the evolution of these new sites. Under its direction, and inspired by the objective of homogenization, numerous urbanized centers sprang up in rural areas (such as those of Jibacoa, Valle del Perú, Triunvirato, Sandino, and others) throughout the island.

In the meantime, investments are concentrated almost exclusively outside of Havana, and all of the major new revolutionary projects are carried out in the country's interior. Industrial centers are built outside of the city to take away its central role; the model schools to train the new man are also placed outside of the city. Such is the case of the Lenin Vocational School (the emblem of the Cuban educational system) and the Basic Secondary Schools of the Countryside (ESBEC). Even the university itself is moved to the country, temporarily in some cases, indefinitely in others (for example, the Escuela de Geografía is moved to the Sierra Maestra).

Culture is "ruralized" through a strategy of founding and promoting institutions outside of Havana. In this way, the Ballet of Camagüey, the Teatro Escambray, and La Yaya groups are founded, and cultural brigades are formed to bring film, music, poetry, and dance to the most remote areas of the country, thus eliminating the urban elitism of the arts. It is the era of the literature of *Los años duros* (The harsh years) by Jesús Díaz, which narrates the "fight against bandits," where the city only appears as the stage for the struggle against Batista.[6] These are the years of proletarian cinema (Pastor Vega's *Habanera*, Tomás Gutiérrez Alea's *Hasta cierto punto* [Up to a certain point], or Jesús Díaz's *Polvo rojo* [Red dust]), of socialist realism in painting—definitely more rural than René Portocarrero's *Interiores del Cerro* (Interiors in Cerro, Havana).

Havana changes, and not just in the imaginary. As the result of all of these policies, it starts to lose its charm and much of its old attraction, its capacity to fascinate. This was so much the case that, according to a recognized urban planner in Havana, by the 1970s, "it is the only Latin American capital that, in the last decade [1965–1975] has reduced its relative demographic weight: from 32.9 percent before the revolution, it has gone down to 20.5 percent at present" (Segre 1977, 325). Thus, the institutional tendency toward rural growth to the detriment of the city managed to take effect. Nevertheless, current statistics seem to demonstrate that such a process was stopped, and what has happened in reality is that today Havana remains the most attractive center of internal migration for Cubans, such that it is not only the largest city in the country but is also twice as large as the second-largest city, Santiago de Cuba.[7] The answer of the government today: it no longer takes pains to make the countryside more attractive through investment; rather, it imposes strict restrictions and controls that impede migration to Havana.

Thus, the great city of the past, represented as the incarnation of sin and of the excesses of pleasure, perversion, and inequality, gives way to the Sovietized city of the end of the 1970s and the 1980s—in which, paradoxically, the first autonomous appropriations of space are produced. Since the objective of all the territorial policies had been to achieve a certain homogeneity between the urban and the rural, toward 1970 the special plans for the development of non-urban zones multiplied. In 1973, with Cuba's incorporation into the Council for Mutual Economic Assistance (Comecon), and from the First Congress of the Communist Party of Cuba (PCC) in 1975 on, these planning policies were stabilized through the so-called Five-Year Plans for Development, through which the Plan Director de la Ciudad (Directive Plan of the City) is specified.

Up to 1970, the population of the city increased as a result of the baby boom of the 1960s and high rates of internal migration.[8] At the same time, the construction of new residences was reduced, so that the scarcity of residences —toward the mid-1970s—begins to become a major issue in Havana.[9] To ease this situation—which was not alleviated, despite the reduction of the average annual growth index of the city beginning in the 1970s—the so-called micro-brigades were created. They were contingents for the construction of new apartment buildings made up of their future inhabitants—that is, people without any construction experience or skills. These led to the growth of the horrendous Alamar neighborhood, very much in the style of the mediocre, massive architecture of socialist countries.

Soviet Havana, with Alamar as its paradigmatic emblem, began to approach the principle of uniformity as the ideal of the city (constructive, spatial, and social), and the imaginary was articulated around the negation of social diversity via the representation of the socialist subject—the new man— as its resident. The new notions of center and periphery, inside and outside, and public and private had already been completely disconnected from the old symbolic representation of the city and its denizens.

Paradoxically, this is also the era of reconstruction and recovery. After thirty years of the city being neglected and forgotten, and of all efforts and investments in development being concentrated in rural zones to homogenize the country, the Havana of the 1980s is a city well on its way to ruin and, as such, renewal is attempted in the Sovietized city. In 1981, and as the result of the effort of the Office of the City Historian, UNESCO designates Old Havana as a World Heritage Site. Beginning with that moment, a policy of reconstruction and rehabilitation of its historical monuments is institutionalized, and it continues to this day. For the first time in history, Havana and its residents recognize the populous neighborhood of Old Havana as something more than a heap of tenements. A process of restoration of the old historical area (previously excluded from the representation of the city) is begun, as well as the reappropriation of its space, both physical—since the restoration includes the remodeling of buildings filled with new functions such as art galleries, restaurants, cafeterias, and so on—and symbolic, as Old Havana becomes representative of Cuban identity.[10]

Moreover, at the end of the 1970s and as the result of the government's dialogue with Cuban exiles, the first exiles return to Havana to make family visits, travelling as tourists. Symbolically, this signifies a reaccommodation of the inside and outside dimensions, since it implies an expansion of the representation of inclusion: exiles begin to repopulate Havana (albeit only temporally and symbolically); their return renders nostalgia and the evocation of the past current; and the images of old property owners in front of their mansions or apartments modify the representation of the exiled city and its relationship with its past. With the events related to the Mariel exodus in 1980, the city once again mobilizes in acts of "revolutionary reaffirmation" and of repudiation against those going into exile. A struggle for the occupation of the "revolutionary" space takes place in front of the "scum."[11]

At the first light of the 1980s—with the beginning of the Reagan era—a return to militarization takes place in the city. It is the era of the Territorial Military Troops, mobilizations for combat preparation, and the construction of underground shelters to resist a possible invasion by the United States. The uniforms return—although with less intensity than in the early years of the revolution—and habaneros joke about the city allegorically turning into an "enormous Gruyère cheese."

This flirtation with the return of the practices and imaginary of the 1960s does not last; rather, it is a stage of transition. By the middle of the decade, public space begins to be appropriated by new generations. The Havana of the 1980s sees a new social subject embodied in groups of young poets, artists, playwrights, and writers who, at different levels, take control of the streets and different places of the city. This movement, which begins in private spaces, little by little invades public space. On G Street, the group Arte Calle (Street Art) stages performances, other groups of artists fill the walls of the public thoroughfare with graffiti, and visual artists appropriate the streets of Havana and organize a baseball game. At the Centro Alejo Carpentier, the Paideia collective begins to call for independent reflection on cultural politics. The Castillo de la Fuerza project holds a space and has a regular audience hungry to find an alternative discourse. The Teatro del Obstáculo (obstacle theater) presents a new dramaturgy that gives voice to the new subject of the city.

Finally, a group of young architects tries to bring these proposals to the reformulation of the city's construction and image.

The Havana of the 1980s is the city retaken by its youth, and the representation of the proletarian and revolutionary city begins to be replaced by a city that reclaims the right to difference and rebels against uniformity. The new autonomous discourses defy state control of the city's image. With this, the very idea of what is public is reshaped and begins to disassociate itself from revolutionary space. The new discourse and the representation of the city call for autonomy, and the new social subject fights to define itself; it is the "rebellion of the new man," or the coming of age of "the sons of Utopia." If the literature, art, and film of the 1960s and 1970s constantly represented the city as that of the working people, in the 1980s the representations of the city are given over to youth and their alternative proposals.

This project of rejuvenating public space ended in the same dramatic way as the Cuban economy. With the fall of the socialist camp, the end of Soviet subsidies, and the ensuing economic crisis, the country falls into what is called the Special Period in Times of Peace—a euphemism that has been utilized to name the crisis that brought the city back down to the lowest levels of existence in all of its contemporary history. Beginning in 1992, transportation problems are exacerbated, Havana fills up with bicycles, and buses almost disappear; the old vehicles are decrepit; the state of residential buildings deteriorates even more; the scarcity of water and electricity worsens; constant blackouts take place; and supplies of industrial and food products are limited to the bare minimum. Faced with this situation, the government must take measures to adapt and to alleviate the crisis.

Among all of these measures, the stimulus of and investment in tourism, plus the appearance of the dual market and the dual currency, put Havana back in a place of protagonism and centrality. The new economic strategy included the acceptance and promotion of foreign investment (mixed, as well as private capital) in diverse sectors; the legalization of self-employment and the possession of foreign currency (with it, the possibility for emigrants to send remittances); the opening of the internal market; the massive cooperativization of agricultural production; the rationalization of the state apparatus and the reduction of jobs; and, finally, the application of a fiscal policy.

Although the measures affected the entire country, their impact on the city and its representation is particularly radical and notorious. In contrast to the planned certainty of the 1970s and 1980s, with five-year plans (that did not exactly look at the city), now incertitude and inequality are put into place. The future is no longer planned by the socialist state, and the new subject of the citizen is faced with the necessity of doing it himself or herself. Tourism, family remittances, and self-employment are the new goals of the city inhabitant.

If, as Iván de la Nuez affirms, "publicity and tourism have converted Cuba into an almost virtual country," Havana is the principal locus of that virtuality:

> The latest propaganda has substituted the word *landscape* with the word *scenography*, within which the population appears as another element. There is something more here than the props that belong in tourist islands, where species—above all the human one—exist to be photographed and classified. That "something" denotes a return. The sphere of prerevolutionary Cuba—cars from the '40s/'50s, "vintage" clothing, tropical flavor, the return of the original *son*, the gerontocracy as the carrier of truth—says to us that, even under the model emanated by the revolution, a return to the past is already being experienced. (De la Nuez 2001, 14)

Virtual Havana is the one that makes ruin a virtue and that shows itself off to be contemplated and enjoyed by strangers who are willing to pay for it (and have return tickets). The new man who lives there (and seems to follow the script of survival), for his part, turns to the whole old repertoire of the criollo picaresque to collect the toll. It is, to repeat the title of Antonio José Ponte's work *La fiesta vigilada*, the "monitored party" of *paladares* (private restaurants) and inventiveness, that of resolving and escaping, that once again bring money, fun, and time to the habanero and that films such as *Buena Vista Social Club* and *Suite Habana* spread throughout the world in full color.

The difference (which could never be eliminated) between the capital and the rest of the country becomes more evident. Although Havana—everyone agrees—is now in ruins, for its inhabitants it is still the place with the highest quality of life. The territorial inequalities that have been stimulated by tourism and remittances have generated an increase in internal migration—in spite of government controls—and have given rise to a very peculiar form of discrimination against immigrants, especially those who come from the easternmost areas.[12] Other inequalities—in terms of race—and subtle forms of discrimination have begun to make themselves visible in a city where the majority of residents in the least favored areas, those who do not receive remittances from abroad and those who devote themselves to illegal activities, are not white.

Nevertheless, even more important than the accentuation of inequality is the appearance of phenomena that symbolically had been identified with the republican past. Such is the case of poverty—a concept that was only employed before to refer to other countries and that begins to be recognized and discussed in official forums—prostitution, and the consumption and trafficking of drugs. In the face of a discourse that had proclaimed the elimination of poverty and "other scars from the past" as the goal and sense of its political and economic project, the reappearance of these phenomena constitutes a challenge that is difficult to take on.

With this, there is a return (sans glory) of the Havana of the 1950s: a locus of pleasure for tourists and a showcase of inequality. The city is once again imagined as a setting for tourism. The very political discourse recognizes it and legitimizes the segregation of citizens from the recently restored, resplendent hotels and restaurants, moving them to parts of the city that are in ruins and recreation centers that operate in national currency. In 1995, Fidel Castro explained it this way:

> Tourism for us is an exportation of services, only a relatively small part, although still of some importance, can be set aside for national consumption, and we principally reserve it for the workers. . . . We have to export a great part of the tourist services because otherwise we could not sustain them; we would practically have to close the hotels because we have to invest convertible currency even in the part of tourism we dedicate to national consumption. (Castro 1995)

The symbolic axes of inside and outside and before and after are modified once again: the city confronts the watershed of the crisis, and nostalgia roots itself in the glorious 1960s or in the years of the *mercaditos* (little markets) and the Plaza de la Catedral.[13] The mirror relationship with Miami is intensified and repaired with the increased flexibility of the migratory policy that fosters the visits and economic aid of emigrants to their families. In their cultural and symbolic dimension, the monetary remittances transnationalize the imaginary, as well as languages. The fashions of Miami come to Havana along with the money and the people (*quinceañera* parties, brands of clothing, prejudices, and lifestyles). What is said in Miami, what is used in Miami, what is seen on television in Miami, forms part of the life and the imaginary of Havana.

With the new representation of the city, the citizen is now faced with diversity. In opposition to the immobility of the ideology in power, the emptiness of values and the urgency of subsistence signal the proliferation of very diverse subjects: *jineteros* (hustlers), *macetas* (nouveau riches), employees of joint venture enterprises, the poor, beggars, working-class people, and the revolutionary masses that have the lead role in the "Battle of Ideas." Hence, while the statue of President José Miguel Gómez is restored to its original place on the Avenida de los Presidentes, restoring the past of the republican city, the space across from the U.S. Interest Section is repurposed as the Anti-Imperialist Tribune to reject terrorism and to call for the liberty of the Cuban Five, or the "five heroes imprisoned by the empire."

If something unifies this heterogeneity, it is the recuperated centrality of the city for the imagination and symbolic universe of Cubans today:

> Havana, without a doubt, has acquired an enormous symbolic value in the perception of Cuba in recent years. If, for decades, Cuba was represented (almost essentialized) with images of peasants or fields of sugarcane, flourishing lands, emerging peoples, schools in the countryside—images, that is, that showed the vigorous torso of the nation—beginning in the '90s it is Havana (and above all its crumbling side) that is erected as symbol of the country. The phenomenon—which I have called the "rhetoric of demolition"—is not exclusive to literature, and has been exploited ad nauseam by film and photography, both Cuban and foreign; but its presence in our narrative is notable. (Fornet 2007a)

The literature, film, and art of the 1990s and today show the capacity of the city to bring that immense variety together. The dirty realism of the novels of Pedro Juan Gutiérrez, portraying a miserable, destroyed Havana populated by marginal and desperate people, coexists with the nostalgia for the 1960s of Senel Paz, films like *Suite Habana*, with co-productions made to suit the taste of potential visitors from Spain, as well as with independent shorts with an ironic, critical view of the current reality, and Kcho's collective murals in homage to the *Granma*, with the irreverent satire of Lázaro Saavedra.[14]

In sum, in the midst of the catastrophe, Havana survives, reinventing itself—tenacious, obstinate, frivolous, and fickle—confronting the weight of a nation that has imposed and continues to impose austerity, grandeur, and history upon it. The new before and after of Havana will be, without a doubt, this resurrection from its ruins, this moment of storms and upheavals, of hopes for renewal.

Notes

1. The area called Little Havana arose quickly, populated by immigrants who established diverse businesses with the names and styles of those they left behind: the restaurant La Carreta, the sweet shop La Gran Vía, the La Moderna Poesía bookshop, and many, many more.

2. "Turning the gaze of the people toward the countryside, Fidel Castro is erasing class distinctions and the social relationships of what was once a traditional Latin American society. Cuba is the only country in Latin America where boots, coarse hands, dirty clothing, first names, and conversations about agriculture are considered signs of honor and status" (Fagen 1969, 179).

3. This was the name of an enormous (although it had scant productive success) government plan to promote the cultivation of vegetables and coffee in barren lots on the periphery and outlying areas of the capital.

4. The Revolutionary Offensive, carried out against "urban capitalists"—called "parasites"—ended with the closure (within twenty-four hours) of more than 58,000 private businesses (bakeries, cafeterias, bars, *quincallas* [dime stores], barbershops and hair salons, fried-food stands, and even shoe-shining chairs).

5. The new man is not identified with the traditional city-dwelling subject; he is defined by his dedication to the revolutionary cause, his deferral of individual interests to those of the collective, his rejection of money and material goods, his solidarity, responsibility, honor, generosity, ability to overcome, and usefulness. Given that the principal task of those years was that of agricultural work, the new man was always prepared to go off to the country and to do without all of the comforts, luxuries, and pleasures of the city.

6. "La lucha contra bandidos" was the term used by the Cuban government to describe the fight against a counterrevolutionary guerrilla group of farmers and small landowners who, with the support of Cuban exiles and the CIA, operated in the Escambray Mountains in the early 1960s.

7. In 2002, the city of Havana had 2,201,600 residents, while Santiago de Cuba had 1,036,300, making up 19.7 percent and 9.3 percent of the total population, respectively (Montes Rodríguez 2007).

8. The indexes of the average annual growth of the city's population decrease from 2.1 percent (1953–1970) to 0.7 percent (1970–1981), before reaching 0.6 percent in 2002 (Montes Rodríguez 2007).

9. "The deliberate abandonment of Havana, the deterioration of its infrastructure, and the deplorable state of its buildings have been the source of many commentaries . . . in 1979, only 13 percent of the urban residences of the province [of Havana] had been built since 1959 . . . close to half of the national shortage of urban dwelling was located in the Province of Havana, and the province in general had a similarly high proportion in terms of projected replacement needs for 1970–1985" (Gugler 1981, 1473).

10. Álvarez-Tabío Albo (2001) points out rightly that during this time new ceremonies contributed to strengthening a new Havanan identity centered in Old Havana, one of them the celebration of the city's founding at the centenary Ceiba tree where El Templete had been built.

11. During the Mariel exodus, those who had put their name down in order to leave the country were declared "scum" by the revolutionary government. So-called acts of repudiation were organized against them by the Committees for the Defense of the Revolution (CDR), the neighborhood committees.

12. "The effect of the contraction of the economy was most sharply reflected in the eastern region of the country, where 30 percent of the urban population lived, of which 22 percent was at risk of not having its basic needs met" (Álvarez and Mattar 2004, 80).

13. *Mercaditos* were markets that in the 1980s sold food and other stuff, in local currency and without the regulation of the state ration book (*libreta*). On the Plaza de la Catedral a popular art market also sold handcrafted shoes, purses, clothes, and jewelry in local currency.

14. In the case of literature, for example, I refer to *En el cielo con diamantes* (In the sky with diamonds), the most recent novel by Senel Paz (2007), which narrates the city from the perspective of the candid surprise of students on scholarship in the 1960s; this is juxtaposed with the marginal subject of *El Rey de La Habana* (The king of Havana) or *Animal tropical* (Tropical animal) by Pedro Juan Gutiérrez, for whom Havana is the setting of physical catastrophe and moral ruin. In the case of film, I refer to Cuban and Spanish co-productions such as *Hacerse el sueco* (Playing Swede) by Daniel Díaz Torres or *Cosas que dejé en La Habana* (Things I left in Havana) by Manuel Gutiérrez Aragón, in which Havana and its residents show a sympathetic face, while independent shorts like *Utopía* (Utopia) or *Buzos* (Divers) show the new man in a much more somber light. Finally, in terms of the visual arts, there are celebratory projects such as the mural created at the National Museum of Fine Arts in 2006 and the work of other artists who maintain a critical stance on the current situation, a good selection of which was on display at the exhibition *States of Exchange: Artists from Cuba*, in London in the spring of 2008.

2

The Bitter Trinquennium and the

Dystopian City: Autopsy of a Utopia

MARIO COYULA

Translated by Elisabeth Enenbach

Why a Name

With the term Gray Quinquennium *(1971–1976), Ambrosio Fornet condensed not only a more expansive time period of sad memories but also a twisted conception of the world built upon intolerance, exclusion, and the rejection of everything new and different. For Cuban architecture, this period began earlier and some of its consequences continue today, totaling at least three quinquennia (a period of five years). Hence my use of the term* trinquennium, *as nonexistent as that place* utopia, *where we all want to go without knowing how. On the other hand, flavors can be more evocative than those deceptive colors, as a brilliant neurotic observed upon dipping a madeleine in his tea, and hence the* bitter. *Writing about urbanism and urban culture entails an ever-increasing component of imagination. Perhaps for this reason I have recently resorted to writing fiction, a novel where I am condemned to the frustration of pursuing the most beautiful woman in Cuba, who died before I was born.*

In the Beginning Were the Principles

In contemporary cities, as well as Cuban architecture, there appeared—with some distinctive nuances—the effects of the same rigid and authoritative cultural politics that damaged thought, literature, theater, and other intellectual and artistic works in the 1970s. That persistence is largely due to the extent, cost, social repercussions, public placement, and lasting nature of the construction works, and above all to their ties to politics and politicians. This last point makes criticism and debate on the subject of construction particularly difficult. The 1970s began earlier for Cuban architecture, masked by the nostalgic charm of the Prodigious Decade of the 1960s, and still have not ended. The dogmatism denounced in 1962, as being consubstantial with a Sovietizing sectarian microfaction whose flame did not last long, turned out not to be exclusive to a determined generation or political militancy.[1]

That deviation had been dismantled by a genuine, young, and iconoclastic revolution, which had triumphed because of its transgressive and renewing nature that had allowed it to mobilize the expectation for change that had seemed dormant among Cubans. However, the Manichean dogmatism that systematically erases difference and suffocates individualism would continue to survive, sealed off like an opportunist and recurring virus. It was associated with a mediocrity in ascent that crushed any manifestation of creativity for being suspicious. Just like herpes simplex, dogmatism has no definitive cure, but there are ways of keeping it in remission.

There are essential principles for the sustainment of ecosystems that are also valid for all human activities and institutions, such as tending to current needs without compromising the possibility that future generations might resolve their own, even those that are as yet unknown; remaining within the capacity of the system to allow for its self-regeneration; or the need for one element to be able to develop various functions, and for allowing the same function to be carried about by various different elements. All of this requires the preservation of diversity and plurality and that the population be allowed active and conscious participation in the identification and solution of its own problems. Curiously, these healthy principles awoke the distrust of those who were dogmatic.

Tolerance, that shameful variant of the recognition of diversity, was seen as a weakness inappropriate for revolutionaries, and intransigence came to be seen as a virtue instead of a defect. A provincial xenophobia rejected that which was different and that which came from outside the island, including fashions and tastes that were considered too "foreign" and penetrated culturally by the decadent capitalist world. Ironically, those who thought that way tried to impose models from a much more distant, cold world—both geographically and culturally—that lasted as long as the life of a person. That other cultural penetration, by a socialism that proclaimed itself *real*, has left some dusty manuals in Cuba, a collection of conventional, grotesque monuments that attempt to give homage to unconventional heroes, and many innocent Ivans and Tatianas, increasingly cornered by the later hemorrhage of Yosvanys and Yumisleidys, where the proliferation of the letter *Y* reveals an escapist air.

Long Die the Difference

In the second half of the 1960s, the Art Schools of Cubanacán were collectively demonized, their creators labeled as elitist pseudo intellectuals, and their influence considered pernicious for young students of architecture. This great construction site, the most publicized of the revolutionary period, was crucified precisely for carrying out what had initially been asked of its architects: to make the most beautiful art schools of Latin America. Its opponents, aligned with a technocratic pragmatism, were inclined to sacrifice beauty to achieve technically impeccable buildings in the large quantity needed by the country. Those people, perhaps unimaginative but technically qualified, were later replaced by improvised builders, who were congratulated for "taking a step forward" without having command of the profession. Thus, the cult of improvisation had begun. Those who celebrated the obedient disposition of inept subordinates in carrying out goals and directives without questioning them, of course, were careful to seek the very best doctors when faced with the slightest problem in personal health.

The youth who dared to wear beards, long hair, blouses, and necklaces of seeds were criticized as extravagant, without the understanding that while the hippie wave—a word that some, stuck in time, still use today—was associated with soft drugs, it also upheld a pacifistic humanism that made them travelling companions with our social project. In fact, that fashion had been imposed on the world by the Cuban rebels of the Sierra, and the failure to recognize it was a marketing oversight that the most obtuse capitalist entrepreneur would not have wasted. That opposition to new fashions was part of a growing static and curiously antidialectic mentality among some decision makers, prejudiced against anything new and, above all, against anything they didn't understand. Curiously, that rejection always occurred from the point of view of a determined trend that the implacable censors had uncritically assumed in their own youth, as if ways of dressing, combing one's hair, or socializing in the 1940s or 1950s were somehow, by definition, more *healthy* than those of the 1960s or 1970s. Those criticisms came from people who generally had a political position that was more advanced than their cultural standards and were marked by a provincial petit-bourgeois, *machista*, anti-intellectual, uninformed mentality with a genetically encoded prejudice against the great capital city that had humiliated them with its cosmopolitanism.

Up La Rampa, Down La Rampa

The creative spirit of the 1960s was condensed in La Rampa. As some contemporary—Paolo Gasparini, perhaps—said, "more than a place, La Rampa was a state of mind." Those few, sloped blocks formed the still brand-new physical frame, with a vivid urban image, for a rich mixture of happenings, buildings, and people. There impressive cultural interventions produced accompanying events such as the Seventh Congress of the International Union of Architects, the Cuban Cultural Exhibition, the May Salon, the World Chess Championships, or the Third World Expo. Some of the most important works of modern Cuban architecture were built in La Rampa at the time, such as the Cuba Pavilion (Juan Campos, 1963), with a perfect urban scale, or the Coppelia ice cream parlor (Mario Girona, 1966). Nearby in the central corner of Infanta and San Lázaro, the first important commemorative monument since 1959 and the first abstract one (Emilio Escobar, Mario Coyula, Sonia Domínguez, and Armando Hernández) was built in 1965–1967, dedicated to the university martyrs; some found it too radical and hermetic.

Part of the awakening of La Rampa was also the remodeling of the old Caballero Funeral Home in 1967 (Joaquín Rallo, Roberto Gottardi, and Mario Coyula), turning it into a multipurpose cultural center. The work was met with immediate success, especially among youths, and became a meeting center for the *enfermitos* of La Rampa.[2] Following the old method of "getting rid of the couch and the lover," the place was closed down and turned into the animation workshop of the Instituto Cubano de Radio y Televisión, which was closed to the public. The "undesirables" could only cross the street and stand on the sidewalk in front. Some blocks of pressed scrap metal that formed the piece donated by the great sculptor from Marseilles, César, at the end of the May Salon, ended up as anchors for the chains that served to enclose the parking lot. For me, that closure symbolically marked the beginning of the Bitter Trinquennium in architecture, already foreshadowed by the paralysis of the art schools.

The following year brought the student protests of May in France, the Soviet invasion of Czechoslovakia, and the Revolutionary Offensive in Cuba, which liquidated what had remained of small private businesses. However, transitions are never black and white, nor can they be defined by exact dates. Together with backward steps in culture, there were also good works other than those already mentioned: 1968 was also the year of Gutiérrez Alea's *Memories of Underdevelopment* and the Command Posts of Agriculture, of which those of Nazareno (Raúl González Romero, with Sonia Domínguez, Rodolfo Fernández, and others) and Menocal (Roberto Gottardi) in Havana and that of Yarey (Sergio Baroni) in *Granma* stood out for their good architecture; while the previous year had seen the inauguration of the famous Cuba Pavilion for Expo '67 in Montreal (Vittorio Garatti and Sergio Baroni). In the second half of that decade, the National Center of Scientific Investigation (Joaquín Galván, Sonia Domínguez. and others) was built, the projects of Lenin Park (Antonio Quintana, with Juan Tosca, Mario Girona, and others) were also begun, while the Medical School of Santiago de Cuba (Rodrigo Tascón) was built, and the town of Velasco appeared on the map with its emblematic House of Culture, finished after the early death of its creator, Walter Betancourt.

The notable emphasis on research and experimentation in building materials and technologies during the 1960s translated into works of high quality affiliated with the brutalist aesthetic that was in vogue around the world at the time and that includes the master work of the Ciudad Universitaria José Antonio Echeverría (CUJAE), 1960–1964 (Humberto Alonso and others). This same time period also gave birth to a technocratic fetishism that always relied on the latest trendy building system to resolve problems as complex as housing. This simplistic focus obviated other urban, social, economic, organizational, and cultural components that come into play in creating a strategy, in the process of conceiving, producing, and consuming a manmade work; the user was almost never consulted by those who presumed to already know what was best for that unknown person. Within the state apparatus itself, the subsequent separation of enterprises into design firms and construction companies further interfered with the organic continuity between the process and the final product. Taking the supervision of the project away from the architect is like stealing a newborn away from its mother and giving it to another person; and supervising it only if one is hired for that purpose is like putting a price on that maternity.

In the first half of the 1960s, the average production had reached a high level of architectural quality that extended to new programs and spread throughout the country. In reality, it was the golden age of modern architecture in Cuba, topping the mythical level of the previous decade. It is useful to underscore that this was achieved at a national juncture even more difficult than the current one, with great consciousness-raising strains and siding with political parties, and the consequent personal and collective splits and ruptures. Along with that came the stampede of the majority of the most renowned architects, the widespread scarcity of materials, and an internal destabilization that included armed aggression supported from abroad. The natural question is: if great things were achieved then, what went wrong later? The other concomitant question is: what can be done to regain that level of construction?

By the mid-1960s, the Ministry of Construction had absorbed other competing building entities such as the National Institute of Housing and Savings (INAV) and the Department of Rural Housing of the Institute for Agrarian Reform (INRA), both having high-quality designs and execution. This process of centralization increased with the subsequent transfer of the building apparatus of the local governments (Coordination, Operations, and Inspection Boards, JUCEI) and of the maintenance and construction equipment of different ministries. In parallel, the classification of projects into fewer building types increased, and norms proliferated that sought standardization at the national level as the supposed only way to industrialize construction, making it cheaper, and achieve mass production. The authority of the architect began to migrate from the project planner to the builders and the investors. This shift in decision making is equivalent to letting printers determine how books should be written.

The Arrival of the 1970s

Apart from a few good works, design in the 1970s began to lose its earlier high standard, and the quality of construction got worse without it reaching the quantity required. The individual authorship of projects was silenced, a custom that continues today in the mass media when they mention workers and administrators but not the architect of a work. In this way, not only is the creator of a project not given credit for achieving an elegant solution, he or she is also relieved of responsibility for anything that turns out badly.

On occasion the supposed beauty and fine execution of frankly bad works were praised publicly, which disoriented the population. This, together with the influence of South American *telenovelas* and kitschy Miami architecture, can explain the appearance of ridiculous styles that deform the urban landscape and distort its identities, as occurs with façades and high garden walls touched up with criollo tiles, low semicircular arches, and the large doors made of nice, varnished wood that have now become a status symbol. Something similar happens with the architecture for tourism, where there is often a vague "Cubanness" that fails to transcend falsified folklore to give the western part of the country a Caribbean flavor it never had but that tourists expect and receive.

The problems that appeared in architectural production were, at the same time, the cause and effect of an excessive centralization that eliminated alternatives and nullified criticism and praise of the merits and defects of a work, confusing social value with cultural significance. Fleeing this claustrophobic framework, many good architectural designers took refuge in physical planning, the restoration and conservation of historical monuments, criticism, and teaching. That escape changed in the 1990s, when several talents crossed over to the better-compensated world of the hard-cash economy, while other younger architects opted to leave the country.

More important than the individual misfortune of "conflictive" architects, humiliated and pushed to the side or else given banal tasks, were the consequences on contemporary Cuban architecture. With few exceptions, it has not been possible to match the high level of quality found in the buildings that are part of the valuable patrimony found in Cuban cities, including that of the first years after the revolutionary triumph. The principal cause should not be sought in the professional qualifications of Cuban architects but rather in the conditions in which they work and especially in their loss of authority over projects and their execution. There was even a stage during the Bitter Trinquennium in which the very title of *architect* acquired a pejorative connotation in the jargon of camaraderie within the establishment, inserted in the traditional *machista* joking that classified architects as weak and untrustworthy.

A combination of anonymous egalitarianism, technocratic bureaucracy, and dogmatism in people who deemed themselves to be repositories of absolute truth imposed rigid models copied from other climatic and cultural contexts, undermined the authority and image of the architect as creator, and killed conceptual and formal experimentation. A few special works, promoted by very high-level authorities, rose above that amorphous mass, but they had little weight in the image of the city because of their inaccessibility, due in part to subjects and users who were also *special*. The best architects were sought for those works. They left their usual work and chose their own collaborators to work in small teams with a creative liberty that others did not enjoy. The results demonstrated that that method works when quality is truly an interest.

At the beginning of the 1970s, the School of Architecture worked inten-

sively on projects built in conjunction with Desarrollo de Edificaciones Sociales y Agropecuarias (DESA), although some of these projects suffered from
changes during the construction process that were imposed by the increasing
power of the builder. Beginning in the middle of the decade, the city of
Havana benefited from the program of Urban Revival and supergraphics that
rapidly improved, and with few resources, the image of important urban hubs
that had seen better days. Two mayors with foresight supported this approach,
but unfortunately, it would later be abandoned due to the increasing fatalism
of the government.

Discrete but continuous achievements were also made in the conservation
and restoration of historic monuments. This paved the way for the impressive
work of the Office of the City Historian, especially beginning in 1993 when it
was allowed to develop its own businesses as independent sources of income,
reconciling cultural and economic interests. In that way, what some had
earlier seen as a burden became valued resources. In earlier times, when
money was not important, a group of good architects that worked for the
Department of School Construction demonstrated that one could make good
architecture even with an inflexible building system as long as there was
architectural talent as well as an equally talented architect as head of the team.
They were responsible for the whole process, from design to the supervision
of works that they had planned. The paradox is that to receive support, one
must first gain it or, rather, demonstrate that one doesn't need it.

City, Country, and Suburb

The small influence that the best works have had on the existing city was also
determined by their almost always peripheral placement. This could have
reflected a rejection, not necessarily explicit, of the traditional city—seen as a
shiny, swindling parasite plagued with vice and bad habits, as opposed to the
healthy rural world. The taste for the remote began very early on with the large
construction sites, in part justified by the need for larger areas of land. So it was
with the first apartment complex built by the revolutionary government, Unit
No. 1 of East Havana, with the CUJAE and the Art Schools of Cubanacán, the
Lenin Vocational School, Lenin Park, the Permanent Exhibition of the Economic and Social Development of the Republic of Cuba (EXPOCUBA), the
Western Scientific Pole that started with the National Center for Scientific
Research (CENIC), the Agricultural Command Posts, and more recently the
University of Information Science (UCI). On the other hand, the plans for

almost all of these installations were larger than necessary: since there was no price for the land, this nonrenewable resource was wasted. Actually, while midsize Cuban cities doubled in population, the urban surface area tripled.

The Monte Barreto complex in the western part of Havana has been a special case, with seven hotels, eighteen office buildings and stores, and a building of condominiums for tourists. Monte Barreto was based on a spread out model of suburban development, dependent on private cars, which has been highly criticized in the countries that went through this model first. This neighborhood is built for a single hard currency, and for a single type of people, those who have access to it. There is no housing for the regular population, nor the everyday services that complement it. All of this makes the development an enclave of wealth, cut off from the rest of the city, running the risk that one day someone will decide to fence it off.

One of the hotels in that subdivision has fixed windows that force the guest to pop his or her head halfway out of the only available opening to smell the ocean that faces the building. The mirrored glass façade—a fashion that has spread like a virus among architects working in State design enterprises—also turns the building into a huge solar heater. The same thing happened with the façade of the beautiful bank on Fifth Avenue and 112th Street by Max Borges, one of the best Cuban architects in the 1950s: The original large panels of transparent glass showed the graceful structure of the columns that open like mushrooms to form the ceiling. Those glass panes were needlessly replaced by reflective ones that no longer allow one to see the interior structure, all because of the same pathetic concept of prestige with which a *maceta* darkens the windows of his shiny car. At the same time, the concentration of investments in historically privileged zones reinforces the tendency toward a dual city, one geared toward visitors and the other toward the rest of the population.

The early policy of urbanizing the countryside translated into more than six hundred new rural towns, including the gem that is still Las Terrazas, inaugurated in 1968. However, that was not enough to stabilize the labor force required by agriculture. Migration was constant but no longer to the capital, but rather it was to provincial capitals and intermediate cities, stimulated by the erroneous strategy of building standard five-story buildings in the middle of the countryside. With this, rural residents encountered all the inconveniences of living on upper floors, quite different from what they were used to, and yet without any of the advantages of living in the city. As a result, they ended up moving to a real city. There has been, in fact, a reverse movement, as the capital has become ruralized with guano palm shacks in a vague neo-

Taíno style, banana trees and livestock in the front yards of many houses, as well as barbed-wire fences, stews cooked over the fire in flowerbeds, animal-drawn carts, and tractors running through the streets.

The considerable investments the revolutionary government made from early on to create jobs and improve the quality of life in the country's interior naturally stopped internal migration to the capital, turning Havana into a special case within Latin America. But that prioritization indirectly worsened the already poor living conditions in the central areas of the city, which are also the most densely populated and those with the greatest cultural value. The physical deterioration increased with the huge crisis that followed the collapse of the Soviet Union, cryptically named the Special Period. That time also brought an increase in internal migration to the capital, as Cubans sought more opportunities. The attempt to slow this phenomenon through regulations instituted in 1997 has not managed to stem that flow but rather to skim off the cream: the best observe the law, and the others keep arriving.

In recent years, the problem has been complicated with the decrease in and aging of the capital's population, which places Havana alongside the majority of large cities in the developed world, sans the development. The overcrowding in its central areas is accentuated by the deterioration brought by time, the aggressiveness of the environment, and the cumulative deficit of maintenance. This bad condition began to show on the exterior of buildings and has spread to all sorts of subdivisions, additions, and enclosures, all the reflection of a growing lack of urban discipline that was never addressed. The policy of taking action first on housing that was in a bad state was understandable in terms of sentimentality, but it resulted in scant resources being utilized in cases that were already lost, while housing that was in a normal, decent state got worse.

Homeowners

The General Housing Law of 1984 turned 85 percent of the population into homeowners, a radical change considering that in 1958 three-fourths of habaneros paid rent, sometimes up to half of their income. The law kept people in the places where they already lived, paradoxically limiting the mobility that is always necessary to adjust to changes in the makeup of the family nuclei naturally produced over time and to changes in the possibilities and expectations of the residents. Those who were lucky to live in high-quality neighborhoods and buildings benefited, but others were shackled to bad conditions, depending on whether they were able to finagle a *permuta* (swap), an exchange of apartments, almost always with money passed under the table. Everyone found themselves in the same situation of having to deal with the maintenance and repair of their homes with their own money and without the resources necessary to carry it out; it was impossible for the state enterprises designed for that purpose to assimilate the enormous cumulative demand.

The conservation of existing buildings turned out to be more difficult in central urban areas, where buildings are taller and of more complicated construction, as well as greater architectural value. As such, the situation worsened for decades because of a policy that prioritized other social and public works programs; in terms of housing, it also prioritized new construction over the conservation of existing structures. This policy even affected housing built by the revolution. Despite a few initiatives to create new solutions, housing continues to be a serious and unresolved problem, with the sad consolation that the same thing is happening nearly the world over.

The Qué-Sadista Era[3]

The problems in the practice of the profession also made their way to the School of Architecture, then the only one in the country. A grotesque personage with an apparently lobotomized sense of humor paraded through the CUJAE costumed with an olive-green uniform and a Makarov pistol at the waist that he carried without having insurrectionary merit. Within only a few years he accumulated an impressive history of ridiculous extremisms, such as placing tents in the middle of the CUJAE to sleep there in solidarity with those who were mobilizing in agriculture. He implanted a technical focus to the course of study and eliminated or mutilated courses with cultural content such as "Visual Arts and Fundamentals of Architecture," replacing them with a Third World–oriented monstrosity that students jokingly called "Underdevelopment I and II." He also sent the teachers he deemed too "cultured" to inhospitable places so that they could "put their feet on the ground," or rather, the mud; and he dedicated his scarce free time to "give attention" to appealing young women with ideological weaknesses. His abuses led him to be publicly thrown out by an absolute majority during an important assembly of workers and teachers in an unusual act of mass public rebellion.

This same person had been as harsh as a whip with those who were different, classified as mannered, extravagant, noncommitted, pseudo intellectuals, or religious believers, who were publicly summoned to the purging assemblies held under the principle that "the university is for revolutionaries." There merciless criticisms were mixed with self-criticism that was more like morbid hara-kiri than honest intellectual exercise. The fate of those who were judged was generally already decided, and the presence of the public was a way to involve the collective in the punishment: expulsion. This aberrant climate fed off of suspicion, opportunism, and envy, unleashing the instinctive cruelty of the human being upon the weak member of the tribe.

Some donned a conformist mask, leaving their religious pendants at home, attending guard shifts and volunteer work, or making suspicious gestures more manly for the sake of not being expelled. Other "deviants" willing to be "rescued" received the benefit of being sent to work in agriculture, as if cutting one's hair, wearing gray khaki, and getting blisters hoeing the fields could keep them on track to meet the parameters that were expected of a young revolutionary college man. The eventual solution of being deprived of the right to study and pursue a career awaited the incorrigible, that expendable human material that in every era has served as a scapegoat. Fear led to a double standard that then spread to those who were purged and those who purged them. It is possible that some of the proponents of that policy and even the victims themselves were convinced that the sacrifices of a few would benefit the whole society. In fact, atheist heterosexuals and revolutionaries were collateral victims of these witch hunts because they made us worse people. I was there, and I did not rise up to object. As did my colleagues, I weighed the pros and cons of the great social project to which I was dedicating my life. I took stock, and I shut up.

As is the case with any other human work, a revolution is subject to mistakes, but when ethical and moral principles that have nothing to do with political trends are violated, such errors turn into abuses. To profess religious beliefs, to maintain relationships with friends and family abroad, or to have same-sex preferences was defined at that time as a problem with one's morals, just as was having voted in the 1958 elections held by Batista. With time, some of those who had been kicked out were readmitted, although others fell by the wayside. The classificatory criteria to exclude them changed, which shows that they were *never* principles, because principles do not change.

Confirming Lenin's phrase about extremists, the lamentable inquisitor of the CUJAE changed his borrowed uniform to a white robe and now is the guru of his own sect, where he contemplates past reincarnations while he cures his followers with holy water. Perhaps he has finally found peace with himself. But the distrust for unpredictable architects did not disappear when this character went off the map. Architecture was later subsumed into a School of Construction at the CUJAE. Although it later returned to being its own school, the other three schools that currently exist in the country still follow that structure, while in other countries architecture as a course of study has the rank of an independent Superior Institute, as the youngest Superior Institute of Industrial Design has in Cuba.

At the beginning of the 1960s, the Spanish professor Joaquín Rallo had revolutionized the teaching of design at the School of Architecture in Havana, amid a climate of experimentation also fostered by other outstanding teachers. Rallo made important theoretical and methodological contributions with a militant, ultra-leftist radicalism that epitomized the spirit of the era. He attracted other relevant creators in music and the visual arts; he also attracted the attention of the mediocre upon himself. Among those who were thrown out the window in that cultural counterrevolution, he suffered more than anybody else. He was exiled to Jagüey Grande, where he lived in deplorable conditions that exacerbated an illness about which he never complained and that killed him at the age of forty-two. However, the moral lynchers were not only resentful, inept colleagues or fundamentalist youth desperately seeking their place. There were also talented architects, though few in truth, who became oppressors of their fellows, demanding austerity, blind obedience, and anonymity from them to atone for the sin of having once defended beauty and personal expression. Curiously, one of the most significant of the renegades later failed to comply with those monastic precepts and dallied in expensive caprices that were allowed and even celebrated, demonstrating that talent is not free from some human trivialities.

Prefabrication Takes Over

While some aspects of the 1970s were positive, they were accompanied by the persistence of a dominant line of thought where supposedly the only possible way to satisfy the enormous needs that had piled up was by means of a tedious prefabrication of large panels that were put into place with large cranes to make high-rises. Despite strong evidence to the contrary, this model was maintained, demonstrating that mental prefabrication is more rigid and long lasting than the technological sort. Year after year, the country became covered with repetitive projects.

The creation of the microbrigades in 1971 was an attempt to find a parallel route to government action on housing construction, supporting the personal motivation of those who were involved. Many were surprised when, in 1984, it was found that two-thirds of all dwellings built since 1959 had been erected by individual residents, despite not really having official endorsement. At the end of the 1980s, the social microbrigade began building to fill in empty lots within the consolidated urban landscape. Although the technology it used was traditional and thus more flexible, the majority of the projects dragged on with the unhealthy inertia of the traditional box, the result of habit. The movement was later dedicated to building social works, leaving many multi-family buildings half-built.

Why Bother Being Architects?

In 1967 the Association of Architects had dissolved and was replaced the following year with the Superior Technical Center of Construction; the Cuban Union of Architects and Building Engineers (UNAICC) was created in 1983, which grouped together these professions, thus diminishing their respective personalities. The presence of the word *construction* in these names established an institutional tie and reflected the preponderance of the builder. The Society of Architects was later created within the UNAICC itself. This organization has promoted City Prizes in different categories, seeking to highlight the good quality of both design and execution, something difficult to combine. The National Prize in Architecture for Life and Work also falls under its auspices, with the good intention of covering an extremely wide occupational spectrum that includes architectural designers, urban planners, material and technical researchers, project directors, teachers, theoreticians, critics, administrators, and activists. Inevitably, this goes against the idea of celebrating the architect as creator, and perhaps there should be separate categories within the prize. It is definitely quite interesting to compare the institutional and popularizing relevance of these prizes in comparison with those in literature and visual arts.

The incorporation of architects into the Cuban Union of Artists and Writers (UNEAC) was initially seen with contempt, not only because of the selective nature of that organization, which revived the ghost of elitism, but also because it constituted a front that was parallel to the UNAICC. The solution was to use the name Environmental Design for that section within the Association of Visual Arts of the UNEAC. Over time it has been proven that there is room for everyone, because their interests and profiles are different.

Technobureaucratic centralization replaced the always-questioning humanism of the architects and imposed models that rested on structural and constructive solutions, turning these into an end in and of themselves. The heavy prefabrication brought from Eastern European countries, where the cold was a good reason to produce large reinforced concrete panels in covered structures, became widespread. With it, the best qualities of in situ concrete were lost from the start, its monolithic quality and capacity to adopt a variety of shapes. At the same time, tall housing buildings became a symbol of prestige for all the provincial capitals, without giving thought to their intrinsic vulnerability, their high cost and consumption of energy, and the resources expended for their construction, use, and maintenance; their inadaptability to traditional ways of life; and the break they made with their surroundings, as well as with local and national cultural identity. Another egalitarian module was the construction of Plazas of the Revolution throughout the entire country, while the one in Havana still awaits a spatial definition to differentiate it from the amorphous asphalt yard inherited from the Batista period.

Cities and Citizens

After delving into the issues that concern us, it would do well to change the focus to the problems Havana has in common with other cities of the world and also their possibilities. Curiously, they are not so different from ours. There seems to be a consensus that cities should be able to pay for themselves, placing value on the giant investment in time, energy, building materials, skills, and even the expectations built up over dozens of generations. The added value thus obtained should directly and visibly revert to the territory and its population. Promoting stronger popular participation can contribute to a more appropriate balance among the people who have the greatest needs, those who think about it, and those who make the decisions. This gives more information to citizens, so that they can choose the alternative that best suits everyone. Theoretically, every problem contains its own solution, but finding the solution requires a sensitive attitude with minimal interventions that preserve diversity and respect for other existing beings and things. However, this balanced line can also lead to a deterministic and passive position that justifies inaction.

Globalization is a reality that is not chosen: at most, one can attempt to steer it. On the one hand, it favors contact between peoples far apart; on the other, it imposes increasingly similar economic, technological, and cultural patterns. This erases particularities separated in time, favors extirpation, and reinforces the dependence of countries on the periphery upon those in the center. This process is accompanied by the relative weakening of nations' economic power, while the regional groupings of countries increases, as well as that of big cities and their spheres of influence.

The potential of public spaces to articulate the urban fabric, orient displacements, reinforce a sense of place, and sustain civic culture still has not been sufficiently explored. Its role in facilitating interaction among different social strata and leveling inequalities is also not understood, and this function is increasingly important in our case. It is certain that the accelerated development of communications and information technology does not eliminate the vital need to see real people face to face. The long history of human dwellings shows sad examples of flourishing cities that disappeared or fell into decadence, but it also shows many other cities that have learned to adapt to change with ingenuity and grace, following the few enlightened cities that foresaw such change and led the march forward.

Havana Today

In the current difficult economic situation, with little being built, it would be desirable for those few buildings to at least have the best design possible; unfortunately, that is not the case. In general, there appears to be an influence diluted from the worst commercial architecture of Miami or Cancun, pathetically taken on as if it were advanced. Nonetheless, there are a few recent projects that are quite decent, which set a high standard of quality. At the level of urban design, Villa Panamericana (1991) was the first and, until now, only example of New Urbanism in Cuba, an alternative to the chaos of Alamar, Reparto Bahía, and other similar complexes that the Spanish have called *sopa de bloques* (block soup). Its clear structure is in homage to the traditional city, that which everyone recognizes; and it gallantly supports a less creative architecture, affected in its variety by the velocity with which it was built. It is certain that cities cannot be built all at once, even by geniuses such as Le Corbusier or Niemeyer.

One of the most interesting recent buildings was the expansion in 2000 of the International Financial Bank on Fifth Avenue in Miramar, by José Antonio Choy and team. It achieved a complex integration of contrasting styles by framing and crowning the old classical-modern building with a contemporary deconstructionist addition resulting in the creation of a work that seemed to have always been like that. On a different scale focusing on interiors, something similar was attained with the restaurant A Prado y Neptuno (Roberto Gottardi, 1998), continuing the pioneering angle of integrating the old and the new that the same architect explored in 1968 with the later very ill-treated pizzeria Maravillas in the district of Cerro.

There is a generalized perception that good architecture is inevitably expensive. But there are fine examples all over the world built with humble materials, and many others that are absolutely execrable, yet built with the most expensive materials. At the same time, the concept of *expensive* is relative: in its day, the No. 1 Unit of East Havana was criticized for being too expensive. However, when the numbers are looked at today, they are laughable. This continues to be the best social housing complex made in Cuba. Almost a half-century later it remains unchanged, not only because it was well executed but also because the residents know very well that if they do not take care of what they have, then they will not have another chance to find something similar.

The reluctance to call for competitions of architectural designs persists, although this selection process is used around the world; and when they do occur, they are of limited scope—often internal competitions within state design enterprises and without adequate rewards for the effort. This is most likely due to the resistance against delegating the pleasure of deciding to a jury. There are good plans for architectural projects, including those of commemorative monuments, that have won competitions and yet remain shelved, while other, worse projects are built that have not passed through the filter of a jury. This kills the confrontation that is necessary to raise quality and makes it difficult for younger, potentially more renewing architects (or those who do not have institutional backing) to make themselves known.

Raising the Bar

There are avant-garde works, a type of architecture for architects, that are essential for marking patterns, setting trends, and raising the bar for average architecture, which is definitively that which *makes* the city. The economic crisis has reduced the opportunities for that type of exceptional work, and with the few opportunities that do appear—generally financed by joint-venture enterprises—foreign partners attempt to impose their tastes, which they often manage to do.

Precisely because of this dependence upon a few investors, it is more difficult to refuse those impositions and risks that seem insensitive to the needs of the country. That is another of the unhealthy effects of a centralization so strong that it only permits dealing with a very few foreign associates. It also impedes the restoration of the network of commercial streets in the central city, with its thousands of small stores side by side, now empty or converted into caricatures of housing. Such a restoration demands thousands of small and mid-level investors, who cannot be attended to centrally. A phenomenon exactly the opposite of that in Centro Havana occurs in El Vedado and especially Miramar, where many mansions are converted into caricatures of stores.

Many urban planners in Cuba are weakened by an informational anemia that includes the difficulty of obtaining decent, current magazines on architecture, as well as limited Internet access. This last point also concerns other professionals, affected by an isolation based on the contempt for ideological bombardment by the enemy. That lack of knowledge of what is going on in the world leads them, from time to time, to "discover" what is already known or to fall to their knees like gullible natives before a false, alien god when confronted with fashions that are often already passé in the global centers where they began. This has happened in Cuba with mirrored glass, which is also completely unsuited for our climate.

It is interesting to compare the high national and international level reached by visual artists from Cuba with that of its architects. Obviously, there are essential differences in the products of each, but there are also differences in processes, institutional frameworks, compensation, and social recognition work. Leaving aside individual wounds, the leveling that characterized the cultural politics of the 1970s in literature, theater, and the visual arts could be restored, in good part, with a later opening up that included the public reinstatement of creators who had been persecuted or removed. In the production of the built environment, the blow was more impersonal, but it also lasted longer. In architecture, the creator does not produce in isolation and of his or her own accord, with the exception of multimillionaires like Philip Johnson. The architect needs someone to commission a work, and in post-1959 Cuba that someone has always been a government entity. Those works are large, expensive, survive their creators, and should satisfy functional needs as well as the expectations and, to some extent, the taste of whoever commissions them— and these tastes do not always coincide with those of the architect. In reality, it is a process of constant mediation that ideally culminates in a mutually agreeable compromise. That is even more difficult when there are multiple intermediaries and interpreters between the architect and the future user, who often never meet face to face.

The role of the professional is, without a doubt, to make sure that the project and the work itself turn out well, but this requires a decision maker who is truly interested in obtaining a product of high quality. That is the tragedy of the advisory boards, which need someone who wants to be advised in order to function. Ironically, whoever requests advice is, in general, the person who least needs it. This artificial separation between the creator and the user is complicated by the institutional separation of the project and its actual construction.

Another quite serious problem that affects the urban environment is the lack of control over its works, as much by the state as by the population. The regulations that are in force are not applied, and if they are, they do not achieve their objective. It is evident that the amount of fines to violators is not enough to dissuade them, compared to the resources that are mobilized for any building project. In reality, the uncontainable proliferation of distortions that deform the city and make it vile are even more harmful than a few new works that are ugly or anodyne. Those deformations waste the important efforts and achievements of the restoration of the patrimony of older buildings. It is known that the only effective brake is to stop the work and to demolish projects that have been built illegally, as was done decades ago. That demands a firm political will, convinced that harsh initial action is enough for the message to be understood and for violations to cease.

But the zeal applied to pursuing illegalities in housing or in the acquisition of materials does not extend to works that are also illegal and furthermore remain for many generations. Ironically, the current strategy seems to be to validate them and for that the Community Architects are used. Their role had been conceived of as advising the population during interventions inside their homes, and now they have been turned into inspector-officials. A paternalistic laissez-faire, the disempowerment of the population, and the confusion between popular culture and populism have allowed that sad mutant, the culture of *aguaje*—much ado about nothing—to flourish out into the street. The citizen is crushed by amorphous junk that falls on top of him or her upon walking through the streets and is subjected to a constant bombardment of equally scandalous bright colors and music. This is a caged city where people move with difficulty between two friendly or at least known points, crossing hostile territory dominated by marginal hustlers and their revered exemplary model, the maceta.

The deformation of the urban image and patterns of behavior can be attributed not only to the uprooting created by rural immigration—which partly filled the space left by the mass exodus of the previous dominant class that was white and urban—but a preexisting urban *otherness* also holds great weight. It is expressed in ways of speaking and dressing, manners, and a certain kind of music more aimed to fray one's nerves than to stimulate emotions or thought; it is also reflected in mass media. The situation is complicated by the kitschy contribution of a persistent petit-bourgeois provincial culture, triangulated in a round-trip journey to and from Hialeah. This all comes together with what Héctor Zumbado called the petit-proletariat.

One can observe a deterioration of civic culture, an internalization of norms of shared living and patterns of conduct that no longer translate into respectful use of public space. Urbanity has been done away with, along with other traditional values that cannot be called elitist, classist, or racist. It seems necessary to give value to values or, to articulate it more clearly, for the citizens who practice them and incorporate them into their lives to benefit from them. As always happens, what is important is who is in charge and to what interests that person responds.

The city is increasingly dystopian, with a topos that is damaged, uncomfortable, and dysfunctional and with a corresponding loss of a sense of place. Every day we see ourselves reflected in a cruel mirror that shows a worn face, once animated by the utopia that called us together with its ideal non-place. Birth, growth, maturity, aging, and death are the inevitable stages of any type of life, including that of cities. However, just as humans do, cities should know how to age with dignity, without wallowing in a useless nostalgia for their lost youth, and to direct their own inevitable renovation before it imposes itself by following the perverse laws of entropy, to introduce chaos. Architecture is not enough to resolve these great problems, but it can help.

What Is the Purpose of Debate?

The commotion around the recent *guerrita de los emilios* is due to the indefinite postponement of analysis that should have been done earlier, not just for reasons of justice but also to preserve the health of the social project in which we are all involved.[4] The idea that a problem does not exist if it goes unmentioned is not only antimaterialist but suicidal. Pressure builds up and leads to an explosion or—what is even worse—brings on disillusionment that drags the bad in with good when it arrives and stays for a good long time. At this point, the debate has not even transcended academic spheres. It remains a topic for the initiated, within the conventional conception of culture limited to art and literature, incomprehensible for those who did not intervene in the exchange of messages. When the power of information is not shared and socialized, there is not only a fatal backwardness of culture but also setbacks in the economy. The future of this country does not lie in producing *things* with badly paid workers, or training servants for tourism, but in producing *knowl-*

edge and thus taking advantage of Cuba's principal resource: its many qualified and hardworking people.

Analyzing the problems from the past forty years should not remain an academic exercise, or simply a liberating catharsis, or a vendetta that removes wounds and injustices and seeks to repress old repressors. The most important thing is to learn from these deeds and to make sure that they are not repeated. That enormous figure of the twentieth century, Nelson Mandela, showed the way: make offenders recognize their abuses and mistakes and then move forward. But other new mistakes could be made, and we should not wait another forty years. Returning to the often forgotten principles of dialectics, one must know how to advance by using contradictions as a starting point, not by silencing them. We should think and act with the freshness and energy of youth, or let them take the lead when we start to repeat ourselves. To do otherwise leads to stagnation and regression, which is living death. I hope that this debate both clears and finishes the path at the same time, so that one day we can laugh at the idea that back then—now—we viewed this discussion as something exceptional.

Making the city work and maintaining control over it require moving forward to make change, but imagining the future is always an exercise that can turn from something fun to something terrifying. Perhaps it is better to concentrate on this very moment and answer this question: are we making the kind of architecture this country deserves? From this half-century of shared desires, dreams, and risks, I want to see from within what will happen and to help, along with all of you, so that it turns out the best possible way.

Notes

This chapter is taken from a lecture given by the author on March 19, 2007, in the Instituto Superior de Arte (Superior Institute of Art), Havana, as part of "The Cultural Politics of the Revolution: Memory and Reflection," a conference organized by the Centro Teórico-Cultural Criterios (Criterios Theoretical-Cultural Center).

1. The three major revolutionary organizations that opposed Batista's dictatorship in the 1950s became one after the triumph of the revolution. They were called the Integrated Revolutionary Organizations (ORI). Some members of the old Cuban Communist Party (Partido Socialista Popular) tried to take control, putting aside the Movimiento 26 de Julio and Directorio Revolucionario, who actually had carried the bulk of the armed struggle. An ORI slogan was "la ORI es la candela," using *candela* (fire) as in a popular interpretation referring to the best.

2. *Enfermito* was a pejorative term used to refer to homosexuals or youngsters who dressed or acted differently and were supposed to be "sick" members of society.

3. Gonzalo de Quesada was the name of the director in the 1960s and 1970s of the Higher Polytechnic Institute José Antonio Echeverría, which includes all the engineering careers plus architecture. He was a typical demanding extremist. Que-Sadista plays with his name and refers to sadism.

4. *Guerrita de los emilios* is a popular name for an e-mail "war" that started among Cuban intellectuals protesting against the TV presentation of three characters who had led the repressive culture of the Gray Quinquennium. Protests reached the higher levels of the government and public presentations were made about different fields of Cuban culture.

3

Barbacoas: Havana's New Inward Frontier

PATRICIO DEL REAL AND JOSEPH SCARPACI

The recent documentary *Habana: Arte nuevo de hacer ruinas* (*Havana: The New Art of Making Ruins*, 2006), by the German filmmakers Florian Borchmeyer and Matthias Hentschler, examines the lives of habaneros inside the decaying buildings of a ruined city. The filmmakers bring to the foreground elegant works of eclectic architecture from the beginnings of the twentieth century that mirror the people living inside them. The Campoamor Theater, the Arbos Building, and the Hotel Regina serve as evocative spatial and figural backdrops for the personal narratives of Reinaldo, Magdalena, and Misleidys —local inhabitants who speak about leaving Cuba, death, history, decrepitude, beauty, resignation, *resolver*, and the overall sadness, which, in their view, envelops the city.

As if these narratives were not enough, the filmmakers also deploy the Cuban writer and intellectual Antonio José Ponte, who serves as guide, interlocutor, and interpreter of the devastated landscape of the city alongside the personal narratives of common people. The presence of Ponte is crucial: his voice as an intellectual gives political meaning to the everyday narratives of average Cubans. In perhaps the most poignant of observations on the ruined condition of Havana, Ponte states:

> If in your private space you cannot rebuild what has fallen down, then you cannot do it any place else. That is why the rulers of the country have a purpose about these ruins: to show their subjects that they cannot change anything. If

you cannot renovate your house, you cannot renovate the kingdom. This private failure precedes public failure. And that spurs Cuban political discouragement, Cuban civil discouragement: the mindset that you cannot do anything about it. Let the buildings collapse, but you cannot change anything. And I think that has been the most important contribution of the revolution to urban thinking. The idea that nothing can be restored. Nothing can be repaired. Then the country cannot be repaired. Let it be. (Ponte in Borchmeyer 2006)[1]

This is an insightful interpretation since it sees the ruined state of Havana as the morphological manifestation of the ideological manipulation of the city and its population by the power of the state. Ponte's elucidation reminds us of the revolution's distrust of the capital city, always depicted as more cosmopolitan than Cuban. Its ruined state is the punishment for its prerevolutionary success in the international concert of world cities. This is a discourse that the film systematically reinforces by the inclusion of black and white footage of late 1950s and early 1960s Havana and the music by La Lupe and others. The classic images of bars, beautiful women, and crowded streets were used in the beginnings of the revolution to construct a city of moral ruin, and they are now used in the film to construct a cosmopolitan city of beauty, wealth, and excitement that contrasts the current material ruin of Havana.

The ruined city serves as a metaphor for the ruined political subject, which, as Ponte claims, cannot change anything. In the film, following Ponte, contemporary Havana is but a metaphor of the ruined lives of its inhabitants, ruined not because they lived in and among ruins, but because they are unable to rebuild themselves, their home, their city. These passive subjects, who escape only through dreams, nostalgia, or pets—like Omar and Totico who raise pigeons on the rooftop of the Arbos Building—are condemned to a static reality in which no meaningful emancipatory agency is possible.

We believe that this notion of a passive subject is an ideological discourse supported by the misleading ideas of a heroic political subject, nostalgic views of a cosmopolitan capital city, and elite cultural perspectives. The film presents the harsh reality of everyday life in Havana, but it does so in an overly pessimistic way. By portraying its inhabitants as victims of a life in ruined houses, it casts a shadow over the entire city. We aim to bring to light another Havana, a city in which one can see, among the ruins, the melancholia of its people and the harsh reality of everyday living, not a happy, bright, and musical city but, rather simply, a city built by its inhabitants.

A Complex Problem

The question of minimal standards of inhabitation, defined either through biological, psychological, or rational means, frames the urban transformations brought about by the processes of modernization. This is not the place to elaborate on this complex issue, which, in architectural studies, is traced back to the late eighteenth century in Europe. For our purposes, it suffices to say that the housing question became a core concern of modern architecture since the International Congress of Modern Architecture (CIAM) that met in 1929 in Frankfurt to discuss the topic of *Die Wohnung für das Existenzminimum* (minimal existence or low cost dwellings). Following the success of the 1927 *Siedlung* or housing development exhibition of Weissenhof (a small town outside Stuttgart, Germany), the second CIAM congress lead by Ernst May addressed a question that the 1927 exhibition had avoided: the condition of social housing.[2] The German wing of CIAM proposed anti-aesthetic positions where Marxist views on property, class struggle, and management of production set the sociopolitical foundations of the housing question along the terms of agency, political involvement, and social commitment.

In 1942 Josep Lluís Sert's book, *Can Our Cities Survive?*, synthesized CIAM's urban theories as presented in the 1933 Athens Charter. The charter takes up Le Corbusier's views on urbanism. He had rejected the notion of minimal existence and forwarded housing as an integral part of urban planning, thus displacing the individual as the central preoccupation of social housing. Unlike the German branch of CIAM, Sert, following Le Corbusier, insists on the priority of an aesthetics of architecture, on the leading role of the architect, and the primacy of the general bourgeois values of architecture. *Can Our Cities Survive?* became a mouthpiece for the rational organization of the city as a whole. Using several case studies, Sert analyzes the slums inherited from the nineteenth century.[3] However, the critique of style is at the core of his argument, highlighting an aesthetic and professional agenda under the guise of social betterment.

In early-twentieth-century modern architecture the housing question is thus framed in two distinct yet overlapping perspectives. Both positions were put to the test in the postwar period. The social consciousness of the postwar period came to fruition in Europe's reconstruction effort, in the United States in the rise of corporate capitalism, and in Latin America in developmentalist ideas that dominated housing issues. An important change was introduced by the eruption in architecture of anthropological language and ideas in the 1950s and 1960s; this, as well as the use of photographs as an ethnological tool, would bring slums, shantytowns, and bidonvilles to the center of the question of social housing. It is no coincidence that the newfound concern for slums is coincidental with the early processes of decolonization. The disruption of traditional societies had been a constant theme in the European discourse of modernity. The question of what constitutes the vernacular in an industrial and industrializing society came to the foreground as the great housing projects in Europe, the United States, and Latin America were being built. The attempt to understand the anonymous history of displaced rural populations became paramount as their life-styles and social organization were being spatially reconstituted through new housing developments. This novel approximation helped establish a new line of thinking along the theme of *habitat*.

Latin American attempts to create a welfare state were constrained by the region's economic and political developments. Housing projects like the Pedregulho (1946–1958) by the architect Affonso Eduardo Reidy in Rio de Janeiro; the Unidad Habitacional Presidente Miguel Alemán (1948–1949) by the architects Mario Pani, José Luis Cuevas, and Salvador Ortega in Mexico City; the mammoth 23 de Enero complex (1955–57) by the architects Carlos Raúl Villanueva, Carlos Brando, and José Manuel Mijares in Caracas; the Unidad Vecinal Portales (1954–1966) by the architectural firm Bresciani, Valdés, Castillo, and Huidobro in Santiago; or the Unidad Vecinal Habana del Este (1959–1963) by the architects Reynaldo Estevez, Hugo D'Acosta, Mercedes Alvarez, and Mario Gonzalez in Havana presented and constructed new social collectives.

Although successful housing strategies were deployed, these worked to the benefit of only a portion of the population, and the ensuing imbalance created *asentamientos marginales* (marginal or informal cities) that are today a common feature of any Latin American city. These barrios, favelas, *villas miserias*, *barriadas, pueblos jovenes, poblaciones*, ranchos, *callampas*, and so on developed without legal permits, technical assistance or planning, and without basic urban infrastructure (water, electricity, sewage). In the 1960s, ideas brought about by dependency theory helped explain these enclaves as products of the territorial organization of capitalism itself. Informal cities grew in peripheral urban areas, "filling" interstitial spaces in the city proper, developing in lands outside the legal urban limits or even as satellite cities, as in the case of Cidade Livre—an informal settlement born out of the building of Brazil's new capital city of Brasilia.[4] Informal settlements also developed in the historic centers, blending with their general decay and abandon. As a manifestation of the structural discriminations of capitalism, these "abusive cities" manifest a politics of marginalization that transforms the worker into a marginal subject (Benevolo 1986, 1008). The spatial disarticulation of the subject—

suffered through his or her separation from the city proper or through the lack of public space in the marginal settlements themselves—brings to the foreground questions of citizenship and the social bond that any city presupposes.[5] This line of thought, prevalent in the 1960s and 1970s, assumes or identifies an unfolding of cities into two: a formal and an informal, popular versus official, peripheral versus central, and so forth. This dichotomy based on polarized patterns of land use became the source of all programs of "betterment" that, as Mike Davis (2006, 98) argues, reveals class conflicts over urban space. Massive evictions or removal of "human encumberments," beautification projects, the criminalization of the slums, and so on that Davis maps throughout the Third World, need to be contextualized in the case of Latin America with the economic assault on the region spearheaded by the Alliance for Progress and the military regimes of the period. The inheritance of the structural economic and political changes of the 1960s and 1970s needs to be measured in space. Squatter settlements, in Brazil for example, cannot be separated from the industrialization of agriculture, which produced in the 1980s O Movimento Dos Trabalhadors Rurais Sem Terra (The Movement of Rural Landless Workers).

Housing in Cuba

In *La vivienda en Cuba*, José Manuel Fernández Nuñez (1976) presents a series of statistical charts that illustrate the "disastrous" condition of public housing in Cuba before the revolution. For Fernández Nuñez the "painful tragedy" of social housing in Cuba was the consequence of the neocolonial structural condition of the republican period. However, if the Cuban Revolution inherited the housing problem from the republic, it also inherited the concerns and intellectual debates that had developed after independence. The period between 1902 and 1959 saw the growth of ideas, projects, solutions, and laws (albeit poorly implemented) to address the housing question in Cuba.

In 1923 the Junta Cubana de Renovación Nacional, presided by Fernando Ortiz, published the *Manifiesto a los cubanos*. In it, leading intellectuals of the period accused the government of Alfredo Zayas and the Congress of abandoning social and public works. Social housing is never directly mentioned. Even though the junta complains of the abandoned and ruinous state of the capital, this abandonment refers to the state and lack of public administrative buildings. Public works are still understood as infrastructure, like waterworks, roads, rail lines, and, above all, education. However, the junta's comments on the state of the rural population, on the beggars that roam all cities, on the need for the betterment of the life of workers, start to delineate the intellectual framework that will manifest a housing question.

Early attempts to address the problem of worker housing can be seen in the Barrio Obrero Redención development (also known as Barrio Pogolotti) of 1910–1912 or the Ludgardita development by the architectural firm Govantes y Cobarrocas and architects Manuel Perez de Mesa and Luis Echevarría in 1929 (De las Cuevas Toraya 2001, 186). Apart from these special instances, housing for the rest of the population remained dependent on private enterprises that would exploit existing buildings by turning them into *cuarterías* for the lowest of classes. For example, when the cloister of the eighteenth-century Convent of Santa Teresa was sold by the Carmelite order in 1923,[6] it was transformed by its new owners into a cuartería. For the lower-middle class and the working class, private entrepreneurs would build two-room apartment buildings called *solares, ciudadelas,* or *casas de vecindad*. This was a practice that had been a common occurrence since the beginnings of the nineteenth century and continued undisturbed after independence (Weiss 1996, 248).[7] The ciudadelas, which possessed communal bathrooms and washbasins, can be viewed as the first forms of mass housing in Cuba, as well as in Latin America (Mesías-González 1995, 13). They have received relatively little attention because, being a business venture, they fall outside the established definition of social housing as a state or public sponsored affair.[8]

The concern for the general conditions of housing in the early years of the republic was the domain of the Secretaría de Sanidad y Beneficiencia. It is within this setting that the *barbacoas* first appear officially. Article 80 of the *Ordenanzas Sanitarias para el Régimen de los Municipios de la Republica*[9] of 1914 states:

> La habitación más pequeña de toda casa de vecindad, no podrá tener menos de nueve metros cuadrados de area y cuatro metros de altura. Queda prohibido dividir habitaciones de las casas de vecindad por barbacoas u otros medios, cualquiera que sea el material que se emplee para ello. (Cuba 1923, 59)

> [The smallest room in any casa de vecindad cannot be less than nine square meters in area and four meters in height. It is forbidden to subdivide rooms in casas de vecindad with barbacoas or other means, whichever material may be used for such.][10]

The fact that the sanitation regulation does not define the barbacoa evidences the currency of the term; that it legislates against its use confirms it as a widespread phenomenon necessitating legislation. The barbacoa is a platform that subdivides a room along the horizontal axis into an upper and lower level. The *Ordenanzas Sanitarias* establish a legal height for rooms with an area of ninety-eight square feet in speculative housing buildings or casas de vecindad. However, we must note that the stipulated height of thirteen feet enables the vertical subdivision of rooms. This most likely has to do with the continuation of colonial typologies and building regulations, which we will address later.

The *Ordenanzas Sanitarias* were issued under the presidency of Mario García Menocal, a member of the Conservative Party, at the beginning of the economic boom caused by the First World War. The "sugar fever," which reached its peak in 1919 and abruptly ended by mid-1920, produced a building boom that resulted in the westward expansion of Havana. But no area of the city was left untouched. Guided by speculation, the traditional city greatly transformed. Small skyscrapers started to appear along the commercial axis of the dense colonial city. Large colonial buildings were bought and demolished, like the Convent of Santo Domingo (San Juan de Letrán) in 1917, bought by Zaldo and Salmón, who planned to build a ten-story building (*Arquitectura* 1917, 39).[11]

As Lilian Llanes points out, the economic bonanza saw an increase in the prices of basic food staples and consumer goods, as well as housing rents. It was accompanied by the reduction of salaries, as foreign workers were imported for the sugar harvests (1993, 64). The general destabilization caused by what was euphorically called the "dance of the millions" had a double effect on Havana; construction of luxurious mansions was followed, as the local and professional press reported, by mass evictions (69).

The professional journal *Arquitectura* commented on "the anguished state of the working classes" (*Arquitectura* 1919, 11). In its general review of the works done in Havana in 1918, the journal commented that there was no incentive for private enterprise to attend to the housing of the middle class and the poor:

> La causa principal de esta anomalía se presume fácilmente. El negocio de construcciones humildes no es, según parece, muy productivo, porque si lo fuera abundarían capitales dedicados a este ramo de especulación. Un propietario de casas nos ha dicho que mientras haya inspectores de Sanidad no será productivo el capital empleado en viviendas para pobres; porque las exigencias sanitarias han introducido un verdadero pánico en el constructor. (*Arquitectura* 1919, 11)

> [The main cause of this anomaly can be easily gathered. The business of building modest homes is not, it would seem, very productive because if it

were, capitalists would abound in this speculative branch. A homeowner told us that as long as there are public health inspectors, capital used to build housing for the poor would not be productive because health and hygiene regulations create panic for builders.]

It is clear that social housing was an entrepreneurial affair that under the liberal economic policies of the 1920s flouted or disregarded any form of regulation. The battle for profit, and thus the tenability of a housing market for the poor, was fought, in the views of the authors of the aforementioned article—which interestingly enough remained anonymous—against the standard set by the *Ordenanzas Sanitarias*. The article stressed the need to establish definitive and invariable sanitary requirements for a building, stating that the root cause of the insufficient availability of housing for the lower classes was the "continuous and unending sanitary impositions that strike as implausible" (*Arquitectura* 1919, 12).

It may be that the legislation, which was introduced as a presidential decree in 1914, was an attempt to regularize what had grown to be an unsustainable health hazard. The *Ordenanzas Sanitarias* must be understood as part of the infrastructural modernization of the city, which introduced trams, telephones, electricity, and paved streets, among many other technological advancements. However, as anyone can notice simply by walking down the former main commercial strips of Old Havana, dotted still today with eclectic skyscrapers, violations of the building codes, which limited the height of buildings in the colonial center, were the order of the day. One can logically conclude the same for the sanitary regulations. This may be the reason why the *Ordenanzas Sanitarias* were officially republished under the Zayas government in 1923, the same year as the *Manifiesto a los cubanos* (Padrón Larrazábal 1975, 85–97). But by 1924 the dance of the millions had ended and the new liberal government had to come to terms with its aftermath (see Comisión de Asuntos Cubanos 1935).

What characterizes the early revolutionary period of the 1960s was the intent to solve, once and for all, the housing question in Cuba. Revolutionary zeal at last brought social housing to the foreground. A brief history of the housing question[12] during the revolution would start in 1959 with the Instituto Nacional de Ahorro y Vivienda, which fomented savings among the population, the creation of the Construction Department of Housing, the reduction of rents, and the expropriation of empty lots, as well as all those buildings that "go against progress and urban planning" (Fernández Nuñez 1976, 94). These first moves by part of the revolutionary government set the stage for the Law of

Urban Reform of 1960, where the bourgeois concept of property was demolished in favor of a "social function of property" (Fernández Nuñez 1976, 96). As thousands of émigrés left empty houses, entire areas of Havana became demographically transformed, as rural students, military units, and needy families were moved into vacated apartments, houses, and mansions.[13] By 1976 the Socialist Constitution enshrined housing as one of the three fundamental rights—along with health care and education—of a Cuban citizen.

The creation in 1960 of the Esfuerzo Propio y Ayuda Mutua program marked the early process of eradication of the slums and shantytowns in Cuban cities. This program called for a social mobilization supported by technicians and architects. The use of the Novoa-Sandino prefabricated system and the involvement of architect Fernando Salinas, who designed the Multiflex system, are from an architectural perspective perhaps the best and most successful example of interactions of this kind.[14] Although this program, as well as others, was always under the guardianship of the state in one form or another, it opened the door to a popular solution and expression of social housing. The Esfuerzo Propio y Ayuda Mutua program was abandoned in the late 1960s for reasons of overall inefficiency and due to the move to centralize the economy of the socialist state. Yet, as the Population and Housing Census of 1970 clearly demonstrated, even with the lack of materials and limited technical support of the state, the population had produced, through self-management and self-building, more than double the number of houses supplied by the state (Mesías-González 1995, 53). Further research needs to be done on the Esfuerzo Propio y Ayuda Mutua program; nonetheless one can say as a working hypothesis that its influence on the attitudes and propensity of the population to take housing matters into their own hands was great.

During the period of institutionalization of the revolution—a period marked by the Zafra de los Diez Millones (The Ten Million Ton Sugar Harvest)[15]—the housing question fell within the ministerial domain. The answer to the census of 1970 was the creation of the so-called *microbrigadas* under the Ministry of Construction. These organisms were connected to work centers and thus serviced a specific social group, creating a gap between these groups and the general population. The guiding idea behind the microbrigades was a reconceptualization of "the housing problem" by Cuban policymakers. Housing ceased to be considered a need of the general population and became associated with specific groups. This brought housing into the fold of a socialist economic organization, as part of a wide array of material goods distributed as incentives for production (Pertierra 2006, 42). The microbrigades declined after the 1980s and were openly criticized for their general lack of efficiency and quality. Essential is the consideration of the relationship between self-construction as exercised by the population and the governmental agencies that attempted to manage and direct these forces. Different ministries, governmental agencies, and laws have—with various degrees of success and failure—attempted to control and regulate the networks (social and economic) and actions that enable self-construction. Yet, as the abandonment of the microbrigades shows, institutionalized forces have never been able to completely control and regulate popular practices like self-construction (Mathéy 1989).

The economic crisis of the 1990s—the Special Period—that resulted from the collapse of the Soviet Union and the end of economic subsidies to the island clearly revealed that urban housing had never experienced the level of attention or success that other revolutionary initiatives, namely health and education, enjoyed. By the 1990s housing conditions in most cities had worsened in comparison to previous decades. The lack of maintenance of the existing housing stock due to the unavailability of materials, and the dearth of new housing units, exposed two of the three structural problems that Fernández Núñez (1976) had identified at the beginning of the revolution: a degraded material condition and the lack of planning, which thirty-five years later had transformed into ineffective planning.

This condition was precipitated and exacerbated by heavy migration to the capital due to the extreme economic situation. Despite official caps on urbanization in the capital, today 50 to 60 percent of the inhabitants of the historic center of Havana are from other places, primarily from the eastern provinces (Chinea 2003, 49). "Esto está lleno de orientales" (This place is full of Orientals or those from eastern Cuba), states one local habanero.[16] Such heavy migration puts tremendous pressure on the already stressed housing stock and infrastructure of cities.

Barbacoas are partly a result of overcrowding that intensified during the economic collapse of the early 1990s. But they also serve as an indicator that the inhabitants' capacity to build and transform the city has remained intact. The Housing and Population Census of 1995, the most recent and comprehensive, concluded that 51.4 percent of the buildings in the historic center had been transformed with barbacoas, approximately 10,813 buildings. This represents 7,580 housing units of forty-five square meters, or 37,942 rooms of nine square meters (Mesías-González 1995, 37). The census of 1995 detected that in the historic center 44.5 percent of these transformations occurred between 1981 and 1995. However, a study by the Havana School of Architecture dated the transformations a decade earlier, to 1971. In either case, both time brackets are well within the time frame of the revolution; and we agree with Mesías-

González when he states that the barbacoa phenomenon fully developed during the revolution.

One outcome of the housing crisis of the Special Period was the state's encouragement of grass-roots initiatives by communities in urban developments to form *talleres* (workshops) dedicated to urban renewal and the improvement of public spaces (Ramirez 2004). Such initiatives varied in success depending upon a range of social, economic, and infrastructural practices, but individuals made even more important transformations to Cuban cities and households and sought to overcome the shortage of space and material through their own informal initiatives. The creation of informal settlements and extensive transformations of the existing urban fabric was a phenomenon that negotiated the ambiguities of an economic period in which the capacities of the state had receded and the population's access to material resources was unpredictable. Buildings in Havana were transformed through locally built structures, such as the barbacoas.

Building a Barbacoa

As mentioned previously, a barbacoa is a platform or a mezzanine constructed in the interior of an already existing space. It is composed of wood beams that serve as a frame for planks of diverse materials, providing a surface or floor on which to stand on. The most traditional material for the construction of a barbacoa is wood. However, since materials are scarce and are intricately related to personal economies, one sees ad-hoc assemblies of disparate materials: wood, steel, and tubular beams are the most common materials used for structural purposes; cardboard sheets, wood boards, and cement are the most common flooring surfaces. Most of these materials are recycled from collapsed buildings, as in the case of the beams that Consuelo, a resident of Old Havana, used to renovate her barbacoa.

Patricio del Real has conducted field research on the barbacoas since 2000, interviewing residents and photographing and documenting different vernacular typologies. In 2003 he met Consuelo, a fifty-seven-year-old divorced and retired woman living on a 132 pesos pension (approximately five U.S. dollars a month), who, like many in Havana, had built her own home inside a nineteenth-century colonial mansion. Throughout the years Consuelo had transformed the space she occupied, and now it was "time for another change." She presents an especially rich case study, particularly because del Real assisted in the construction of her barbacoa and has followed up for several years to document the progress of the transformation.

Barbacoa in the eighteenth-century Convent of Santa Teresa, Havana.
PHOTO BY PATRICIO DEL REAL.

"I need to rebuild the barbacoa. It's all rotten," she explained in 2003. "But this time I want it permanent. I want a *placa*." In order to support the placa (a thin concrete slab poured on top of the wooden planks of the floor), Consuelo —working with her son-in-law Gidalberto—"found" two steel beams at 240 pesos.

"They were from a building that collapsed. We had to carry them by hand, just imagine!" Gidalberto explained.

Del Real met Consuelo in time to help her finish her project. Stunned at his proposal to help her, she agreed to his offer in disbelief. The next day, del Real showed up as promised, and even though he came to work in his worst clothes, they appeared to Consuelo and her son-in-law as being too good for the job. They offered him a change of clothes, and, with this taken care of, they all started the arduous job of mixing concrete by hand directly on the white marble floor that covered her living room. The project consumed five cement bags at 100 pesos, bought on the black market (state stores price is 150 pesos or six U.S. dollars per bag.) Cement is mixed with gravel and sand, using a total of ten bags of each (at 25 pesos each). The tools, shovels and buckets, were borrowed from friends. These were in poor condition and made the work even more difficult. Consuelo and Gidalberto had received no professional or technical assistance and had not looked for it. Gidalberto had built his own barbacoa years ago for which he had consulted his cousin who worked in construction. Personal experience plays a very important role in these constructions. Ninety percent of these actions have no professional technical assistance, and only 10 percent have building permits (Chinea 2003, 3). Technical assistance remains a crucial concern, since most of these constructions are structurally over-dimensioned, that is, the load-carrying members—like beams and columns—are usually bigger or greater in number than they need to be. This overloads the existing building, as well as being an extra economic cost that could have been avoided. Del Real did offer some technical pointers, more in the form of questions, realizing that the decisions were already finalized and that what was required now was simple, hard work.

After four mixings and what seemed to be an endless number of buckets of concrete carried up a locally made spiral stair, the barbacoa was complete. The process took an entire day. Throughout it, people came in and out, more to look at the work and get informed about the enterprise than to offer physical assistance. Word had spread that a foreign architect was helping to build barbacoas, so some people arrived asking when del Real had time to help with theirs.[17] The visits allowed for small breaks from the hard work. Of all the people who visited the "construction site," only one, a seventy-year-old man, offered to help with the actual construction.

An economically affluent family would have installed brand new linoleum tiles as finished flooring and painted plastered gypsum boards as a ceiling, covering the underside of the beams. Just the linoleum tiles, covering an area of about twenty-five square meters, would have cost five hundred U.S. dollars, a small fortune.[18] These materials can be acquired in government stores and on the black market, the source most frequently used. The quality of the finished surfaces reveals the economic and social standing of each home.

In the case of Consuelo, the concrete finishing of the floor, with some gray paint over it, was good enough. The ceiling, notwithstanding, was covered with plastered gypsum boards and painted white. We wish to underscore that, in this world, even paint is a luxury item. These simple material elements reveal the economic standing and social network of those who have access to them. Access is not only a matter of economics. Consuelo had been working on her apartment for three years, living in a construction site, as she found the materials, stored them in her home, and slowly transformed and rebuilt her home and life.

For the general standards of the historic center and of her building, Consuelo lives in luxury. She has three bedrooms, a living room, a kitchen, and one bathroom in her home, with only extended family visiting her. The high level of material finishes, the good condition and amplitude of the spaces, and the quality of the appliances sets her apart from most of her neighbors. The general comment in the building is that Consuelo lives in El Vedado—a reference to the upper-middle-class neighborhood of prerevolutionary Havana.

The aim of the barbacoas is to gain more livable space by dividing rooms with a horizontal platform in two sections, an upper and a lower one. The general disposition is for public activities (eating and living) to be in the lower level and private activity (sleeping, sexual relations, and private conversations) to be in the upper level. In this sense the barbacoas are built to provide a retreat from the public domain. Since individuals and family are strongly dependent on neighbors and friends, they have to provide a semipermeable link to the community. In his visits to Consuelo, for example, del Real observed during the course of several weeks that doors to homes were rarely fully closed and are generally left more than ajar. This is a sign of occupation—letting it be known that someone is home—and of physical connection to the community. Any "movement" in the building would prompt the immediate presence of the master of the domain—invariably women. For example, every time del Real would visit Consuelo's building, the entire community was curious to find out who was entering the communal space and their faces would appear and vanish at the threshold of their homes, peering through partially open doors and peeking through windows.

That the barbacoas exist in interior spaces and that these spaces exemplify a gendered realm of domesticity should not be easily disregarded or overlooked. In most of the homes interviewed, it was the woman who would describe and narrate the transformations of the home, even when performed by men (husbands, sons, brothers-in-law, and so on). Caridad, a forty-seven-year-old housewife, is a typical case. She has lived in her home for thirty-one years and helped her husband build the barbacoa. Even though Caridad's husband was present during the interview, he receded into the background as Caridad narrated the family history. Caridad explained how her husband, managing the tight spatial constraints, created a three-by-two-meter bedroom by making a barbacoa on top of their current kitchen and bathroom. This was a great relief, since they had lived for several years in a one-room space. Although she recognizes that the stair is extremely steep, she claims she does not mind and is most proud of her husband's ingenuity. "I rebuilt the kitchen," she confidently stated, not to forget that she was no mere observer of the entire process.

The barbacoa is generally the first major *self-built* transformation of the home for those who live in Havana. It expands the living potential of a single room. These transformations are prompted by necessity and centered on the person and the family, as is manifest through the spatial reorganization of the home and its functions (living, eating, sleeping, and *aseo*, or personal hygiene). The history of a person or a family is literally recorded in their home. This spatial history—the need for more living space or a new form of privacy because of a marriage, a new daughter, son, or grandchild, the subdivision or selling of space because of economic need, a divorce, or a family member leaving the country—makes the barbacoas, and all the transformations it subsequently deploys, a diary of the family's lives. When talking to Consuelo for example, it was clear that many of the transformations that she has executed were direct reactions to her divorce and later to her daughter having a child. Her actions, like all those interviewed, were the response to a specific need materialized in space.

Existing space clearly imposes its limits, limits that serve to define the acts of transgression and transformation of any barbacoa builder. In the historic center of Havana, the barbacoa developed from a specific spatial typology of Spanish colonial buildings in which rooms have minimum heights of twelve to fourteen feet. The typical colonial home in Havana developed into a longitudinal parcel and is organized around two interior patios: the *patio soleado* and *patio sombreado*. The consolidation of the urban parcels gave way to a centralized patio type, in which the sun patio (patio soleado) served as the focus of family life and the shadow patio (patio sombreado) that of the servants. There are several colonial building typologies (*casa baja sin zaguán, casa baja con zaguán,* and *casa alta*) that served as single-family residences. The development of these typologies spans several centuries. They consolidated during the nineteenth century, and the hierarchical distribution of spaces followed a prescriptive social order.

What is most relevant for our discussion is that the subdivision of the traditional *puntal* or ceiling height is already present in colonial construction. The development in the casa alta of the *entresuelo* or mezzanine, a level built between the ground floor and the *piano nobile* or the main floor of the house where the family lived, established a precedent of vertical spatial subdivision. As Joaquin Weiss, in his classic *La arquitectura colonial cubana,* states, the development of the entresuelo, which housed the servants and slaves, prompted authorities in the mid-nineteenth century to regulate the height of the puntales to a minimum of 2.78 meters (Weiss 1996, 384).[19]

With the entresuelo, the casa alta claims the space between the ground and the main floor. This frees the ground floor for business-related activities, allowing for rent spaces, workshops, stables, housing, and so forth. The casa alta, representative of the great landowners and industrialists connected to tobacco and sugar, locates the family above the business activities that sustain it. This is an important condition, for one can see that even the most economically prominent examples of the traditional Cuban house were understood and spatially organized as a multifunctional productive unit and did not follow contemporary bourgeois ideas of home habitation, which seep into restoration programs and efforts through the need to respond to the tourism industry.

The barbacoas present a new bond with the existing structures. Occurring in and within the existing city, the barbacoas act directly on the architectural patrimony of Havana. Their builders manage and manipulate a system of values (economic, social, cultural, historic, aesthetic, and many more) that reveal the city itself as a contested territory. In the case of the historic center, managed by the Office of the Historian, the confrontation is evident, since the desires for preservation counter those of inhabitation.

When Consuelo removed the early-nineteenth-century stained glass on the colonial arch, called *sol de medio punto,* of her house to establish a corridor between her barbacoa and a new expansion she built, she acted like her colonial predecessors who would also transform their house to suit their needs. Consuelo saved the stained glass pieces, "for the future, one never knows when these will come in handy," she explained. Although Consuelo understands the historic value of the house she lives in—she is most proud of the perfectly preserved stained-glass window in her kitchen, one of few remaining in the entire building—she acts on the house, transforming it. This appropriation of the values of culture (of the built patrimony) challenges the institutionalized forms that crystallize around these same values to put them to work for the tourism industry.

Barbacoas as New Landscape and Frontier

In contemporary Cuban society the barbacoas are illegal and informal constructions. They are illegal because the government does not officially recognize or sanction these constructions. They are informal because rarely do these enterprises get any form of technical or design assistance by professionals sanctioned by state institutions. In this dual condition of illegality and informality, the barbacoas share similar instances and characteristics with other forms of illegal and informal settlements, like the favelas in Rio de Janeiro, the ranchos of Caracas, the *villas miseria* in Buenos Aires, or the barriadas and pueblos jovenes in Lima. However, what differentiates the barbacoas from all these examples is that the barbacoas are transformations of existing structures. It is not that such transformations do not occur in other Latin American cities; in fact, in Mexico City these platforms are known as *tapancos*. What is singular about the Cuban case is the prominence and the impact that these transformations have had on the city of Havana. More importantly, barbacoa construction represents the most meaningful type of new construction for the average Cuban who copes with a quotidian landscape full of uncertainty and penury.

In Caracas, Rio de Janeiro, Lima, and Buenos Aires the city has been transformed through developments that establish clearer spatial lines and boundaries at an urban scale. In Havana these types of transformations have been minimal. Instead, it is the constructions that Cuban art critic Gerardo Mosquera calls "indoor favelas" (1996, 6) that have marked the city to the point of becoming the subject of songs, short stories, and novels—by the Cuban music group Los Van Van and by writers such as Reinaldo Arenas, Pedro Juan Gutiérrez, and Antonio José Ponte.

In Ponte's short story "Un arte de hacer ruinas" ("A Knack for Making Ruins"), the narrator describes the spatial generosity of the buildings in Havana; the high ceilings offer a new space for modest conquests and for adapting to the housing dilemma:

> When you need to add to the size of your house and there's no courtyard in which to build anything more, no garden, not even a balcony; when you need more room and you live with your family in an interior apartment, the only thing left to do is to lift your eyes and discover that the ceiling is high enough so another level could be fitted in, a loft. In short, you discover the vertical generosity of your space, which allows the raising of another house inside. (Ponte 2002, 21)

This suggests that the barbacoas really represent a version of the new frontier in the new millennium. They provide the only available option for an individual or a household to conquer new and unclaimed spaces. Ponte shows the agency of everyday Cubans, a condition that was left unexplored in Borchmeyer and Hentschler's film with which we opened our analysis of Havana.

Ponte's story articulates the desires that are woven into the detritus of the city. Receiving powerful impulses from everyday life, the characters in his story accumulate objects, animals, maps, and more and develop the Havana that they desire. In "Un arte de hacer ruinas," Ponte turns to the ruin, to decay and death. The ambivalence between generosity and decay ties the barbacoas to the art of making ruins. This art is not a condition of time but rather the primacy of the present, a present excluded from the fossilized historical time of the revolution. The internal spatial growth of Havana becomes the image of another possible city. Those whom Ponte calls "Tugures" or slum builders remake Havana. These builders, nomads who inhabit the city, seek the horizon. In a small island like Cuba such a quest has to be internalized. Unlike the nineteenth-century settlers of the American West or the Argentinean Pampas or even the early *bandeirantes* of Brazil who developed the mythology of the frontier, these spaces in Havana are vertical and not stretched out over the horizon. Thus, in Ponte's narrative these builders turn inward and upward, to the only expansive space left to them.

In the city of Havana we observe that selected locations are being scooped up by national and joint-venture hotel and recreational companies. Since there is no formal real-estate market in socialist Cuba, residents must swap homes (*permutarse*) when trying to coordinate their work lives and their home. At the same time, the city's skyline tells its own story, as several residents of Habana Vieja are fond of saying, "wherever there is a crane, there is a hotel going up." Accordingly, the only spaces available for many habaneros remain the vertical dimensions of a city that continues to manifest itself in creative ways. Cuban ingenuity in resolving problems and finding a fix has a long history. Louis Pérez (2001) shows that nineteenth-century Cubans' reactions to hurricanes did as much to promote a cultural identity and sense of neighborhood as did the independence movement in that same century. Since the demise of the Soviet Union and the rise of the Special Period, a dearth of literature has assessed Cuban resourcefulness in "making ends meet" (Scarpaci and Portela 2009). These are the attributes delicately inscribed in the makeshift lofts known as barbacoas, interior spaces that provide individuals and their families and friends with improved material comfort and express the indelible mark of the new Cuban frontier.

Notes

1. This quote comes at one hour and fifty-two minutes into the film. The English translation, which I am quoting here, is provided by the subtitles.

2. For an excellent account of the CIAM internal debates on these issues, see Ciucci (1981).

3. These case studies are far from the shantytowns created with salvaged materials, which are indeed included in *Can Our Cities Survive?*, but remain marginal in the book.

4. For an account of Brasilia, see Holston (1989).

5. For contemporary questions of cities and citizenship, see Appadurai (2002).

6. Weiss (1998, 248) dates this transformation of the convent to 1923. One of the oldest residents dates it back to the early 1930s.

7. There is no clear usage difference between the terms. *Solares* and *ciudadelas* appear to be popular voices; while *casas de vecindad* appear as an official legislative appellation. Diverse authors interchangeably use these. The main taxonomic categorization that we are trying to introduce is that of buildings transformed into mass housing structures and those built purposely for that function.

8. In Cuba, Obdulio Coca has studied the ciudadelas for several years; Francisco Liernur the Casa Chorizo in Argentina; María Ximena Urbina Carrasco the *conventillos* in Chile; and Sandra Lauderdale Graham the *cortiços* in Brazil.

9. We have to thank Cleidy Vázquez for bringing this document to our attention.

10. Author's translation.

11. Weiss gives the acquisition date of 1916. He also states that the economic downturn stopped the demolition process that had started with the church, leaving the cloister standing until the late 1930s or early 1940s (Weiss 1996, 138).

12. These themes were first developed in del Real and Pertierra (2008).

13. For an ethnographic study of social change and neighborly interaction in one such apartment block in 1960s Havana, see Lewis, Lewis, and Rigdon (1978).

14. See the monographic issue on Salinas of *Arquitectura y Urbanismo* 23, no. 3 (2002), Revista de la Facultad de Arquitectura de La Habana Instituto Superior Politécnico José Antonio Echeverría.

15. This was the name of the titanic effort by the revolutionary government to obtain a sugar cane harvest of ten million pounds. The failure to reach this target goal, but more importantly the collapse of the international sugar market in expectation of this enormous surplus, marked the end of the heroic, manifesto-based management of the revolution and finalized the establishment of a bureaucratic machinery that would organize and control the revolutionary process until this day.

16. Heard in conversations with the local population.

17. This resulted in the development of an architecture studio with local architecture students and faculty Orlando Inclán the following year. The studio Taller Barbacoas developed research concentrating on several case studies. The intent was to develop these case studies into a design and subsequent building project with the participation of the population.

18. From interviews with the inhabitant. The local inhabitant was very proud to have been able to spend such an amount just on the flooring of the house, including the barbacoa.

19. One finds *entresuelos* built in the seventeenth century, although as Weiss states, these are rare. On the functional aspects, see Weiss (1996, 194).

4

The "Slums" of Havana

JILL HAMBERG

Foreign visitors to Havana—while charmed by its stunning architecture, friendly residents, vintage cars, and tropical pleasures—can hardly escape a sense of dilapidation and seeming impoverishment. Steps from Old Havana's elegantly restored colonial edifices, they may easily stumble upon shored up buildings and crumbling facades. On the way from tourist hot spots on La Rampa to Old Havana, they may catch a glimpse of decaying structures.

For long-time Havana residents, the severe economic crisis starting in the early 1990s—known as the Special Period—was not only socially, economically, and psychologically wrenching, but they also experienced a disorienting loss when the long-term, slow deterioration of the city's older districts accelerated into frequent building collapses, including structures on such iconic settings as Old Havana's Plaza Vieja (Old Square), the Malecón seawall drive, and the San Rafael pedestrian mall in the heart of downtown Havana.

But has Havana really become a city of slums, little different from those of other developing nations? To be sure there are *slums* in Havana. However, the meaning and context of this term is quite different in Cuba than elsewhere.

Indeed, the term *slum* does not have a universal meaning. Since its inception in early-nineteenth-century Britain, the word *slum* generally signified not only overcrowding, poor housing conditions, and lack of basic services but also disease, poverty, vice, squalor, and immorality. Governments in developed and developing nations often designated neighborhoods as blighted slums to justify clearance of richly textured and socially thriving urban communities. But the use of social and behavioral characteristics to define slums has been highly criticized. In an attempt to develop an operational definition for future international use, in 2002 a United Nations expert group proposed defining a slum as an area that combines, to various extents, poor structural quality of housing, overcrowding, insecure residential status, and inadequate access to safe water, sanitation, and other infrastructure. Social and behavioral characteristics were excluded. Based on the thresholds for each indicator, UN-Habitat (2003, 14) estimates that nearly a third of the world's urban population lives in slums, with the highest proportion in sub-Saharan Africa (72 percent) and the lowest in developed regions (6 percent). Latin America and the Caribbean have near the world average (32 percent).[1]

This chapter explores several aspects of Havana's slums. What types of slums exist in the city, and how do their characteristics compare with the United Nations' indicators? Who lives in Havana's slums, and do they conform to the stereotype of slum dwellers? Which policies have accelerated, halted, or rolled back the deterioration of Havana's housing?

First, in order to provide context for answers to the above questions, there will be a brief introduction to Cuban housing, urban planning, and economic development policies influencing slums up to 1990. This is followed by a detailed discussion of the characteristics of Havana's slums and their residents. Finally, housing policies starting in the early 1990s will be analyzed.

This discussion will show that, despite their highly visible concentration in certain areas, Havana's slums only partially fit the definition and stereotypes of slums in other developing nations. Moreover, they are somewhat less prevalent than in other Latin American large cities.

Policies Affecting Slums before 1990

The policies pursued since the Cuban Revolution of 1959 prevented the explosion of shantytowns found in other Latin American cities but also resulted in widespread deterioration of Havana's housing stock. The basic urban and regional policies enunciated in the early 1960s were largely followed for the next thirty years (INV 2001b; PNC 1996). These policies were designed to promote balanced regional growth by directing resources to areas other than Havana; diminish urban and rural differences by improving living conditions in the countryside and concentrating the rural population in small settlements; foster the development of a network of settlements; and assure rational land use through comprehensive urban planning. The government hoped to accomplish these goals by coordinating economic and social development with physical planning. At least until the early 1990s, these policies were largely successful, although with contradictions and problems in achieving rational urban land use and stabilizing the rural labor force.

Despite fleeting antiurban rhetoric in the late 1960s, Cuba sought to increase the proportion of its population living in urban areas, reaching 76 percent by 2005 (ONE 2005b). But its annual rate of urban growth has been one of the lowest in Latin America, and, unlike other countries in the region, urban growth occurred primarily away from the capital. Havana's share of the country's economic activity and social and educational institutions declined significantly (PNC 1996). Major new industries, institutions, and housing were located on the outskirts of cities, preserving existing central areas but leading to a form of "socialist sprawl."

The decline in Havana's relative importance was matched by a shift in migration patterns and urban growth rates. In the 1970s and 1980s, small towns and provincial capitals swelled rapidly, in contrast to Havana, which generally grew at a slower rate than the country as a whole. This shift took place in the absence of *direct* migration control measures until the late 1990s, making Cuba one of the few developing nations to contain the growth of its largest city (CEDEM 1996).

Except for brief periods housing has received low priority compared to "productive sectors" of the economy. Even among "nonproductive" sectors priority went to building educational, health care, and other community facilities. Havana received even lower priority for housing and community services since it started at a much higher level than the rest of the country and to discourage migration to the capital.

Given the government's limited direct investment in housing and its concentration in priority locations and economic sectors, residents took the initiative to build their own dwellings with and without public support and authorization. At least two-thirds to three-quarters of all housing created in Cuba since 1959 has been self-built, including subdivisions of, or additions to, existing units as well as conversions from nonresidential uses (Hamberg 1994).[2] Even in Havana at least a third of the dwelling units have been self-built.

New construction, rather than maintaining and repairing the existing stock, was emphasized, although this has shifted to a small extent in the last several decades. Most new, government-sponsored housing was built in large developments on vacant land on the outskirts of all major cities and many towns, but since the 1980s, there has been more "in-fill" building on vacant lots.

Together these policies meant that until the 1990s, Havana was spared the explosive growth in shantytowns found in the rest of Latin America and the developing world. Its inner-city slums were shielded from deliberate clearance for the most part. This preserved the physical and social fabric of neighborhoods, including those with cultural and historical importance, making it almost unique in Latin America and the Caribbean. But it also meant that Havana—with the country's largest stock of old, dilapidated housing and crumbling infrastructure in 1959—suffered continued deterioration, which accelerated in the 1990s.

Havana's Slums and Their Characteristics

As previously discussed, the UN indicators for slums are poor structural quality of housing, inadequate access to safe water, sanitation, and other infrastructure, overcrowding, and insecure residential status. Although excluded from this definition, it is also useful to look at the social characteristics of the residents of areas where most slums are concentrated.

Physical Quality of Slum Housing

Although the generic term *slum* (or *tugurio* in Spanish) is seldom used in Cuba, there are several ways that substandard housing is described: by housing type, housing conditions, building materials, and settlement type. This roughly coincides with the UN category of "poor structural quality" but takes in a broader range of indicators.[3] The location of different types of slum housing is also important.

The Cuban government regards three housing types as inherently substandard—tenements, rural thatched-roof *bohíos*, and improvised units. The typical inner city slum dwelling unit is a room in a tenement, known by the terms *ciudadela, cuartería, casa de vecindad, pasaje,* or *solar* (Mathéy 1994; Ortega Morales 1996).[4] It is usually a single room with shared bathing and sanitary facilities in a common courtyard or passageway, although such rooms are often upgraded and expanded to include indoor plumbing.[5] The great majority of these single-room units are located in older multifamily buildings in Havana's central areas. But individual, stand-alone rooms are also found in the backyards of inner-city blocks and in outlying shantytowns. A "hybrid" between a tenement and a small shantytown appears when additions to a former mansion subdivided into rooms extend out into the backyard until they become individual units detached from the original building.

Most census reports and the National Housing Institute generically refer to all such single-room units as cuarterías or "rooms in cuarterías"—which is translated in this chapter as "tenement" as opposed to apartments, houses, or bohíos. In 2001 there were 60,754 tenement units in 6,932 buildings in Havana, representing nearly three-quarters of all such units in Cuba (INV 2001a). However, most of these appear to have been upgraded with kitchen, bathing, and toilet facilities since they were categorized as "apartments" in the 2002 Census (ONE 2005a). This census reported that only around 21,000 units (3.1 percent of the total) were tenements.[6]

Almost nonexistent in Havana, bohíos are thatched-roof shacks that were once common in rural areas. In 1996, 6 percent of all units in Cuba were bohíos (Bauzá 1997). They represented about a fifth of rural units in 2002, a considerable improvement since 1981, when they represented nearly two-fifths of rural units.[7]

Dwelling units built mostly of scrap materials are considered "improvised." Only about a hundred units in Havana were categorized as "improvised" in the 1981 Census (CEE-ONC 1984). In 1996 there were 3,574 units located in shantytowns categorized as "improvised" (ONE-OTECH 1997). At the end of 2001 Havana was one of five provinces that had virtually eliminated dirt floors according to the National Housing Institute (INV 2001a), but with new shantytown growth, the number has undoubtedly risen (Pérez and Orta 2008).

In addition to dwelling units originally built for housing, a small but significant number of occupied units have been converted from nonresidential uses, such as stores, garages, and warehouses. Moreover, with the drop in tourism in the first decades of the revolutionary period, most of the smaller inexpensive hotels and boarding houses also became permanent dwellings. In 1981 some 34,000 dwelling units—or 6.5 percent of Havana's total—had been adapted from nonresidential uses (CEE-ONC 1984) and since then a growing number of conversions have occurred.[8]

Although not a specific building type, many older buildings with high ceilings—whether tenements or not—have added *barbacoas,* which are mezzanines or loftlike structures that create an extra floor, potentially doubling the unit's floor space. As of 2001 some 51 percent of Old Havana's historic district units had barbacoas (UNESCO and Oficina del Historiador de la Ciudad 2006, 41), which is a native word for a rustic hut or platform, also extended to mean grill or barbecue. They are a creative way to stretch space, achieve greater privacy, and ease overcrowding, but unless well designed and well built they can be unsafe and poorly ventilated; moreover, their bricked up windows can deform building facades. Barbacoas—together with their furniture and appliances—add considerable weight to load-bearing walls, already weakened by leaks, corrosion, and heavy rains. This is often the cause of partial or complete building collapses. Wooden barbacoas are sometimes replaced with well-designed concrete structures, improving safety but adding weight.

Another source of extra residential space, as well as extra building weight, are *casetas en azoteas*—literally "shacks on roofs"—which are usually wooden structures built on top of multifamily buildings. There are also well-built units on roofs of such buildings, creating informal penthouses. Indeed, well-built units on roofs of single-family units are one of the main forms of creating standard housing and increasing Havana's density.

Another common measure of housing adequacy in Cuba is housing conditions based on the degree of deterioration and need for repairs regardless of building type. Three categories are used—good, fair, and poor—although it's unclear what the criteria are for these categories. According to official figures, 64 percent of Havana's 586,768 units were considered in "good" condition in 2001, up from 50 percent in 1990 (INV 1990; INV 2002). Some 20 percent were in "fair" condition, and 16 percent were in "poor" condition. In the mid-1990s about 60,000 units needed to be replaced (Lee 1997). In spring of 2008, nearly 1,000 buildings with almost 8,000 units, housing 25,700 residents, were listed in "critical condition," and there was a plan to start replacing them (J. A. Rodríguez 2008).

Partial or total building collapses are not uncommon, although the number had been cut in half by the end of the 1990s as the worst units disappeared and others were repaired. The municipality of Old Havana averaged about two partial or complete collapses every three days in the late 1990s (PDHL 2000), and that average jumped to more than one a day in the early 2000s (UNESCO and Oficina del Historiador de la Ciudad 2006, 38). By spring of 2008, there were one to three partial or complete collapses a day in the entire city (J. A. Rodríguez 2008). Partial building collapses range from part of a balcony breaking off to a roof or wall falling down. The National Housing Institute estimated that 4,064 units—0.7 percent of the total—were lost from the city's housing stock in 2000 for a variety of reasons, including collapses (INV 2000).

Buildings in Old Havana and Centro Habana are especially exposed to the elements: high humidity, heavy rains, the corrosive effects of salt spray from proximity to the coast, and flooding (Murray 2008). These factors, as well as its much larger stock of older deteriorating buildings and greater neglect, resulted in Havana having many more highly visible slums in its central areas than found in any other Cuban city, and this was the case before 1959 as well.

In 1999 some 26,000 Havana households with 88,000 people were desig-

nated as *albergados*, that is, their current or former dwellings were so deteriorated or damaged by a storm or partial building collapse that they were placed
on a special list for replacement housing (Lee 1997). Most live in less dangerous dwellings or temporarily reside with friends or family. Others have
moved back to their condemned, vacated homes, technically living as squatters in highly precarious situations (Murray 2008). But in 1997 about a tenth
of albergado households actually resided in transitional homeless shelters,
which are discussed below (Reinosa Espinosa and Vilariño Delgado 1998). By
2004, according to the National Housing Institute, the total number of albergado households had dropped to 20,000 (Núñez Moreno 2008, 21).

Of all units in Havana's housing stock, 78 percent were categorized as Type
I (the best) in 2001 in the National Housing Institute's five-category system
based on building materials used for walls and roofs (INV 2002). The great
majority of all structures in inner-city slums are "permanent" in that they are
built of masonry or good quality wood. However, in some cases their perma-
nency is challenged by severe deterioration that could lead to building collapses. There is more variety in shantytowns.

Two settlement types are considered to be inherently substandard: shantytowns and transitional homeless shelters. At the time of the revolution, 6
percent of Havana residents lived in squatter settlements, a relatively low
proportion compared with other Latin American capitals at the time (Hamberg 1994). They were known as *barrios de indigentes* (literally, neighborhoods
of the poor, indigent, or destitute). The largest and worst of these shantytowns
were demolished in 1960 and 1961; their residents built replacement housing
through the Self-Help and Mutual Aid Program. The remaining shantytowns
were officially renamed *barrios insalubres* (unhealthy neighborhoods) to make
clear that the issue was the quality of the housing and settlements, not the
economic status of their residents. Residents, journalists, and researchers also
call shantytowns *barrios marginales* (marginal neighborhoods), *asentamientos
precarios* (precarious settlements), and *llega y pon* (literally "arrive and stay").
But aside from those early efforts—and a brief one in the late 1960s—shantytowns were largely ignored.

But many shantytowns continued to grow, and new settlements were
formed. The official policy had been to "freeze" them: no new dwellings were
allowed and repairs could only be made using the same type of materials as
the existing dwelling. Nevertheless, residents upgraded their dwellings.[9] The
government provided schools and health clinics, and transportation routes
were extended where necessary. At the same time, most existing residents were
able to legalize their situations as rent-free leaseholders. Government policy

gradually changed and improvements and upgrading became permitted. A number of such shantytowns were sufficiently upgraded so that they fully or partially attained the status of regular neighborhoods.[10] Indeed, even still "illegal" shantytown settlements composed of recent migrants to Havana often have access to water, electricity, cooking fuel, electric appliances, and local health services as well as functioning local community-based "mass organizations," such as the Committees for the Defense of the Revolution (CDR) as shown in the documentary *Buscándote Havana* (Rodríguez Abreu 2006).

By 1987 Havana had 15,975 units in shantytowns, representing less than 3 percent of all Havana's dwellings (ONE-OTECH 1997). But by 2001 the number had grown to 21,552 units, representing a little more than a quarter of such units nationally (INV 2001a). This growth of 35 percent was seen as the result of an increase in net migration to Havana, especially from the less developed eastern provinces and was one factor leading to a new migration law in 1997 discussed below. Despite the new law and the policy of "freezing" shanty-towns, new settlements have continued to spring up, and existing ones expand, in Havana itself as well as in the surrounding municipalities of Havana Province (Pérez and Orta 2008; García Alfonso 2007).[11] Local officials and planners are especially concerned about shantytowns that appear on flood plains or over the city's main aquifer as well as those whose layout makes it difficult to add streets and other infrastructure at a later date.

Albergados receive an official form sending them to a government-run shelter for the homeless, officially called *comunidades de tránsito* (transitional communities). But only about 10 percent of albergados actually go to live in these transitional homeless shelters (Reinosa Espinosa and Vilariño Delgado 1998). They were originally considered temporary, until adequate dwellings could be provided. A group of shelters was first established in 1969–1973; most of their residents were relocated to permanent housing, especially in an up-surge in residential building in Havana during the 1980s. But when it became clear that the stock of new dwellings would not meet all the accumulated needs, a new form of shelter was created in buildings with individual cubicles for each family and shared bathroom, cooking, and dining facilities. With the virtual halt to new building in Havana in the early 1990s, these shelters took on a semipermanent character. By the mid-1990s almost all had been up-graded to contain bathroom and cooking facilities in each cubicle. In 1997 there were seventy-six transitional shelters lodging 2,758 households with a total population of 9,178 (Reinosa Espinosa and Vilariño Delgado 1998), but by the end of the decade the number of shelter residents had declined by about a fifth. Given continued building collapses—and therefore the need for temporary dwellings—there is debate about whether additional shelters should be built and if so, where.

Slum housing is located in areas where there are tenements, shantytowns, and units in poor condition. Most tend to be concentrated in about five or six of Havana's fifteen municipalities; even in these areas—except for tenements in central areas—slum units represent a small percentage of all dwellings.

As to be expected, tenements are concentrated in inner-city municipalities. In the 1990s and early 2000s, tenements represented some 40 to 50 percent of all units in Old Havana's historic district and the neighborhoods of Cayo Hueso and Atarés (Ortega Morales 1996; Padrón Lotti 1998; Plan Maestro 1996). However, the number of units in tenements with shared services in central areas appears to have decreased since the early 1990s because of building collapses, demolitions, and upgrades to full apartments.[12]

Shantytowns are virtually absent from central areas. Nearly half the residents of such settlements, according to a survey in 1996, lived in just two municipalities—Marianao and Arroyo Naranjo—where they represented about 10 percent of the areas' inhabitants. The much smaller municipality of Regla had 9 percent, while Playa and La Lisa around 4 to 5 percent. Five municipalities had less than 1 percent, and four municipalities ranged from around 2 to 3 percent (ONE-OTECH 1997). A *Juventud Rebelde* exposé of shantytown living (Pérez and Orta 2008), stated that nearly half of Havana's forty-six "illegal settlements"—somewhat fewer than found in the shantytown survey of 1997—were located in the municipality of San Miguel de Padrón.

Transitional homeless shelters are located in all fifteen municipalities, and most are at least fifteen to twenty years old (Reinosa Espinosa and Vilariño Delgado 1998).

According to official figures for 2001, the worst housing conditions regardless of building or settlement type were concentrated in five municipalities—Old Havana, Arroyo Naranjo, Centro Habana, San Miguel del Padrón, and Diez de Octubre—which together had two-thirds of the city's units in "poor" condition. These municipalities (plus Regla) also had the highest proportions of units in "fair" and "poor" condition, with Old Havana having two-thirds and the others with 40 to 47 percent of such units.

To summarize, the magnitude of the slum problem in Havana based on the physical quality of housing is somewhat smaller than that of Latin America, where an average of 32 percent of the units are considered slums using UN indicators. Table 1 provides an estimate of the dwelling units and population of each major type of slum housing and its proportion of the total population.

Typical tenement in Atarés with barbacoas in first floor units.

TABLE 1. HOUSING UNITS AND POPULATION OF HAVANA SLUMS (1997–2002)

	Type or condition	Year	Units	Population*	Percent of total population
Housing type	Tenements (all)**	2001	60,754	206,564	9.4
	Tenements (shared services)**	2002	20,969	71,295	3.2
	Shantytowns***	2001	21,552	72,986	3.3
	Shelters	1997	2,758	9,178	0.4
Housing condition	Condemned units (*albergados*)	1999	26,000	88,000	4.0
	Units in "poor" condition	2001	94,000	319,600	14.5

Note: Categories overlap.

Sources: INV (2001a), ONE (2005a), and Reinosa Espinosa and Vilariño Delgado (1998).

*Assumes average household size is the same as in 1996 for shantytowns (González Rego, Rúa de Cabo, and Blanco Sánchez, 2000) and 3.4 for tenements, an estimate based on case studies in central areas in the mid-1990s.

**The Population and Housing Census of 2002 classified tenement units with exclusive use of kitchen, toilet, and shower facilities as "apartments." Most of the 20,969 units classified as "other" in Havana are *cuarterías*, although the category includes *bohíos* and "improvised" units (ONE 2005a).

***By the mid to late 2000s, there were 18,000 people living in 6,200 units in forty-six "precarious settlements" (Grogg 2008).

There is considerable overlap in the table—for example, some units in shanty-towns are categorized as "tenement units,"[13] and virtually all condemned buildings are in "poor" condition, as are most tenements and shantytown dwellings. This table does not include an estimate of units in "fair" condition because in most cases they are basically sound dwellings needing repairs rather than slum housing.

Access to Water, Electricity, and Sanitation

Virtually all residents of Havana have access to electricity (CIEM 2000). In some cases residents have illegally tapped into nearby power lines, but they do have access—indeed, the vast majority of slum dwellers have an array of electric appliances.[14] But given the shortage of spare parts during the 1990s, not all these appliances were necessarily working. Moreover, the economic crisis led to frequent blackouts during the early and mid-1990s. By the end of the decade, power outages were reduced, and by the mid-2000s blackouts had diminished substantially. At the same time, new energy-efficient appliances and light bulbs were made available to most households (Grogg 2007). A crackdown on illegal hookups led to their being metered, and subsequently more residents had to start paying their light bills.

Water and sanitation are almost universally available, although not always inside the dwelling unit (CIEM 2000).[15] Because Old Havana and Centro Habana are at the end of water supply and sewer networks, they get less water and have more trouble disposing wastewater into already full pipes. Half the city is beyond the reach of the sewer system; most of these residents use septic tanks. Moreover, extensive water loss through leaks—by one estimate 58 percent of the total (InterPress Service 2007)—means water is only available several hours a day or even every other day, leading families to install cisterns and water tanks for storage. Water has to be pumped up from the cisterns to the tanks. Leaks, cisterns, and other water delivery problems contribute to deteriorated quality, and many residents boil water, putting further pressure on energy supplies. In some areas, such as Colón, the water mains were in such disrepair in the early 2000s that all water was brought in by water trucks (Rey et al. 2005). However, during the 2000s there has been a substantial improvement in water mains in Old Havana as part of a more extensive project to repair most of the capital's leaks by 2011 (InterPress Service 2007).

Overcrowding and Doubling Up

In comparison with the situation in slums in most developing nations, Cuba's household size is small and overcrowding moderate. But it's not just the number of people per room or the average floor area per person that influences the perception of overcrowding; extensive doubling up in multigenerational families and with nonrelatives also plays a role.

Average household size in inner-city areas and shantytowns ranges from 2.9 to 3.4 persons per household.[16] Average floor space per person in tenements is close to the minimum standards for habitability, meaning roughly half the units are below standard.[17] Available measures of overcrowding in shantytowns are based on household size and the number of rooms, indicating that nearly half had more than two people per bedroom (González Rego, Rúa de Cabo, and Blanco Sánchez 2000).[18]

The degree of doubling up in multigenerational families is related to rates of population growth, births, and household formation. Children born during the twenty-year baby boom starting in the early 1960s began forming their own households in the early 1980s. Nationally, from 1981 to 1995, the population grew by 0.9 percent annually, but households grew by 2.4 percent (Benítez Pérez 2002, 93). Although housing creation nationally outpaced population growth, housing in good condition couldn't keep up with the sharp increase in family formation and far less so in Havana (Gazmuri Núñez 2004, 4). This led to doubling up, living in substandard units, or both. In the mid-1990s, nearly half of Havana's households were either "extended" (with relatives other than unmarried children) or "composite" (including at least one person unrelated to the household head) (Benítez Pérez 1999). In the inner-city neighborhood of Atarés, 53 percent of households were in those categories (Ortega Morales 1996).

The housing deficit and consequent doubling up are also thought to be contributing to the steep decline in the birth and fertility rates and the high divorce rate (Núñez Moreno 2008, 24–25). Several authors have noted the vicious cycle of doubling up contributing to divorce that in turn increases the demand for additional dwelling units (Wolfe 2000, 9–10).

Security of Residential Status

With some exceptions, Cubans have a high degree of security in regard to their residential status, also known as "tenure security."[19] By the early 1990s, more than 85 percent of Cuban households were homeowners, paying little or nothing for their units except for maintenance, repair, and utilities. An additional number were rent-free leaseholders, mostly those living in dwellings rated "inadequate."[20] There are no mortgages or property taxes. Financing for purchases of units or repair materials is considered a loan, not a mortgage, and therefore dwellings are not used as collateral. Nonpayment of rents or loans is addressed by garnishing wages or bank accounts, not through eviction or foreclosure.

Within this overall system of substantial tenure security, there are, nevertheless, potential challenges facing a relatively small number of residents. The most likely sources of displacement include dislocation due to public action, loss of housing through natural disasters or a building collapse, and eviction of guests or renters by the homeowner. Residents designated as "illegal occupants" may be fined, evicted, or eventually legalized depending on the nature of the infraction, ranging from failure to have paperwork in order to construction without a building permit or with stolen materials.[21] Violators of the migration regulations of 1997 discussed below—some of whom are squatters in condemned buildings or shantytowns—can also be evicted.

Who Lives in Slums and What are Their Characteristics?

Although social indicators have been excluded from the United Nations' definition of slums, it is useful to examine to what extent Cuban slum dwellers resemble those in other developing nations.[22] In market economies most of the urban poor live in slums and most slum dwellers are poor. However, in Cuba this is much less the case because of relative tenure security and generally low-cost or free housing. Restricted legal housing and land markets, despite the growth in the informal sector, have also had an impact—although such restrictions may soon become more "flexible."[23] Moreover, the demographic characteristics of people living in substandard housing are fairly similar to those of the general population, and they generally have access to the same education, health care, job opportunities, and social security. In practice, nevertheless, some opportunities are not equally available because of the subtle persistence of racial and social prejudices and growing income inequality. But compared to other countries, Cuban slums are quite socially diverse, poverty is relatively dispersed, and social indicators are similar for most areas.

Although slum dwellers were "fixed" in place when the Urban Reform Law of 1960 granted them long-term leases to their dwelling units, other policies and informal practices favored increased geographic heterogeneity. For instance, in the early years after the revolution, many vacant units in "good" neighborhoods were turned over to low-income residents or migrants to Havana, or newcomers simply squatted in vacant units. Also new state-built housing has a mix of residents since units are assigned to a range of employees of workplaces as well as those living in shelters or seriously deteriorated dwellings. However, since the 1990s there have been early signs of a modest resegregation by social class as a result of growing income inequality.

Most slum areas have roughly the same percentage of women as in Havana as a whole, 52.5 percent, with men having a slightly higher proportion in some slum areas.[24] The average age in Havana is higher than the country as a whole—15.4 percent of the population in Havana were over sixty years old in 2000 compared to 12.9 percent for Cuba (MINSAP 2000). In part because of tenure security, Havana's inner-city slum areas have a generally older population than the city. In contrast, the elderly are underrepresented in shantytowns.[25]

Havana's slum neighborhoods were racially diverse according to the 1981 Census, although there was a slightly lower proportion of whites and a higher proportion of blacks and mulattos in municipalities with the highest concentration of slum housing. Whites comprised 63.4 percent of Havana as a whole, and they averaged between 53 and 58 percent of the population in municipalities with the highest proportions of tenements (Old Havana and Centro Havana) and shantytowns (Marianao and Arroyo Naranjo). Blacks represented 16.4 percent of Havana as a whole and between 19 and 21 percent of the population of these four areas (CEE-ONC 1984). More recent surveys in some of these communities indicate a similar racial distribution, with some exceptions.[26] Specific blocks or tenements may have higher concentrations of blacks and mulattos.

As of the mid-1990s roughly three-fifths to two-thirds of residents of slum housing were born in Havana, in many cases in the same neighborhoods as they lived then, although in some areas the proportion was somewhat lower.[27] Most of the domestic migrants come from Cuba's eastern provinces, and most of these had been in Havana since the 1970s. More recent migrants are found in the more outlying areas, while those who arrived before or just after the revolution are concentrated in the more central, consolidated settlements.[28] However, there is some evidence of continued movement into central areas from other provinces, directly or after a time in the periphery of the city, which is discussed in more detail below (Dávalos et al. 2005).

All residents of Havana—as well as the rest of Cuba—have free access to health care in hospitals, local clinics, and neighborhood family doctors. Despite their possibly illegal status, new shantytown residents are usually added to the roster of local health clinics and family doctor offices.

In spite of medication shortages and other challenges in its health system, Cuba's infant mortality rate in 2006 was 5.3 infant deaths per 1,000 live births —in Havana the rate was 4.9 per 1,000—lower than many developed nations (ONE 2007b). Differences among Havana's municipalities were minimal.

Cuba's health indicators are similar to those of developed countries. Most deaths are from chronic noncommunicable diseases, such as heart disease and cancer, rather than infectious and parasitic disease, as is more common in developing nations (PAHO 1999). Nevertheless, the economic crisis of the 1990s did lead to a short-lived increase in rates of some communicable diseases, such as tuberculosis and hepatitis, as well as low–birth weight babies and nutrition-related neurological disease (MINSAP 2000).

Despite the relatively even coverage of the Cuban health system, death rates for both communicable and chronic noncommunicable diseases are slightly higher in such slum areas as Centro Habana (Yassi et al. 1999). The spread of some infectious waterborne diseases like hepatitis is sometimes the result of leaks in water mains and sewers. Kerosene stoves, high humidity, dust, and air pollution in central areas contribute to asthma and other respiratory diseases (CSVC 2002; Spiegel et al. 2003). Cuban researchers have linked overcrowding and noise to anxiety and stress.

All Cuban children have access to free public education. The percent of Havana's children between the ages of six and fourteen in school in 2000 was 98 percent (ONE 2001). School enrollment in Old Havana for children between six and fourteen years of age was virtually 100 percent, and enrollment for fifteen through sixteen year olds was 97.5 percent (PDHL 2000). The educational quality in Cuba and Havana was also ranked highest in Latin America in two UNESCO studies in 1997 and in the mid-2000s.[29] Nevertheless, children in Havana started falling somewhat behind other areas in Cuba. By 2000 the situation of primary education in Havana was quite deficient: the average class size was thirty-seven children, and the schools were in serious disrepair after a decade of neglect (F. Castro 2002). A crash program was soon instituted to train and recruit more teachers, repair and build schools, and lower class size, but there are still persistent teacher shortages.

Adult educational levels of Havana's slum dwellers are relatively high, averaging between tenth and eleventh grade. Indeed, by the mid-1990s to the early 2000s, some 10 to 13 percent in Cayo Hueso, Colón, and Old Havana had completed university degrees, although in Atarés it was only 3 percent.[30]

In short, compared to slums in other parts of Latin America and the Caribbean, Havana's slums are characterized primarily by substandard housing and a certain degree of overcrowding and doubling up. Tenure security and access to water, sanitation, and electricity are largely assured with some exceptions. Unlike slums in other countries, those in Havana are socially diverse, and their residents are relatively well educated and enjoy generally good health.

Policies Regarding Slums Since 1990

When Cuba's economic crisis hit in the early 1990s, housing was the population's most significant unmet need. By 1993 the economic crisis resulted in the contraction of the economy by one-third and the reduction of imports by 75 percent. Food, transportation, employment, and energy shortages rapidly replaced housing as the most pressing issues. Measures to address the crisis were successful in slowly reviving the economy. These measures included a cautious expansion of self-employment; the growth of foreign investment through joint ventures, including real estate; the legalization of U.S. dollars, which created a dual currency situation; and some decentralization in public administration through the creation of the People's Councils (Consejos Populares), first established in Havana in 1990. Housing production largely ground to a halt as crucial inputs disappeared. But new nongovernmental organizations (NGOs) and public agencies started experimenting with appropriate technology and soon construction picked up again. The crisis itself and some of the policies designed to address it led to growing inequality among Cubans.

The major policies regarding Havana's slum areas in the 1990s and 2000s included the migration restrictions of 1997, new forms of community development, programs to renovate and repair inner-city slums and address shantytowns, and the new nationwide housing initiative launched in 2005. By taking a closer look at these major policies and initiatives, we get a better sense of which have expedited, constrained, or reduced the degradation of Havana's housing, as well as some of the dilemmas and debates.

The Migration Restrictions of 1997—"La Habana No Aguanta Más"
The economic crisis and measures to address it had a predictable impact on internal migration. Rapid expansion of tourism and legalization of the use of U.S. dollars attracted workers to tourist areas, accelerating migration to Havana. In the 1950s domestic net migration to Havana averaged 20,000 to 25,000 people a year. It nearly doubled just after the revolution, but it dropped to an annual net average of 10,000 to 11,000 migrants until the late 1980s. In 1990 Havana still had net migration of only 13,000 people. By 1994 this had grown to 16,000 migrants; in 1995, 22,000 migrants; and in 1996 to 27,000 migrants (CEDEM 1996; OTE-CLH 1997; March 11, 1997, issue of *Trabajadores*). Migration took place in a context of further housing deterioration aggravated by heavy storms in 1995, which led to a spurt in building collapses. Many migrants rented rooms, doubled up with family members, moved to shantytowns, and squatted in vacant condemned buildings in central areas.

Throughout the revolutionary period, proposals to institute direct restrictions on migration to Havana had been considered, but they were rejected in favor of more indirect measures like labor force policies and development of areas outside Havana. Although some urban planners and government officials argued that "Havana can't take any more" ("La Habana No Aguanta Más")—to quote a popular 1980s song title—and a few even called for a smaller population, most believed that the level of migration was acceptable. Havana's growth rate was far lower than those of other Cuban cities or capital cities elsewhere in Latin America. Moreover, many researchers and officials doubted that direct restrictions could be enforced (Acosta 1998). However, by the mid-1990s even those favoring balanced development strategies to address migration reluctantly agreed that some form of regulation was warranted, especially given the scarcity of resources to address simultaneously the development needs of the rest of the country and the infrastructure, employment, food supply, and housing needs of Havana during the depths of the economic crisis (CEDEM 1996, 101–2; see also the May 13 and 14, 1997, issues of *Granma*).

The outcome was Decree Law 217 of April 26, 1997, designed to regulate migration to Havana based primarily on the availability of housing (see the April 26, 1997, issue of *Granma*).[31] The migration law stipulates that those seeking to live permanently in Havana must prove that they have guaranteed housing in a dwelling with at least ten square meters of floor space per resident. The dwelling must meet minimum "conditions of habitability," and it cannot be located in a barrio insalubre. The law also requires that residents of Havana who wish to move into the capital's four most overcrowded and deteriorated neighborhoods (Old Havana, Centro Habana, Cerro, and Diez de Octubre) pass the "adequate housing" test.

Simultaneously, there were renewed calls for enforcement of building and land use regulations to prevent the growth of shantytowns and squatting in dangerous buildings. A housing census was launched in 1997 to assess the level of housing conditions and detect illegal or irregular situations like squatting, illegal house sales, lack of building permits, use of stolen construction materials, nonpayment of rent or mortgages, illegal sublets, and incorrect titles on deeds (see the June 8, 1997 issue of *Tribuna de La Habana*; and the June 3 and July 3, 1997, issue of *Granma*). In the vast majority of cases of irregularities, violators were granted the opportunity to rectify the situation or pay a fine. Only in a limited number of cases was more drastic action taken (see the February 14, 1998, issue of *Granma*).

Although the migration law primarily focused on housing, it also mandated that government employers minimize the number of people temporarily or permanently transferred to Havana, in recognition of the fact that 20 percent of previous migrants were transferred workers (CEDEM 1996). In Havana, however, unemployment coexisted with labor shortages in several occupations, leading to recruitment in other provinces. Indeed, President Raúl Castro, in his speech to the National Assembly in July 2008, discussed at length the practice of "importing" thousands of people from other provinces, especially *Orientales* (a term used to describe migrants from the eastern provinces of Cuba), to work in Havana as construction workers, police officers, and teachers.

Did the new migration policy work? In the following two years, officially recorded net migration dropped sharply (OTE-CHL 1997; Acosta 1998). In response to infractions detected by the housing census and the conditions imposed by the migration law of 1997, more than 200,000 people applied for new identification cards to legalize a change of address. But some migration to Havana has not been reflected in official statistics—newcomers have developed inventive ways to successfully get around the law. However, it does seem to have reduced but certainly not prevented migration. Over the following decade migration to and within Havana continued apace, whether or not reflected in official statistics. For instance, in 2002 a survey of residents of the inner-city Colón neighborhood (Dávalos et al. 2005, 61–65) found that more people arrived in the community from 1998 to 2002—after the law went into effect—than in the previous four years, although most came from other Havana municipalities. Indeed, 20 percent of those surveyed moved to the area after 1997. Similarly, *Juventud Rebelde* journalists interviewed many recent migrants living in a large shantytown in the Havana municipality of San Miguel de Padrón (Pérez and Orta 2008; Orta and Pérez 2008). Most came for economic opportunity and, at least initially, worked in the informal sector. Others had lost their homes in hurricanes. However, at the same time Havana's total population—at least as officially reported—has been declining since the mid-1990s due to plunging birth and fertility rates and accelerating emigration abroad, half of which comes from Havana (ONE 2007a; ONE 2007b).

Perhaps more striking, since the late 1990s as the population of Havana appeared to decrease, that of the area surrounding the province spiked (ONE 2005a; ONE 2008).[32] Two-thirds of the 29,000 residents added to the province between 2002 and 2007 lived in municipalities adjacent to Havana and on the seacoast. To the extent that new residents to these outlying suburbs seek housing in new or existing shantytowns, it means that some of the potential housing pressure on Havana has been displaced to its periphery, at the same time creating even more urban sprawl.

Although the migration law enjoyed some support from residents of Havana, it sparked considerable controversy (see the May 5, 1997, issue of *Trabajadores*; and the May 13 and May 27, 1997, and July 29, 1998 issues of *Granma*). Officials emphasized that the law does not prohibit migration but rather regulates it and noted that over a third of Havana's residents were born elsewhere. Indeed, in the first half of 1998, less than 8 percent of applications for residence in Havana were denied. Responding to accusations that migrants from the eastern provinces—who are thought to be disproportionately black and mulatto—have been unfairly singled out and blamed for increases in street crime and prostitution, officials have stressed that migration controls are not intended to weigh more heavily against people from any particular area of Cuba. Nevertheless, anecdotal information suggests that police are more likely to request the identification cards of darker-skinned Havana residents—whether born there or newcomers—than lighter-skinned ones. It also creates a class of "illegals" in their own country, leading to possible difficulty in obtaining certain services and rights, such as a ration card and full-time work contracts. As one shantytown dweller noted in the documentary *Buscándote Havana*, residents do not refer to themselves or their settlement as "illegal," but rather "undocumented" due to lack of official papers for their housing (Rodríguez Abreu 2006).

Enforcement of the new law has proven tricky. While early rumors claimed that 1,600 people had been forced to leave Havana when the law went into effect, in fact these people were displaced as the result of the stepped-up enforcement of the housing law regarding squatting on land and in unsafe buildings (see the April 27, 1997 issue of *Tribuna*; and the May 11, 1997, issue of *Juventud Rebelde*). Officials insisted that they are relying on fines and persuasion rather than force. But by late 1998 reports claimed that 3,353 people had been "returned" to their previous residences and 5,393 fines valued at over a million pesos had been imposed (InterPress Service 1998). Since then, there have been various waves of "deportations." According to city officials, in the first half of 2008 some 2,400 people were returned to their previous locations, and from 2006 to 2008 more than 20,000 were sent back, including some more than once. Indeed, recently "deported" migrants report returning to Havana almost immediately (Orta and Pérez 2008; Pérez and Orta 2008).

Public officials, urban planners, and researchers recognize the limited effectiveness of the migration law to stem movement to Havana. They urge, on the one hand, a return to more balanced regional development to the extent that resources permit and cite some recent successful examples of economic revival and population stability and growth in some parts of the island. Reforms to address severe shortages of agricultural labor and improve food production include greater decentralization and the distribution of land and inputs for production. On the other hand, they urge creating incentives, training programs, and other measures to assure that the city's residents fill most of Havana's jobs (see R. Castro 2008; Orta and Pérez 2008; Pérez and Orta 2008; and García Alfonso 2007). The reduction of 500,000 jobs in the state sector in late 2010 and early 2011 may also increase the supply of local workers available for construction jobs in Havana (Grogg 2010).

Community Development Related to Slums

Even before the economic crisis hit, new forms of decentralized, comprehensive, and coordinated community initiatives were under way. The first attempt to bring government closer to the neighborhood level was the People's Councils. Composed of locally elected officials and representatives of organizations and workplaces, they do not directly control any resources. But they try to foster local, horizontal collaboration among entities that usually function within their own sectors and are vertically integrated (Uriarte 2002).

The Neighborhood Transformation Workshops (Talleres de Transformación Integral del Barrio, or TTIB) were created in 1988 by the Group for the Comprehensive Development of the Capital (Grupo para el Desarrollo Integral de la Capital, or GDIC), an agency that advises the city government on urban policy (Coyula, Oliveras, and Cabrera 1998; Uriarte 2002). TTIBs are small teams of architects, planners, engineers, economists, sociologists, and social workers that work and often live in target neighborhoods—usually those with a concentration of slums—and advocate for alternative, participatory, bottom-up planning. The original three workshops grew to twenty by mid-2002. They have developed strategic plans for each neighborhood and work closely with the People's Councils. The twenty Havana TTIBs together cover a population of nearly 500,000. Since TTIBs do not have special budgets —the city government only pays their salaries—the GDIC has promoted collaboration projects with foreign NGOs that address neighborhood improvement. Some of those projects paid for the repair or rehabilitation of deteriorated dwellings, including the creation of small shops to produce local building materials and recycle rubble. But the total output of these housing projects has been small, and most of the TTIBs' programs have instead focused on neighborhood-based social, educational, and cultural activities that require fewer material resources and, in some cases, target vulnerable populations.

The 1990s also witnessed a veritable explosion in community-based organizations and activities (Fernández Soriano, Dilla Alfonso, and Castro Flores 1999). An estimated seventy community development projects have been sponsored in Havana by People's Councils. They have used strategic planning, encouraged participatory planning methods, garnered some resources from foreign NGOs and Cuban organizations, and developed capacity building and training for local residents. Researchers have noted both the potential and limitations of these approaches (Uriarte 2008).

Slums and Housing Construction

Except for some shantytown clearance and replacement and new developments in the early days of the revolution, there was relatively little built in Havana in the 1960s.[33] Construction labor shortages, especially in Havana, led to the creation in 1970 of the microbrigades. They consisted of employees from the same workplace who built housing for their fellow workers that was allocated based on need and "merit." Although a unique form of "collective self-help" that initially produced many units, the microbrigades had their limitations. Building quality suffered from the use of unskilled workers. The program was restricted to key economic sectors. It had little effect on existing slums except allowing some families to "undouble." Building in outlying areas meant the journey to work increased.

By the early 1980s microbrigades were largely limited to Havana and building lagged. Although about a fifth of the microbrigade units in the past had been assigned to albergados and others in great need, during the urban building boom of the late 1980s, new forms of microbrigades more directly addressed the issue of slum housing. One form consisted of brigades—called "social microbrigades"—of community residents who received a salary to build infill structures or rehabilitate slums in their own neighborhoods. Another was brigades from different workplaces that built infill housing closer to their jobs. And finally, there were brigades of residents of homeless shelters. But workplace brigade members were often pulled off housing jobs to help state brigades complete higher priority community facilities, leaving thousands of units under construction when the Special Period began, and many weren't finished until nearly two decades later. Other challenges included materials shortages exacerbated by endless delays in delivery, inadequate storage, and theft, which in turn stretched out the construction process interminably. Completed units often remained unoccupied because of delayed electric, water, or sewer hookups.

In the 1990s construction was practically halted, except for programs like building hotels and condominiums for foreigners that would bring some desperately needed hard currency into the country. Once construction picked up again in the mid-1990s, social housing was limited to programs for workers of key industries or agencies, with priority going to finishing buildings that had been halted in the early 1990s and to meeting the needs of people living in shelters. Alternative technologies that minimize the use of imported or energy-intensive materials were also introduced, but these technologies were used more on the city's outskirts and in other provinces.

Although the economy improved in the early 2000s, housing construction nationally and in Havana plummeted. Between 2001 and 2007, hurricanes, tropical storms, and flooding damaged more than 584,000 units nationally and destroyed 76,000 units, with all these units requiring extensive repairs and rebuilding (Martín and Jiménez 2008). Three more hurricanes in 2008 damaged 444,000 units, destroying 63,000 of these (Gazmuri Núñez 2009, 59). Although Havana was not as affected by these weather events as other parts of the country, the availability of construction materials was severely reduced. At the same time, other construction resources were devoted to repairing and renovating schools and health facilities. The total of government and officially recognized self-built completions plunged from around 40,000 to 50,000 units annually in 1995–2000 to only around 15,000 in 2003 and 2004 (ONE 2007b).

In response to insistent concerns expressed by national legislators at the semiannual meeting of Cuba's main legislative body (the National Assembly of People's Power), the government launched a major housing initiative in September 2005 (see Carrobello 2006a, 2006b, and 2006c; Heredia Reyes 2008; Martín and Jiménez 2008; Mayoral 2008; and Lage Dávila 2008). Initial goals were so ambitious that fulfilling them rapidly would have been virtually impossible, given the shortages of construction materials, labor, and transportation. Nevertheless, 110,000 units were reported as completed out of the 150,000 projected in the first sixteen months. Most completions were of units already well under way before the new initiative. Nearly 70 percent of these were self-built. They represent a part of the 300,000 self-built units under construction in 2005, more than a third of which lacked building permits. Pressure on municipal and provincial agencies was so great that some officials reported phantom units completed, judging from the warnings about avoiding fraudulent reporting in 2007. In that year the goal was reduced to a more realistic, but still overly ambitious, 70,000. It was further cut to 50,000 in 2008, but would require more resources since most dwellings were to be built from scratch and moreover would incur extra costs for infrastructure. In addition, more materials and labor have been allocated for repair and rehabilitation. With 20 percent of the country's population, Havana was allocated around 10 percent of new housing units but about 25 percent of resources for repair and rehabilitation. Nationally, most of the rehabilitation and repairs budget went to replacing or repairing roofs of hurricane victims.

According to public officials, challenges in implementing the housing program include shortages of certain construction materials; insufficient transportation to deliver materials to sites and distribution centers for sale to residents; poor management; extensive red tape in getting permits and financing despite some recent streamlining; shortages of skilled and unskilled labor; diversion of labor and materials to other projects; and instances of theft, corruption, and fraud.

Future policy directions can perhaps be seen in the housing section of the draft program of the Cuban Community Party to be discussed at its Congress in April 2011 (PCC 2010, 31). It gives priority to maintenance, repair, and rehabilitation; highlights the role of self-building and other non-state forms of building and renovation; and focuses on the use of local construction materials and labor-saving technologies that use materials efficiently.

A Tale of Two Neighborhoods: Rehabilitation and Repair Programs
Two experiences in the 1990s with rehabilitation and repair in inner-city slum areas illustrate several dilemmas in housing and social policy. Cayo Hueso is a working-class neighborhood in the heart of Centro Habana where housing is a major problem.[34]

One of the first TTIBs was created in Cayo Hueso in 1988. After a thorough inventory of the community, the TTIB mobilized local resources and assistance projects from international NGOs and UNICEF to improve living conditions and reinforce a sense of local identity. This aid was used to finance the repair of several tenements and to create a small plant to recycle rubble into mortar blocks.

In 1995–1996 the neighborhood received strong assistance from many national ministries in what became known as the Cayo Hueso Plan. Residents were offered building materials at affordable prices, while government agencies were responsible for neighborhood infrastructure improvements, structural repairs, and facades. Differences from previous efforts were the targeting of an entire neighborhood for rehabilitation rather than a few tenements; focusing on upgraded community facilities and neighborhood infrastructure as well as housing repair and rehabilitation; and the "adoption" of specific streets or blocks by individual ministries, which provided technical assistance, specialized construction labor, tools, machinery, and materials. But the strong involvement of the national agencies gradually resulted in some of them assuming most of the work, which moreover was often cosmetic. Nevertheless, around 10,000 units were repaired, eight schools, and fifteen health facilities were improved, and street lighting, waste disposal, streets, and sidewalks were upgraded.

A before-and-after study comparing Cayo Hueso and Colón, another Centro Habana area that had not received a similar assistance program, indicates the relative effectiveness of the Cayo Hueso Plan (Spiegel et al. 2003).[35] In 1999 the program was extended to central areas of other selected provincial capitals and to some other Havana neighborhoods but with reduced resources in each community. The reliance on national ministries with other goals for resources limited the role of local government in planning and implementation.

A contrasting model is represented by the restoration of the historic parts of Old Havana and the rehabilitation of its most deteriorated area, San Isidro.[36] The difference is local access to and control of resources. After becoming a UNESCO World Heritage Site in 1982, restoration of historic buildings proceeded slowly. Finally, in 1993 Havana's Office of the City Historian was granted the right to run its own for-profit companies in the real estate, building, retail, and tourism fields and to use part of its earnings—as well as taxes from other workplaces—to resume restoring the historic district. In addition, it started devoting a third of its resources to financing community facilities and social programs for local residents and to repairing and rehabilitating dwellings, even in nonhistoric areas (Mas 2001; Peters, 2001).

Gentrification of the sort seen in historic areas in other countries has been largely avoided since housing for local residents is included in the upper floors of most restored buildings. By 2004 more than 3,300 units had been rehabilitated and 437 built, benefiting 13,200 residents who represented about a fifth of the population (UNESCO and Oficina del Historiador de la Ciudad 2006, 197). Most residents stayed in the area, but some moved to apartments built and financed by the Office of the City Historian in Alamar and Rancho Boyeros on the outskirts of the city. Around 500 families had been moved by 2004. Temporary relocation housing is often provided in Old Havana itself while rehabilitation is under way.

Local economic development includes residents receiving training and jobs as skilled construction workers for the restoration process, incentives to produce crafts for sale to tourists, and employment in the tourist industry— although hiring preferences for local residents are not always honored in practice (Robainas Barcia 1999). Of the 11,000 jobs created up to the end of 2000, some 60 percent went to residents of Old Havana, Centro Habana, and Regla—all municipalities with a high percent of tenements—and 40 percent went to women (UNESCO and Oficina del Historiador de la Ciudad 2006, 66). Another 2,000 indirect jobs were created as well. Community facilities and social programs include a rehabilitation center for disabled children and another for those with Down syndrome, a maternity home for women with problem pregnancies, programs and assisted housing for the elderly, special equipment for schools, and a program of holding primary school classes in museums. In addition, until the early 2000s the UN Program for Local Human

Development (PDHL 2000) sponsored dozens of social projects throughout Old Havana, promoting local economic development, job creation, protection of vulnerable groups, and the upgrading of the environment and public services, including education and health care.

Once the Office of the City Historian had sufficient revenues in 1995, it started financing the Comprehensive Revitalization Program in San Isidro, located at the southern tip of the historic district. Modeled to some degree after the TTIBS, it had a multidisciplinary staff that dealt with social, cultural, and educational activities as well as residential, commercial, and infrastructure upgrading. It was not until the program became an official part of the Office of the City Historian that it fully controlled the use of its resources in an autonomous and decentralized way (Coipel Diaz and Collado Reyes 2000).

As in the Cayo Hueso Plan, residents were sold materials for repair and rehabilitation at affordable prices, but starting in mid-2000, building enterprises with specialized skills were brought in to tackle the complexities of major work on such old, deteriorated, and often historic buildings (Mayoral 2001). In addition, aggressive emergency repairs have helped prevent building collapses. No other community-based project in Cuba had this degree of relative autonomy and stable resources.

Community Residents: Self-Building, Repairs, and Rehabilitation
Aside from special projects such as those in Old Havana and Cayo Hueso, official figures indicate that residents of Havana were active in repairing, rehabilitating, and, in some cases, building their own units. In 2001, 96,696 repair and rehabilitation jobs were completed in Havana—43.2 percent by residents themselves—representing two-fifths of all those in the country (INV 2001a). In contrast, legal self-building of new units in the capital was almost impossible from the early 1990s until 2005; only 366 new self-built dwellings were officially completed in 2001, just 2.5 percent of the nation's total self-built units, and of these, a little over two-thirds were replacement units (INV 2001a).

In an effort to direct low-cost building materials to those with the greatest need (rather than those with the most money), complete the self-built units under construction, and prevent the development of shantytowns, a series of new regulations was issued in 2000–2001. One regulation established neighborhood-based committees to allocate to households the right to obtain a building permit and buy low-cost materials based on need. It also sharply reduced permits for new construction—which had been the policy in Havana for more than a decade—in the belief that units already begun should be finished first.[37] Another set of regulations drastically increased fines and penalties for any building activity that violates the law and is undertaken without proper permits.[38] While some materials were distributed under this system, the virtual prohibition on building new units fostered illegal building and even more shantytowns.

Materials for purchase for repair and new construction became somewhat more available starting in 2005 with the new housing program. It made it possible for many families to complete half-built dwellings and for others to make repairs. But problems noted include expensive transportation to retrieve materials from distribution points, limited access to equipment, and the high cost of private, skilled labor.

Several major changes in policy occurred in spring 2010 (Cáceres 2010; Martín González 2010). Rather than allocate building permits and the right to buy low-cost materials through neighborhood committees, almost any owner of a place to build or repair can be granted a building permit. Moreover, construction materials can be purchased without prior authorization in nonconvertible currency. This initiative started on a limited basis in February 2010, but is slated to be substantially expanded in early 2011. It remains to be seen whether supplies will be sufficient—given the pent-up demand—and prices are set at appropriate levels. The expansion of permitted self-employment in 2010, combined with substantial layoffs of government employees, is likely to expand the supply of construction workers, whether individually or in cooperatives, for hire by self-builders for specialized tasks (Martínez Hernández 2010).

La Güinera is an example of three large adjacent shantytowns that mobilized to respond to community needs (Fernández 1997; Pérez Callejas 1997). Located on the outskirts of Havana, these shantytowns had a combined population of nearly 9,000 people with 2,500 housing units. In 1987 a group of women from the community initiated participation in the newly formed social microbrigades, and a year later the La Güinera TTIB was founded. Streets were paved, sidewalks built, and work begun on five-story walk-up apartments similar to the standard designs of those built elsewhere in Havana. A woman directed the microbrigade, and 70 percent of its members were female as well. By 1997, 270 units in nine buildings had been completed, with another several hundred units in buildings under construction halted since 1990. The buildings were criticized by some experts as ugly, monotonous, inappropriate for the area, and very dependent on materials, equipment, and energy, often from abroad. The community turned to alternative technologies, establishing a Materials Production Shop that made soil-cement blocks using soil found locally and a donated manually operated block-making machine. By 1997, 36 units had been built using this method. Other activities were also undertaken, such as local economic development and building a community center.

Havana's Unique Slums: The Challenge of the Future

Havana's residents and public officials are in a race against time to save as many of its crumbling inner-city slums as possible with the growing but still scarce resources available. The still relatively intact urban fabric was largely spared from massive clearance and redevelopment as occurred in so many other Latin American cities, but the ravages of weather, time, and neglect place it in danger. Meanwhile, makeshift shantytowns are proliferating on the outskirts as migrants continue to move to Havana. However, compared with cities in other developing nations, Havana's slums are largely characterized by substandard housing and some degree of overcrowding. Access to basic services and tenure security is relatively assured, and the residents of slum neighborhoods are socially diverse, generally well educated, and healthy.

Public officials face serious dilemmas about priorities. Should they focus on saving Havana's inner-city slums, or should they devote resources to repairing and replacing dwellings destroyed or damaged by hurricanes in the city and elsewhere? Should they upgrade Havana's shantytowns or allocate investments to achieve balanced regional growth to stem migration to the capital?

Despite still inadequate resources, at least there is renewed attention to the issue of housing. Models exist—such as the efforts in Cayo Hueso and San Isidro as well as extensive building and repair by residents—of effective work to restore, repair, and rehabilitate the city's built heritage in a way that will benefit existing residents.

Notes

This chapter draws on excerpts from a case study on Havana slums written by Mario Coyula and Jill Hamberg (2003), and it is updated with more recent information. The case study was one of several dozen city studies commissioned as background by UN-Habitat (2003) in preparation for *The Challenge of Slums: Global Report on Human Settlements 2003*. The case studies were compiled by the Development Planning Unit of University College London and published on CD-ROM and the web. A brief summary of each case study appears in the Global Report itself (195–228). The Havana case study was later reproduced as a working paper of the David Rockefeller Center for Latin American Studies in 2004 (Coyula and Hamberg 2004).

1. See UN-Habitat (2003, 8–16); Angotti (2006, 961); and Davis (2006, 20–26).

2. Indeed, one estimate indicates that only 21.3 percent of units created between 1959 and 1985 were state built (Benítez Pérez 2002, 85–86).

3. The UN indicator focuses on the materials used in construction and their sturdiness.

4. *Ciudadelas* consist of a single or double row of rooms built along a long, narrow courtyard. A *cuartería* is a large mansion, older hotel, or boarding house subdivided into rooms, sometimes with over sixty families, while a *casa de vecindad* is a smaller subdivided house, generally with twelve rooms or less. *Pasajes* are a double row of small dwellings (similar to efficiencies) consisting of a living and dining room, kitchenette, one bedroom, bathroom, and a small service courtyard set along a long, narrow alley usually open to streets at both ends. *Solar* and *ciudadela* are the popular terms to refer to all forms of buildings subdivided into single-room units, usually with shared services and a common courtyard.

5. Indeed, according to the 1981 Census, 44 percent of tenements had water inside the unit and that number continued to increase in the following three decades (CEE-ONC 1984). By the 2002 Census most tenement units were classified as apartments since they had exclusive use of kitchen, toilet, and bathing facilities (ONE 2005a).

6. This was actually the number in the "other" category—that is, neither "houses" nor "apartments"; most of these were "tenements" since there are virtually no *bohíos* in Havana and relatively few "improvised" units. Havana's "other" units represented about a quarter of the country's urban dwellings in this census category. Definitions from the national 2002 Census (ONE 2005a) and surveys and local censuses of neighborhoods may be different. For instance, although the national 2002 Census reported 14.4 percent of units in Old Havana municipality in the "other" category (almost all tenements), the 2001 Population and Housing Census, conducted of only Old Havana's historic district, reported that 20 percent lacked an internal toilet and 24 percent an internal bath or shower (see "Resúmenes: Censo de Población y Viviendas 2002" [Havana, n.d.]; UNESCO 2006, 41).

7. According to the 2002 Census (ONE 2005a), nearly 79,000 rural units were classified as "other" (not "houses" or "apartments"), representing 20.7 percent of rural units. The great majority of these units are *bohíos*.

8. Of these dwellings adapted from nonresidential uses, two-fifths became "houses," nearly a third became tenements, and the rest became apartments. Three-quarters of these converted units had full plumbing (CEE-ONC 1984).

9. For instance, in Playa municipality, which has some of the oldest shantytowns, some two-fifths of the units were already considered "houses," ranging from a third to two-thirds in individual settlements in 1996 (ONE-OTECH 1997).

10. The minimal housing standard for change of status was *vivienda adecuada* (adequate or standard housing), requiring at least twenty-five square meters, three separate rooms, and the building type had to be I, II, or III. This meant that thatched roofs, scrap materials, and the like would automatically not qualify. The neighborhood could not be in a dangerous location such as in a flood plain or under high-voltage

power lines and had to have a street layout with electricity and water supply and acceptable treatment of wastewater.

11. An August 2008 article in *Juventud Rebelde* states that there are 46 "illegal settlements" scattered throughout Havana's fifteen municipalities (Pérez and Orta 2008). Núñez Moreno (2008, 21) cites a National Housing Institute source from 2004 as indicating that there are 22,170 units in shantytowns.

12. Indeed, the 2002 Census (ONE 2005a) indicated that only 14.4 percent of the units in Old Havana municipality and 10.5 percent in Centro Havana were tenements with shared services, since units with exclusive use of a kitchen, toilet, and bathing facilities were classified as "apartments" even if they were in tenement-type buildings.

13. For instance, nearly two-fifths of the units in shantytowns in Playa municipality were tenements in 1996 (ONE-OTECH 1997).

14. A survey in 2000 estimated that 90.1 percent of Havana's households owned electric fans and 87.5 percent owned refrigerators (Pérez Villanueva 2002). In the slum neighborhood of Atarés, it was estimated in 1987 that on average virtually all households had radios, televisions, refrigerators, and electric fans and nearly half had washing machines (Ortega Morales 1996).

15. In shantytowns 17.5 percent lacked water in the unit in 1995, and 25.6 percent did not have their own sanitary facilities, although shared sources were available (ONE-OTECH 1997). In Old Havana municipality about a fifth of the units lacked water in the unit. About a third had to manually carry water to their dwellings because of problems with water tanks, pumps, and water pressure (Collado, Mauri, and Coipel 1998; PDHL 2000), although this improved to some extent in the mid-2000s (UNESCO 2006). In 2001 a fourth of Old Havana's units lacked exclusive use of a bath or shower in their units; a fifth of households used toilets outside their units (UNESCO 2006). In Atarés 83.8 percent had water inside their units and nearly as many had exclusive use of a toilet, most of which were inside the unit. The 2002 Census found that around 85 percent of the units in the Old Havana municipality had exclusive use of kitchen, toilet, and bathing facilities, as did 90 percent in Centro Habana (ONE 2005a).

16. Average household size in inner-city areas in the mid-1990s to early 2000s ranged from 2.9 people per household (Centro Habana, Cayo Hueso), 3.3 (Old Havana's historic district), 3.5 (Colón), 3.6 (Malecón-San Isidro), to 3.9 (Atarés). In shantytowns, the average was 3.4. Around three-fifths of the units consisted of 1–3 occupants. In 1995 average household size for Havana was 3.43 (Benítez Pérez 1999) and by 2002 it had decreased to 3.24 (ONE 2005a). The smallest average household size in 2002 was found in inner-city areas such as Old Havana and Centro Havana (3.06), with much larger averages in several outlying municipalities (3.35 to 4.00). For information on neighborhoods and shantytowns, see Arranz González (1998) and Vázquez Penelas and Cantero Zayas (1998) for Centro Habana and Cayo Hueso; Rodríguez Alomá (1996) for Old Havana; Rey et al. (2005) for Colón; García Fernández et al. (1998) for Malecón-San Isidro; Ortega Morales (1996) for Atarés; and González Rego, Rúa de Cabo, and Blanco Sánchez (2000) for shantytowns.

17. The average floor space per person in tenements is around 9.5 to 10 square

meters, and per unit it is 39 square meters (ranging from a low of 20 square meters to a high of 60 square meters, depending on the presence of *barbacoas* and other expansions) (Rey et al. 2005). Cuban planning indicators and laws have established 10 to 10.5 square meters per person as the minimum standard for habitability.

18. One-seventh of units have only one room, and of these, 18.2 percent consist of more than three occupants, representing 3.6 percent of all shantytown residents. If having more than two people per bedroom is considered overcrowding, then 32.8 percent of the units and 45.7 percent of residents were overcrowded. There were 1.64 bedrooms per unit in shantytowns (in 1996), smaller than the average for Havana as a whole in 1981 (1.95 bedrooms per unit) (González Rego, Rúa de Cabo, and Blanco Sánchez 2000).

19. For more information on housing tenure, tenure security and homeownership, see Hamberg (1994, 2001) and Vega Vega (1986).

20. For instance, 42 percent of households in Old Havana's historic district were homeowners in 2001, 45 percent rent-free leaseholders (roughly the number of tenement units), and 8 percent paid rent to the government (UNESCO 2006, 43). In the late 1990s nearly 14 percent of Malecón households had illegal residencies (Garcia Fernández et al. 1998).

21. Some 135,000 unfinished, self-built units lacking building permits have been legalized as part of the major new house-building program started in 2005 (Miguel Coyula 2009, 46). This has led to rumors that shantytown dwellings will be legalized as well (Pérez and Orta 2008).

22. Except for the census of shantytowns in 1996, there are few published studies of the characteristics of residents of slum housing. Even the nationwide 1981 Population and Housing Census did not publish demographic characteristics by type of residence. Therefore, case studies conducted in the 1990s of neighborhoods or municipalities with a high concentration of tenements and deteriorated housing will be used here to approximate the attributes of residents of inner-city slums, meaning the municipalities of Old Havana and Centro Habana and the neighborhood of Atarés. Because different information was collected or published for each area, generalizations from trends are presented here when consistent data is not available.

23. The Cuban Communist Party's draft Guidelines for Economic and Social Policy (PCC 2010, 31), discussed at the party's congress in April 2011, proposes that "flexible formulas be implemented for housing exchanges (*permutas*), buying, selling and renting to help respond to the population's demand for housing."

24. Centro Habana, including Cayo Hueso and the San Isidro-Malecón area: Arranz González (1998) (53.6 percent women), García Fernández et al. (1998) (51 percent women). Old Havana, including the San Isidro area (all 52–53 percent women): Collado, Mauri, and Coipel (1998); PDHL (2000); Plan Maestro (1996); Rodríguez Alomá (1996); Atarés: Ortega Morales (1996) (52 percent women). Shantytowns: González Rego (2000); González Rego, Rúa de Cabo, and Blanco Sánchez (2000) (higher proportion of men in shantytowns than in surrounding municipality).

25. For ages in inner-city slum areas see Collado, Mauri, and Coipel (1998); García

Fernández et al. (1998); PDHL (2000); Plan Maestro (1996); and Spiegel et al. (2003). For shantytowns, see González Rego (2000); González Rego, Rúa de Cabo, and Blanco Sánchez (2000); and ONE-OTECH (1997).

26. A survey of Old Havana in 1995 (Plan Maestro 1996) and a survey of two rundown Centro Habana neighborhoods in 2001 (Spiegel et al. 2003) indicate a similar racial distribution to that of 1981. However, a survey in 2002 of one of those same neighborhoods—Colón—indicated a somewhat lower proportion of whites (around 40 percent) and a higher concentration of mulattos and blacks (about 30 percent each) (Dávalos, Cárdenas, Muñoz, and Vilariño 2005, 59).

27. For inner-city slums, see Arranz González (1998); Collado, Mauri, and Coipel (1998); Ortega Morales (1996); Plan Maestro (1996); Rodríguez Alomá (1996); for shantytowns, see ONE-OTECH (1997).

28. Data on inner-city slums in this paragraph is from Arranz González (1998); Collado, Mauri, and Coipel (1998); Ortega Morales (1996); Plan Maestro (1996); and Rodríguez Alomá (1996). In terms of shantytowns, nearly a fifth of the household heads in the mid-1990s lived in their current location since before 1959, and roughly a fifth arrived in each of the following periods: the 1960s, 1970s, 1980s, and 1991–1996. In some cases migrants from the same towns and provinces clustered together in shanty-towns (ONE-OTECH 1997).

29. In 1997, UNESCO conducted a major comparative study of language and math achievement in third and fourth grade pupils in thirteen Latin American countries. Cuba's children scored considerably above both public and private school students in all the other countries. Moreover, unlike other countries, there were minimal gender or rural and urban differences. Similar results were found in a UNESCO study in sixteen countries in 2005 and 2006 (Israel 2008).

30. In Atarés (1992), residents ten to forty-nine years old completed an average of 9.6 years; 3 percent completed university (Ortega Morales 1996). In Old Havana his-toric district (1995), of residents six to forty-nine years old, 9.8 percent completed university, 1.9 percent completed teachers college, 17.0 percent completed technical school, 24.7 percent completed academic high school, 1.4 percent completed vocational high school, 27.5 percent completed junior high school, and 16.8 percent completed primary school (of course, the children hadn't yet completed primary or junior high school) (Plan Maestro 1996). In Cayo Hueso, in 2001, the average adult educational level was slightly more than 11 years (and around 10.5 years in nearby Colón neighbor-hood) (Spiegel et al. 2003); in 1997, around a third with ninth- and twelfth-grade educations, respectively and 12.7 percent with university degrees (Vázquez Penelas and Cantero Zayas 1998).

31. A decree law is like an executive order since it is approved by the Council of State rather than the National Assembly. Although technically a decree law, not a full-fledged law, here the term *migration law* is used.

32. While Havana had a net domestic migration rate of 2.3 per thousand in 2006, the then "Province of Havana"—which surrounded the "City of Havana" province— reached 9.1 per thousand, more than doubling since 2001. In the five years between

2002 and 2007, Havana province's population grew by a remarkable 4.1 percent. Indeed, San Antonio de los Baños municipality gained 11.3 percent in this short period (ONE 2005a; ONE 2008). In mid-2010, City of Havana province regained its original name of Havana and Havana Province was split up into two provinces named Artemisa and Mayabeque (*Juventud Rebelde* 2010).

33. See Hamberg (1994) and Mathéy (1997) for more information on microbrigades.

34. Information on the Cayo Hueso Plan is based on Díaz Gutiérrez (2001), Rey et al. (2005, 88–89), Spiegel et al. (2003), Vázquez Penelas and Cantero Zayas (1998), and Yassi et al. (1999).

35. Compared with Colón, Cayo Hueso had fewer serious housing problems, greater improvement in neighborhood conditions, less need for housing repairs, and fewer perceived new community needs. Moreover, the self-reported health status of certain vulnerable subpopulations such as women over sixty improved dramatically in Cayo Hueso when compared with Colón (Spiegel et al. 2003).

36. Information on Old Havana and San Isidro is based on Coipel Díaz and Collado Reyes (2000), Collado et al. (1998), Mayoral (2001), Peters (2001), Rey et al. (2005, 88), Robainas Barcia (1999), and UNESCO (2006).

37. Resolución No. 500/00, "Reglamento para la construcción de Viviendas por Esfuerzo Propio de la Población," September 29, 2000.

38. Decreto No. 272, "De las Contravenciones en Materia de Ordenamiento Territorial y de Urbanismo" (Havana: Comite Ejecutivo del Consejo de Ministros, 2001).

5

Havana and Its Landscapes:
A Vision for Future Reconstruction
of Cuban Cities

NICOLÁS QUINTANA

The title of the project "Havana and Its Landscapes," currently under way at Florida International University's School of Architecture, is predicated on the fact that cities, which are urban landscapes located at strategic points in the regional landscape, are part of Cuba's overall rural landscape. The word *landscape* is used to suggest a territory whose ecological characteristics are basic and important in providing sustainability to the city's growth and development.[1] It clearly expresses the ecological connectivity between the natural, physical, social, and cultural aspects that we are dealing with in this project, and, at the same time, that the street grid system and residential clusters, jointly with the greenway networks, tie together.

The Problem

During the past fifty years, Cuban cities, and particularly Havana, have suffered the ravages of time and have been the victims of neglect, resulting in a level of urban destruction rarely seen anywhere except perhaps during times of war. Despite it all, one thing they have not lost is their majestic presence as works of art worth preserving.

The architect Carlos Dunn, a participant in the "Havana and Its Land-scapes" project, who lived for many years in Castro's Cuba—today he is in exile—and worked brilliantly in the preservation of Old Havana, has this to say:

> On January 1st, 1959 profound tectonic shifts took place in Havana. A revolu-tion triumphed and the city entered into a unique phase in its history. A phase that involuntarily saved it from destruction, but at the same time immersed it into a dangerous sleep that eventually turned into a nightmare. . . . In the 1950s the marked differences between the capital city of Cuba and the rest of the country were striking. In order to quickly and profoundly change this, the new regime decided to stop all investment and development in Havana and began intensive social and economic programs in the rest of the country. Thus Ha-vana—one of the most important Latin American capitals of the first half of the twentieth century—was literally frozen in time. It could be said that Havana sequestered its urban structure and buildings in a time capsule. Without know-ing it, by pure coincidence, this initial political, economic, and social strategy of the Cuban Revolution saved the city and its historic areas. Fundamentally through neglect and disregard its image of the 1950s is preserved, but for how long? . . . Saving it is beyond doubt a worthy project. The question is where to begin. It has been left to decay, almost completely unmaintained, for over fifty years. If a major urban action plan does not come into effect in the coming years, it will be too late. . . . Havana is a jewel threatened by the cumulative effects of decades of neglect and by, what could be perhaps worse, the future actions of man." (Dunn, n.d., 2–3)

The city has been treated as hostage, since 1959, by a political process that has penetrated the organizational structure, developed over 400 years of constant care and development, negatively altering its physical appearance and social atmosphere, breaking the delicate balance between the environment and its citizens.

Lately a new situation even more damaging to our urban environmental quality has been created. Due to the national economic collapse and as a way to face it, Havana's best urban sites have been placed on the auction block, on a "first come, first served" basis. The area of Monte Barreto, in Miramar, is a good example of this situation. In this area prime sites are being offered to foreign capital in an indiscriminate manner, authorizing developers to build —without any intelligent guidance—mediocre exploitative projects that ig-nore local traditions, destroying, possibly permanently, the aesthetic quality typically predominant in the island's urban centers.

Cuba's present political situation will inexorably end, and change will come in time. The country will then enter a transition period moving it toward becoming a democratic, free-enterprise system of government. The whole atmosphere of the place will then burst into a feverish rhythm of growth, with a will to produce and build, no matter what!

We are not prepared to face this radical situation that might at long last destroy Havana's identity and its urban atmosphere. We are not prepared to face the demolition—without any serious professional evaluation—of buildings that should be preserved, retrofitted, and recycled; demolition of existing structures without considering what could be the proper environmental evaluation, the most appropriate urban model applicable to the city's future growth, or the most adequate architectural typologies to be used in the new constructions. If we are not careful this period of activity could obliterate the existing rich, dense urban fabric typical of Cuban cities and introduce the mediocrity of suburban sprawl. Our cities will then cease to be the expression of our culture.

This consideration has to take into account, urgently, the execution of proper urban plans, based not on imported, foreign concepts and ideas but on basic urban criteria emerging from Cuba's cultural traditions and way of life in a free society. By doing so, we will help preserve, orient, and intelligently guide future development, protecting that very special atmosphere and character that has always been proper to the island's cities. This work is basic and unavoidable.

Another important obligation is to creatively address the critical overcrowding situation presently occurring in Cuba, especially in Havana. The reconstruction of its dilapidated, but nevertheless inhabited, areas constitutes one of Cuba's top priorities.

A similar emergency situation exists with the public service infrastructure, and its prime historical sites and buildings, where lack of maintenance and overcrowding have provoked a high degree of blight, causing dramatic changes in their typology. Careful planning will have to be done to reconstruct in situ these blighted areas, with the minimum social and psychological disturbance to the citizens.

These are two of Cuba's most delicate urban problems that have to be analyzed in depth, recognizing that Havana presents a most dramatic crisis in its housing, lacking the most elemental public service facilities, showing a collapsed overall quality of life.

The Objective

The objective of the project "Havana and Its Landscapes" is to visualize the future reconstruction and development of Havana in order to create a total sustainable environment that recognizes the historic values and, at the same time, provides for the needs and aspirations of a free modern society. Havana is Cuba's urban paradigm, its capital city; its vision will surely have some bearing —as proven historically—on the development of the rest of the Cuban cities.

One final, very important consideration that has to be accentuated is the fact that due to the "dormant condition" in which Havana has been surviving for over forty-five years, it lays waiting in ruins but, at the same time, has not been ruined beyond repair by uncontrolled development.

Related to this reality this is what Paul Goldberger, the renowned architectural critic and academic, had to say:

> This is the only major city in the world that has not been damaged by the scars of 1960's and 1970's and 1980's overbuilding. Havana is the only place that has not yet been disfigured by the kind of senseless overbuilding that has made so many cities so unappealing; by the anonymous over scaled modernism that has made so many cities cold and bland. And it has not remade itself entirely to serve the automobile, as so many places have . . . this is an architectural and urban design laboratory unique in all the world, the only place in which we can look at a metropolis that has not been disfigured by the development of the last generation, and therefore it is the only place in which we can plan a metropolis for the twenty-first century that does not contain within its core the mistakes and problems of every other city of its size in the world. . . . Havana is like a person who has been in a bubble, and has never been exposed to a certain virus that has worked its way into all the rest of us. It is a unique clinical condition. (Goldberger 2001, 26–31)

Havana offers an exceptional opportunity for the implementation of creative town planning. It is our serious professional duty to be ready when Cuba is finally incorporated—by democracy and free enterprise—into the community of free nations, to work together in a joint effort to save our cities. To prepare for this moment, by providing the proper instruments and the suggestions needed to help creatively guide its urban development, is what "Havana and Its Landscapes" is all about.

We cannot help but feel that the highest form of wisdom is exerted by humanity when they place cities and families in nature to facilitate orderly interactions.

The Urban Model: The Grid

The grid is the urban model that will be used logistically to focus this project, as according to Spiro Kostof "orthogonality is a method of creating urban order, not just a simple formula of urban design. If the urban grid is ubiquitous in the history of cities, it is neither standard nor predictable. The virtue of the grid is, in fact, its unending flexibility" (Kostof 1999, 116). It has its origins in the basic plans of the castra, the Roman military camp, whose "idea of order" Vitruvius perspicaciously noted in his *The Ten Books of Architecture* (*De architectura*). The grid is, in fact, the same model that inspired Philip II to write the *Laws of Indies* (1573), a document that helped guide the development of the Spanish colonial cities in America; and it is the basic urban design model under which Havana was founded and developed for over 400 years.[2]

The studies that we have undertaken indicate that—with adaptations to different moments in time—the city grew and changed creatively by a process of *connectivity* and *continuity*, always respecting the basic urban design model. In this same way it will adapt itself to modern times. There is no need to make any new, different major urban statement—it already exists and it is proven to work. An in-depth analysis of El Vedado's urban design will provide most of the needed answers.

El Carmelo (1859) and El Vedado (1860)—both paradigmatic neighborhoods—were designed by grouping city blocks into a series of typical mixed-use residential clusters, each approximately seven city blocks by seven city blocks in size. Peripheral avenues or wider streets encircled these clusters, and all sorts of commercial and service mixed-use facilities were available in them. A recreational park was supposedly placed in the center of each cluster.

Facing the peripheral avenues and the parks in our studies are tall buildings that framed the residential clusters and have coded maximum heights: in the wider avenues and around the parks, two times the right-of-way. In the remaining more private streets of the clusters the maximum allowed building height is one times the right-of-way. The end result of this approach is that a mid- to high-density level is achieved, a variety of building typologies is also achieved, and all kinds of service and recreational facilities are located at pedestrian distances from housing.

There has been great consistency in applying this mixed-use urban clustering concept during Havana's history. The design of El Carmelo and El Vedado, being among the most advanced urban models of their time, were inspired by Ildefonso Cerdá's design for the extension of Barcelona. They constitute a paradigm that—with adaptations to modern contemporary needs—is perfectly applicable in the city's future development.

To become great, cities have to be responsive to their site's physical and environmental conditions; responsive to their social and economic needs; responsive to their symbolic image: religious, historic, and so forth; aesthetically well conceived and properly structured; and contemporary. Cities cannot exist hermetically alienated in a nostalgic atmosphere or in a futuristic abstraction. To be contemporary—thus real—cities have to establish a creative presence in the present, standing on the broad shoulders of tradition and providing a creative vision of their future; without this outcome, they become pathological human conglomerates.

Shadrach Woods, a famous architect and town planner, stated the following:

> We are concerned, not with "architecture" or "town planning," but with the creation of environment at every scale. . . . The problems which we face in making our world are entirely new, for our society is entirely new. . . . We cannot think of planning in static terms, in three-dimensional space, when we live in a four-dimensional world. The realization, for instance, that the scene of action of reality is not a three-dimensional Euclidean space but rather a four-dimensional world, in which space and time are linked together indissolubly, sets our civilization apart from any others. (Shadrach 1964, 151)[3]

Throughout most of its history Havana has been contemporary, dynamically incorporating into its urban fabric any and all styles, but only after retaining its own essential characteristics and mutating each style into its regional imagery of Cubanness. Alejo Carpentier, a famous Cuban writer, said that Havana was a city erected in no particular style but executed with great style (Alejo 1970, 20). That is how it became a work of art, a depository of history and the most appropriate stage for the unraveling of Cuban culture.

Cuba's traditions are influenced by a variety of cultures. It is a Mediterranean country with strong Mediterranean cultural roots. Spain was invaded and conquered by the Romans (218 BC to 17 BC) and later by the Moors. All left their imprint: physical, social, and cultural. Spain and the Mediterranean, as a whole, constitute the cultural base of Cuban traditions.

Research, Creative Approach, and Recommendations

During colonial times Havana developed as a multicentered city with no recognition of a dominant urban center, facing the Bay of Havana, its main resource of commercial activity. The original villa's economic survival depended on the operation of the Royal Fleet for almost two centuries (1543–1740). On November 30, 1665, Havana was officially designated as the "Key to the New World" by the Spanish Crown. To secure the bay, the Spanish Crown created a formidable defense system by building a series of fortifications that gave Havana a monumental urban scale. Later on, Cuba's socioeconomic base was grounded on the exports of tobacco and sugar, and the bay kept its importance.

The recognition of Havana's monumental urban scale and of the traditional importance of its bay is fundamental in any project dealing with the future of the city. The Bay of Havana is today one of the world's most contaminated. This is another significant factor to take into account.

Havana should develop around its bay, and it should become the geographic center of its development into the foreseeable future. The land available for development toward the east up to Guanabo, packed with excellent beaches, could best accommodate a sizeable portion of the city's future growth. This would undoubtedly require major engineering and planning. It would also be likely that another tunnel would have to be built under the bay's entrance channel to provide adequate access to the entire area.

The analysis of the bay's extraordinary tourism possibilities and Havana's good highway connection with the Bay of Mariel led to the following basic recommendations:

1. Move the industrial, commercial, and major supply activities present today in the bay area, to the Bay of Mariel.
2. Convert the Bay of Havana into a major cruise-ship port and tourist attraction offering all sorts of water-related activities. The bay would become a monumental "Plaza on the Water," bordered by Casablanca, Regla, Atarés, and Old Havana and accessed via its entrance channel protected by the colonial castles, El Morro, La Punta, La Cabaña, and La Real Fuerza, making this a truly unique setting.
3. The bay's coves, Ensenadas de Triscornia, Marimelena, Guanabacoa, Atarés, and the bay front of Old Havana, would provide unique venues where marinas could be located around the bay's edges. A fishing port and fish market could be developed in the Atarés cove. In Old Havana,

the view of the bay from the Alameda de Paula should be opened again, and the main cruise ship docking facilities should be located at the piers of Santa Clara, La Machina, and San Francisco, backed by the customs building and opening onto the Plaza de San Francisco. Regla could provide additional cruise ship docking facilities.

4. All the elements that will structure the bay as a "Plaza on the Water" should be tied together with a water taxi and public transport system.

Additionally, the project's work has explored the following urban elements and studied their interrelationships as they historically structured the city: urban centers, urban corridors, city edges, urban nodes, the street network system, and the green network system.

All these elements, grouped together, interconnected with efficient public transport systems—tramways being, again, one of them—are being studied. The end result should constitute a creative urban composition unique in the Caribbean, both in size and in aesthetic quality.

Explaining how to deal with the regional approach to ecological sustainability, the architect Juan Antonio Bueno—who also serves as the co-director of "Havana and Its Landscapes"—had this to say at the initial presentation of the project on August 18, 2004:

> Planners should be sensible to the economic, sociological, and cultural implications of the population distribution throughout the city. This takes the project beyond just buildings and includes issues such as parks, open spaces, and the sustainable development of all of these components. The environment in which the city is set is as important as the city itself, be it the basin of the Almendares River, the surrounding rural areas, or the mountains to the south. That is why we bring all of these components into the project. By working as a team, we are making sure that this is a holistic endeavor that includes everything from building facades, to city planning, to how the city harmonizes with the geography and ecology of that part of Cuba. (Bueno 2004, 2)

Three Study Areas and Their Findings

The project is being executed at Florida International University's School of Architecture under the direction of architects Nicolás Quintana and Juan Antonio Bueno. Architect Felipe Préstamo—recently deceased—was invited to participate as an associate investigator and provided a significant contribution. At the project's start three study areas were established: the regional approach to ecological sustainability (under the direction of Bueno); urban

Urban Activity Center Project. Students Jorge Atick, Gilbert García, Yanina Corbea, and Andrea Rodríguez. COURTESY OF NICOLÁS QUINTANA.

planning of the sociopolitical structure (under the direction of Préstamo); and urban design and architectural typologies (under the direction of Quintana). It was agreed that the three study areas should work jointly to achieve a new urban vision by way of a multidisciplinary approach. Each of the study areas would produce a document explaining its research and recommendations.

The conclusions arrived at in the three study areas would help to conceptually guide urbanism in the future in Cuba. Based on these conclusions—including the rural, natural, and sociopolitical components—an urban vision will be recommended to structure a modern Havana. This vision will constitute the main armature inside which the development of the city's barrios occurs, always respectful of their traditional historic values. The modernity inherent to the approach will propel the city into the future.

In the study area of urban design and architectural typologies a total of fifty students during four semesters—in three groups of twelve students and one group of fourteen—developed thirty-two projects and thirty-three scale models; all this work is supplemented with project posters, written reports, site photos, plans, digital images, and three-dimensional animations.

One of the typologies developed was the "Urban Activity Center." One of the students' main objectives was to avoid the occurrence in the future of the antiurban shopping center—typical of the sprawling development of modern

Introduction of a modern building in Plaza Vieja. Graduate project of Gabriel Fuentes. COURTESY OF NICOLÁS QUINTANA.

suburbia—surrounded by open-air parking areas that are inefficiently used almost year round. This innovative concept, still not present in Havana, could well be implemented by incorporating future primary shopping centers as part of the Urban Activity Centers that would also offer multiple services for high-density, mixed-use, mixed-income urban living. Parking buildings will provide accommodation for resident and visitor vehicles. These centers could be developed in approximately twelve acres of space.

A student, in his graduate thesis, analyzed how to introduce a modern building into a colonial context, in this case, Plaza Vieja in Old Havana, enriching its urban quality. An essay about the urban history of Havana was also incorporated into this project, and it examined the historic models and critical thinking that have influenced the city's urban structure from its historical foundation up to the present.

In addition, a group of specialized professionals have cooperated with different studies, involving environmental, economic, legal, sociological, and psychological aspects as well as research into infrastructure, transportation, telecommunications, and much more. Their proposals open a wide informative horizon and offer important suggestions in their reports.

A series of approaches, attitudes, and suggestions as to how to deal creatively with the urban environment will be recommended to protect and orient the new vision. They will be useful to the execution in Cuba—when it is free and democratic—of the codes and ordinances needed to implement any urban vision. These codes and ordinances will provide the legal framework within which the engineers, architects, investors, developers, and other individuals will work.

Finally, a series of suggestions are made to deal with the order of procedures applicable during the process of reconstruction, new development, and the overall recovery of the city. To be successful this process has to start based on the existence of a rule of law, the recognition of human rights, the establishment of private property, the presence of a free market economy, and so on. The process should be guided by the National Institute of Territorial Studies and Urban Design (Instituto Nacional de Estudios Territoriales y Diseño Urbano), which will be created for this purpose.

Conclusion

The basic component in Cuba's continuous urban growth and development during the days of the republic was the guaranteed liberty of its citizens—even in our worst political moments—to question, research, and create in a constant, never ending process of cultural enrichment. Today the ugly face of destruction and despair is present and evident everywhere. To face this situation we must be aware that we need to create a new urban vision and work diligently in our cities to achieve their historic preservation, evolution, and insertion into the modern world.

Our cities must not be interpreted as nostalgic copies of what they were because that urban manifestation, logically, belongs to the past, and the value of its imagery is only useful as the cultural platform from which to start to delineate the immediate present and visualize the future. They should also not be interpreted as the product of imported dogmatic urbanisms that utilize and enforce concepts empty of modernity or urban structuring systems that do not originate from the in-depth investigation of culture—whose preconceived decisions are arrived at in short reunions (*charretes*) of accelerated rhythm.

The paradigmatic city, the Havana we have to rethink should create a historic continuum with the best that existed and whatever is good that exists today, because those images constitute the cultural base to create the future city that lies deeply within and waiting to emerge from the intelligence and soul of the Cuban people. It will be the creative product of the symbiosis between the internal experience of those living in Cuba with the external experience of Cubans in exile, both the same people (*un solo pueblo*).

Metaphorically this symbiosis can be expressed as the convergence of two effluents that flow independently to come together in what can be called the river of Cuban culture, enriching and transculturizing it. The new city should be the product of a meaningful research of experiences, needs, ideas, and projections. It should never be the product of intellectual improvisations, much less if they are delivered by elements foreign to our culture.

Cubans should not consent to be taken as laboratory mice for urban experiments done by others. We have an example of this dangerously superficial and disrespectful attitude in *The Havana Project*, which includes a series of individual proposals—most of them devoid of any creative or useful conclusions—issued hastily by a group of well-known foreign architects during and after a short stay in Havana.

The answer to the problems we are going to face will emerge from the study of our history and our context; in the Cuban person acting privately and publicly; in the Cuban intellectual armature; in the capacity of the Cuban people to work once motivated and in their creative spirit. All these qualities are fully verified as existing during the fifty-seven years of the republic.

Anything else constitutes opportunist "siren songs" to which we should not pay any attention. There is not an easy way out of Cuba's present situation. A lot of hard work and sacrifice lies ahead of us. The answer, I repeat, will come after a serious analytical process and creative decision making that should contain the following elements that have steered my professional life along fifty-seven years of unceasing work: passion, searching, vision, and work.

Notes

The project "Havana and Its Landscapes" at Florida International University's School of Architecture is being privately financed by donations from Sergio Pino, as president of the Board of Directors of Century Homebuilders, LLC, and Anthony Seijas, as regional vice president of Lennar Homes Inc. in Dade and Broward Counties.

1. The term *sustainable development* was defined in 1987 by the World Commission on Environment and Development (WCED) in their report to the UN General Assembly as "development that meets the needs of the present without compromising the ability of future generations to meet their own needs," adding that a sustainable development requires serving the needs of all (WCED 1987, 44).

2. Pietro Cataneo (1567), in his essay "L'Architettura," developed those ideas on the

grid that had been interpreted in Spain by a Catalonian Franciscan friar named Francesh Eximénic (1340–1409). This information reached Philip II with the translation of the very influential book by Sebastiano Serlio undertaken by Francisco de Villapando. Philip II later proclaimed the Ordinances in 1573. The Laws of the Indies were not mandated until 1680, and by then more than two hundred new towns had been founded by Spain in America, based on the Roman camp design, guided by the Archaic Ordinances of Castile and the instructions given to Pedro Arias de Ávila in 1513 by King Ferdinand "the Catholic." Numerous books document this process: Leopoldo Torres Balbás's *Resumen Histórico del Urbanismo en España* (Madrid: Instituto de Estadios de Administración Local, 1954); Erwin T. Galantay's *New Towns: Antiquity to the Present* (New York: George Braziller, 1975); Enrique Browne's *Otra Arquitectura en América Latina* (Mexico: Gustavo Gili, 1988); and Nicolás Sapieha's *Old Havana, Cuba* (London: Tauris Parke Books, 1990).

3. Shadrach Woods, a very important member of Team X, was instrumental in changing CIAM's approach to urban design.

6

The Illegible City: Havana after the Messiah

RAFAEL ROJAS

Translated by Eric Felipe-Barkin

Is there history after the messiah? How should one think about the historical period that follows the messianic kingdom? As leftovers of the past? As child abandonment? As a new Fall of humankind that will reinitiate its growth? In his book *La potenza del pensiero*, Giorgio Agamben returns to Walter Benjamin's philosophical thesis to investigate the type of sovereignty that is established after all the means of a utopian state have been left behind by history (Agamben 1999, 160–77). Reading his work may prove useful in thinking about the tribal Havana that is beginning to survive Fidel Castro, the Revolution, and socialism—three symbols of Cuban power over the last half century.

Agamben does not accept Derrida's belief that posthistorical time is that point where events do not take place. Following his line of reasoning on the quotidian nature of the state of exception, he asks what kind of sovereignty could be imagined in the rabbinical tradition of the messianic kingdom, as reformulated by Benjamin in his philosophy of history. The Italian philosopher finds the answer in the political theology of Carl Schmitt: the sovereignty of the utopian state is nothing but a dictatorship (Agamben 1999, 161). When the sovereign places himself above the law to decree a permanent state of emergency, establishing that "there is no law" beyond its own power, we are clearly in the messianic realm. A realm, as Agamben says, that is double, triple, or multiple, and, therefore, paradoxical.

One of the paradoxes of the messianic kingdom is that another world and another time must make themselves present in this world and time. This means that historical time cannot be simply canceled, and that messianic time, moreover, cannot be perfectly homogeneous with history: the two times must instead accompany each other according to modalities that cannot be reduced to a dual logic (this world / the other world). (Agamben 1999, 168)

The question could be shifted to the Cuban issue to explore the moment in which the messianic kingdom—the Revolution—is exhausted and historical time ceases to coexist with its ideal future. The product is then a volatilization of destiny, as explored by José Quiroga in *Cuban Palimpsests*, and manifests itself in nostalgia for the three pasts of the island: colonial, republican, and revolutionary (Quiroga 2005, 197–205). In the works of some writers from the late 1970s and 1980s (Senel Paz [2007], Leonardo Padura [2005], Marilyn Bobes [2005], Abel Prieto [1999], and Artura Arango [2001]) there is nostalgia not for the republican era but for the first decades of the Revolution, when the people were guided by the cultural values of socialist ideology and not money, individualism, or the popular culture of the 1990s or 2000s.

The Sum of Times

For writers who define themselves in their intellectual politics as "revolutionaries" or "socialists," it is also evident that the time for the Revolution and for socialism is over. Their novels refer to the revolutionary period in the simple past or historical past tense, even if "reality" is presented at times inside a temporal ambiguity that confuses the present with the past. Since these authors are individuals shaped by the first decades of the Revolution, their reporting of the social change that occurred in the post-Soviet period takes the form of the general denunciation of today's decadence and egoism, set against the epic and glorious past. This alienation from the present often results in the counterpositioning of literature (the past) and the market (today) or intellectual culture and popular culture, which marks their discourse with a melancholic and conservative tone.

The juxtaposition of characters like Jacqueline, the mature and well-versed writer, versus Benvenuta, the young and postmodern *jinetera* in Bobes's novel, or like Little Marco Aurelio and Freddy Mamoncillo in Prieto's novel, reveal a certain kind of "criticism" of the Special Period's present time (1992–2008), articulated as a restorative thrust for the stable and Soviet socialist period (1961–1992). In this narrative time is guided by well-established and hierarchical aesthetic and ideological values, while the post-Soviet period is associated with the fracturing of the national literary canon, the emergence of multicultural subjects, the invasion of the market, and a flood of popular culture. The market, as Esther Whitfield (2008) has observed, has become widely accepted in one sector of contemporary Cuban narrative (Zoé Valdés, Pedro Juan Gutiérrez, Eliseo Alberto, Leonardo Padura, Ena Lucía Portela, and Wendy Guerra), but in another it is depicted as a device that threatens professional literary order.

The work of Leonardo Padura is a curious intersection of both currents. For instance, every possible sort of nostalgia for Cuban culture coexists in *La neblina del ayer* (*Havana Fever*) (2005). The Montes de Oca family reconstructs the lineage of *criollo* and republican elites whose few remaining descendants on the island ended up taking refuge exiled in the mansions of El Vedado, Miramar, and Kohly, where the ex-policeman Mario Conde arrives to search for old libraries to buy and sell. The book catalogs tell us of a community of readers from the republican era that begins with the chroniclers of the Indies (Las Casas, Fernández de Oviedo, Díaz del Castillo, and Andueza), continues with the first historians of Cuba (Arrate, Valdés, Urrutia, Humboldt, and La Sagra), goes into nineteenth-century literature and thought (Heredia, Saco, Bachiller, and Villaverde), and culminates with the republicans exiled after 1959 (Novás Calvo, Labrador, Montenegro, and Cabrera Infante) (Padura 2005, 25, 68, 78–79).

Some characters in the novel, more steeped in popular culture than in the island's literary traditions, are nostalgic for the modern Havana of the 1950s, and others from the generation closer to the protagonist and the author are nostalgic for the 1960s and the beginning of the 1970s. These temporal cuts are produced from the perspective of a present-day writing defined as the era of Crisis (with a capital letter) that begins in 1992 with the collapse of the Soviet Union when: "his end as a policeman and forced entrance into the world of business coincided with the official pronouncement of the Crisis' arrival to the island—that galloping Crisis that made all previous ones pale in comparison, . . . crises that now began to appear, as a result of inevitable comparison and faulty memory, glorious times or simply nameless crises, and therefore ones without any claim to that terrible personification suggested by capital letters" (Padura 2005, 16).

Nostalgia for the socialist past—as seen from the social decay of the present—is most notable in Senel Paz's *En el cielo con diamantes* (In the sky with diamonds) (2007). Set in the same time period as his other works *Un rey en el jardin* (A king in the garden) and *El lobo, el bosque y el hombre nuevo* (The wolf, the woods and the new man), the novel takes us back to the flirtation of Cuba's youth with morality during the 1960s and 1970s—when political commitment was more demanding but, at the same time, simpler. The solid construction of ideological and aesthetic values of those decades accelerated not only the politicization of the country's intellectuals but also gave rise to a literary canon, reconstructed by Paz in his own text. The works of Carpentier, Guillén, Lezama Lima, Diego, and the Latin American Boom writers (García Márquez, Vargas Llosa, Cortázar, Bryce Echenique, and others) are a counterbalancing force to the influence of Soviet socialist realism on that generation (Paz 2007, 279–95, 320).

It is interesting to observe that Paz, like Padura, destabilizes time as he interweaves the current text's post-Soviet present with the socialist past in which the narrative takes place, while not drawing too much attention to the interruption of the 1990s "crisis." Paz's allusions to republican writers in exile, like Enrique Labrador Ruiz, Carlos Montenegro, Lino Novás Calvo, Gastón Baquero, Jorge Mañach, and even Guillermo Cabrera Infante, are a way of fusing past and present, particularly since some of these authors are being reread in Cuba since their "literary rehabilitation" in the 1990s (Paz 2007, 332). This fusion of time periods offers a symbolic solution to the "crisis," equipping the period of Soviet influence with the ideological flexibility of the post-Soviet period, while simultaneously reconciling it with the utopian ideals of the Revolution's first decades.

Another writer from the same generation of Paz and Padura, Eliseo Alberto, who has been exiled in Mexico since the 1990s, relates to Havana through literature in another way. In his last two novels, *Esther en alguna parte* (Esther in some place) (2005) and *El retablo del Conde Eros* (Count eros's altarpiece) (2008), the city is presented in two different periods: during the 1940s and 1950s, the decades of republican modernism, and the present, Havana at the dawn of the twenty-first century, after the Special Period. The memories of Lino Catalá and Larry Po, along with the urban experiences of Julián Dalmau, achieve such a familiarity with the lost city of Havana that they place Alberto's writing beyond the republican nostalgia of Cuba's first wave of exiles and beyond the obsessive temporal break that characterizes the novels from the post-Soviet period.

The Havana that emerges from Alberto's symbolism is a collage of different time periods. The city's narrative, as realized on the island and in exile, manifests a temporary decoupling of the character in order to capture its multiplicity of feelings. The transition from the Soviet to post-Soviet period that took place in Cuban culture around 1992 could be seen as a movement from "political utopia" to "urban heterotopia," as branded by Manuel Delgado in *El animal público* (The public animal) (1999). In it, Delgado defines this transition as a mutation of citizens and pedestrians that turns public space into an unintelligible text. The coexistence of characters living in different times, and on occasions ideologically opposed, turns the city into a discourse that cannot be narrated:

> An illegible, senseless gibberish, without meaning—or at least without a *single* meaning or a *single* purpose—that says nothing, since the sum of all voices creates just a murmur, a rumor, at times a clamoring, an incomprehensible sound incapable of being translated since the words are without order, and instead consist of an unclassified noise resembling a great buzzing. (Delgado 1999, 189)

The superimposition of times on Havana's stage creates a ritualized chaos among its inhabitants. Citizens learn to accommodate different cities under the same roofs and in the same streets. From the beginning of the 1990s, people in Havana felt nostalgias for all Havanas, including nostalgias for the most immediate past, the one just before the "crisis." However, since Fidel Castro's convalescence in the summer of 2006 or, more precisely, since the transfer of power in 2008 the future is being lived alongside every imaginable past and present. The future, that kingdom subsequent to the messiah, begins to show its strange legality, unaware of the "state of emergency," in which the community, which is barely alive, manifests itself as the end of the prior civic model and the end of the socialist era.

A song from the mid-1980s by Juan Formell and Los Van Van repeats the refrain "la Habana sí, que sí, sí, que sí." The song, which was conceived as a call for the remaking of Havana in its entirety—not just for the remaking of its colonial facade—incorporated an ideological message as well. The song says, "Havana, yes, Havana the socialist, city of traditions, wants that they consider her pretty / All of Havana wants to be the most beautiful capital in Latin America, in Latin America." The song came out at the same time that two phenomena converged on the city: the beginnings of the restoration of colonial neighborhoods in Havana spearheaded by the historian Eusebio Leal Spengler and the beginnings of perestroika and glasnost in the Soviet Union under Mikhail Gorbachev. As they had so many times before, Juan Formell and Los Van Van captured the political sentiment of the moment: according to the island's elite "socialist Havana" was to be a slogan capable of surviving the reform or even the collapse of communism.

As a slogan that affirms half a century of continuity and that erases temporal breaks, not only of politics and culture but also of architecture and urbanism, "socialist Havana" presents itself as a city in which the development of the 1960s and 1970s coexists with the crisis of the 1990s and 2000s. As a matter of fact, however, the readings of the city produced by the intellectual field in the past two decades have had recurring themes such as decadence, ruin, nostalgia, decomposition, poverty, precariousness, and tribalization. These readings are not new. At the end of the nineteenth century and during the middle of the twentieth century similar discourses had emerged, although never as persistent or extensive.

Of Chronicles and Decadence

Throughout the history of Cuban literature there have been narrative strategies for dealing with the city where the writer has presented himself as the city's reader in times of symbolic mutation. Duanel Díaz has alluded to some in his study of criollo nostalgia in Jorge Mañach's *Las estampas de San Cristóbal* (The imprints of St. Christopher) (Díaz 2003, 67–91). If we take three of the best known, Julian del Casal's chronicles of the late nineteenth century, José Lezama Lima's *Tratados en la Habana* (Havana treatises) (1958), and Antonio José Ponte's *La fiesta vigilada* (The supervised party) (2007), the three cities of these books are depicted at a point of decadence of a historical order, stable for at least fifty years: colonial Havana, republican Havana, and revolutionary Havana.

Casal, for example, wrote his chronicles in the waning years of the Spanish colonial rule. The feeling that an era is ending pervades Casal's text in many ways. Decadence can be felt in the festivities in the palace ballrooms, "notable for their past splendors" but now "converted into expansive museums of antiquities." The festivities of the 1860s during the times of the Captain Generals Francisco Serrano and Domingo Dulce are transformed under the government of Sabas Marín in the beginning of the 1890s into boring and solemn affairs bereft of Havana's high society and filled instead with colonial functionaries: "Bureaucrats are the most faithful attendees of General Marín's vulgar receptions" (Casal 1963, 27).

Casal follows the example of Sainte-Beuve's literary *Portraits*, measuring society's cultural refinements through the analysis of the reading salons of the nobility (Sainte-Beuve 1996, 115–200). Consequently, he is constantly searching for the Countess of Fernandina, the Marquise of Calderón, the Marquis of Real Socorro, the Count of Mopox and Jaruco, the Count of Jibacoa, the Count of Casa Barreto, and the Marquis of Aguas Claras. Casal himself, who signed his chronicles as the Count of Camors, lamented the decadence of the old nobility and its disappearance under the new class of merchants and bureaucrats dominating Havana's society.

It is interesting to note Casal's counterpositioning of this community of readers and the salon festivity on the one hand, and, on the other, the world of another kind of party, that of Havana as a "provincial Ireland," where actors, playwrights, journalists, painters, baseball players, beggars, and even lion tamers mill about (Casal 1963, 100–104). That other Havana, part circus and part bohemian, exposes itself most vividly to the flaneur's gaze, appropriated directly from Count Paul Vasili's Madrid chronicles with added undertones from Casal's readings of Joris Karl Huysmans and Max Nordau. In *Memory of the Modern* (1996), Matt K. Matsuda notes the importance of these last two authors in the creation of end of the century urban archetypal characters like "the vagabond," "the criminal," "the doctor" and "the judge"—all of whom fill the pages of Casal's chronicles (Matsuda 1996, 121–42).

Casal presents this urban underground of characters as the other face of Havana's high society and as a Simmelian world in which the fiesta and the market, which were suppressed in the premises of the General Captaincy, are set loose into a frenzy (Casal 1963, 100–104). The euphoria of money and merrymaking is felt in his chronicle about the Centro de Dependientes (Sales-clerk's Hall) and also in his splendid description of the grand ball of the Bomberos de Comercio (Trading Firemen) held in the Almendares park grounds. He recalls that the bright lights of the party with dancing until dawn "overtook the night's vigil," rejecting the somber festivities in the salons of the aristocracy: "the illuminated gazebo, seen through its carved openings, looked to us like a grand field full of unmoving fireflies, with eyes wide open" (Casal 1963, 105–8).

If Casal was the voice of colonial decadence, some fifty years later Lezama would be the voice of republican decadence. Money and merrymaking re-emerge in Lezama's "Sucesivas o las coordenadas habaneras" (Succesives or the Havana Coordinates) that he wrote for the *Diario de la Marina* through-out the 1950s, later collected and published in *Tratados en la Habana* (1958)—just one year before the revolution. In these chronicles Lezama describes the advance of the market over the Cuban economy in the republic's last years as an inexorable sign of the end of an era. Phrases like "pay day" and "window shopping" are like "pinches of the moment," as employees sweep through the stores of Havana, the city transfigured into the Baghdad Bazaar, searching for a "nameless commotion of solicitations" (Lezama Lima 1991, 41–42).

Lezama writes of "Byzantine ballplayers," "debauched buses," "syrupy drinks that unreel the mind," and "tunnels of the subconscious" (Lezama Lima 1991, 51–52, 55–58). But underneath so much sharp-witted praise, we can read a lament for the past that has been lost. In the gardens, cafes, and parks one no longer finds real "discourse" as before. The "exercises of the soul" have been displaced by the "desire for luxury," the beaches are stuffed with tourists, the *ordo caritatis* or the "spirit of volunteerism" that once characterized the village of San Cristóbal and its patron saint has become commercialized, the universities have been overrun with scholars studying the "mystery of the enthymeme," and a new type of reader surfaces in the bookstores, the nouveau riche who "devotes himself furiously to indexes and titles, without any desire to lose himself in a succession of chapters, or dynasties of the development of ideas" (Lezama Lima 1991, 95).

For Lezama, the equivalent of this reader, outside the world of literature and inside the city's commercial life, is the "arrogant, unibrowed, truly original character . . . , who likes to disguise himself as an 'artist,' ratifying style abuse for brown pants and a plaid jacket, with a domino-patterned scarf screwed round his throat" (Lezama Lima 1991, 199). The appearance of these new civilian archetypes is presented by Lezama as a marker of the coming of a new future society linked to modernity, capitalism, and democracy in the most Western sense. A modernity received by the poet with ambivalence in the same manner as in Casal or even Martí.

With respect to the nonreligious aspects of the city, Lezama tried to counteract the existing decadence under the aegis of money and market by praising the "nutritive influence of the Catholic calendar": Carnival, Lent, Christmas, and the Feast of the Three Magi (Lezama Lima 1991, 133–34). This family feast, he thought, fitted the city's colonial and republican architecture better than the American way of life that was spreading in El Vedado and Miramar. Set against that other emerging Havana, mainly chronicled by Guillermo Cabrera Infante, Lezama champions the "style" of the Quinta San José, the grand old mansion of Lydia Cabrera and María Teresa de Rojas, which also provoked a well-known article in *Bohemía* by Maria Zambrano.

Lezama writes:

> To have a house is to have a style capable of combating time. Combating time can only be achieved if an essential sense of tradition is fused with creativity that continues to grow and has not stopped. Lydia Cabrera and Maria Teresa de Rojas have made and own such a house. They are and have style, they challenge, transgressing with great elegance through the weight of tradition. . . . They have gained respect for what must always be known as: *La Casa*. (Lezama Lima 1991, 222)

What does Lezama mean by "combating time"? Tradition affirmed in his historical poetry is understood as a form of resistance against the immediacy of the present. In a letter written in 1961 to his sister Eloisa, Lezama writes that he understands his literary purpose as a "transcendence, rising above the walls and living in a futuristic dimension" through his internment into the "essence" of Cuban and universal culture (quoted in González Cruz 2000, 421). That notion, when transferred to Havana and his condition as a habanero, means an exercise in citizenship, which has been inscribed with the traditions of criollo high culture since the eighteenth century. For Lezama, the Quinta San José is the tangible inheritance of the "noble" colonial and republican architecture: spaces built for the last descendants of the insular Cuban aristocracy (Álvarez-Tabío Albo 2000, 227–58).

The discovery of the vestiges of criollo civilization goes hand in hand with a vision of modern, urban apocalypse and a vision of the future that is, at minimum, disturbing. In his "Havana coordinates" Lezama refers to visionary tales of impending catastrophes, such as that of "tropical Nostradamus or the infused closures," where the image of the "sugar coated lion" is interpreted as a symbol of the Caribbean and the "two fiery peaks battered by cascades" are seen as an omen of the Revolution: "two armies hold at a short distance, awaiting the authentication of some prophetic text to begin shooting their arrows and destroying each other" (Lezama Lima 1991, 131–32). In other chronicles, Lezama makes reference to UFOS, "discs possessed of matter brought to life by a breath or a spirit, keepers of an interplanetary secret, eroded by the communicating desperation of multiple talkative worlds. Here, the dawning of a new era! A new age!," they shout. And he speaks of the "atomic war" as the highest "irony of the species":

> What refutation of our times, to conceive of the destruction of everything, the moral question of our days: Will man achieve the destruction of his own planet? And thus, through a paradoxical limitation, wars will become museum wars. In the wise, old, and magnificent halls of any country's artillery museum one might find an artifact with a concise, little inscription by its side: "capable of destroying half of the world." (Lezama Lima, 203–4)

This revelation of the nuclear age, in conjunction with the prophecy of the Revolution—the true prophecy of the tropical Nostradamus, not the one interpreted by Cintio Vitier in his "Secularidad de José Martí" (The secular José Martí) (1953)—leads us to the last of the Havana chronicles of Cuban literature, where the city is perceived as a world of decadence: Antonio José Ponte's *La fiesta vigilada* (2007). Here, Lezama's apocalypse has become a daily and museum worthy affair; it has lost its eschatological sense because it has made destruction into an architectural entry from the past. Ponte's vision of the city as a postbattle landscape is an intrinsic element of his work. The parties and the commodities reappear as rituals or simulations among the ruins of a city. Here, the "end of an era" does not take the connotation of something that is about to happen, that announces itself as it does in Lezama and Casal's work, rather, it is something that has already happened and has begun a process of normalization before the arrival of the new era.

Ponte begins his work with a reference to Graham Greene's novel *Our Man in Havana*—a spectacle of spies, policemen, tourists, nuclear arms, and young revolutionaries published in 1958, the same year as Lezama's *Tratados en la Habana* (Ponte 2007, 50–67). In Greene's novel, the giant vacuum cleaner sketches that the false British agent James Wormold draws to make them look like missiles installed in the mountains are prophetic. The events that begin in Havana, the year after Lezama and Greene's works are published, proved to be an overwhelming manifestation of the new era, both desired and feared by the republican chronicles of the city. Ponte recognizes this temporal advent, but unlike Padura, Paz, Prieto, Bobes, Arango, and the island's other writers, he does so with full cognizance that a new place will follow after the Revolution and socialism.

The time Ponte describes will come after the messiah, when the city becomes illegible and during which the exception will become the rule. In this era there is no temporal ambivalence: the revolutionary and messianic time occurs during three decades and runs out in the 1990s. The city ends up in ruins, as if an imaginary war had savaged it—a war that was constantly announced but never verified. Ponte cites Benjamin's writings on the Paris Commune, when clocks were shot full of bullet holes, to allude to the great mission of the revolutionary era to "tame time," "fix an hour forever," and to "interrupt Chronos himself" (Ponte 2007, 119–20). This is why Havana's revolutionary history can be thought of as a "parenthesis in ruins" (Ponte 2007, 143–204).

If Havana is, as Ponte claims, "less a city full of life and more a landscape for political legitimization," it is then necessary to read Havana in terms of power dynamics. The end of *La fiesta vigilada* concerns itself chiefly with the state, or more specifically with the "State Security," where Agamben's issues of sovereignty are resolved (Ponte 2007, 207–39). Ponte explores how the ambiguity of the postmessianic period manifests itself in relation to the memory of power; in Havana the repressive apparatus has a museum, a school, and even its own army of historians at its disposition. The very same institutions charged with destroying the city are those claiming to archive and narrate the brief history of its destruction.

The major paradox of the postmessianic period resides precisely in the limited memorization of its past. By failing to recognize that the messianic kingdom, in a duality outlined by Agamben, has ended, the past, present, and future become unmoored from their meanings, and subjects begin to lose their sense of historical orientation. The temporality of the island begins to function in a synchronic sense instead of a diachronic one; in a sort of carnivalesque simultaneity that makes it difficult to establish the new sovereignty. As a citizen, the reader of the city can experience time as he pleases, encapsulated in the nostalgia of some past or progressing toward some personalized future as if on a one-way street. As a subject of the state, however, that very same reader has no alternative but to remain within his subaltern condition until a new legal code and a new sovereignty is established.

The illegibility of the city as a public space and of the citizen's roles within the city is, therefore, related to the temporal and semantic ambiguity of socialism as a concept. It is evident that this concept, while being the signifier of a historical time, that of the revolution and of the entire repertoire of Marxist and Leninist political values and revolutionary nationalism, nevertheless, functions as a symbolic, gravitational center in Cuba's insular culture. Thus, in order to read the city, to orient oneself inside it and, above all, to be a part of it, an inhabitant of the island must somehow socialize the socialist identity, must derive a meaning from calling herself or himself and being called by others a citizen of a socialist republic.

The New Tribes

The phenomenon of "new urban tribes" (rastas, emos, punks, *repas, miquis*, vampires, werewolves, and others) in the streets of G and Malecón and other public spaces in Havana speaks to an experience of globalization that must in turn be read as part of the collapse of socialism's hegemonic forms of sociability (Leafar Pérez 2001a and 2001b).[1] In every other American or European society, these tribes form part of a network of self-elected communities and civil associations. As the French sociologist Michel Maffesoli has written, these alternative groupings make the fabric of society more complex, diversify interventions in the public space, and reproduce the "tribalization of the postmodern world" (Maffesoli 2005, 11–17).

In Cuba, however, where a bundle of "social and mass organizations," the language of Article 7 of the Cuban Constitution, are meant to "group together the different sectors of society" (*La constitución cubana* 1994, 9), the emergence of these new urban tribes is as much the result of the cultural impact of globalization, as the impact from the crisis or the debilitation of the socialist model of citizenship. Some writers from the generation of 2000 (Michel Encinosa Fu, Orlando Luis Pardo Lazo, Yanet Fernández Labrada, Agnieska Hernánez Díaz, Gabriel Pérez, and others) have captured this crisis, and the role that Havana has played in it, through emerging works of fiction, mostly short stories.

One of the characteristics of this new Havana narrative, which also appears in the work of poets from the same generation like Javier Marimón, Pablo de Cuba Soria, or Noel Castillo González, is the transgression of the barrier between Spanish and English, both of which had been characterized as hostile languages in Cuban literature both before and throughout the Cold War. Unlike the rather rhetorical anglophobia that Gustavo Pérez Firmat has observed in the work of Nicolás Guillén and other revolutionary authors (Pérez Firmat 1999, 142–47), English has begun to take roots as a language and to take part in writing, generating in some cases, a bilingual phenomenon in Havana that should be put into dialogue with Cuban American literature.

Orlando Luis Pardo Lazo's story "Sweet Habana" (2005), for instance, shows us Havana in two moments: on the eve of 1989, before the fall of the Berlin Wall, when the reform of Cuban socialism seemed possible, and the decadent Havana of 2000, as depicted in Fernando Pérez's film *Havana Suite* (2003), from which the story draws its title and atmosphere. The text begins with a narrator, located among the ruins of the city, giving a speech that draws directly from the visual ambiance of Pérez's film but at the same time referring to an earlier time, when Havana's last utopia was insinuating itself:

> sweet havana, i am not desperate, i am not desperate, i am not desperate. today it has been exactly ten years since i last felt someone's gaze, a decade not so much decadent as peeling off, the trapped air of your broken-down boulevards always stalking silent streets, parking spaces without parking meters, inhospitable hospitals, and plazas displaced by the doldrums of their inhabitants— myself excluded. and even if i were to hate you already with all my heartbroken love, sweet havana, i assure you, i am not yet desperate, i am not desperate, i am not desperate. (Pardo Lazo 2005, 43)

From there, the narrator jumps in time to the end of the 1980s, when he and three other characters, Ipatria, El Sagys, and Ian, "discovered" that "everything was as easy as saying it . . . that there was sex and liberty . . . and they wanted to engage in them even if the city were to execute them in revenge"

(Pardo Lazo 2005, 43). With the invocation of "decadence" and "peeling off" signaling the moment of change in the century, the city of the late 1980s gave the strange impression of being an enclave with Soviet elements, generated by the illusion of a full and "appetizing" universe not exempt from the desiring temporality that is so typical of utopian discourses:

> Granma, Sputnik, pork sandwich, Juventud Rebelde, Novedades de Moscú, pork sandwich, Workers, Pravda, pork sandwich, Tribuna de la Habana, Soviet Women, pork sandwich, Palante, Soviet sports, pork sandwich, Misha, Pioneer, pork sandwich, DDT, Verde Olivo, pork sandwich . . . and an appetizing etcetera. (Pardo Lazo 2005, 46)

The list of diverse publications provoked a contrast against the monotony of other types of consumption that seemed appetizing, all the same, to the post-Soviet habaneros. The community articulated by the characters began with the disintegration of a greater community, the communist community, which guided the values and cultural customs not only of the Cubans but also of a great part of Central and Eastern European countries along with a large swath of Asian and African nations. Pardo Lazo insinuated, then, the exercise of an "uncommunist flight," borrowing a phrase coined via Jean-Luc Nancy by the Puerto Rican scholar Juan Duchesne Winter (2005, 37–49). This uncommunist gesture had no connection to the anticommunism of the Cold War, but instead it was grounded in the search for an autonomous sociability and in the "identity fatigue" provoked by the crisis of the symbols of legitimacy of a false socialist homogeneity (Duchesne Winter 2005, 17–36).

The post-Soviet community of uncommunist habaneros renegotiated its relationship with public spaces in much the same way as the new urban tribes would do it at the close of this decade. The Malecón would not be the site of triumphal, revolutionary parades, of the carnival, or of mass demonstrations against imperialism right in front of the offices of the U.S. Special Interest Section, but rather it would be a pilgrimage site for citizens looking to explore the limits of the city. In this literature, the Malecón emerges as a wall that separates the city from the rest of the world; one that must be visited in order to get closer to the rest of the world. The narrator of "Sweet Habana" explores the symbolic significance of the Malecón in a nightmare where the city loses its sea and with this loss the little contact it has with the outside world:

> sweet havana: i dreamed that you no longer had your sea; the wall of the malecón was nothing but a useless luxury separating the dry reefs: the dog's teeth, the living rock. in my dream, you remained vaginaless, walled in, wrapped up in a

constrictive belt of concrete: asphalt-town on cold, rigid rock. in my dream, your story, your history without a sea, was burning, a continental crematorium: waterless dream world where the word *isla* is just something to rhyme with the words *vivas* and *pingas*. that's how it was, sweet havana. your history without histology, your organless corpse, your corpus sans organist, your dramaless trauma, or maybe it was the other way round: the salty sleep of your miasma. (Pardo Lazo 2005, 48)

In another, more recent writing, "Espero la noche para no soñarte, Revolución" (I Wait For Night to Dream You No More, Revolution), from Pardo Lazo's blog *Lunes de post-revolución* (The post-revolution Mondays), the poet reconsiders the placement of the Malecón proposed in the literature of the new tribes.[2] Pardo Lazo recounts a trip along Route 23 from Fonts and Beales, Lawton, the English-named residence in Havana, to the Vedado. In one of his recurring homages to Guillermo Cabrera Infante, the narrator reaches la Rampa, opens his arms into the air, and advances toward the wall, Samsung camera in tow. The Malecón, says Pardo Lazo, "is a literary icon, now without the glittering baptismal waters of commercial advertisements (including the most vulgar sort from the 1990s), but still always with that spontaneous phosphorescence capable of reflecting the moon on one side and of containing the absolute darkness of the night on the other" (Pardo Lazo, "Espero la noche para no soñarte, Revolución").

The narrator then sits on the wall and notes that he is surrounded by hundreds of people, sitting like him, on the "winding concrete." Pardo Lazo describes these citizens as subjects "on the edge, unafraid to get lost in the late hours of the night, because around them sits an entire nation on the edge of the city" (Pardo Lazo 2008). Waiting for nightfall in front of a collision of slogan-stuffed billboards from the U.S. Interests Section, the Anti-Imperialist Tribune and its hill of flags, makes him recall the title of Nivaria Tejera's memoirs *Espero la noche para soñarte, Revolución* (I wait for night to dream of you, Revolution). However, in contrast with Tejera, who was a writer for the 1950s generation and who initially supported the revolution and later opposed it from her exile in Paris, Pardo Lazo considers himself to be a subject of the aftermath of the revolution, tied to the hope of not dreaming it, that is, of simply forgetting it (Tejera 2002, 11–23).

The Havana that emerges from this writing, created by authors belonging to the communal tribalization being experienced by Cuban society today, is no longer a place of the past, depicted nostalgically, nor a future city imagined as a utopia. Although the 1980s references to Havana introduce a certain yearning that could be compared with the longing of the narrators of the previous generation of the 1960s or 1970s, nostalgic and utopistic elements are minimized and subordinated to a prose that reiterates ruthlessly the decadence of the present. In this sense, the new Cuban narrative seems to abandon the dialectic, so recurrent in the intellectual history of the island, between disenchantment and utopia, decadence and nostalgia.

For some of the youngest Cuban writers, born around 1980, the post-Soviet era is tied to the tribalization of society under a state system bent on preserving Soviet-modeled institutions and ideology. The city then begins to be lived as staged decadence and not staged transformation, where the subject must break the closing of historic time through new associations in public space. Tribalization accentuates the illegibility of the city, not because a legible city is one in which its citizens respond to traditional forms of socialization but because diverse and dysfunctional interventions are added to the superimposition of different time periods.

A new social structure set on an old stage produces a dissonance between the discourse of the subject who intervenes in a public space and the hegemonic meanings with which the ruling power seeks to mark them. Avenida de los Presidentes or G Street, for example, is a road designed as a heroic pantheon where one finds that the old monuments to José Miguel Gómez and Tomas Estrada Plama have been joined more recently by statues of Simón Bolívar and Salvador Allende. This correction of the public space by the state attempts to counteract the presence of statesmen from the republican period—seen as neocolonial leaders—with figures from the Latin American nationalist or socialist tradition better suited to the symbolic needs of the Revolution.

Just like the *graffiteros* of the 1980s and 1990s, the new tribes represent a new symbolic correction with their own interventions into these spaces, one that does not emanate from the state but from civilian society. Under a heroic pantheon that seeks the homogenization of the citizenry, whether under a republican code or a revolutionary one, these alternative communities articulate a discourse about fragmentation and diversity. The dissonance created between the public space and the intervening subjects, therefore, demands a refunctioning of the space that only the state can assume. The ever-imaginative state could habilitate a specific location for tribal socialization, but doubtlessly, the tribes themselves would always prefer an old stage where a new language could be superimposed over it.

The alternative communities that manifest themselves in the public spaces of Havana, spaces codified in their architecture and urbanity by colonial, republican, and revolutionary narratives, invoke in any case a fourth city not yet built. However, with respect to the cultural practices of the tribes, that future Havana does not seem to fit the symbolic repertoire of an ideal habitat for a citizenry yet to come. In this sense, the new urban social orders are more global than national and have a virtual—or rather mental—notion of space in which the stage only has meaning as a discourse that must be refuted or repurposed but not rebuilt. The strategy of the tribes is unconnected to the foundational mechanisms of republican and revolutionary ideology.

Threading this tribal literature back to the ideas of Benjamin and Agamben laid out at the beginning of this chapter, it could be concluded that from a cultural perspective post-Soviet Havana is a city where lectures and discourses are organized that are known to come some time after the messianic time of socialism. The Cuban government, nevertheless, continues to present itself to its citizens as a totalitarian and providential entity that either controls or voids the rituals of civil society and the theatrical staging of the public space. This symbolic tension between the city and the state masks public discourse and at the same time obstructs the invention of new citizen sovereignties that desire to congregate either well beyond or at the margins of the legitimizing apparatus of Cuban socialism.

Notes

1. *Emo* standing for *emotional*, this group, a variation of the goth movement, dresses in black, proclaims an androgynous aesthetic, and is preoccupied with suicide. *Miquis* derive their name from Mickey Mouse; they associate themselves closely with U.S. American pop culture and with Hollywood, are well dressed, and live in elegant neighborhoods like Vedado and Miramar. *Repas* are those who have lower incomes and live in more popular *repartos* or in neighborhoods like Old Havana or Centro Havana; they listen to Cuban pop music. While rastas, emos, punks, vampires, and werewolves belong to global youth culture, repas and miquis are local, Cuban "tribes."

2. A play on the title of the Cuban weekly cultural magazine *Lunes de Revolución* (The Revolution Mondays), which ran from 1959 to 1961 before being closed by the Cuban government. It was founded by Carlos Franqui and edited by Guillermo Cabrera Infante.

Havana: A Photo-Essay

ORLANDO LUIS PARDO LAZO

Olimpabana.

PHOTO BY ORLANDO LUIS PARDO LAZO.

Bicúbica.

PHOTO BY ORLANDO LUIS PARDO LAZO.

Hola, olas.

PHOTO BY ORLANDO LUIS PARDO LAZO.

Hasta siempre, Comandante.

La Gran Muralla.

PHOTO BY ORLANDO LUIS PARDO LAZO.

Infanta para una Habana difunta.

PHOTO BY ORLANDO LUIS PARDO LAZO.

Calle Cárcel.

PHOTO BY ORLANDO LUIS PARDO LAZO.

Habanabelisco (Alamar).

Habanarús (Russian Orthodox Church).

Watching the Wheels (Parque Lennon).
PHOTO BY ORLANDO LUIS PARDO LAZO.

PART II

HAVANA'S SHIFTING

MARGINS

The City in Midair

EMMA ÁLVAREZ-TABÍO ALBO

Translated by Eric Felipe-Barkin

They too wanted to make prophecy, to design
the grace and destiny of our tomorrow's cities.
—José Lezama Lima

The Metaphor of the Ruins

It was to a city "abandoned the night before by all of its inhabitants" that José Lezama Lima compared Julián del Casal's poetry. According to Lezama Lima (1988, 192), Casal's poetry "at times, follows a line of inhabiting with pleasantness a unique land" one that for Lezama Lima (1970b, 182) represents the Orplid, "the city of stalactites where the real and unreal interlace in undulating remoteness."[1] Both poets have lost themselves in a poetic and domestic space where the texts they construct take them into "the mysterious and refracted palace of bliss" (Lezama Lima 1988, 192). When the poet abandons that palace, his travels take him through an abandoned city, where the whirr of an insect wandering between columns makes silence more ominous and evocation more unattainable. But there, everywhere, the footprints of the man who inhabited it can be found, "like the wicker rocking chairs in the ruins of the sugar mill" that Lezama Lima found forgotten in his "Oda a Julián del Casal"—objects close to the iconographic landscape of the ideal Lezamanian city (1999, 476).

Casal's forsaken city—which stands in contrast to the city of pronounced silhouettes that teem beyond the walls of his modest accommodations, near the lively streets of Habana and O'Reilly—is a more abstract and universal city; it is definitely the modern city to which he declares his "impure love" (Casal 1945a, 304). The abandoned city that Lezama Lima evokes symbolizes the fate of the inexpressible, that which resists representation. A poem without a poet and a city abandoned by its inhabitants sum up the paradox of Havana's textual destiny as begun by Casal and depicted by Virgilio Piñera in his devastating tale *Presiones y diamantes* (Pressures and diamonds). Like Casal and like Lezama Lima, the narrator of this strange and disturbing novel remains in the city while its inhabitants abandon it—or, conversely, he is abandoned by his city, though he will not leave her.

Some go and others remain. But those who stay are unwilling to engage in the tradition of resistance—the imagined besieged plaza, interwoven with the very foundations of the city, that unique act that poets attempt to recreate. Casal never renounces his "unquenchable thirst to travel" (Casal 1945b, 99). Lezama Lima replies with this aphorism: "he who wanders the world may find a snake on the table of the *Meistersinger*; he who never leaves home may find a *Meistersinger* in a snake" (Lezama Lima 1970c, 11). Piñera stays, because, as he himself explains, "who gives up a cherished habit?" (Piñera 1988, 117). The narrator of Piñera's "Frío en caliente" and the protagonist of Tomás Gutiérrez Alea's film *Memories of Underdevelopment* remain in the city, too, while others leave. However, the lucid and skeptical observations of both about those who leave and those who remain undermine their explanations about their own decision to stay—reasons that would supply substance for the barricades of the besieged city. Gutiérrez Alea himself made a vicious caricature of that form of resistance in *The Survivors*. In that film, the ruins of the house in which the characters entrench themselves reproduce an ambiguous journey reminiscent of Alejo Carpentier's "Journey Back to the Source," in which the life of Don Marcial is reconstructed from the very ruins of his family manor.

Carpentier himself often refers to the ruins of Havana that always seem to threaten the gesture of writing his monumental city. "Havana is the unfinished city, limping, asymmetrical, and abandoned," he writes in an article after returning from a long stay in Paris in 1940 (1996, 65). One hundred years earlier, in 1840, the Countess of Merlín also arrived from Paris to visit the city. "I walk among nothing more than a pile of lifeless rocks and an undying memory," she writes in *Viaje a La Habana* (Journey to Havana) (Santa Cruz y Montalvo 1974, 109). In his own *Viaje a La Habana*, Reinaldo Arenas (1991) describes a decrepit city, one that is almost in a state of siege. Piñera also chews over this vision of a city defined by ruins in "Hecatombe y alborada" (Catastrophe and dawn), where a "second self" watches as Piñera buries the shady mansion of the past in "clouds of dust, bodies savagely killed, and blazes of green." This "second self," however, allergic to dust, abandons the debris "in search of more suitable ruins" (Piñera 1987a, 296). Perhaps the ruins are those between which Casal, who might well be Piñera's "second self," wandered, considering himself as "pensive, wandering among the ruins / of the old, stately homes" (Casal 1945c, 119).

The ubiquity of these ruins isn't necessarily a consequence of material destruction; it may be the product of absence and abandonment. They are ruins lodged in the writer's gaze, evoking a feeling of nostalgia, loss, or emptiness, the look of *what could have been and never was*: a rebellion, a breakdown, a discord. It is a permanent disjuncture with the inadequacy of the present. These writers explore the space between the extremes of a far-off utopia and an imminent apocalypse. Piñera's "Hosanna! Hosanna . . . ?" describes the destruction of the city and the hope of the body's resurrection, a coming with "no signs in the sky, no announcements and no symbols" (1987b, 318). With that, one can imagine that the Final Judgment has come and gone, and that the ruins that remain, contemplating those who go and those who stay, are a testament to the forgotten memory of the eternal Father.

The metaphor of the ruins represents the frustration of destiny: personal, familial, national. Lezama Lima (1988, 205), however, saw Casal's frustration as "the achievement of a harmonious destiny," while Piñera (1994, 172) was interested in him precisely as a "frustrator." Yet it would be Lezama Lima who recast his works into a representation of what he calls "the spirit of the ruins." In his "Homenaje a René Portocarrero," he decrees that "the home represents infancy." He goes on to add that, "furthermore, very frequently the Cuban family, whose delicate fabric of resistance always establishes the house as a center for the extensions of the imagination, is forced to receive at some moment of its unfolding that which we've already called the spirit of the ruins" (Lezama Lima 1970a, 390). I suspect that if we half-closed our eyes we would find those ruins not only in the Havana landscapes of Portocarrero's paintings or Lezama Lima's *Paradiso* but in the scenery that surrounds us.

Through abandoned houses and empty neighborhoods, through "the spirit of the ruins," I could also retrace a large part of my own childhood. At that point, I experienced it not in metaphorical terms but real ones—an abandoned city filled with ruins. I suppose that in other neighborhoods some had similar experiences, but the Havana I knew was no bigger than the Miramar area and limited to the dozen blocks that surrounded my childhood neighborhood, which I did not then know was a *zona congelada* (frozen zone). I close my eyes to walk around the block in my mind, and I can recall no more than three or four houses occupied by regular families. If I continue down adjacent streets, the results are similar. In the surrounding empty mansions, they had set up a school where I went to elementary school; there were polished marble floors, sprawling chandeliers, colorful stained-glass windows, iron-worked banisters, and luxurious bathrooms. Today, that school has ceased to exist and the houses have been taken back and made into offices for foreign businesses and joint ventures. A former teacher, who himself had become a prep cook, told me with bitter irony that the slogan from the first years of the revolution, "We will make barracks into schools" has had as its coda, "and schools into corporate headquarters."

But if I half-close my eyes I can also make out, resplendent in the midst of those ruins, "the mysterious and refracted palace of bliss," in the same way that Portocarrero's Havana landscapes let us make out his cathedrals. On the outskirts of Havana—"on the road to Santa Fe," as the children's song goes— you'd find the Tahoro sugar mill. On Sundays, at a noontime that my memory now recalls as always sunny, we would go picnicking on the old, abandoned grounds, buzzing with the hum of the insects that lay between the overgrown stalks of grass. Though we preferred running through the *batey* (sugar mill town), overgrown with vegetation, or around the bell tower, we would sometimes slip through the ramshackle planks of the plantation house's main door. I can't think of any place where I've been so intensely pervaded by a feeling of being frozen in time. Inside the house, the only things that seemed to move were the particles of dust that would find their way into the faint streams of light fanning in through the blinds. The heavy drapes sagged off to the side, the big family portraits hung crooked on the walls, and the furniture was preserved under layers of dust and sheets of cobweb.

Many years later, on a trip to the Aegean Islands, I visited the ruins of the city of Akrotiri. The village was destroyed and buried by a volcanic eruption in 1500 BC; when it was discovered in the 1970s, it was very well preserved. There were narrow, recognizable streets, city plazas, and thresholds of houses that sharply held up roofless walls. Inside there was furniture petrified by lava and a great many pithoi—large earthenware pots that were used for storing food—that still had the remains of cereals and grains at their bottoms. As I walked through that sixteenth-century BC city, it gave off a troubling sense of immediacy. It looked as if it had been "abandoned the night before by all of its inhabitants," as if its visitors might at any moment find themselves surrounded by a band of chlamys-clad people.

In the plaza of Akrotiri, all of my childhood feelings from the batey of the Tahoro sugar mill came back to me, and I was able to recognize a feeling of imminent catastrophe that I hadn't been able to understand before, that feeling that Carpentier called "the apocalyptic immobilization of a catastrophe" represented in the painting *Explosion in the Cathedral* that appears at the beginning and end of his novel by the same title (1990, 18–19). At the same time, I was aware that for those remote and unknown inhabitants of the plazas, the catastrophe had already happened. Both of the grounds conveyed an immediate sense of ruination, an illumination of the present that muddles the directionality of time, like that night in "Journey Back to the Source" where the past and future occur simultaneously. In much the same way as Piñera does in "Hosanna! Hosanna . . . ?," Carpentier leaves the possibility of existence beyond Judgment Day in suspense, in a negative or inverted time and space, and in the midst of ubiquitous ruins. In the plaza of the abandoned city, time was suspended, left hanging "in midair." Within that frame, the time of memory and the time of hope existed concurrently. The past was prophesized and the future was remembered.

The Citizen's Decade

The city has its neighborhoods and its eras, different spaces and times that have superimposed themselves over each other and over the years, each one illuminated by the memory of its own specific inhabitants. More recent Cuban literature has told us, prolifically, of those memories and their desires; it has charted a sentimental map of the city. I too would now like to speak about these illuminations and cast a ray of light into one of these strata, a time and place when it seemed as if a more "democratic" city was being constructed. I ask myself again, in what direction should I cast my gaze to find *what could have been and never was*, as I look over the ruins, because it seems to me that there is as much prophecy as memory in it. The landscape of this inquiry is that of the "happy '80s," a time I dare to call the Citizen's Decade.

I refer to *citizen* both in its proper and subversive sense. On the one hand, it presupposes the recognition and even the exaltation of the city, and on the other, it indicates brokenness and a certain capacity for dissent. Perhaps I should remind the reader that *citizen* has had pejorative connotations, that it assumes a certain ideological distance. Being a citizen does not mean being a *comrade*, but rather someone of dubious affiliation, probably a *gusano*, a traitorous worm, as Cubans going into exile to Miami were called. But we should also recall that the gusanos, as the popular saying goes, "grew into butterflies." The 1980s began with the arrival of the Cuban exile community and then saw the massive exodus from the port of Mariel in 1980. Under pressure from this two-way movement of coming and going, the walls that surrounded the city became porous, began to crack, and never quite closed again.

In 1982, Havana was included in UNESCO's World Heritage Site list. The designation may have gone unnoticed by the majority of the city's inhabitants, but in practical terms, it translated into financial aid for enormously challenging reconstruction and restoration projects that were being carried out in La Habana Vieja by the National Commission of Monuments, which was founded in 1963, and the Office of the City Historian, headed since 1967 by Eusebio Leal Spengler. La Habana Vieja was reactivated as a historical and cultural center; once again the city radiated from its "magnetic center," located by Lezama Lima in the Plaza de Armas (1989, 421).

From that moment on, the anniversary of the city's founding—celebrated each November 16, the day that a mass was held in 1519 to bless the city and celebrate its charter and settlement on the west side of the port of Carenas—became increasingly important. The city was consecrated with new rites, like walking around the Templete's ceiba tree three times and dropping newly-minted one-centavo coins by its roots or attending high mass at midnight in the Cathedral of Havana. Leal Spengler himself, more or less transcending his usual occupation of heading conferences in the Palacio de los Capitanes Generales or leading guided tours of La Habana Vieja, would assume the role of television host each week on the documentary program *Andar La Habana* (Exploring Havana), which at the time was one of the most popular shows in Cuba's languid television lineup.

The biggest consequence of this recovery of the city and what made it lasting is that high culture and popular culture began to overlap and speak to one another. The Symphony Orchestra and the National Ballet events held in the Plaza de la Catedral coincided with Los Van Van or Irakere shows, where the attendees danced to tunes like "La Habana sí," "La Habana no aguanta más" (Havana can't take any more), "La Habana ¡oh! La Habana," and other similar and often excessively didactical songs that dealt with eminently urban themes like restoration and renewal work, urban emigration to the city, or illegal construction and building modifications. The "Castillo de La Fuerza" project and the workshops by plastic artists coexisted with the "Sábados de la Catedral" (Saturdays of the Cathedral), an unforgettable weekly arts and crafts fair.

But strolls through La Habana Vieja did not make solely for contemplative experiences; rather, they made the city available for active use. In addition to going to the events the city held, there emerged the possibility of consuming in the modest restaurants that surround the Plaza de Armas, like La Casa de la Natilla, La Casa del Agua, La Casa del Café con Leche, La Casa del Té, or El Mesón de la Flota. This ability to use the city moved beyond the limits of the old city and spread from there to the rest of Havana. An important element of this reacquaintance and appropriation of the city was, precisely, the possibility of choosing and taking advantage of the offerings that included film festivals, theater and ballet shows, concerts, exhibits, and even the restaurants, bars, and "pilot" beer halls. There also was the "parallel" market with its network of little stores or *mercaditos* for food, clothing, and household goods that ran along San Rafael Boulevard or even the short-lived *mercado libre campesino* (free farmers' market).

Another symptom representative of this sedimentation of traditional city culture in the 1980s was the consolidation and popularization of a certain middle-class aesthetics—if I can use this term to refer to the *cuadros* (squares), party leaders with certain levels of responsibility within the revolutionary state apparatus, also called *pinchos* (big bosses). Apart from being characterized by having certain specific possessions and a certain behavior, in architectural terms, this aesthetic espouses the popular notion of *soap houses*, like the Villa Jabón Candado. Flat roofs, eaves running down the sides, a carport, and Miami-style Venetian blinds all typify this kind of urban dwelling. You find them principally in Nuevo Vedado, the outskirts of Monte Barreto, or the Coronela area—neighborhoods where these houses proliferate and are copied infinitely in more modest, privately built homes.

With respect to the "interior baroques," as Carpentier would call it, there is wicker furniture, Art Nouveau lamps (real or fake), paintings or silkscreens of habaneras by Servando Cabrera Moreno, bracken ferns hanging from macramé cords, railings salvaged from a collapse, traffic lights, a tin sign with the former street name from the old city, objets trouvés expected to attest to the naturalness of well-established codes, recognized and interpreted according to everyone's means and social level. Pastor Vega's ineffable film *Habanera*, staring Daysi Granados, helped popularize this aesthetic. Indeed, the humorist Héctor Zumbado crucified the film in his review "¿Habanera tú?" (You, a habanera?), alluding to the famous song by Eduardo Sánchez de Fuentes.

In the context of this Citizen's Decade, there emerged a space for intense intellectual reflection—space that even if to some extent was capitalized on by young visual artists, nevertheless found its way into nearly every creative medium. The young architects who made up the 1980s generation engaged in these reflections with profound implications for the city and architecture. Although the existence of this generation has been obstinately rejected by many of its predecessors, it distinguished itself by its clarity and capacity to orchestrate mechanisms of collectivization and action and its willingness to participate in the new intellectual social order that sought a more "democratic" city.

Between May and June of 1986, the Centro Provincial de Artes Plásticas y Diseño exhibited the architectural works of Emilio Castro and Rafael Fornés in *Detrás la fachada* (Behind the Façade). Perhaps the most significant thing about this show was that not a single one of the works on exhibit had ever been constructed. From this perspective, the show itself represented the only possibility of realization, even if ephemeral, for projects condemned from the start to being no more than projects, shown by their authors in a deliberately negligent setup as projects relegated to being useless or superfluous junk. This planned protest symbolically began a debate and a new relationship between architecture and art. At the opening, on May 29, 1986, Fernando Salinas, the most lucid theorist of the architecture of the revolution, claimed that the fact that an architectural exhibit was being celebrated in an art gallery—something unusual in the context of Cuba at that time—only expressed that architecture in a new society deserved "to create a new societal architecture" together with nature, history, and culture.

The young architects argued that architecture was a historical and cultural product opposed to the technical modernization and trivialization of the "myth of the new" as labeled by Roberto Segre, whose body of theoretical and critical work on revolutionary architecture and urbanism is the most systematic. The preoccupation with context—a reaction against aggression and lack of respect toward the city—manifested itself in a reappreciation of the traditional Havana and an investigation into its urban and architectural heritage. The 1980s generation was characterized by a sense of social and cultural responsibility for the city and its inhabitants as well as by its sense of studious discipline and a thirst for information. Twenty years later, I look back with more melancholy than nostalgia on the dreams we had—melancholy for our sincere belief that we could provide a reinvented, urban, architectural tradition as part of a much more ambitious intellectual project of renovation.

Those young architects planned for a city that longed to be built and presented an intense reflection on the part that architects should play in society; in the majority of cases, it remained a plan, to be realized on paper only. Flipping through a portfolio of their architecture is another way of looking at ruins. Although it is necessary to note that in those years the ruins we loved and admired were actually unfinished projects or ones that had not been started—ones which we thought would never be built. That unrealized "paper architecture," far from being a sign of frustration, embodied hope. Those ruins represented neither destruction nor decadence, nor the past's footprint, nor the basis of sublimated nostalgia; rather, they represented the map of a project to be completed in the future, something yet to come.

The "Havana-on-paper" that emerges from those drawings can be confused with *La Habana desaparecida* (The disappeared Havana), the city exhumed from the splendid architectural sketches of Francisco Bedoya. The drawings represent the writing of sorts, the text of the architecture of the 1980s. Because of the enormous gulf between planning and realization, they themselves are the work. For that reason, emphasis is put on the presentation of these projects, assembled from a large volume of visual and conceptual information, using a number of unconventional media. Highly skilled graphic expression was encouraged by the fact that the documentation of architectural plans was the only possible end product. The 1980s, in fact, saw an abundance of brilliant draftsmen who had to focus their skills on other artistic avenues of professional and material creation.

Nevertheless, the architects did not lose themselves in their work; rather, they sought to establish a dialogue between cultured and popular codes, between high culture and kitsch, between professional control and the spontaneity of the popular initiative. Instead of suggesting the demolition of some fragments, the 1980s architects, who could only plan for a Havana-on-paper, hoped to engage in dialogue with all texts. Ultimately, assimilating marginal schemes to the professional codes was also a strategy for subordination and control of a city whose residual spaces were being occupied by new inhabitants.

In 1987 in conjunction with the government's "process for the rectification of errors and negative tendencies," a period of exuberant construction began. Decentralization of planning increased the decision-making power of municipalities over their territory. The spate of new apartment and medical clinic construction that followed in turn revitalized the microbrigades movement. In this environment, opportunities for construction in the empty lots of the city materialized and the young architects, faced for the first time with the real possibilities of seeing their projects realized, greeted it with enthusiasm. Sadly, however, the promising, bustling racket of buckets, pulleys, hammers, wheelbarrows, and cement mixers could not long drown out "the sound of the instruments."

In January of 1990, the Centro de Desarrollo de las Artes Visuales opened the *Arquitectura Joven Cubana* (Young Cuban architecture) exhibit. The exhibit preceded another now infamous show, which was held in the very same space, *El objeto esculturado* (The sculptural object). In the architectural exhibit's program—the only testimony remaining since the projected catalogue was never made—three buildings, each one representing one of the three blue stripes of the Cuban flag, rise impetuously toward a triangular sky with a star, which has apparently had some trouble reaching its summit. In spite of its efforts, the star didn't manage to stay fixed in that triangular sky very long. What looked to be the ringing in of something new, turned out to be, in reality, a death knell, the swan song of the Citizen's Decade. The exhibition would be the last joint event for the 1980s generation until 1992, when the magazine *Arquitectura Cuba* published its 375th issue dedicated to young architects. By then, events had dispersed the 1980s generation and ended the Citizen's Decade.

Back to the Future

The only things left standing from the "democratic" city that seemed possible during the Citizen's Decade were set designs for a kind of Potemkin village, a mask to hide fear of the future. Meanwhile, the majority of professionals that dealt with city planning maintained the same expectations of a city under siege, as if "waiting for the barbarians." After the passage of the Foreign Investment Law in 1995, drab buildings of the speculative developer sort began to flourish in Havana like malignant tumors. Nevertheless, at the end of the 1990s, the fundamental concern of Cuban architects and urban planners was the wave of investment that would come pouring in from Miami after a hypothetical lifting of the embargo. This outward gaze directed toward Miami also strikes me as ambiguous. It supposes, at the same time, a look toward the future and a waiting for the past.

Reading the scant reflections generated to date by this waiting, I have come to think of them as a dialogue between two professionals who are representative of the positions of each side, even if for now the potential for their participation in the city's future seems to me rather limited. Besides a well-known reputation in their respective fields, they have the added value of mutually acknowledging each other and of being acknowledged as spokesmen. The figures in question are Mario Coyula, the head of the Provincial Department of Architecture and Urbanism for the City of Havana before he became deputy manager of the Group for the Integral Development of the Capital, and the Cuban American architect and city planner Andrés Duany. The latter is an eminent new urbanism theorist and member of the Cuban

National Heritage Foundation, an institution for the conservation of Cuban patrimony; his projects include Seaside, the development where *The Truman Show* was filmed.

The inclusion of Coyula in the Group for the Integral Development of the Capital, created in 1987, signaled the end of the Provincial Department of Architecture and Urbanism, which employed several of the young architects from the 1980s generation and was where some of the more interesting projects around the city were taking place. To judge from the information to which I have access, in Coyula's eyes the group's most important works—aside from the apparently difficult drafting of the strategic work paper—are the Comprehensive Workshops for Neighborhood Change, on the one hand, and the *Maqueta*, the Model of the City of Havana, on the other.

The workshops were an experiment launched in 1988 in the central neighborhoods of Cayo Hueso, San Isidro and Atarés, and the precarious southern settlement of La Güinera. Each workshop was made up of a team of three to eight members from different disciplines, including architects, sociologists, engineers, and social workers, with the objectives of improving housing conditions, developing the local economy, educating children and young people, and developing a sense of neighborhood identity. The experiment, no doubt, would have brought to full fruition the "medieval ideal of the vicinity" where, according to Lezama Lima, "people were proud of growing up in a barrio that in turn grew inside the city" (1991, 50). Until now, however, it has failed to adequately account for the new necessities of urban planning and development that have come with the introduction of foreign capital into the construction business.

What Coyula seems to be truly proud of is the 1:1000-sized scale model of Havana. According to Coyula, the model is not only a convivial fixture for the benefit of foreign tourists but also a tool for growing the relationship between Havana and its residents. It also allows for the impact of new projects to be evaluated. If, for instance, authorities had seen how the Hotel Melía Cohiba looked next to the Malecón, they surely would have never allowed for it to be built, Coyula argues. I fear greatly that the city model has transcended its role as a model or representation of the real city to stand in for the real city in the imagination of its creators. My worries deepen all the more when I see the cover of the book *Havana: Two Faces of the Antillean Metropolis*, which features an aerial shot of Havana that, as it turns out, is actually a photograph of the model.

The book, published in 1998, was cowritten by Coyula, Roberto Segre, and Joseph L. Scarpaci, a North American sociologist who specializes in human geography. The volume is stacked with dates and features an exhaustive analysis of Havana's development. At this point, however, I am only interested in its last chapter, "Havana's Future," where I expect to find predictions on the city's future. I am in for a surprise, though: rather than being about *what will be*, the chapter is about *what would have been*. That is to say, rather than confronting the delicate issue of the city's future, the authors turn sharply and begin to describe what would have happened in Havana if the revolution hadn't triumphed in January of 1959 and if it had been possible to implement Josep Lluís Sert's 1957 proposed plan for Havana—which, although never implemented, has become a scapegoat for all the city's real and potential calamities.

In that case, according to the authors, Havana would have had three or four million inhabitants. It would have had a forty kilometer skyline of glass and steel structures—hotels, clubs, apartment buildings, offices—extending from Guanabo in the east to Santa Fe in the west. Speculative development would have exploited two markets: apartment buildings and offices in the central zones—La Habana Vieja, Centro Habana, and El Vedado—and urban luxury developments in the west—Country Club, Biltmore—around which great shopping centers, private schools, and private universities would have been built. Around the axis of Rancho Boyeros Avenue, garden neighborhoods would have flourished for the middle class, and along the Carretera Central you'd find the improvised settlements and modest homes of the manual laborers. Neighborhood houses, operated by speculators looking to take in minimum wage earners and emigrants from the rest of the country, would have grown. La Habana Vieja, Centro Habana, and El Vedado would have lost their original form: they would have likely taken on new administrative and service functions, but would have also brandished brash billboards advertising McDonald's, Pizza Hut, and Burger King.

Having reached this point, the authors, perhaps thinking they have gone too far into the future, return again to Sert to accuse him of attempting to widen the main streets of Havana at the cost of demolishing the very heart of the old city. The very inertia of their futurist accelerations, however, impels them forward: gleaming, shining buildings would have been constructed all over the entire city, designed, no doubt, by architects of renown. But these buildings would have dimmed the cultural splendor of the past, the footprints of history recorded in the urban landscape, and the comforts that make Havana a special place and so on.

I know how hard it is to make predictions, especially when dealing with a subject where the factors change with such speed that the only thing possible is a tangential approximation, like waving one's hands over a crystal ball. But I confess I had expected some thoughts that didn't cling to the same apocalyptic vision that the authors explicitly reproach in the professionals of Miami. All the same, before taking on the challenge of imagining the future, they return again to the past. It is much more compromising, as far as doubts go, to imagine *what will be* than to speculate *what would have been*. However, it is even worse to suddenly suspect that *what will be* could end up resembling *what would have been*. As one reads the conclusions of the book about *what would have been* the city, one gets the troublesome feeling that the authors are making just as dire predictions about *what will be* Havana.

Continuing along, I glance through an interview with Duany published in *La Gaceta de Cuba* from March and April of 1999, dedicated to Havana. The interview is interesting, not only because of what Duany says, but because of what the interviewer thinks, an architect herself who was linked for many years to the planning of the city and who collaborated with Coyula. Like many of the professionals who have worked in Cuba after 1959, she seems incapable of conceiving of urbanism in market terms—an understandable limitation after forty years of living with state-owned property at the base cost of four pesos per square meter, without distinction.

The first thing one notices is that Duany also defends the idea of the structural recuperation of neighborhoods as opposed to a system of specialized districts. However, the notion of neighborhood that Duany has in mind—apart from the principle of mixed-use associated with the traditional neighborhoods—does not look too much like the neighborhood workshops, just as Seaside and Cayo Hueso don't resemble each other either. Whatever the case, though, Duany is not a naive architect. When his interviewer forces him to denounce the construction of high-rise buildings along the coast, Duany tells her: "I think that each city, or each sector of a city, has its natural typology that's based on objective things like the width of its street, or its vistas, or the quality of its infrastructure. . . . The Malecón is huge and very efficacious, and because of that it has the ability to assimilate high-rise buildings" (Duany 1999, 11)—just the opposite of what she expected he would say. Nevertheless, she goes on insisting that the coast must be protected, that a strip of three hundred meters must be left free of buildings that would block views of the sea.

Duany, in turn, offers her a small lesson in the logic of the market: "But there's a determinism in that. If the price of land is too high, investors have to build big buildings because they're not going to pay more for the land than for the building. . . . All the same, they can be charged in more subtle ways; for instance, through annual taxes" (Duany 1999, 12). The interviewer notes that in La Habana Vieja they are charging taxes. "And that's why business is doing well," remarks Duany, referring to Leal, Spengler, and Habagüanex S.A. As he goes on he clarifies his analysis of the market, noting the necessity for mechanisms of control: "In the whole world over there are city codes that determine the configuration of buildings and establish for each lot the way it opens onto the street, its height, etc." (1999, 12).

Finally, Duany manages to get away from the shadow of high-rises: "One of the things that anchors the tourism industry is urbanism. Havana, as a city, has the potential to be a kind of Rome in the Americas. . . . Havana's urbanism, as a cultural artifact, has tourism potential comparable to the best cities in North America" (Duany 1999, 12). The interviewer then asks him what it is that attracts people to Havana and Duany responds: "The yearning for the urban experience. In many parts of the world, being able to walk happily through a city is something almost exotic. There are very few high quality cities in existence and people want to live, even if only during a vacation, the lifestyle that they offer. . . . You have to reinforce urbanism to attract tourism. That's what Disney sells in an artificial way with its streets, plazas, and stores. It charges visitors $40 a day to enjoy a pseudo-urban experience" (1999, 13).

Duany continues to insist on the subject of the "civic" quality of the city in the prologue to Eduardo Luis Rodríguez's book *La Habana: Arquitectura del siglo XX*, published in Barcelona in 1998, where he writes "Sólo nos queda La Habana" (Havana is all we have left). In this brief text, Duany lays out his thoughts on the end of the U.S. embargo and the consequences that the wave of investment, channeled through Miami, would have as it pours into Havana. "What ill might come of this?" he asks himself. "After all, the Cuban exiles love Cuba passionately. They wouldn't want to hurt her, the way others do; others who exploit her in cold economic calculations, without any emotional investment in the results. Would the exiles exploit their beautiful capital? Not one of them would want to, but it's possible that they may not know how to do anything else" (Duany 1998, 10). As Duany shows us, the system of applied urban planning in Miami, and in the United States more generally, is "categorically hostile" to the traditional concept of urbanism that is still represented in Havana. Faced with such a disheartening perspective, it looks as if the only thing we have left to count on is the "good will born of patriotism" and the fact that it may be too late to "disgrace" another city (1998, 10).

Despite the vagueness of the terms used to reflect upon the future of the city, it seems to me that there are three preconditions that must be discussed urgently. First, there is the need for a clearly defined, modern, urban body of laws since, in essence, Havana is operating under the Construction Ordinances of 1861. Secondly, there must be a shift in the way we think about the city. Third, it is necessary to modernize and adapt the teaching curriculum for students of architecture and urban planning. In short, less naïveté and more pragmatism will help better protect the future of Havana.

In the interview with Duany, his interviewer complained about demolishing a perfectly good house in order to put up a building. Coyula, too, believes that "we should think more about rescuing what we are losing instead of constructing new buildings" (Coyula 1999, 19). That's the naïve mentality that Duany criticizes in "Sólo nos queda La Habana" when he observes that Havana's city codes and, implicitly, the professionals who protect the city "don't take into account, for example, that a block devoted to parking in Centro Habana might be more valuable than leaving all of its original buildings intact. Nor can they understand how a rural piece of land, far from everything else, might be a more valuable place for a superstore than one of the elegant spaces in La Rampa" (Duany 1998, 10).

The notion of the compact city has been exploded into pieces with the universal diffusion of the suburban model of development of the United States. Reconciling these visions in the Havana of the future will be a difficult task, and one could expect the worst. However, one can also believe, full of optimism, that there are things that could hardly get worse. I think, for instance, that the conservation of the old city will hardly be questioned. I think about the maintenance that the buildings will receive, after decades of abandonment have condemned a high percentage of Havana's buildings to irreversible deterioration, which will in turn justify demolition and new construction. I also think of the modernization of the technical infrastructure— the roadway, waterworks, sewer systems, power lines, phone networks, gas lines—which are in dire states, even if the roadway system, without a doubt, will have an impact on the structure of the city. I think about the improvement of the environment and in particular the cleaning of the bay—one of the ten most contaminated bodies of water in the world—and the relocation of polluting industries.

Leal Spengler once told the Spanish writer Manuel Vázquez Montalbán, in an interview for his book *Y Dios entró en La Habana* (And God entered Havana), that many of the city's neighborhoods just needed a coat of paint. In an interview from the same issue of *La Gaceta de Cuba* dedicated to Havana, Coyula declared, with an apparent jocular sparkle, that some neighborhoods just needed trees to hide them. But when they asked him what he expected of Havana in the year 2059, he gravely pronounced: "In 2059, Havana will be the city we deserve" (1999, 21). Beyond that, nothing is clear. But that, at least, is true—no more and no less.

Flying Over Havana

From any perspective, it is difficult to explain the fascination Havana exerts over its inhabitants and strangers alike or, more precisely, over the gaze from inside Cuba and that projected from outside. During the latter years of the twentieth century, both gazes have converted the city into a literary myth. Perhaps a minor myth or a myth limited only to certain cultural areas, but, nonetheless, a myth that enjoys an enviable health, although its most noteworthy theme could be described, in a way, as its "lack of health."

Truth be told, Havana has never lacked artisans for creating this myth. Since its founding in 1519, the city has embodied a successive and simultaneous series of archetypes, shaped by the mandates of a culture of service to which the city was fated by its position and duties within the organization of the Spanish Empire. The "fortress city," the key to the defense and conquest of the New World, the "convent city," from which the continent's religious colonization was launched, the "inn city," waiting for the annual reunion of the Spanish silver fleet, from where all the expeditions were organized, or the "port city," through which sugar and tobacco were exported; originally, these all presented the extroverted and, to a degree, carefree faces of a city that did not need to question itself.

In the nineteenth century, as a result of the weakening of Havana's strategic position, the city, for the first time, consciously assumed its role as the capital. Shortly thereafter began the writing about a city that came to symbolize the writing of Cuba's nationality as such. Cirilo Villaverde is undoubtedly the most exemplary of this budding readiness to inscribe with national themes the fabric of a city whose construction seems to be posterior to its texts. This trend continued and was cemented during most of the twentieth century, when it reached its most polished expression in the works of Carpentier and Lezama Lima, the most conspicuous proponents of the constructive, positive mythic exaltation of Havana.

Toward the end of the twentieth century, however, something different began to occur. The image of Havana, which had been created by the Cuban intellectual elite, underwent two simultaneous but opposite processes of erosion. On the one hand, La Habana Vieja, the nucleus, where the city had been founded, began to undergo a recovery and revitalization, especially after being designated a UNESCO World Heritage Site in 1982. When the city opened up to tourism, this would become important and offer possibilities to order and arrange the urban past decoratively for its manipulation and more effective exploitation as a service industry. On the other hand, and harder to tackle, is the allure of Havana's ruins over its own people and foreigners alike.

It is true that ruins have always aroused man's imagination. It is also significant, even though ultimately one of the hazards of her eventful exile, that it was in Havana in 1951 where the Spanish philosopher María Zambrano wrote her essay "Una metáfora de la esperanza: las ruinas" (A metaphor of hope: The ruins), first published in Havana's magazine *Lyceum* and later included in her book *El hombre y lo divino* (Man and the Divine). In this text we read: "Ruins are a historical category and allude to something very intimate in our life. They are the dejection of that act which defines man among all: edification. To edify, to make history, constitutes a double edification: architecturally and historically" (Zambrano 1951, 9–10). But Havana's ruins are neither "beautiful," as Lezama Lima would write, nor witnesses of remote times and modes of life. Havana's ruins are recent ruins, brought about by the sloth and the abandonment that the city has suffered for half a century. Something, when mentioned in passing, also paradoxically gives the city the unspeakable charm of anachronism.

Beyond La Habana Vieja, that ordered, painted, rejuvenated city, custom-built or reconstructed for the untroubled tourist and dotted with places where one can linger, with comfortable and neat walking routes, lies a city rotting away and about to collapse—what is, in reality, the true Havana. These "third style" neighborhoods, as Carpentier would call them, comprise the center of Havana and provide the most coherent image of the city. They are neighborhoods built in accordance with an eclectic city code, at times pretentious but generally modest and controlled by the middle class that lives in them, neighborhoods turned into the stage from where a somewhat morbid gaze is cast over the ruins.

It is not as if the theme of ruins had been missing from Cuban works up until this time, though. Ruins were present not only in negative discourses about the city as exemplified by Casal in the nineteenth century and Piñera in the twentieth; they were also included in the positive discourses of Carpentier and Lezama Lima. However, at the end of the twentieth century and the beginning of the twenty-first, Havana's ruins have stopped existing just in the poet's gaze and have overtaken the real city. The optimism about the future invoked by Lezama Lima when he talked about "futurity's tradition" or about the "great myths based on the future" (quoted in González 1988, 123), has been harshly broken and supplanted by the mythologization of memory. The gaze to the future is plaited like a telescope, leaving a trail of ruins. Those ruins do not symbolize nonconformity with the inadequacy of the present being projected into the future, but passive nostalgia that finds comfort in looking to the past. The active gaze into *what could have been and never was* turns into a mindless gaze upon everything that was. The ruins, then, represent only an imprint of an absence, the wreckage of *what was*.

"And thus in the ruins," continues María Zambrano, "what we see and feel is an imprisoned hope of what was perhaps not so present, when the wreckage of what we now see was intact, and had not attained with its presence, what it can in its absence" (1951, 10). It is difficult, nevertheless, to identify that hope in Cuban writing from the last decade, like in the novels of Abilio Estévez or Pedro Juan Gutiérrez, or in the controversial film *Suite Havana* by Fernando Pérez. In barely fifteen years, Cuba has gone from proudly displaying buildings swarming with scaffolding, announcing the new era of construction, to glorifying dilapidated, old buildings that can barely remain standing with the help of braces. It would be enlightening to examine this trend in a wider cultural perspective, yet all that needs to be asked is whether the aestheticization of decadence will lead to the destruction of the real city, whether this "deconstruction" of Havana will have the same effect as the prior "construction" by the intellectual Cuban elite of the nineteenth century and the first half of the twentieth century.

The two contemporary movements that gaze over Havana from inside Cuba and from abroad share a somehow "reactionary" attitude toward the "revolutionary" city. They are both fascinated with the exaltation of "the spirit of the ruins," manifested in the obsession of Cuban culture at the end of the century as it reinscribed experience into the devastated territory of the city. On the other hand, the almost obscene curiosity and enthusiasm awakened in its idle or supposedly concerned visitors by the destruction of the city is regarded with pained stupor and even some irritation. As a consequence of this trivialization of nostalgia, destruction or flight, ruins, or the metaphor of the abandoned city stop being literary images and turn into literal expressions; they cease being text and are transformed into context. When viewed from this perspective, it is not surprising that on the one hand the ruinous splendor of Havana and on the other hand the *balseros*, the rafters, should have become its defining icons in the mass media at the end of the century.

The foreign view of Havana reveals a fascination with ruins that has notable origins in the work of the photographers of the U.S. occupying forces—in particular with the photographs taken by Charles E. Doty between 1899 and 1902—or in Walker Evans's photobook, *Havana 1933*. However, what was a self-serving vision in Doty's case, documenting the cruelty and backwardness

of imperialist colonial Spain, and praising the superiority of the U.S. government, or the result of professional restlessness in Evans's case, becomes the
only possible vision. The countless photographic collections published during the 1990s and films such as *Buena Vista Social Club*, produced in 1999 by
Wim Wenders, consecrate this vision of the city. To find another one would
require turning to the more specialized and less subjective architectural
books, which are less abundant and harder to find.

Aerial views of the city are superimposed over these "street scenes." Film of
the raft exodus toward Miami, shot from a helicopter during the balsero crisis
in August 1994, were seen on television sets all over the world. The images
inspired U.S. musician John Adams to compose a "Habanera" for his 1998
album *John's Book of Alleged Dances*. "Too many rafts headed for Miami . . .
watched from the wings," goes its refrain. The images of the city fraying,
unraveling, and dissolving into the ocean were reminiscent of a dam burst-
ing—a dam that might well be represented by the Malecón—or of the *desmerengamiento* ("unwhipping") of the city under siege: meringue peaks over a
custard ocean, like the "floating islands" of the classic dessert.[2] From living
with their backs to the ocean to launching themselves into the ocean, the city
and its inhabitants had embarked on a long journey. Havana and the ocean,
"gigantic, blue, open and democratic: / in short, the ocean" as celebrated by
Nicolás Guillén in "Tengo" (I have) (1979, 250) are categorically united in the
image of the rafters, acquiring a dramatic face with the Elián González affair—
foreseen by Lezama Lima in *Paradiso* as the boy "going forward into the sea on
a diving board that has been sawn off" (2000, 418).

The city abandoned by its inhabitants is contemplated from the air. It is a
gaze that has its own antecedents, as does the fascination with ruins. Looking
among them we would have to recall the beautiful nineteenth-century etchings
rendered in bird's-eye view, or the balloonist's-eye view. Beginning in 1796,
with the first launch, balloonists took to the skies in Havana's first aerostatic
ascensions, followed by Robertson's on March 20, 1828, in celebration of the
inauguration of the Templete, or the flight of the famous Matías Pérez, who
disappeared while attempting an aerostatic flight from Havana in 1856 and is
immortalized in the colloquial phrase "Voló como Matías Pérez" (He flew like
Matías Pérez). We might also remember photos of Havana taken in 1899 from a
U.S. military observation balloon or the French landscape architect Jean-
Claude Nicolas Forestier flying over Havana in a plane with Carlos Miguel de
Céspedes, minister for public works during the government of Gerardo Machado. Likewise, from a plane and imitating Forestier, but especially Le Cor-
busier, Carpentier discovers the city in *The Lost Steps*. Lezama Lima also dares

to fly over the city in one of his chronicles written for the *Diario de la Marina*, although his flight seems more indebted to the devil's intervention than to modern aviation.

In the 1990s, the city's textual "maquette," the ideal model for the intellectual strategies of Cuban modernity begun by the Cuban writers of the first third of the nineteenth century, is realized in the *Maqueta*, the city model, which substitutes the real city with a true-to-scale representation. From the catwalks of the building where the model is housed, it is possible to fly over the entire city to the tune of John Adams's "Habanera." With a simple flick of the wrist, it is possible to rearrange or eliminate a building, just as Virgilio Piñera's Sebastian would do from the rooftop of his building, feeling in *Pequeñas maniobras* (Small maneuvers) like "the captain of a ship giving orders to his crew" (Piñera 1963, 20).

Sebastian's gaze from the rooftop represents an unusual view of the city, a point of view Carpentier milked for maximum literary yield in *The Chase*, in which the city is revealed not only on the level of the street but through the displacement of successive points of view. The city is uncovered and clearly acquires the protagonist role in the pendulous movement between street and the rooftop. The streets of the quotidian city turn into a subterranean labyrinth when viewed from above, while the rooftop, a kind of elevated street, offers the safety missing in the streets. These displacements of perspective, that subvert the physical stability of notions of street and rooftop, likewise represent the moral drama in which the protagonist of *The Chase* lives and that plays out in the oscillation between the "earth" and the "sky." But in the 1990s this gaze turns into something more than just a skillful literary device; it represents the reality of a city whose residual spaces are occupied by a floating and frequently marginal population, contemplating its city from its old basements and rooftops.

The perspective from the city's "underground," in a metaphoric sense, and from the rooftops in a literal sense, the oscillation between the "earth" and the "sky," is expressed at the end of the 1990s by Pedro Juan Gutiérrez in *Dirty Havana Trilogy*. Like Piñera's Sebastian or Carpentier's protagonist in *The Chase*, the narrator of *Trilogy*, Pedro Juan, is an antihero, a marginal figure living in the center of the city but displaced to its fringes—fringes that in the 1990s are extremely volatile. It is no coincidence that the book begins with images of the balsero crisis and the Malecón, the principal stage of the action, representing the edges of the city blown apart by the rafters' escape after suffering an irreversible breech. Nevertheless, just as in Miguel de Carrión's novel *Las impuras* (The impure ones) eighty years earlier, where the story of

Havana of the early twentieth century is told only through marginal characters, the marginal protagonist of *Trilogy* turns out to be the one best suited to describe Havana in the 1990s.

Unlike Carpentier's omniscient narrator, who leaves nothing to chance and controls all points of view, Pedro Juan offers only his version of the facts, his personal vision of the city, with barely enough fragments to compose a sketch. Also unlike Carpentier's stable narrator, the narrator of *Trilogy* finds himself under a great duress. The narrator is always Pedro Juan, but Pedro Juan is not always the same: he does not have the same experiences, he's not always the same age, he doesn't always use the same vocabulary. This may explain his somewhat enigmatic remark: "Maybe there is no other place in the world like Cuba to be one and many at the same time" (Gutiérrez 1998, 203).[3] Nevertheless, even though the various Pedro Juans have different pasts and a varying present identity, they all share an uncertain future, like the chased one in Carpentier's *The Chase*. But if the chased one is fleeing, Pedro Juan is "escaping," which in Havana at the end of the twentieth century is not the same.[4]

Both Pedro Juan and the anonymous protagonist of *The Chase* live in rooms on rooftops. In *The Chase*, the room is the Mirador, the Belvedere, rented from an old black nanny in an El Vedado residence turned tenement. That is, in the rooftop of a two-story house in the traditional city, which during the twentieth century, as Carpentier shows in *Reasons of State*, was transformed into "a kingdom forbidden to the eyes": the horizontal city turns vertical and the rooftops become an "Invisible City," a "city upon a city" where "there were no eyes now that could see it and know it" (Carpentier 1976, 133). This is the city where Pedro Juan lives, in a room of unstable construction, with corrugated roof sheets, on the rooftop of a building finished in 1936 that could very well be the "modern building" of *The Chase* if it were located in El Vedado and not on the Malecón. It is a monumental building, "with a Boston-style façade," but inside "it's falling to pieces, and it's an incredible labyrinth of stairs without banisters, darkness, foul smells, cockroaches, and fresh shit. And makeshift rooms crowding the hallways and black men's quarrels and brawls" (Gutiérrez 2001, 82). In short, it is a building that has been destroyed "by the profanity of a tenement," as Lezama Lima would say (1991, 81). Nevertheless, the tourists come and photograph it, amazing Pedro Juan, who once again confirms the fascination Havana's ruins hold for foreign eyes.

The city's corruption, both in *The Chase* and in *Trilogy*, parallels the moral decomposition of the main character or the narrator. "Sometimes I remember what a nice, polite guy I used to be," reminisces Pedro Juan (Gutiérrez

2001, 207). Now he is unemployed and has his obvious vices: alcohol, marijuana, or a sexual voracity that's not above living off women and taking advantage of them like a pimp. In both works the city is undergoing a profound crisis. In *The Chase* it is a political crisis after Machado's fall. In *Trilogy* it is crisis at all levels in the beginning of the 1990s: "Everything is in crisis: ideas, wallets, the present. And the future, let's not even go there" (Gutiérrez 1998, 146). During this decade, the model of success of the *pinchos* was substituted by the *macetas* (newly wealthy), behaving not even like *picúos* (squares) or *cursis* (posers), but like *cheos* (rubes) or the vulgar nouveau riches of precariousness. The songs are no longer the civic-minded songs of Los Van Van but the corrosive songs of timba or hipersalsa, like the one hummed by Pedro Juan as he reflects on the "mercenary spirit of the age": "Búscate un temba que te mantenga. / Pa' que tú goces / pa' que tú tengas. / De más de treinta y menos de cincuenta. / Un papirriqui con guaniquiqui" (Find a sugardaddy to support you. / So you can enjoy / So you can have. / A sugardaddy older than thirty and younger than fifty. / A rich daddy with plenty of dough") (Gutiérrez 1998, 208).

From the rooftop, Pedro Juan flies over the city and himself: "I like to fly over me, look at Pedro Juan from afar" (Gutiérrez 1998, 15). From that point of view, which is, ironically, somewhat privileged, the ocean and the city can be seen, "each place with its people, its sounds and its music" (1998, 15). However, the city that Pedro Juan contemplates from his rooftop looks like a city "which has been bombarded and abandoned," the ruins are no longer "suitable ruins" like the ones described by Piñera. The metaphor of the ruins and the image of the abandoned city have acquired a more prosaic meaning. Nevertheless, it looks like a beautiful city to Pedro Juan: "It is falling to pieces, but this bitch of a city where I have loved and hated so much, is beautiful" (1998, 206). Pedro Juan's indolent attitude is congruent with that slight gaze, which climbs and leaves the city as it loses weight and intensity, like an aerostatic balloon. The images of a bombed city and the beauty of its ruins speak of an acceptance of material destruction that has no relation to "the spirit of the ruins" Lezama Lima wrote about. Turned into topical themes, sold as typical products, these are the images representing Havana at the beginning of the twenty-first century.

Therefore, it is not its characterization of the city that distinguishes this book from others published during the 1990s. Its point of view is not even rare or uncommon, or lacking antecedents. What I think is unique in *Trilogy* is the devaluation of the act of writing about the city, something unprecedented in Cuban literature. The degradation of the real city occurs simultaneously with that of the ideal city in *Trilogy* or that of the text. Pedro Juan Gutiérrez does not reach any conclusions, he does not care whether he repeats himself over and over again and even boasts of not knowing how to write. When his first novel, *El Rey de La Habana* (The king of Havana), was published in 1999, a year after his *Trilogy*, he said: "I don't misspell, but my grammar is a disaster. It is a good thing that there is a magnificent editor at Anagrama." Perhaps due to the intervention of this editor, the same vices of language that Pedro Juan criticizes in the *jineteras*, who absorb the sayings of their Spaniard clients, are ironically smoothed over in his own text.

The colloquial language of the book—driven by the narrator and not the author—is economical: barebones, chocked with plain and violent adjectives, fragmented and made staccato by copious use of interjections. But it's precisely due to its repetition, accumulation, and scatology—in the excremental sense, not transcendental as is the case with Carpentier—that it succeeds in transmitting to the reader the narrator's disgust, boredom, emptiness, and hopelessness. Nevertheless, Pedro Juan does not give up: "Shattered but not destroyed" seems to be his motto (Gutiérrez 1998, 60–61), a personal commentary on Hemingway's parable in *The Old Man and the Sea*, which also describes the condition of Havana at the end of the century. Sitting on the ledge of the eighth floor, Pedro Juan finds solace in the illusion of flight: "I always dreamt that I could jump and take off flying, feeling like the freest guy in the world" (1998, 168). If going down into the streets is like descending into hell, as in *The Chase*, it is indeed better to remain in midair.

Flying. Surviving.

Notes

The epigraph by Lezama is quoted in Cintio Vitier's "La aventura de *Orígenes*" (1994).

1. Lezama's Orplid alludes to Eduard Mörike's poem "Gesang Weylas," which evokes a land of fantasy, called Orplid.

2. *Desmerengamiento* was the term used by Fidel Castro in an obviously pejorative sense to refer to the unraveling, the desmoronamiento of the socialist bloc after perestroika, glasnost, and the fall of the Berlin Wall in 1989. Reinaldo Arenas had imagined Cuba as a "floating island." Thus, the idea of the meringue and of its desmerengamiento can be associated also with the most symbolic Cuban wall of all, that of the Malecón.

3. The published English translation departs at times from the original Spanish. Quotes refer therefore to the English text (Gutiérrez 2001) when using that translation and to the Spanish one (Gutiérrez 1998) when the published translation has been modified.

4. To "escape" in the street language of Havana in the 1990s is not so much to flee but to "resolve" problems in informal and often illegal ways, "inventing" ad hoc solutions, living from day to day, and generally "surviving" using every available resource. All these terms come to be associated during the Special Period with resourcefulness on the one hand, illegality, prostitution, and extensive trading back and forth on the black market on the other.

8

Made in Havana City:
Rap Music, Space, and Racial Politics

SUJATHA FERNANDES

"*Niche niche*"
that's how the emcee is born.
For everyone here,
made in Havana City.
And you know how I am
I don't believe in nuthin.'
—Magia, "Niche, Niche"

In her rap song "Niche Niche," Cuban slang for black or dark skinned, Magia declares, "I am what my image shows, a black woman." She raps, "Representing those women who dare to get out there / My skin is the color of night, it reveals secrets already known / To show that which is hidden is seen by all." Through rap music, young black Cubans began to speak about race, breaking silences that had existed for several decades. Magia was part of a new breed of emcees, agnostic and irreverent, the voices of an urban culture that was—as the chorus to her song went—made in Havana City.

The emergence of rap music in Havana has opened a window into the complex relationship between racial identity, urban public space, and cultural politics in the contemporary post-Soviet era. Young black people in the marginal sectors of Havana were attracted by the street art of b-boying (a hip-hop dance style, sometimes known as breakdancing) during the 1980s. In the 1990s rap music, as another element of hip-hop culture, continued to provide a means of leisure, survival, and voice for young black Cubans as the city was being remade for global investors and foreign, mostly white, tourists. Whether through concerts or gatherings in open spaces of the city; in lyrics promoting the *jineteros,* or street hustlers who siphon off dollars from tourists; or through the promotion of a militant and visible black identity; rappers accessed and defined new relationships to public space.

"All the B-Boys Know That I'm Alexey of Regla": Locating Rap

Growing up in the '80s, Alexey Rodriguez, who forms the rap duo Obsesión with his wife Magia, was attracted by the raw energy and soul of the hip-hop music that came along the airwaves of 99 Jams FM. In a song called "Hip Hop," a genealogy of Cuban hip-hop, Alexey describes how as a kid he would build antennas from wire coat hangers and dangle his radio out of the window, "crazy to get the 99." On episodes of *Soul Train* that came through broadcasts from Miami television, Alexey saw b-boying for the first time, and he copied the steps and then showed them to the kids in the neighborhood.

> Everything began as a kid, I struggled
> with a piece of wire, a coat hanger, and a "radio"
> stuck it all out the window, and there it was
> crazy to get the 99.
> I got *Soul Train* without static or nuthin' . . .
> I copied the steps and later in the barrio we beatboxed
> And me like many others in Havana,
> dancing and listening to American music, nuthin' else.
> My papa bought a tape recorder for me,
> and my first cassette was Public Enemy.

Alexey remembered the ciphers in the park El Quijote. Kids would form a circle, "mulattos, whites, blacks," and in the center the b-boys would polish the concrete with their back spins and windmills, while others broke into a beatbox or rhymed. "You had to live it, you had to see it, feel it, know it to describe it," rapped Alexey. He recalled that time nostalgically as one when money and designer clothing were not the main thing. "If you had money, good, and if not, well brother, same thing / the women in those times, they treated you normal / it didn't matter if your clothes were better or worse / the love for the music was super-superior." Black youth living in the poor barrios, *solares*, and housing projects of Havana identified more with the sounds and beats being produced by young emcees and deejays in the Bronx than the sterile socialist realism of the Soviets.

This musical culture of hip-hop that gave young Cubans a means of diversion and a channel for their frustrations during the 1980s offered them a voice once Cuban society entered the Special Period of the 1990s. As Magia noted in an interview with me, "At the start doing rap was more a hobby than a necessity. It allowed us to play at being artists and deal with those difficult moments that can take you down other paths. But then it gave us the opportunity to overcome the sudden and deep crisis that hit us during the nineties."

The fall of the Berlin Wall in 1989 and the consequent decline in Soviet aid and export income caused a major crisis for the Cuban economy. Blackouts became a common part of life, people were unable to get to work because of lack of transport, and food was scarce. The Cuban government attempted to rebuild the Cuban economy through food policies promoting self-sufficiency, the reintroduction of wide-scale rationing, and the earning of hard currency through tourism. During this process of transition, black Cubans fared worse than white Cubans, as they were less likely to receive remittances from abroad, were generally excluded from working in the more lucrative sector of the tourist industry, and were faced with an increasingly visible and blatantly open racism. The urban terrain was stratified by a deepening inequality, but it was simultaneously the stage for the emergence of a new racial politics.

As a cultural form, rap music has been strongly identified with the city and urban spaces. Murray Forman (2002, xviii) argues that, "in the rhythm and lyrics, the city is an audible presence, explicitly cited and sonically sampled in the reproduction of the aural textures of the urban environment." Local affiliations, such as the neighborhood or particular sites in the city such as a street, a park, or a housing project are repeatedly mentioned in songs and in the imagining of collective identities.

Rap music has also altered the sonic landscapes of the city. For the first five years of its evolution in Cuba, up until 1992, rap was produced and consumed within the specific social context of the local community or neighborhood. At parties people would play music from CDs that had been brought from the United States, or music recorded from Miami radio, and they would pass on recorded cassettes from hand to hand. There would be breakdancing competitions and people would rhyme in private houses, on the streets, or in parks. In the summer of 1992, the Asociación Hermanos Saíz (Brothers Saiz Organization, AHS), the youth cultural wing of the official mass organization of Cuban youth, Unión de Jóvenes Comunistas (Union of Communist Youth,

UJC), created a space for rap in La Piragua, a large open air stage by the Malecón. In 1994 this space ceased to exist and the movement began to dissipate, that is until DJ Adalberto created a space at Carlos III and Infanta. Up until this moment there was no real movement of rappers, only individuals improvising or "freestyling" (Fernandez 2000). From the scene at Carlos III emerged the pioneers of Cuban rap: SBS, Primera Base, Triple A, Al Corte, and Amenaza. An association of rappers called Grupo Uno, relatively autonomous from AHS, was created by a promoter known as Rodolfo Rensoli, and this network went on to organize the first festival of rap in June 1995.

Rap music in Havana has been identified predominantly with black, working-class neighborhoods such as Old Havana, Central Havana, Regla, Santos Suárez, and Playa. Yet the spirit and soul of hip-hop culture in Cuba came from the housing projects of Alamar, on the outskirts of the city of Havana. If Havana was hard hit by the crisis of the Special Period, then Alamar was even more so. The gasoline shortages meant transport into the city was less frequent and there were longer waits, making it difficult for people to get to work. There were no tourists around to hustle dollars from, and the enclosure of the dwellings made it harder for residents to start up small businesses, like the bodegas cropping up around Central Havana, with people selling ice cream, pastels, or pizza from the front windows of their homes. There were frequent blackouts, water problems, and shortages of cooking gas. And for the young people of the projects, there was nothing to do.

Alamar has been referred to as Cuba's South Bronx. According to Tricia Rose (1994, 30), black communities in New York, impoverished by the shift from blue-collar manufacturing toward service sectors, were displaced from their neighborhoods by "slum clearance" programs designed to make way for commercial districts in the 1960s. Relocation to areas such as the South Bronx destroyed community structures that had been built up over many years. Projects such as Alamar were propelled by the same spirit of modernism that animated projects such as the South Bronx, with little concern for how communities would rebuild their networks and function in a vastly new environment. Like in the South Bronx, hip-hop culture was one of the forms that allowed for the renewal of local networks (Rose 1994, 34).

The five- and six-story buildings were designed by Soviet architects and built by microbrigades, or ordinary people organized into work teams, as a solution to housing shortages in Havana in the 1970s. As part of slum clearance programs, black communities from slum areas such as Llega y Pon, Las Yaguas, and Palo Cagao were relocated to Alamar. The 1970s were a grim era of Cuban history, known euphemistically as the *quinquenio gris* (gray five years), when the orthodoxy of Soviet socialism overshadowed cultural and social life on the island (Scarpaci, Segre, and Coyula 2002, 219). The heavy and somber buildings immortalized the spirit of those years. With a population of 300,000 in over two thousand buildings, Alamar is the largest housing project in the world. Each prefabricated building bears a stencil of its number, D 42, Zona 2, the impersonal stamp of the assembly line.

Racial Consciousness and Urban Space

In May 2001 the annual music contest sponsored by the Cuban music industry was held in the beachside district of Playa. One of the last acts of the night, the group Hermanos de Causa came onto the stage. "Buenas noche, Playa" said Soandry. "We're Hermanos de Causa. We're from the barrio, from Alamar." A synthesized beat came into the background, overlaid with conga. After a four bar interlude, a sampled drum kit brought the rhythm, and Soandry began to rap, "I have a race that is dark and discriminated / I have a workday that demands and gives nothing / I have so many things but I can't even touch them / I have so many resources that I cannot even step on / I have liberty between parentheses of iron / I have so many rights without benefits that I imprison myself / I have what I have without having what I had." The song borrows the title and format of a poem written in 1964 by celebrated Afro-Cuban poet Nicolás Guillén entitled *Tengo* (I have), where the poet lists the changes that the revolution has brought for blacks, highlighting the differences between the generations.

The performance illustrated the ways in which rap music has become a forum for articulating a set of concerns about racial inequality in the current period, linked to the projects of Alamar as symbolic of the failure of a set of modernist principles that have undergirded state socialism. As the city is being remade once again, this time in the interests of global investors and white tourists, new axes of marginality and exclusion are occurring, mostly along spatial lines. Investment is being channeled into those areas deemed to produce considerable returns, while others—those on the margins of the city and in working-class neighborhoods—are left to deteriorate. Like Hermanos de Causa say in their song "Tengo," "The years pass and the situation is the same / Time is not forgiving, just ask Havana / Now that it's on the world map, nobody gives a shit."

In the contemporary transformation of greater Havana, different groups are making claims over urban space. As Saskia Sassen (1998) has argued, the city itself becomes a strategic terrain for new conflicts and contradictions.

According to Sassen, global cities are increasingly becoming sites for the servicing and financing of capital. While Havana was also partially incorporated into a global capitalist world, during the 1990s it still retained a largely state-managed economy. The necessity of adopting market mechanisms in selected areas of the economy led to what has been called a "dual economy," described by Haroldo Dilla (2002, 61) as the segmentation of the economy into two spaces: "a dynamic one linked to the world market and called upon to finance the second, which remained in crisis, ruled by central planning and generally concentrated on the internal market and traditional export activities." The dual economy led to the formation of a dual city, what some have referred to as a tourist apartheid.

During the 1990s the tourism sector expanded dramatically as the major source of foreign exchange income; production and distribution functions of state-owned enterprises were transferred to foreign business through the mixed firm; traditional export markets were recuperated; and the dollar was legalized, so that the Cuban economy functioned as a dual currency economy with both the peso and U.S. dollar (Gonzalez Gutierrez 1997, 8; Valdés 1997, 103).[1] The hotels, streets, and beaches of the city were increasingly designed to cater to the pleasures and desires of white tourists, while working-class black residents of the city were policed and harassed for identification cards. Some thirty thousand Cubans from the east of the island, often referred to as *palestinos*, migrate illegally to Havana every year in search of work or income (Scarpaci, Segre, and Coyula 2002, 179). Policing of black residents is intended to root out these illegal migrants and also ensure that black youth are gainfully employed or studying and not "vagrants."

At the same time that the city is being reshaped to meet the demands of corporate capital and tourists, it is also facing a growing marginalized minority struggling for recognition and claiming their rights to the city (Sassen 1998). This contestation, argues Sassen, is being expressed through the new politics of culture and identity. Young black people in Havana have found a variety of forms for self-expression, from timba, to salsa, and most recently reggaeton, but it is rap music that has most strongly invoked an emergent racial consciousness as young people make claims on the city.

In their song, "Lágrimas Negras" (black tears), Hermanos de Causa question the invisibility of blacks in Cuban society. "Lágrimas Negras" is a famous Cuban song, which was created by the Matamoros Trio in the 1920s and has been performed by many other groups since. Hermanos de Causa sample the song, rapping with particular racial implications not present in the original song. The rappers point to the exclusion of blacks from the tourist industry, as

Cuba's fastest growing source of hard currency, as well as their ongoing absence from television programming and cinema. When blacks do appear, it is in "secondary roles of last resort," or the "classic role of slave: faithful, submissive, or the typical thief without morals." Hermanos de Causa expose the absences and stereotypes of Afro-Cubans in the media, which is particularly ironic in a society that has claimed the end of racism.

In "A Veces," the group Anonimo Consejo connect the history of Cuban slaves with the situation of contemporary Afro-Cubans. The rapper begins with his geographical location, he identifies himself as "a Cuban from the east." He is lying in his "poor bed" thinking about slavery and the struggle of black people in his country when the similarities of the present situation occur to him:

> You think it's not the same today,
> an official tells me, "You can't go
> there, much less leave this place."
> In contrast they treat tourists differently,
> people, is it possible that in my country
> I don't count?

The rapper uses the critique of racial hierarchies in the past as a way of identifying contemporary racial issues such as police harassment of young black people and the preferential treatment given to tourists over Cubans by officials. He identifies himself as "the descendent of an African," as a *cimarron desobediente*, or a runaway slave, drawing his links to an ancestral past rooted in a history of slavery and oppression.

The critique of police harassment is strongly present within rap music, and it points to one of the sites of conflict that have emerged over the uses of public space, mostly the city's streets. Officials attempt to discipline and regulate the movements of young people, controlling where they can go, who they are with, and checking their identity cards to make sure that they are residents of the capital and not another province. Cliente Supremo challenge the futile practice of asking for identity cards, asking, "in reality what will become of me when my youth is gone? Will I have to be worried about my personal documents like you all? What ID? For what?" Los Paisanos also talk about police harassment of young black Cubans in their song "El Barco" (The boat) and the ways in which they are constantly questioned by the police and asked to produce an identity card. When the police threaten the rapper, he shouts "seremos como el Che" (we will be like Che). The rapper repeats this slogan, recited daily by children in daycare centers and schools, partly as a way of invoking the youthful rebelliousness of the revolution's founding martyr and partly as a way of inoculating himself against reprisal.

"Run for the City": Black Youth Accessing the Tourist Mecca

"I was thinking of finding myself a foreigner / one that has a lot of money," Magia began a rap skit between herself and Alexey, also known as el tipo este.

"Of course," el tipo este interjected.

"I don't care what he's like / I just want someone who'll resolve my problems," continued Magia. "It's a sacrifice but you get results / Love in these times that we live in is relative / I'm a young woman who has to secure her future, you get me? / I'm not the kind to look for work or nothin' / I want to travel and help my family from abroad / My wedding has to be beautiful, like in the Hollywood movies."

"Run for the city, a commentary," they both chanted on the chorus, "Is it a jinetera, a bunch of crazies doing tourism, tell me where, chico?"

"I was thinking that an intellectual such as myself . . . ," el tipo este rapped in a pompous tone.

"Like you?" asked Magia.

"Shouldn't be wasting time with these people / who don't have a sufficient cultural level / to have a conversation that matches my social position / I don't support this language everyone is using / 'asere,' 'qué volá,' you find it all over the place / you know, with these people of the solares."

"Yo, yo, yo, I was thinking," responded Magia, "All the hours I've studied haven't served for nothin' / whole mornings studying / I'm going to leave my career, papa / I'm very sorry, I won't be an engineer / My girl just called, there's a job in tourism / Tourism, papa / It's cleaning floors, but who cares? / It'll give me a few bucks and I can resolve some problems."

"I was thinking, why don't I / form a combo and start performing traditional music?" rapped el tipo este. "I'll be part of the *farándula* [new elite] / I'll play Son de la Loma, and Chan Chan."

"And Guantanamera," added Magia.

In their song "Run for the City," Obsesión discuss the contradictions of Havana in the 1990s, where education is no longer a ticket to social mobility and professional qualifications are less remunerative than those who can hustle on the side or market themselves by performing traditional Cuban songs to metropolitan consumers. Obsesión are critical of this reality, and the song is a polemic against consumerist mentalities that have been emerging with increased access to a market economy and a condemnation of the desire of young people to find an "easy fix" rather than working hard.

By contrast, for other groups such as Orishas, hustling has been presented as a strategy to get by in the Special Period. In the song "Atrevido" (Daring) from the album *A Lo Cubano* (2000), Orishas tell the story of a couple who manage to take advantage of tourists as a way of bringing themselves out of rural poverty. Over an upbeat salsa dance track and heavy bass, the rapper describes the situation of the poor couple in the countryside:

> Once upon a time a deprived couple
> without money were thinking of a chronic
> tonic to live,
> to leave the black mud in which they
> drowned, plotting.

The couple leave the countryside and come to the city, where the husband, acting as a pimp, sets his wife up with a tourist, and she begins to work the tourist for money and gifts. The song parodies the clueless tourist, who thinks that he is the one taking advantage of the woman. The rapper portrays the woman as the agent and the tourist as her helpless victim. The song continues with the following chorus:

> Everything that she asked for, the idiot paid out,
> a pretty room in the Cohiba, the idiot paid out,
> a dress for her, and a shirt for me, the idiot paid out,
> if she wanted to go to the beach, the idiot paid out,
> he was running out of money, but the idiot paid out,
> to dance at a concert with Orishas, the idiot paid out.

In the song *jineterismo* is presented as a vacation for the woman who is taken to the beach, receives new clothes, and has a fancy room in the hotel Cohiba. The Orishas even write themselves into the song, saying that the woman gets the tourist to take her to an Orishas concert, but also suggesting that the Orishas are somehow themselves jineteros, producing suitably exotic music for an international market. The woman tricks the tourist into buying her new clothes and giving her money. She and her husband use the money for themselves. Finally the husband comes to take the jinetera from the hotel room, and on his way out they rob the tourist of all that he has. The song concludes with the victory of the couple who have come out of poverty, and it is the tourist who has lost out. Orishas celebrate jineterismo as a practice that puts agency and control in the hands of the women and men who use it to rob tourists in order to support themselves. Jineterismo becomes a strategy by which to raise oneself up. For Orishas it is a practice that resists the objectifying intent of the tourist and turns his voyeuristic designs back on himself by making him an object of ridicule. In contrast to the traditional values of work and study put forward as a way of improving one's conditions, Orishas suggest that tricking and robbing tourists is a worthwhile means to rise from poverty.

The relative autonomy of commercial groups such as Orishas, that derives from being based outside of Cuba and funded by a transnational record label, allows them the scope to broach topics such as jineterismo that are threatening to the Cuban socialist government in several ways. The ability of jineteros to hustle for dollars from tourists challenges the regimes of labor discipline that the state seeks to impose. Through hustling, jineteros can bypass official avenues for earning an income. Jineterismo disrupts the attempts of the state to justify new forms of labor discipline related to Cuba's insertion into a global economy. As the Cuban state seeks to regulate foreign currency toward a centralized state bureaucracy, black and mulatto youth siphon off some of the dollars that have begun to enter Cuba, and they access the tourist mecca that Havana is becoming.

"537 Cuba": Hip-Hop and the Emergence of New Transnational Spaces

One of the main dynamics of Cuban culture in the 1990s was the opening of new transnational spaces of cultural production. Foreign artists and visitors have frequently attended and performed at Cuban rap concerts, and less frequently Cuban rappers have toured abroad in Canada, England, and Europe. In September 2001 there was one tour of New York City for three Cuban groups—Obsesión, Raperos Crazy de Alamar (rca), and Anonimo Consejo. But the tightening of travel restrictions since April 2003 under George Bush made it more difficult for Cuban artists to obtain visas to come to the United States, and so these exchanges have since halted.

Since 2005 there has been a large exodus of Cuban rappers to different parts of the world. Orishas was the first to leave Cuba in 1999; they moved to Paris and signed with the record label emi. In September 2001 Julio Cardenas from rca stayed behind after the tour of New York City. Since then various other rappers have also emigrated from Cuba. Promoter Ariel Fernandez left Cuba in 2005 to live in New York City. The rap producer Pablo Herrera moved to Scotland. The three rappers from Las Krudas all left Cuba and reunited in Austin, Texas; DJ Leydis moved to San Francisco; Miki Flow from Explosión Suprema is in Washington DC; Randy Akosta from Los Paisanos is in Caracas; Janet from Instinto lives in the Canary Islands; and Jesse Saldrigas from Los Paisanos went to England. In the contemporary period it is possible to speak more broadly of a Cuban diasporic hip-hop, given that there is a considerable amount of musical production taking place outside the geographical boundaries of the island.

The reasons for this mass migration of Cuban rappers are multiple. Some left for personal reasons, to follow a foreign spouse or partner, or because they needed to experience life outside of Cuba. Others felt that given the travel restrictions imposed by both the U.S. government and the Cuban government, it would be easier to have a base outside of the country where they could travel freely to perform and tour. The migration of Cuban rappers was part of a general trend of migration among Cubans. But there was also a sense that the hip-hop movement in Cuba had been incorporated and co-opted by the state, and that much of its vitality and energy had been sapped. Internal divisions and political differences within the hip-hop movement led to greater disunity, and rappers began to look to outside opportunities as a way of reaching broader audiences and continuing their art.

But given the strong connection between rap music and place—urban public space and the city—what value does Cuban rap have outside of this geographical space? Made in Havana, and made for habaneros, how can this music speak to a public that does not share its same context? How can Cuban rappers reconnect in the diaspora? It has been difficult for rappers, as new immigrants, to pursue their art, given the demands for everyday survival. They are often separated from their group members, making it necessary to reinvent themselves as solo artists or move into other fields. When Julio Cardenas moved to New York City in 2001, he experienced what many rappers after him were to encounter: without professional qualifications or credentials, without family in the States, he was forced to abandon his music and bus tables like many other immigrants in the city. Since then, he has moved into the area of hip-hop theater, and with a grant from an arts foundation he wrote and acted in a play called *Representa!* From his base in Helsinki, Randy Akosta was able to earn enough money from his tours in Venezuela, Peru, Ecuador, the United States, and Canada to support himself. The Orishas have been the most commercially successful group, going platinum in several countries and winning a Grammy award. Las Krudas moved into a cooperative in Austin, where they earned their keep by participating in shared household and production tasks, leaving them sufficient time as a group to write songs, rehearse, and tour.

Havana as a locus for memory and place still acts as a powerful imaginary in diasporic hip-hop. There is a certain nostalgia toward the city that is both a marketing tool to attract global audiences and a way for the rapper to anchor themselves in relation to an increasingly dispersed movement. This former aspect can be seen in the Orishas song "537 C.U.B.A." on their album *A Lo Cubano*. The international code for dialing Cuba is 537:

> Cayo Hueso, San Leopoldo
> Buena Vista, Miramar
> Alamar, La Victoria
> Habana Vieja, Barrio Nuevo
> Bejucal
> Where are you my Rampa?
> The son that sings, La Catedral
> The Capitolio rises
> as it hears these voices
> 23 y 12, Vedado, Paseo del Prado

The song lists the neighborhoods in Havana that have meaning to the rapper, "Cayo Hueso, San Leopoldo, Buena Vista, Miramar," even listing certain streets and landmarks such as 23 y 12 in Vedado, Capitolio, and La Rampa. The list reads somewhat like a map of tourist sites in Havana, not unusual given Orishas's adoption of a marketing strategy that seeks to sell a nostalgic vision of Cuba to foreigners. In 2002 Orishas followed up on the success of their first album with another album entitled *Emigrante*, which narrates their journey from Cuba to Europe.

The connections between Havana and other urban spaces can be seen in the play *Representa!*, written and performed by Julio Cardenas and the Chicano poet Paul Flores and directed by actor Danny Hoch. The play passes through three moments and distinct urban locales, as it explores the developing relationship between Cardenas and Flores and their differing investments in Havana. The first moment is in the year 1996. Flores is finishing up college and using his school loans to fund a trip to Cuba. He wants to see the country where his grandmother was born and reconnect to his Cuban roots. Cardenas has finished a degree in civil construction, but unable to find a job he is working with his grandfather in a nearby fishery. The actors stand side by side: Flores in his college dorm planning the trip, and Cardenas riding a *camello* bus, both of them speaking their thoughts aloud. Flores wants to see the Cuban hip-hop festival. Cardenas wants to perform in the hip-hop festival. Flores wants to dance salsa and drink Cuban rum. Cardenas wants to go to the Palacio de la Salsa and dance with a beautiful woman. Ironically Flores, a minority in his own country, has access to certain privileges in Havana that are not available to marginalized youth such as Cardenas.

Their differential access to and experience of the city is dramatized in a scene where they are both walking through the streets of Havana. "Today I'm walking in Havana," says Cardenas. "For the police, I'm just another jinetero. I can't walk along La Rampa, or sit on a wall by the Malecón, because they stop me all the time," Flores repeats after him. "Today I'm walking in Havana. People look at me like I represent the dough. I can't shake the hustlers. If I want to smoke a cigar in the street, they want to sell me ten boxes" (Performance, Lehigh University, April 2008). Both feel besieged within the urban space of the city, yet while Cardenas is policed and his movements restricted by the authorities, Flores's discomfort comes from the perception of him as a rich tourist, a position he is not used to occupying.

In the second moment of the play, during 2001, the geographical focus shifts to New York City. Flores wants to host a tour of Cuban rappers, including Cardenas, and show them his landmarks of the city, including the Nuyorican poets cafe, the "home of spoken word"; the graffiti hall of fame in Spanish Harlem; and marches in Union Square. But the tour, which takes place in September 2001, ends up being dominated by one prominent site, the World Trade Center. This site becomes the focus for a series of reflections over identity and belonging, American hegemonic power, and terrorism as a pretext for war. As a site that is discussed in New York, Havana, and countless places in the world, it is symbolic of the transnational nature of urban space and the meanings that certain landmarks generate even for those who do not reside within the same territory.

Cuban rap takes the spaces of the city, Havana, and its periphery, Alamar, as central to cultural production, the formation of identity, and the experience of racial inequality in the Special Period. Even as Cuban rap has moved into the diaspora, it has retained a notion of place as central to its concerns. As Cuba became a major tourist destination, questions of access to space and the exclusion and policing of black youth in the city became increasingly contested. Through b-boy battles in the park, concerts in open spaces, and, less frequently, graffiti, Cuban hip-hoppers reclaimed their rights within the city. In lyrics, rappers rhymed about hustling and robbing tourists as a means of siphoning off funds from the tourist industry for their own survival. As images of Havana piqued the nostalgia of metropolitan consumers, diasporic rap groups played on that nostalgia in their own representations of the city. The spaces of the city, real and imaginary, have continued to provide the point of cohesion for an increasingly dispersed movement, as well as means of entry into a competitive global music industry. As Arjun Appadurai (1996) has argued, globalization has increasingly allowed the possibility for deterritorialized culture. At the same time, relocation presents new hierarchies and spaces that must be negotiated, but whether it will produce corresponding communities of resistance in the diaspora remains to be seen.

Note

1. In October 2004, Castro once again banned the circulation of the U.S. dollar in Cuba. The dollar has been substituted by the convertible peso, which is equivalent to the dollar but has no value outside of Cuba.

9

Urban Performance Pieces
in Fragmented Form: A Reading
of Pedro Juan Gutiérrez
and Antonio José Ponte

CECELIA LAWLESS

Tell a story. This is what we do in life and especially in academia where we weave stories in and out of texts to prove certain theoretical arguments. In this case, I wish to address the intersection between literature and the socio-cultural environment as understood through the textual experience of dwelling spaces and buildings, in particular the home.

Trilogía sucia de La Habana (*Dirty Havana Trilogy*) by Pedro Juan Gutiérrez (1998) and *Cuentos de todas partes del Imperio* (*Tales from the Cuban Empire*) by Antonio José Ponte (2000) will serve as a foundational base for my investigations and concerns regarding the making of home in Havana since the advent of the Special Period. *Home* here relies on both its phenomenological and physical connotations. That is to say, that many things—a meal, a song, a person—can represent home, not just four walls and a roof. As Edward C. Relph comments, "home is not just the house you happen to live in, it is not something that can be anywhere, that can be exchanged, but an irreplaceable center of significance" (1976, 39). As a tourist site of increasing economic exchange Havana is becoming a place of quotidian performance where the actual ordinary, everyday, or homey activities are overwhelmed and obscured by the pressures of the market. The homesite is also invested with a sense of identity and belonging that in the English language in particular has a broad range of implications.[1] Can a sense of home even exist in a socialist post-Soviet Havana? Both of my chosen texts perform an unraveling of a traditionally understood city and homesite. To understand this deconstruction I will move discursively amidst the architectural theory and history of Havana as well as performance theory and personal narrative.

My impetus for working with Havana's architecture came about through a small episode of destruction as I was walking through the dilapidated streets of Havana on my first trip there in 1999. I hold my son's small hand as we search for a place to get a glass of water. He is thirsty. Standing uncertainly before a run-down house in Centro Habana, a woman beckons to us from a doorway.

"¿Qué busca?" (What are you looking for?), she asks.

I explain my son's thirst and she invites us into her apartment on the second floor. She leaves us to wait in a room streaked by bars of light, that enter through the broken lattices of a wooden shutter pulled across the window. As she returns with a glass of water there occurs a resounding crash, and through the opposite end of the room falls a column from the floor above and crumbles on the floor in front of us. I let out a screech. My son begins to cry.

"No se preocupe señora—es sólo una más" (Don't worry señora—it's just one more)," the woman tells us.

Another broken column in the midst of decay. This is the homesite. And in our reaction to the decay lies the difference in our cultures and histories.[2]

In my further work in Havana I began to realize that in the often unpoetic struggle for daily living, the nuances of language accompanied by gesture open up spaces for understanding. If Old Havana is being promoted as the homesite of the nation-state, where this neighborhood with its patrimony and the country at large are conflated into one representational entity, how does that urban story include the individual homesites of city dwellers? As Joseph Scarpaci explains, "historic places allow nation states to create a national identity, forge ideologies and to ground abstract notions into tangible forms, for example the renovation of certain buildings" (2000, 289–90). Everyone in Havana has a house, but not everyone feels the need to describe this site as home. The inarticulateness regarding such a situation stems from a reluctance by many habaneros to transform a contextualized experience into a decontextualized discourse. The stories by Gutiérrez and Ponte specifically use architectonic language to convey Havana as a lived-in space different from the one promoted through brochures about Old Havana. In their stories the *textures* of everyday practice take precedence; that is the dense, vivid, detailed inter-woven narrative, relationships, and experiences one needs to make the density of life bearable.

Piece 1

The Special Period in Cuba during the 1990s emphasized the "special" place of Cuba in the Western world and the sheer survival of its people. Some critics today doubt that this period is over, but all agree on the euphemistic quality of the term. In the wake of the collapse of the Soviet Union and therefore the economic subsidies for Cuba, the island found itself in a state of paralysis, unable to feed its people or provide for basic necessities such as electricity, petrol, or job stability. Habaneros in particular had to *adaptarse*, and this has left its mark on the urban psyche to this day. Although the economy has been revived with its renewed dependence on tourism, the people remain resigned and often despondent about their future. The perspective on recent events becomes inverted so that they have less impact on the collective unconscious than more distant events. In other words, there occurs a renewed impact of revolutionary ideology to offset practical difficulties. Strident socialist slogans continue to appear on billboards, and recent events such as the Elián González affair of 2000 and Castro's evocation of massive political rallies still dominate the social scene to offset the unwelcome concern about the continuing lack of basic, daily needs being met, such as having access to aspirin or basic foodstuffs like chicken and rice. Such shortages of course affect the popular sector, those people who live in Centro Habana, for example, where the official or touristical discourse has not yet penetrated. These are people who appear in the stories by Ponte and Gutiérrez and not on the covers of brochures, except as a folkloric touch. Such a gap between an official discourse and a popular lived experience is further complicated by the dimming of hope and expectations in Cuba, where the past needs interpretation, the present appears static, and the future is full of uncertain change, particularly in the wake of Raúl Castro's takeover of power from his brother.

To speak or understand the present one must consider the past. After 1959 and the "triumph of the revolution," the mission of architecture would show solidarity with the island's dispossessed through a twofold subtext: ideological containment that linked architecture with the natural environment, and a foregrounding of massive projects so as to prove a certain power status to those outside Cuba, thus further isolating the island and disregarding the individual. The wildly experimental National School of the Arts (1961–1963) located in

Cubanácan and designed by the renowned architects Ricardo Porro, Vittorio Garatti, and Roberto Gottardi, serves as an example of such grand projects, while the Urban Reform Law of 1960 demolished the bourgeois concept of property in favor of a social function that provided housing for the individual. Now a ruin amongst vegetation, the National Art Schools today is under consideration for much-needed rehabilitation, and the overcrowding of Havana's core speaks to the failure of providing decent dwelling for all habaneros. Thus Castro's distrust of the bourgeoisie and all it represented meant that the city and its planning, design, and renovation would be abandoned for a focus on the rural. The effects of this kind of policy can easily be seen today in the "growing ruins" of the city center outside Old Havana.[3]

As representatives of a decadent architecture, houses and apartment buildings constructed by Catalan craftsmen at the turn of the twentieth century were allowed to fall into decay. The state became the only client for architects, and as many of the brightest and experienced architects had left Cuba by 1961 (some say up to 85 percent) individually designed dwelling spaces in the city were no longer viable (Segre 1977, 122). Until recently, the design, style, and goals of the 1950s, as representative of the Batista regime of dictatorship and corruption, were disdained in favor of the ideologically safe colonial style. Of course, this turn toward the past is also an ironic move considering that the colonial period reflects an imperialistic and exploitative period, too.

When UNESCO designated the Havana port as a World Heritage Site in 1982, a key date, the process of equating a particular area of Havana with the nation as a whole and even to the world at large took further shape. The city center became the site of reconstruction and renovation, key terms in the Havana narrative, and a space that Castro and his government viewed as a bourgeois holdout. Around the same time there emerged, under the guidance of the architect Mario Coyula, the Group for the Integral Development of the Capital (1987); it stressed preservation instead of new construction and a grassroots base as opposed to state-directed planning. This rectification process took advantage of the microbrigade system to rehabilitate existing residences in the central city in order to move fewer families to the monotonous, industrial-type housing on the outskirts of the city in such projects as Alamar constructed in the 1970s. Such peripheral housing developments ironically helped to solidify downtown Havana as a bourgeois holdout. Today, for example, Alamar is the center for the Cuban hip-hop scene and the Havana Rap Festival—musical genres that feed on rebellion against traditional authority. Vital to this progressive engagement with Havana, at least in the old city core, was the reevaluation of the barrio, that is, the historically grown neighborhood, which complemented the renovations of buildings as undertaken by the Office of the City Historian represented by Eusebio Leal. The understanding of the meaning of *dwelling* in a city, that in the words of Coyula "is sustained by the thick web of relationships and meanings that transcend the material plane of building facades and extend to the people who move through the streets" (1996, 94), was crucial to this initiative.

In the Special Period during the 1990s, with all the shortages and economic problems that it embodied, there emerged the task of protecting and validating a patrimony—the colonial period—that had become designated as an integral part of the collective conscious, even though Havana had also come to be seen as the site of modernity. This represented an ambitious and complex proposal that ultimately ignored individuals and their homes. As buildings crumbled leaving holes in the urban fabric, the house turned into a non-place, both literally and metaphorically. Both Gutiérrez and Ponte write these holes into existence, giving voice to emptiness in a unique and unusual way. They are not so much captivated by the architecture of these buildings, as they are interested in translating an architectural world into a literary one.

Both Gutiérrez's *Trilogía sucia de La Habana* and Ponte's short stories collected in *Un arte de hacer ruinas y otros cuentos*, present stories fragmented in style and content that not only demand a performance from their readers, but also engage them in a reconfiguration of the imaginary and real urban space of Havana, whether it be through an almost visceral reaction for or against Gutiérrez's provocative voice or a certain bewilderment with the density of Ponte's. In *Trilogía* Pedro Juan, a journalist and writer who has lost his job, wanders the streets of Havana looking for ways to make money, have sex, and observe the life around him. Reminiscent of a nineteenth-century flaneur, his urban wanderings no longer rely on a sense of economic and gender privilege, rather he becomes part of the inversion of such criteria—his privilege to wander is premised on the fact that he has no money, and, like a female "streetwalker" in the nineteenth century, Pedro Juan has no problem in prostituting himself when the occasion and need arise. In Ponte's "Un arte de hacer ruinas"—which originally appeared in his *Cuentos de todas partes del Imperio*—the city represented is Havana and Tuguria simultaneously. The latter is an underground city and an exact replica of the city aboveground, a mirror image; yet not quite because as the aboveground city is falling down, it is literally being translated into Tuguria—its underground equivalent.

The story of the "saving" of Old Havana in the 1990s may serve as a counternarrative to Gutiérrez's and Ponte's stories. Its main protagonist is Habagüanex, headed by the City Historian Eusebio Leal. Old Havana consists of 214 hectares, 242 city blocks, 4,000 buildings, a quarter of which have heritage value. The significance of the term *heritage* is that it involves using the past as an economic resource for the present, and to a large extent it is manufactured like a commodity. Habagüanex runs autonomously and receives its budget, in U.S. dollars, from tourism—restaurants, bars, and such. In 1995 it generated 5 million dollars, in 1997, 10 million dollars, and in 2002, 200 million (Scarpaci 2000, 291). As we can see, money plays an important part in this chapter of the Havana story, money to which neither the characters of Gutiérrez nor Ponte have access.

An example of a Habagüanex project is the renovation of the Hotel Saratoga (1998) that used gut-and-preserve tactics; that is, the facade is stabilized, the interior is hollowed out, and the shell then stands as a twenty-first-century core constructed behind the old skin. This is not always the case (see the Hotel Ambos Mundos or Hotel Florida), but it represents a quick and efficient method of renovation quite common to projects in Havana. The questions arise, of course: Whose history and collective memory will be forged in saving Old Havana? Whose story is being told? And what about the residents, the Cubans who inhabit these spaces? Cooperation with the civil society is not part of the joint operations in Havana. Gutiérrez and Ponte see and understand beyond these facades, making that which is disappearing reappear in their works. While renovation processes take the precarious, unstable, and unofficial urban sites and make them viable living spaces, they simultaneously lose the sometimes dirty "spirit" that Gutiérrez and Ponte tend to emphasize.

In the words of Michel de Certeau, we are "walkers whose bodies follow the thick and thins of an urban text [we] write without being able to read it" (1984, 24). To understand *Trilogía* and *Cuentos* we want to decipher this map of mobility that their characters trace. The emphasis in these texts lies in the body and in the interstices of traditional urban spaces. If we look for the "ex-centric" site of experience, as Homi Bhabha (1994) has called it, we must therefore search for those areas not presented for tourists and economic progress. This involves wandering past the facades of Old Havana, past that which is two-dimensional and encountering the territory of lived space distinguished among cultural geographers as *place*. Much has been written recently in cultural studies about space and place, but as early as 1976 thinkers such as Relph claimed that: "space is amorphous and intangible and not an entity that can be directly described and analyzed. Yet, however we feel or know or explain space, there is nearly always some associated sense or concept of place. In general, it seems that space provides the context for places, but derives its meaning from particular places" (1976, 8). Following the lead of Relph's six categorizations of space, Linda McDowell (1999) later used the phrase "spatial scale" to encompass different levels for potential study.[4] In my reading I generally refer to space as mathematical, abstract, and without human content. In contrast, place is active, dynamic, and a lived-in space.

In moving northwest from Old Havana toward Centro Havana or El Vedado, where official preservation has not penetrated, we experience more and more the "architexture," the sensuous fabric of intimate space, that Giuliana Bruno (2002) speaks of in her work. These are the neighborhoods, the places where the stories of Gutiérrez and Ponte unfold. They form part of the cityscape and are areas of rich architectural treasure that have been overlooked by or excluded from renovation, as they do not fall within the official parameters of the colonial history. Instead, the eclectic buildings date from the turn of the twentieth century and display a wide palette of art deco details and Catalan modernist curves, now lost in many other Latin American capitals during the rage to renovate in the 1960s, as evidenced in Caracas or Lima or Santiago.

To understand a place such as Havana we must remember that a city represents a labyrinth of identities both real and imaginary. Ultimately, the city we experience in reality, as well as through written texts—the city as a state of mind—is always already symbolized and metamorphosized. What we imagine adds one more layer to the urban palimpsest in our minds. When speaking about the use of Havana in Cuban film, for example, Laura Podalsky articulates this layering effect as "an implicit critique of the increasingly visible disjunctions between urban renovation projects aimed at attracting more tourists and the increasing physical degradation of surrounding neighborhoods . . . wherein the individual has become unmoored" (2003, 281). Unmoored or homeless in an existential sense, many Cubans do not have access to Old Havana because of the high prices and unwelcoming guardians in many hotels and restaurants run, in fact, by Habagüanex. Old Havana and its tailoring through renovation functions as an accessible product mainly for tourists. As a cultural product, it can rarely be consumed by Cubans, while outsiders with dollars and euros have become the primary consumers. Although Cubans have walked the paths and navigated the neighborhood for many years, foreigners now read a map carefully prepared by Habagüanex that highlights the shops and hotels that they need to visit in order to validate their tropical tour. But what is said can never incorporate all that which is *not* said. You cannot arrive at a totalizing narrative—even in history books or the now famous maquette of Havana, a precise reproduction of every individual downtown building. Thus, any discourse leaves us with certain holes, with certain moments of silence. Gutiérrez and Ponte fill in these gaps with more holes. Automatically, since these are written urban texts we experience a representation of a present already past. Doreen Massey (2005) in her research sees space, or in my view place, as a product of interrelations based on the immensity of the global to the intimacy of that which is most small. Hence the global interacts with the local through social relations. Place encompasses a multiplicity of trajectory and voice. Lastly, place also represents a constantly unfinished product of social and material interrelations because it is in a continual state of *process* (2005, 54). Thus, place is inherently based in rupture, the disruptive, or the uncanny and entails a performative level. We build space; we make place. Spaces and places are in a constant state of change, either through perception and interpretation or through climatic and temporal elements. Havana as presented textually by Gutiérrez and Ponte sets the stage for a performance of radical displacing.

Piece 2

In literary studies the extensive use and abuse and the debate that occurs regarding such terms as *performance* and *performativity* are well known. Multiple books have been written on the subject straddling various disciplines.[5] One of the founders of this field, Richard Schechner, defines performance as "the totality of the event for both performers and audience" (2003, 99). Dwight Conquergood (1985) outlines five areas of performance studies: cultural process, ethnographic praxis, hermeneutics, scholarly representation, and the politics of performance. If we consider the conceptual consequences of thinking about cultural space as a verb instead of a noun, a process instead of a product, then we have an interesting door into an analysis of *Trilogía* and *Cuentos*. What happens to our thinking about performing space when we move it outside of aesthetics and situate it at the center of lived experience? What is the relationship between performance and power? Through the acts of making and dwelling in homes we can see how housing becomes a site where the material forms of buildings and building interiors are impacted by sociopolitical changes and the desires and needs of the individual. This philosophical and active practice forges Cuban domestic architecture through the concept of *inventar*, a term commonly used in Cuban colloquial speech to describe improvising creative solutions for everyday problems.[6] Inventar embodies a performative act at many levels: the pragmatic, political, and social. Keeping this in mind, I offer up the two Cuban works of Gutiérrez and Ponte as urban performance texts.

   If we acknowledge the postmodern urge to view the reader as an active participant, in not only the reading exercise but also in the construction of the text, then theorists such as Iser (2000) and Dufrenne (1973), to just name two, would point out to us that in reading a novel we must imagine it with the text's help. The reader does to a text what the actor does to the script of a play except that the activity takes place in a mental space; although, often as in our two examples, one that references a real space. But as Ponte himself suggests in Nestor Rodríguez's interview, "Cuba is a fiction. All countries are, life is, but this country, in my opinion, is more fictitious than others."[7] My two chosen texts not only invite the reader to perform, but as pieces of writing I would suggest that they themselves are performing an urban space—Havana. It becomes a space that for many Americans is as much a fiction as it might be for the Cubans that live there, although we negotiate it and perform it in different ways.

In neither *Trilogía* nor *Cuentos*, however, is the city space communicated as only Havana; rather, there surges a supplement, as Derrida would say, the sign "Havana" overflows its possibilities. Havana with its cultural, historical, and sociopolitical difference is simultaneously present and absent in the enunciations of these stories. Havana becomes a liminal space, between here and there, both words I leave unadorned of their mere indexical connotations. Not quite universal, nor just symbolic, Havana in these stories has become, perhaps, globalized, for as a background for the Havana in these stories lies the heritage site of the tourist package that is aesthetically pleasing, easy to consume, and strictly a commercial product. Indeed, these texts are highly local, grounded in details of an everyday lived life experience situated in Havana, distinct from all of its Western counterparts ideologically and economically. Simultaneously, Gutiérrez and Ponte are conscious of their restored behavior, that is, twice behaved as Schechner (2003) calls it, making Havana constantly a performance and, at least in the case of Gutiérrez, very marketable. Daniel Garret in reviewing *Trilogía* calls it a "fun book full of sad facts" where the hero tries "to forget the despair of a meaningless space in a hopeless place" (2001, 215).

Piece 3

Trilogía begins by making reference in its first pages to a postcard from London, modern dance in Liverpool, the "Snake Rag" of Louis Armstrong, Allen Ginsberg's poetry, the magazine *Sphincter* and its personal ads, and to Miami. These are not the typical signifiers that immediately come to mind when thinking of Havana. We have left behind the Hotel Nacional and the nostalgia for gambling delights, nearby beaches, Cuba Libres on a terrace, or the rhetoric of "the triumph of the Revolution." In fact, in the next page of this opening story, "New Things in My Life," the first person narrator, a fictionalized and simultaneously autobiographical voice, meets with people who are trying to leave the island, to escape. If we know the context, then we realize that this is taking place during the depths of the Special Period, and this apparently nameless place, a placeless place, is Havana, Cuba. But, as Gutiérrez writes, "nothing matters," a phrase that ends the story and appears repeatedly throughout the volume. And then the narrator performs sex and performs his poverty in this urban non-place as if there were an observing eye on him, as there is of course: his own. As if, perhaps, to alleviate the oxymoronic fun and despair of his life, he writes himself into the urban fabric of his dwelling place, feeling more vibrant, more conscious, and earning some U.S. dollars in the process.

Trilogía can be seen as carnivalesque and multivoiced in the Bakhtinian sense, but ultimately it represents stories of survival, a performance of an everyday liminal period—the Special Period—and individuals will be reinserted or reinsert themselves into their defined place in society. In many ways this collection can be related to Richard Schechner's direct theater defined as: "multivocal and multifocal, a popular deconstructing of hierarchy, often blasphemous, irreverent and obscene, full of small scale dramas and guerrilla theater, the direct theater plays to the roving eyes of many cameras simultaneously ingesting images" (2003, 104). The difference with both *Trilogía* and *Cuentos* lies in the fact that there are no Cuban cameras: these are events that the Cuban public is censored from viewing, and hence they turn into voyeuristic scenes for a paying foreign public. These are unofficial performances that in fact, ironically, must be published outside of Cuba.

When behavior becomes self-conscious behavior, whatever that may be, then it becomes performance. Performances mark identities, bend time, reshape and adorn the body, and tell stories. To see the everyday presented by Gutiérrez and Ponte we must take into consideration that it involves years of training, of learning appropriate behavior, of finding how to adjust and perform one's life in relation to social and personal circumstances. Performance is always performance *for* someone, even when that audience is the self. In the case of *Trilogía* all these levels are addressed and enacted in a blatant way.

Pedro Juan, the main protagonist of this collection of stories or vignettes in the shape of a novel, actively performs throughout the text the dismantling of the traditional concept of home, just as Pedro Juan Gutiérrez the author performs this same dismantling through the very denial of form with his text. Often referred to as a novel, *Trilogía* is, however, a series of moments that capture the everyday life of the disenfranchised protagonist. The text's only connectors are space, Havana, and personality, Pedro Juan's. There is no linear chronological narrative, as each titled segment has no visible transition to the following segment. For example, a chapter might end with talk of Pedro Juan in a prison cell describing his interactions with his cellmate and the next chapter begins, "Two men came to the door. They knocked. Betty opened the door but she left the grille locked" (Gutiérrez 2001, 249).[8] At this point in the text we are trained to know that this "door" and "grille" have nothing to do with prison, and that we have jumped in time and space, although we do remain in Havana. Each segment can stand independently but is enhanced by and carries echoes of the context of surrounding segments. And each title of the individual segments helps to place us textually in what would otherwise be a much more incoherent mass without titles. For as we know, space is claimed territorially by naming it. In fact, the narration calls upon us to perform its fragmented urban space almost as a manifesto for movement.

The triptych form of *Trilogía* appeals to a certain aesthetic of balance and harmony, while simultaneously disrupting that harmony through disjuncture, fragmentation, and incoherence when related to a sense of wholeness. There are titles for the three sections and the segments, and the last two sections are even dated and placed by the inscription, "Havana." If we wished, we could easily read *Trilogía* in the manner Julio Cortázar suggested with his novel *Rayuela* (Hopscotch), so many years ago, as a playful game where we use free will to map our reading path.[9] The novel as homing ground for the Western reader of the past five hundred years is being played with here. In fact, the author and the protagonist do violence not only to the form of the traditional novel but also to its content, in part by appealing directly to the most basic of life's qualities—hunger, dirt, and sex—with such an exaggerated and eschatological directness that it forces upon the reader a real participation that is contrary to the distance and disinterestedness of pure taste in the Kantian understanding of aesthetics (De Ferrari 2003, 24). Pedro Juan also dismantles this iconic role of the flaneur as an *errante*, someone who is out of place within this traditional role while also, of course, still remaining in place. Although he does wander, he is not homeless. Instead he appears rather attached to both his dilapidated *solar* and the disintegrating city.[10] This is ironic considering the chronic disrepair of his building and the ruined state of Havana, or on a larger scale the revolutionary project that has failed to keep up with its grand purpose.

While living in his solar, and in Havana, Pedro Juan is also out of place, like refuse in Mary Douglas's study on pollution and purity (De Ferrari 2003, 29). One of the most intimate and solitary places in a home is a bathroom, a space that in *Trilogía*'s Havana has become a communal, overflowing literal wasteland, so much so that it is a space to be avoided at all costs, thus pushing people to convert any other available space into a potential toilet; a place for refuse and excrement, matter out of place. As de Ferrari points out, in *Trilogía*'s Havana "the bathroom behaves as a thinly veiled allegory of the state of the nation, as the characters of *Trilogía* have been degraded to the lowest stratum of civility by a dramatic succession of historical transformations" (2003, 30). The intimate place here resonates with the larger-scale national imaginary. This represents only one of many references to waste—*mierda*—throughout the book that emphasizes how Pedro Juan appears constantly engaged in negotiating his place in the neighborhood as both insider and outsider. One of his defining traits as an outsider is his role as a writer and observer, which he rarely mentions but we are constantly aware of as we read his text.

As a performative text *Trilogía* gives the impression that the reader is receiving, in fact experiencing (sometimes in all too much detail), a direct transposition of what it is like to live in Havana in the 1990s. Gutiérrez's "dirty realism" becomes so detailed, so violent in its eschatological constancy that the reader begins to believe in his hyperbolic performance. In particular the American reader outside Cuba, who must connect to Havana through brochures, photographs, film, or music, can take this fiction home—dwelling in it—as reality. Gutiérrez plays with this possibility throughout his text, thus creating a tension between the "real" or documentary-like home in Havana and the fictive home. When the reader becomes aware of this ambiguity, the homesite becomes one of discomfort, *unheimlich* in its resistance to and slippage with predetermined categories. In other words, Havana here embraces both definitions of the unheimlich—the unhomely, uncomfortable, and the unconcealed but inadvertently revealed. As de Ferrari comments, "a text that has made such a conscious effort to locate the reader in a strongly referential space simultaneously invites her to suspend disbelief as it pushes its own testimonial authority to questionable levels" (2003, 35). For example, the constant asides to the reader remind us that Pedro Juan is giving us reality, even if he must repeatedly emphasize his performativity with comments such as: "But I won't tell those stories; they're too dirty. Though they're absolutely true" (Gutiérrez 2002, 349).[11] Or, even more clearly: "I don't want to talk about that yet because I'm not ready to tell my audience, scalpel in hand, 'Pay close attention and cover your noses'" (Gutiérrez 2002, 228).[12] Obviously, such comments inspire confidence in the narrator if, at the same time, when read in accumulation and with the super abundance of sexual exploits, a reader has to start questioning the setup or performance of this narrative space.

Trilogía offers us a view into the private, secret spaces of Havana not often available to the foreign public eye. In the process of mapping Old Havana's tourist geography, public spaces have become increasingly less accessible to the resident habanero through the management of the Historiador Eusebio Leal. Although Leal's goal is to sustain a living city wherein historical sites and tourist infrastructure coexist with institutions and services for a permanent resident community (de Castillo) such actions remain conspicuously absent from *Trilogía*. As Medina Lasansky notes, "in a process of transculturation that typifies all things Cuban, Castro's key advisors have launched an ingenious form of entrepreneurial socialism that combines capitalist process with socialist goals" (Lasansky and McLaren 2004, 171).[13] The network of hotels, all with different names but owned and operated by Habagüanex, forms a cultural geography from which habaneros are excluded. This tourist topography is segregated from the Cuban geography of Gutiérrez's and Ponte's characters. Leal has packaged the city center as a series of palpable cultural and historical products in a manner that helps the tourist navigate through the city. In contrast, Gutiérrez provides a labyrinthine formless map where we get lost. Rather than Leal's edited version of Havana, the readers of *Trilogía* feel as if they are receiving a homemade version, an authentic copy of Havana, with all of the obvious representational connotations of "reality" that come with such a word. In many ways Gutiérrez's version of Havana is as carefully fabricated as Leal's. Gutiérrez the author, through his writing style and content, becomes like the designers of maps, pamphlets, and postcards, the travel agents and tour guides, scholars and historians who emerge under the tutelage of Leal as the true architects of the city's new image. The latter promote order, cleanliness, a readable urban fabric; the former offers chaos and dirt.

Yet Pedro Juan, although trapped by his room on top of his building, is seduced by the city, even by the building where he lives. His appreciation, however, always comes with a certain sense of distance from where he can share what the tourists also see from afar. To avoid being alone he takes to the streets, his extended homesite, the city as home. As he leaves his apartment in this particular instance he writes,

> I went down the stairs. The building dates back to 1936, and in its heyday it mimicked the massive banks of Boston and Philadelphia, with their solid,

sober façades. In fact, the façade is still in good shape, and tourists are always amazed by it and take pictures, and it even appears in magazines, especially as photographed on stormy days. I've seen impressive photos, with the wild sea crashing against the Malecón, in that gray-blue hurricane light, the building splashed with water but solid and august. A splendid, majestic castle in the middle of the hurricane. But inside it's falling to pieces, and it's an incredible labyrinth of stairs without banisters, darkness, foul smells, cockroaches, and fresh shit. (Gutiérrez 2002, 82)[14]

I quote this passage at length because it illustrates so clearly the tensions between the public facade of the city constructed by Leal and company and the inner guts of a building teeming with people and filth. And in this paragraph about his building, Pedro Juan explicitly connects the state of affairs to the nation and to the revolution at large, thus implicitly mapping trajectories with a failed project that affects everyone. Another more lyrical moment appears later when while drinking rum on a rooftop, Pedro Juan feels himself to be projected outside on a passing ship: "A solitary figure, dressed in white, leaned against the railing on the third deck. He watched the beautiful golden city in the dusk, and I watched the green and red ship lose itself in the fog as it slipped away" (Gutiérrez 2002, 139).[15] Through this stranger's eyes Pedro Juan is able to appreciate and feel the beauty of Havana, although to do so he must displace himself onto a passing ship, into another's body. Ultimately, he realizes: "This was a good place for me . . . It looked bombed out and deserted, and it was tumbling down, but it was beautiful, this city where I'd done so much loving and hating. I went to bed alone and in peace" (Gutiérrez 2002, 224).[16] Pedro Juan can still be captivated, seduced by the city with whom he has a relationship throughout the text, emotional ties that are absent from the multiple women with whom he has sex. It is Havana who has captured his heart and his body as it traps him through his adventures. And, Pedro Juan's ambiguous feelings of entrapment connected to being an outsider and an insider are reflected innumerable times throughout the text when people who do not leave their homes, those who stay inside, become hungry, desperate, get raped, killed. The home is no longer safe, loneliness is dominant, and survival becomes paramount. The everyday is a performance of dismantling the traditional home so as to be able to survive, as we see in story after story that unfolds on these pages.

Piece 4

Like *Trilogía*, *Cuentos de todas partes del imperio* structurally relies on multiple embedded narratives. The prologue evokes both stories of Rudyard Kipling and those of Scheherazade—stories that are embedded in other stories. In all of these texts we are aware of ourselves as listeners, readers, for whom the stories are being performed. In fact, in the prologue we are directed, even commanded to take violent action if we, as readers, become bored: "make Scheherazade's head roll" (Ponte 2002, 2).[17] The stories then demand that we feel safely at home, an attachment to the place of storytelling. Without this base, violence will occur on the home front, a death that will cut off our sense of belonging and membership to the dwelling place of readership that is a cultural forum of performance. The narrators of these stories are usually telling a story for others, while the story and the persons within the story are performing for an audience as well: the woman afraid of men in "Por hombres" (Because of men), the butcher cutting meat in "A petición de Ochún" (At the request of Ochún), and so on. As an almost placeless space rarely identified as Havana is evoked (except in the core story), a peculiar doubling occurs in these embedded narratives. Through this strategy an uncanny Havana emerges, a city unique and globally infused.

The pivotal story of this collection is "Un arte de hacer ruinas" (A knack for making ruins) where Havana and its underground replica, Tuguria, serve as the labyrinthine setting for a new kind of mapping of the city. The protagonist acts as a skilled detective. He follows certain codes that must be deciphered, but the standard he must reach has not yet been established and so his accomplishments for the reader become cloaked in irony.

"Un arte de hacer ruinas" begins with a story. This story sardonically tells the tale of everyday living in Havana that involves cohabitating with many extended family members, building a *barbacoa*, or loft, to augment the living space, and buying a goat to alleviate the apartment's sense of claustrophobia. This latter action reveals how existing in such a cramped space can actually be worse with a goat than without one. By eliminating the goat after three days, life appears immeasurably better although, of course, it reverts back to just what it was before: a paradox, change with no change, or the process of life in a Havana that reveals the process is stasis. Space and time do not change in this city, as is evidenced later in the story when the first person narrator says: "As a child I used to visit my adviser in what seemed like another apartment— this same one, but with the shutters open" (Ponte 2002, 25).[18] In fact, space and time collapse in this story: "Time, as they should have taught you, is another space" (Ponte 2002, 29).[19] Two key spatial phrases appear repeatedly in "Un arte de hacer ruinas": "tugurización" (Ponte 2005, 64, 65) ("tuguriza-tion" [Ponte 2002, 32, 33]) and "estática milagrosa" (Ponte 2005, 63, 64, 65) ("miraculous statics" [Ponte 2002, 31, 33]). The resonances of such phrases are complex—physical deterioration combined with social overcrowding, slum formation. According to Babar Mumtaz, "informal settlements or slums are not only inevitable, they are a mark of success of a city. The formation of slums is an integral part of the process of growth and development of a city. Only in a static (stagnant?) city does the state and status of its constituent parts remain unchanged" (2001, 2). Ponte himself gives a definition of *tugurización* in an interview with Nestor Rodríguez: "the capacity that an overpopulated city has to make divisions within the urbanized space and to convert those places into slums, that is, to devalue them architecturally because of the need to crowd lives into a restricted space."[20] But with tugurization there also occurs the "miraculous statics" described by the actual director of the Oficina de Re-habilitación y Desarrollo: "It is when the building is in a critical condition, irreparable, and it's kept standing through the work and grace of the Holy Spirit."[21] The religious and political irony, if not the legitimacy, of such a phrase is evident, especially in light of the conspicuous slogan throughout Havana, "Revolución es construir" (Revolution means to build). But in Ha-vana construction was paralyzed during the last fifty years; that becomes reflected in the paralysis of its inhabitants in knowing what to do with such a situation.[22] As Florian Borchmeyer comments in an interview regarding his film of the same title *Habana: Arte nuevo de hacer ruinas*: "This was the idea from the beginning, that the human being, in this film, would enter the environment of his city's architecture and of the architecture around him. In this way, somehow, the human being becomes the architecture. The architec-ture and the human being reflect one another."[23] While people and buildings reflect one another, they are also subsumed by one another eventually leaving architectural and psychic holes.

Throughout *Tales from the Cuban Empire*, in fact, the tension between buildings falling apart and the accumulation of dwelling space—a delicate balance, on the abyss—is ever-present (reminiscent of such book titles as *Cuba on the Verge*). The narrator remarks, "The city still had the same fixed borders; it showed no signs of spreading. When a building fell, they didn't replace it. We took the cheapest way out of a collapse by making a park, or leaving the space empty (Ponte 2002, 33).[24] Or, "My advisor and I watched the train station empty out once more, and saw how waves of *tugurs* kept arriving in the city" (Ponte 2002, 33).[25] Empty spaces are created in Havana that echo the empty space left by trains filled by *tugures*—a foreshadowing of how those urban spaces that fall into the underground are in fact populating Tuguria. Or as Ponte writes in *Un seguidor de Montaigne mira la Habana* (A follower of Montaigne views Havana), "There is emptiness in every gesture and, nevertheless, there is persistence: every day the Habanero makes himself believe that he lives in Havana."[26] At the same time, the narrator of "Un arte de hacer ruinas" comments: "My advisor recalled all the cities this was to be" (Ponte 2002, 25).[27] Havana is multiple cities and full of possibilities. Yet simultaneously, Havana is not even a city, as the narrator remarks: "There was a moment when I thought that if I were to open the shutters, we wouldn't find a city out there" (Ponte 2002, 25).[28] Havana is present and not present in these stories, embedded in the story of a goat, a thesis, the lost book "Tratado breve de estática milagrosa" (Brief treatise concerning miraculous statics), the death of two professors, false money, times of cholera in the nineteenth century, the collapse of Havana, the construction of Tuguria, the words of a grandfather who quotes Italo Calvino's Marco Polo from *Invisible Cities* (1978), and so on. In such an aporia of cumulative layers, place can actually be lost. Not only do multiple stories appear but also a variety of genres: detective, essayistic, murder mystery, fable. Time and spaces merge here in less than twenty pages, and from these strands we readers construct a different vision of Havana than the one presented by the culture industry ready to sell us a city contained by monuments and music.

Although place names take precedence over personal names in this story, one name does stand out, or rather its meaning is hinted at. Other characters appear anonymously with only an initial such as "D." standing in for names, or their title "mi tutor," "tu abuelo." But near the beginning of the story, to establish the theme of building, this exchange occurs between the narrator and his tutor:

> "Do you know what your surname means? . . ."
> "Builder," I answered.
> "I always envied your grandfather his name . . ."
> "You're going to be a city planner in a family of city planners" (Ponte 2002, 23).[29]

Not only are stories embedded within stories here but the narrator himself is embedded in the layers of vocation of his father and his grandfather. Thus are constructed the stylistic layers of this palimpsestic city and its inhabitants. Style reflects content. This performative bonding between style and content also occurs in the structure of the story.

Throughout the narration appear eleven breaks or gaps or holes—empty spaces. The reader does not know and is not told what might happen or what might have happened within these holes. Just like the ruins of Havana's buildings that leave gaps in the city texture to be filled in by parks or just left abandoned, so these narrative gaps demand a certain level of performance from the reader. At the same time, the dialogue throughout the story is cut through with dialogistic holes noticed by the narrator himself who also becomes lost in the labyrinth of words, similar to the labyrinthine city; for example: "'Of course,' I said without understanding what connection there could be between this conversation and the coin" (Ponte 2002, 28).[30] Not only is there a displacement between words and objects as in this example, but there also occurs a displacement between words themselves: "'I talked with his ex-wife at the identification of his body. It will be best to leave things as they are' . . . 'I'll make some coffee'" (Ponte 2002, 37).[31] Death, moving things, and making coffee do not seem to really connect especially when taken together with other repeated words such as: "detour" (Ponte 2002, 29), "I asked interrupting his digressions" (29), "I didn't understand" (28), "D. didn't seem to understand me" (34).[32] The written style of the story accumulates a series of signs that creates an uncanny place, where one is sure of nothing, where cities appear and disappear, where for a moment "none of it was real" (Ponte 2002, 41)[33] and "it was impossible for me to find an exit" (Ponte 2002, 43).[34] This is the place that is no place or displaced. This is the reconstructed city of Havana presented by Ponte.

In this story the mirror image of Havana, Tuguria, grows "hacia adentro," or "toward the inside," a theme that catalyzes the protagonist's meeting with his tutor. This literal, architectural idea of growing inward takes on an identitarian resonance when read in the context of Rodríguez's interview with Ponte:

> It is about thinking that Cuba ends in 1959 and that what we live from then on is a limbo between the end of Cuban capitalism and the capitalism that returns after a long interval. And I am opposed to both because it is not possible to deny life to those who leave the island nor to those who have remained on it. I think that in this historic moment the country has to make a double transition. Confined by the border you have to go inward, to the depths of the country, but also outward. I have no distrust for my condition as a Cuban. Although, of course, this condition is always ironic.[35]

In this quotation Ponte makes a distinct link between the spatial metaphor of "inward" and the idea of Cuban identity; that is, his psychological (existential) homesite. And in this inward movement, there is a reciprocal dialectical outward movement that implies a continuous process. In this way, we can read "Un arte de hacer ruinas" not as a merely negative critical denunciation of Havana and its buildings but rather, simultaneously, as a reconstruction of the concept of dwelling. In this act of dwelling, the object, a book, a story, places them, perhaps even giving them a home. As Ponte states in the afore-mentioned interview: "Sharing this talismán [a book] has made us brothers. A chain of co-conspirators is established, the book becomes an object of conspiracy . . . This object of conspiracy links all the people who read it."[36] Of course, there is a difference in creating a community or home base around a book or a city, and in neither case does this link remain unproblematic. We must not forget, as Massey (1994, 137) points out in her work: "places . . . are of course not internally uncontradictory. Given that they are constructed out of the juxtaposition, the intersection, the articulation of multiple social relations they could hardly be so."

Piece 5

In both *Trilogía* and *Cuentos* Havana unfolds as a city in crisis. As Ana María Dopico states, the "allure of Cuba lies precisely in both its suffering and its surviving collapse" (2002, 463). While the characters of these texts live within the confines of an urban setting, they are also out of place with their counter-parts in other Latin American cities. This is in part due to the special circum-stances of Havana as a city that is an island on an island trapped in a political time that is no longer viable in the twenty-first century and breeds a palpable nostalgia for that which is no longer there. For a multitude of Cubans the rewards of work are so minimal and the quest for survival so difficult that they have needed to find other ways to embrace life. Gutiérrez in particular follows the lead of another Cuban novelist, Abilio Estévez, in recounting through his stories sex as salvation from life's problems. He makes time and space visible through flesh and ruins. Ponte sees that "in Cuba between yesterday and tomorrow exists the greatest amount of emptiness breathable" (2003, 15). He focuses on the empty spaces created by the thickly populated Havana city-scape.

Rather than a non-place or even a heterotopia as suggested by Dopico (2002, 457), I would suggest that *Trilogía* and *Cuentos* set up Havana as a theatrical stage where the inhabitants dwell in a place that is in constant motion but always remains the same. Thus we enter the oxymoron of the "growing ruins" and of a home that no longer conforms to a stasis but rather presents an architexture in motion. These stories collapse traditional themes and concepts to force their performativity on the reader as a different manifestation of self and a different manifestation of home. They contest what it means to be postmodern and the relation of art to structures of power. In this context, we must ponder, in the words of Ponte, the immorality in writing about the "accident" of ruins rather than assisting its victims. Protagonists achieve some power through their words in *Trilogía* and *Cuentos*, home becomes a restructured and displaced center, and yet this does not overshadow the ever-present struggle for survival.

Notes

1. Many of the terms used in this paper, such as *home*, *place*, and *space*, are very open-ended and critics agree about their resistance to definition. This very open-endedness attracts me, as it provides a territory of ambiguity. For one source on the various nuances of home, see Sopher (1979). The difference between the Spanish *casa* and *hogar* definitely has less resonance than their English counterparts.

2. This small incident not only highlights the contrast between English and Spanish, an American and a Cuban, but also points to the distinctive role that Havana plays as a UNESCO World Heritage Site compared to other U.S. or European cities. Havana does not promote internal tourism that could be used as a catalyst for defining local and national identity; rather tourism is produced for the Other (Lasansky and McLaren 2004, 181).

3. For an excellent study and meditation on these "growing ruins" I suggest the documentary film *Habana: Arte nuevo de hacer ruinas* (Borchmeyer and Hentschler 2006), where Antonio José Ponte appears as a self-proclaimed "ruinologist."

4. Relph (1976) outlines six broad categories of space: perceptual, existential, sacred, geographical, architectural, and cognitive. This "continuum," as he calls it, is useful, but I prefer to negotiate a spatial scale as outlined by McDowell (1999) that starts at the home place and moves outward toward larger dimensions.

5. These include Sue-Ellen Case and Janelle G Reinel's *The Performance of Power*, Richard Schechner's *Performance Theory*, Marvin A. Carlson's *Performance: A Critical Introduction*, and Philip Auslander's *Performance: Critical Concepts in Literary and Cultural Studies*.

6. Obviously, this is not only a Cuban phenomenon, but it does stand out among other poor urban communities around the world because the Cuban government does tend to involve itself in the management of other aspects of daily life such as health care and education as formulated in the Socialist Constitution.

7. "Cuba es una ficción. Todos los países lo son, la vida lo es, pero este país es en mi opinión, e más ficticio que los otros" (Rodríguez 2002, 184).

8. "Los dos tipos llegaron a la puerta. Tocaron. Betty les abrió pero dejó la reja con el candado" (Gutiérrez 1998, 248).

9. Various Cuban writers and critics claim that, in fact, very few options of "free

will" are left to Cubans on the island, and hence Gutiérrez's "playful" style can be seen as rather liberating.

10. A *solar* is a land lot where a large building has been erected and later divided into multiple dwellings. It is often referred to in English as a tenement building with a central sunlit courtyard and a communal toilet and water source. This kind of constructíon goes back to medieval Spanish buildings still to be found—now chiefly renovated—in downtown Madrid.

11. "Pero no voy a contar esas historias porque son demasiado pornos. Aunque absolutamente reales" (Gutiérrez 1998, 319).

12. "No quiero hablar de aquello porque aún no estoy preparado para tener el bisturí en la mano y decirle al respectable público presente: 'Atiendan cuidadosamente y cúbranse la nariz'" (Gutiérrez 1998, 209–10).

13. According to Lasansky, 45 percent of all profits from the Habagüanex enterprises are reinvested in further renovation, 35 percent into community social services, while 20 percent returns to the central government to be spent at their discretion. This is, needless to say, an unusual method of distributing profits for any large company (Lasansky and McLaren 2004, 171).

14. "Bajé las escaleras. El edificio es de 1936 y en sus buenos tiempos imitó esas moles de Boston y Filadefia, con fachadas de bancos sólidos y eficaces. En realidad conserva la fachada y los turistas se asombran y le toman fotos y hasta aparece en las revistas, fotografiado sobre todo en días de tormenta. He visto fotos alucinantes, con el mar furioso saltando sobre el Malecón, con esa luz gris-azul de los ciclones, y el edificio salpicado de agua. Pero sólido y antiguo. Un castillo majestuoso y espléndido en medio del huracán. Pero adentro se está cayendo a pedazos y es un laberinto increíble de trozos de escaleras sin barandas, oscuridad, olor a rancio y a cucarachas y a mierda fresca" (Gutiérrez 1998, 82–83).

15. "Hay un tipo solitario, vestido de blanco, recostado en la baradilla de la tercera cubierta. El tipo mira la ciudad hermosa y dorada en el crepúsculo. Yo miro el buque verde y rojo que se pierde en la bruma, y se aleja" (Gutiérrez 1998, 132).

16. "Me gusta este lugar. . . . Semeja una ciudad bombardeada y deshabitada. Se cae a pedazos, pero es Hermosa esta cabrona ciudad donde he amado y he odiado tanto. Me acuesto solo y tranquilo" (Gutiérrez 1998, 206).

17. "Haz rodar la cabeza de Scheherazade" (Ponte 2005, 42).

18. "De niño yo visitaba a mi tutor en otro apartamento, ese mismo con las ventanas abiertas" (Ponte 2005, 59).

19. "El tiempo, como deben de haberte enseñado, es un espacio más" (Ponte 2005, 61–62).

20. "La capacidad que tiene una ciudad sobrepoblada para hacer divisiones dentro del espacio urbanizado y convertir en tugurios esos lugares, es decir, devaluarlos arquitectónicamente por la necesidad de apinar vidas dentro de un espacio limitado" (Rodríguez 2002, 184).

21. "Es cuando el edificio tiene un estado muy crítico, no reparable, y se mantiene en pie por obra y gracia del espíritu santo" (Ponte 1998, 2).

22. For a clear explanation and denunciation of this paralysis, see Ponte (2007b).

23. "Esa era la idea desde un principio, que el ser humano, en esta película, entre en el ámbito de su arquitectura de la ciudad y de la arquitectura que lo rodea. De esa forma, de alguna manera, el ser humano se transforma en la arquitectura. La arquitectura y el ser humano se reflejan mutuamente" (Elligiers 2006).

24. "La ciudad tenía los mismos bordes fijos, no daba seña ninguna de extenderse. Donde caía una edificación no levantaban otra. Salíamos del derrumbe del modo más barato, con la construcción de un parque, de un espacio vacío" (Ponte 2005, 65).

25. "Mi tutor y yo veíamos cómo se vaciaba otra vez la terminal de trenes, cómo arribaban a la ciudad oleadas de tugures" (Ponte 2005, 65).

26. "Hay un vacío en cada gesto, y, sin embargo, hay una persistencia: todos los días el habanero se hace creer que vive en La Habana" (Ponte 2001a, 41).

27. "Mi tutor recordó todas las ciudades que iba a ser esta ciudad" (Ponte 2005, 59).

28. "Hubo un momento en que sentí que, de abrir una ventana, no la encontraría allá fuera" (Ponte 2005, 59).

29. "Sabes qué quiere decir tu apellido?" . . .

"Constructor," respondí.

"Le envidié siempre ese apellido a tu abuelo." . . .

"Vas a ser urbanista en una familia de urbanistas" (Ponte 2005, 57–58).

30. "Claro, acoté, sin comprender qué relación había entre esta conversación y la moneda" (Ponte 2005, 61).

31. " 'Hablé con su ex-mujer en el reconocimiento del cadaver. Será mejor no remover las cosas.' . . . 'Voy a hacer un café' " (Ponte 2005, 68).

32. "Desvío" (Ponte 2005, 61), "corté sus divagaciones" (61), "Yo no entendí" (60), "D. pareció no entenderme" (66).

33. "Nada era real" (Ponte 2005, 71),

34. "Me fue imposible hallar salida" (Ponte 2005, 72).

35. "Consiste en pensar que Cuba termina en 1959 y que lo que vivimos a partir de entonces es un limbo entre el final del capitalismo cubano y el capitalismo que vuelve después de un largo paréntesis. Yo me opongo a las dos porque no es posible negar la vida a quienes se van de la isla ni a quienes se han quedado dentro de ella. Pienso que en este momento histórico el país tiene que transitarse doblemente. Circunscrito a la frontera debes ir hacia adentro, hacia lo hondo del país, pero también hacia afuera. Yo no tengo ninguna desconfianza en mi condición de cubano. Ahora bien, esa condición es siempre irónica" (Rodríguez 2002, 181).

36. "Compartir este talisman [libro] nos ha hermanado. Se establece una cadena de conspiradores, el libro se convierte en objeto de conspiración . . . Ese objeto de conspiración vincula a toda la gente que lee" (Rodríguez 2002, 181).

10

Topographies of Cosmonauts in Havana:
Proyecto Vostok and Insausti's *Existen*

JACQUELINE LOSS

What to do with monuments once the figures they represent are no longer viewed as heroes is a subject that many nations from the former Soviet Bloc confront. According to Michael Kimmelman (2008), Hungary adopted one of the most unusual resolutions: "In Budapest statues of Communist idols have been relocated to a park on the city outskirts to become virtual headstones at a kind of kitsch graveyard." Unlike what occurred in many places in the former Eastern Bloc, the government of Cuba, though strongly supported by the Soviet Union, did not erect many statues in honor of its heroes in Havana; furthermore, it forbade statues of living Cubans.

In fact, one of two statues in honor of Lenin in Havana was erected on January 27, 1924, the very day of Lenin's funeral in Moscow and long before the Soviets exerted influence in Castro's revolutionary Cuba. Indicative of the two nations' later state of affairs, in 1984 the site was named a national monument, and that same year at Lenin Park in Havana (opened in 1972) a 1,200-ton white marble Lenin monument, sculpted by the Soviet Lew Kerbel, was erected. Engraved in the statue is an excerpt of a speech that Fidel gave at an event commemorating the one-hundredth birthday of Vladimir Ilich Lenin at the Chaplin Theatre on April 22, 1970, "el año de los diez millones" (the year of the ten million). The words are: "Lenin fue desde el primer instante no solo un teórico de la política, sino un hombre de acción, un hombre de práctica revolucionaria constante e incesante" (Lenin was from the first instant not only a theoretician of politics, but also a man of action, a man of constant and incessant revolutionary practice). Statues dedicated to Lenin are scarce; however, those dedicated to Cuba's national hero, José Martí, are ubiquitous, as anyone who has seen *La muerte de un burocráta* (1966) (Death of a bureaucrat) would know. In Tomás Gutiérrez Alea's film, a bureaucrat is killed by the giant machine that he invented to mass-produce busts of Martí. Illustrative of fiction and history's coincidence, just six years after Kerbel's monument to Lenin was erected in Cuba's capital a proposal was made in Moscow to move "Lenin's body from the mausoleum in Red Square to the Vlokov Cemetery in Leningrad" (Pavlov 1994, 141).

With the advent of perestroika, Cuba did not literally inter or exhume its "Soviet brothers," but it did distance itself from the previous predominant narrative of international solidarity. In 1992 the Cuban Constitution was radically transformed to demote their function by taking away previous references to them, such as "la amistad fraternal y la cooperación de la Unión Soviética y otros países socialistas" (the fraternal friendship and cooperation of the Soviet Union and other socialist countries). To a large extent, everyday Cuban people, politicians, intellectuals, and artists followed suit and claimed that nothing remained of the Soviet Bloc in Cuba. However, in the wake of the most difficult hardships of the Special Period, stories that once again connect the island to the extinct bloc have surfaced in the memory of Cubans. *Ostalgie*, a term that, according to Reinhard Ulbrich and Andreas Kämper, was coined by the German comedian Bernd-Lutz Lange to mean nostalgia for the East, has often somewhat erroneously been viewed only as East Germans' escapism from the present. Actually, the phenomenon is more complex than that. It refers to: "a mixture of memories that gloss over the real problems and an emerging East German consciousness, point[ing] to intra-social problems that can only partly be explained with the legacy of the GDR and the reintegration of East Germany, but perhaps all the more with the twofold crisis to adapt to a capitalist West Germany and a transforming global economy" (Andreas Ludwig quoted in Blum 2000, 230). In a review of Wolfgang Becker's *Goodbye Lenin!* (2003) and Florian Henckel von Donnersmarck's *The Lives of Others* (2006), Slavoj Žižek (2007) points out that Ostalgie is "not a real longing for the GDR, but the enactment of the real parting from it, the acquiring of a distance." The multiple nuances of Ostalgie ought to be kept alive as we examine a distinct, yet comparable phenomenon of Cubans' recollections of their country's alliance with the Soviets that emerged in the late 1990s. By no means are they on the grand scale of Ostalgie, but they do open up yet another nodal point with respect to elucidating Cuba's recent history, present, and future.

Toward the end of the Special Period, at the beginning of the era of the Bolivarian Alternative for Latin America and the Caribbean (ALBA) and within the context of the U.S. invasion of Iraq, artistic and sociopolitical contestation, exhumation, and memorialization of the Soviet Bloc have evolved.[1] The memories of the Cuban and Soviet alliances have expanded, morphed, and taken on new critical meanings. These memories are being hashed out in cultural and political centers, academic and journal publications and conferences, Internet forums, as well in a variety of informal settings.[2] To understand the richness of the temporal framework, we must keep in mind that Raúl Castro, today's tentative transformer, was once the minister of the Revolutionary Armed Forces and was largely responsible for having modeled Cuba's armed forces on the Soviet Union. Taking the artistic renditions of scientific exhibitions in Havana as the point of departure, this chapter focuses on the way in which Cuban artists transform the "great Soviet" into a peripheral character that, in its very marginality, is crucial to provincializing the United States as well as to envisioning the possibility of greater critique within Cuba's present and future public sphere.

The symbolic decay of triumphant moments resides not only within the very city of Havana but also within its texts, as illustrated in an expanding body of scholarship on Cuban literature. The generations denoted as "Los hijos de Guillermo Tell" (The sons of William Tell), who were in their twenties around the time of perestroika, the *perestroikos*, younger generations of the *muñequitos rusos* (cartoons of the Soviet Bloc), as well as Generation Y (from their late twenties to about forty) were affected by a youth steeped in the "great Soviet," as well as an adolescence and adulthood impacted by the dissolution of the Soviet Bloc.[3] Cubans now face a new wave of transnational players that include some of the old actors. Back in the 1970s and 1980s, Cubans had a penchant for naming their children with Russian-sounding names.[4] The grand narratives of liberation and progress that inspired such names are transformed today into paradoxical and critical performances of desire and repulsion. The events explored in this chapter are some of the many instances of a Soviet Havana that belong to the present and evoke strong critiques of some Cuban governmental policies and institutions, of unforgiving capitalism, and of the U.S. blockade. They evidence a non-monumental memorialization entailing rapprochement and reproach.

As is well known, Vostok (meaning east in Russian) was a Soviet spaceflight project with the goal of sending people into orbit around Earth; it used the

Vostok spacecraft designed for human spaceflight. Launched from Baikonur, the first flight with a crew, carrying Yuri Gagarin, took place in 1961; Vostok's last flight, with Valentina Tereshkova (the first woman in space) on board, was in 1963. While these days the Internet, in addition to concrete wars, is an alternative space for carrying out ideological and scientific battles, back in the early 1960s the fight for world domination was also carried out in outer space. The Vostok program manifested the excellence of Soviet political, economic, scientific, and technological command.

This cosmonaut past can be identified not only by the number of Yuri's and Laika's on the island these days (fewer Laika's than Yuri's, given the life spans of dogs), the postage stamps commemorating the space program, but also by the numerous artistic interventions, starting with Manuel Pereira's *El ruso* (1980), that reflect upon the topic. Among the many Vostok-inspired moments of the new millennium are Tonel's "Conversaciones con 'la primera carga'" (Conversations with "the first charge") in 2003; Ramón Fernández Larrea's "Carta a Yuri Gagarin" (Letter to Yuri Gagarin) in 2003; and Gertrudis Rivalta's painting *Todas queremos ser como Valentina Tereshkova* (We all want to be like Valentina Tereshkova), part of the 2004 *Fnimaniev!!* exhibition.

The cosmonaut past has many concrete dimensions in Havana. Not only is there the Taller de Reparación de Aviones "Cosmonauta Yuri Gagarin" (Airplane Repair Workshop of Astronaut Yuri Gagarin), founded in 1966 by Raúl Castro, but there is also another strangely evocative yet somewhat more tedious workshop, the Taller de Reparaciones de Equipos Electrodomésticos Vostok. This workshop, specializing in Soviet appliances, was transformed and re-signified in November 2007 into one of the two sites of the group exhibition *Vostok: Proyecto de exposicion colectiva*, curated by Frency Fernández and Victoria Gallardo.[5] This detail is particularly interesting in light of the significance of material culture within German Ostalgie. Before the exhibition's inauguration, it was briefly announced in *La Jiribilla*, a Cuban cultural journal, and Rafael Grillo published a substantial article about it. Little public discussion ensued around the event—a number of intellectuals deeply involved in cultural affairs in Havana and also alert to artistic and sociocultural phenomena related to the remains of the USSR on the island claimed not to have heard of the project. Regarding the meaning of artwork, Hans Haacke affirmed in his discussions with Pierre Bourdieu that "the problem is not only to say something, to take a position, but also to create a productive provocation. The sensitivity of the context into which one inserts something, or the manner in which one does it, can trigger a public debate" (Haacke and Bourdieu 1995, 21–22). However, with *Vostok*, seemingly no public debate ensued, and, in line with Haacke, the meaning of the exhibition is put into question.

While few knew anything, one source, attributing the information to a rumor, said that some of the works were censored or destroyed and that the exhibition at the Vostok workshop in Centro Havana ended before it was scheduled to. Another spoke of not understanding the youngest participating artists' anger toward the Soviet Bloc when they were too young to have lived through Cuba's solidarity with it. One young artist, in response to my question about the artistic technique he utilized, provided me with a little extra information, saying that his work "fue desaparecido por autoridades políticas" (was disappeared by political authorities) and that another artist's was partially so, greatly affecting the entire exhibition. He attributed this mechanism, like many Cubans before him, to the most repressive legacies of the Soviet Union.

The majority of the artists who showed their work was born in the 1960s and early 1970s and came of age at about the time of the disintegration of the socialist camp. Unlike artists who made their careers in the 1970s and 1980s, were children at the height of the Cold War (a war that was fought, in part, through scientific experiments such as Vostok), and who as adults actually went to the USSR for their higher education,[6] for all of Vostok's exhibitors the actual Vostok program was, for all extensive purposes, inherited memory: Jairo Alfonso was born in 1974, Tessio Barba in 1975, Alejandro Campins in 1981, Diana Fonseca in 1978, José Fidel García "Micro X" in 1981, Hamlet Lavastida in 1983, Ernesto Leal in 1971, Jorge Luis Marrero in 1970, Gertrudis Rivalta in 1971, Lázaro Saavedra in 1964, Ezequiel Suárez in 1967, and Ulises Urra in 1972.

With the *Vostok* of 2007 in mind, let us briefly recall some of the other retrospective moments of the artistic panorama of the 1960s and 1970s that were recycled and re-signified between 2005 and 2008. In December 2006, just five months after Raúl Castro took over command of the island for the first time, debate around the "gray period" of the 1970s heated up soon after Luís Pavón—a former president of the Consejo Nacional de Cultura (National Council of Culture) between 1971 and 1976 who was instrumental in the creation of the policies that led to cultural Sovietization—appeared on television three times. Fierce debate over Pavón's resurgence was carried out on the Internet with Desiderio Navarro, the director of the Centro Teórico-Cultural's *Criterios*, taking the lead. That the debate has already been collected within a volume, *La política cultural del período revolucionario: Memoria y reflexión* (Cultural politics of the revolutionary period: Memory and reflection, 2008), authored by multiple people, several who were not central to the initial debate, and was published by the very same center in Cuba's capital speaks to the practices of containment and dialogue in Cuba today.

In April 2007, approximately four months after "Pavóngate" and just six months prior to the *Vostok* exhibition, *Los 70: Puente para las rupturas* (The '70s: Bridge for ruptures), launched at the National Museum of Fine Arts in Havana. Having been in the making for some time, the exhibition's core objective was to show that the 1970s were not as artistically repressive and static as they are often perceived. Its curator, Hortensia Montero Méndez, argued that the art of the decade possessed commonalities with both the art of the hopeful 1960s and the critical 1980s. That is to say that Cuban artists— many who came from the countryside to take advantage of the new national initiatives—may have created works that reflected the period's principal official rhetoric in favor of the pedagogical value of art, but they did not imitate Soviet socialist realism. Quoting Pedro Pablo Oliva, Montero Méndez asserts:

> Los años 70 fueron los de un mundo muy soñador y vinculado a eso que en política le llaman ahora socialismo utópico. Era soñar un mundo mejor, lindo, hermoso, que llevó a tanta gente a intentar transformar el mundo, por mejorarlo, por hacerlo mucho más lindo.

> [The 1970s was a world full of dreams linked to, what in politics, they call utopian socialism. It meant dreaming of a better, lovely, beautiful world that led so many people to transform the world, by improving it, by making it much more lovely.] (Montero Méndez 2007)

With that spirit of the decade in mind, the exhibition showcased the decade's return to nature, the myths of *Cubanía*, as well as photorealism. On the one hand, not explicitly apparent in any of the works was the extent to which the Soviet Union peopled the imaginary of 1970's Cuba, although Montero Méndez points out that many of the artists, including Cosme Proenza, Arturo Montoto, Rocío García, and Manuel Alcalde, did, in fact, study in the Soviet Union. On the other hand, the very themes of utopianism and a return to nature can be viewed either as the product of Soviet influence or simply as tendencies common to both countries on account of shared ideologies.

As Juan Carlos Betancourt (forthcoming) demonstrates, in the late 1980s and early 1990s, Cuban artists parodied socialist realism using its very techniques, and while some works in *Vostok* utilize this strategy, others apply a myriad of techniques to excerpt objects and moments from the imported Soviet world and recast them within the new topography of Havana's twenty-first century. For instance, snowy landscapes with dachas and churches characterize Alejandro Campins's work, but there is something strange and out of place within these otherwise idealistic images that could resemble Soviet socialist realist art. A flock of birds flies in a church-like building and the text reads: "Entran por la izquierda, Escapan por la derecha" (Enter at the left, Escape at the right). Another Campins painting places an Eastern European-looking landscape in the foreground, with a sea in between, and in the background a tropical island. Both the textual directions and the imagery refer to the artist's position on Cuba's political inheritance from the Soviet Bloc—an entrance into a structure that obliges escape.[7] Through naive stylization, Campins examines the encounter between a dominant territory and a faraway place under its sphere of influence. In another painting, a red cloud-like figure monopolizes a light blue sky and splatters something red onto the landscape below. Handwritten in black, with the second word scratched out in red, with only part of an *I* and an *ó* remaining, is written: "ESTA _____IÓN ES TAN GRANDE QUE APLASTA" (This _____ is so big that it crushes). In an interview with Abél Prieto (2007), Cuba's cultural minister characterized the bittersweet reflection on the Soviet Bloc by referencing an essay that he published in 1995: "Lo que me interesó, obviamente, fue discutir siempre en la cuerda humorística, irónica si nuestro vínculo con los soviéticos significó 'atraso' o 'adelanto'" (What I was interested in, obviously, was to discuss always in a humorous, ironical tone if the link with the Soviets meant something "backward" or "advancement"). Likewise, Campins's bittersweet oil paintings suggest something that is not apparent within Montero Méndez's assertions. Repression is part and parcel of ideological constructions, even if they are construed idealistically, as in Campins's palette of childlike colors that obliges spectators into empathy for the dreams of solidarity.[8]

In a similar vein, Jorge Luis Marrero's work imparts an old pedagogical lesson, wherein Lenin instructs a Cuban who is placed in the role of a child. In *Ya es hora*, for example, the image of Lenin appears alongside children's scribbles, as if the artist were narrating the evolution of the "national" into the "international."[9]

In another of Marrero's works, cutouts of film reels display a medley of Soviet Bloc cartoons, the emblem of *Sovexportfilm*, and V. Borisov's and Y. Seguei's *Como fui mono* (How I was a monkey). Marrero's paintings allude even more directly than Campins's to a form of colonization. However, his many images that evoke childhood transmit a certain odd lightheartedness within this process. International revolutionary solidarity, like evolution, entails a definitive line of progress; the starting point is the monkey and the endpoint is an author of one's own destiny.

Jorge Luis Marrero, "¡Ya es hora!"

Subjugation of the personal to collective body politics is the concern of Tessio Barba's montage of the Kremlin above the emblem of a Zil automobile (the Soviet or Russian brand driven by the Cuban government) that is engraved on a naked body. In another Barba collage, a militaristic Fidel shouts "Todos somos uno!" (We are all one!) beside a military parade. Like other exhibitors in *Vostok*, Barba also recalls another pleasurable part of the revolution and his own infancy through a reference to the Soviet circus ticket and a school notebook that reads "La educación es el futuro del país" (Education is the future of the country).

In a more acerbic interrogation of militarism and solidarity, Hamlet Lavastida engages an undoubtedly inherited memory with graffiti-like stencils of Castro and Khrushchev on stone, along with "Partido del Pueblo Cubano," and the saying "unidad monolítica de pueblo, ejército y partido" (monolithic unity of the people, military, and party). Lavastida's work is immediately exposed to the elements—as soon as they are elaborated on the streets of Havana, they are erased, as they aim to challenge the dominant semiotic codes. As Rafael Grillo (2007) aptly asserts in his coverage of the exhibit: "Si bien predomina la ironía y hasta cierto cinismo, ambas lecturas están presentes en la obra de los artistas convocados" (If irony and even a certain cynicism predominates, both readings are present in the work of the gathered artists). For Grillo, Hamlet Lavastida represents the most radical of the critical visions with his installation and video projection duet titled *Microfracción o Macrofracción* (Microfraction or macrofraction), a collage of images and press headlines that, not in vain, includes the sentence "Return to Colonialism" among its most disturbing messages.

Microfracción, we remember, was the term used by Raúl and Fidel Castro in 1968 to refer to the supposedly pro-Soviet, treacherous faction led by Aníbal Escalante. By calling his installation and video projection *Microfracción o Macrofracción*, Lavastida challenges the limits of this memorialization of a Soviet past. Can artistic defiance be so explicit as to cast these new street semantics over a "revolutionary tribunal" led by Raúl Castro, who is currently the head of the Cuban state?

While, as previously mentioned, a volume of critiques of the gray period has been compiled and published in Cuba, Lavastida partakes in a distinct semiological encounter with a past in a project that he denotes as UMAP. Lavastida re-signifies the abbreviation for Unidades Militares para la Ayuda de Producción (Military Units to Aid Production), the highly repressive and internationally criticized camps established in 1965 and closed somewhere between 1967 and 1969, to mean "unión militante de agitación y propaganda" (militant union for agitation and propaganda), the street art he creates and soon after erases. He proposes to transform the visual universe of Havana's streets through defamiliarization and recontextualization. In the works of Lavastida, made on walls six meters wide and three meters high and displayed on the *Vostok* blog, expressions of commitment to social and political causes are depleted of their original significance. No longer solely part of a national patrimony, objects such as the Cuban edition of *Manuel básico del miliciano de tropas territoriales* (1981) are now housed among other "found" objects.

The *Vostok* project illustrates the desire to work through multiple narratives of "spare parts" originating in the Soviet Bloc. In a similar fashion, Esteban Insausti's (2005) documentary *Existen* recovers old footage of *noticieros* as an explanation for what he represents to be the "deterritorialized" condition of Cubans and the inevitability of resurfacing and rearranging the recent past. The documentary shows sociological, cultural, and political "transition" by evidencing what happens when a principal element within the symbolic order is extirpated. It is as if *Existen*'s subjects cannot help but speak the "real" and desire to restore the symbolic order.

The documentary's frame is the first Soviet exhibition in Havana that, having taken place one year before the first manned spacecraft Vostok, highlighted the same aspects of Soviet greatness. The point of departure for *Existen* was the Soviet exhibition at the National Museum of Fine Arts in 1960, inaugurated by the Soviet statesman Anastas Mikoyan, who, in a conversation with Norberto Fuentes, characterized it as emblematic of the Soviet's first entrance into revolutionary Cuba (Fuentes 1982, 163–66). *Lunes de revolución*, for example, dedicated issue number forty-six to the exhibition. The "Soviet brothers" some years later, in 1976, covered 15,000 square meters of Havana's capital building with another exhibition, *Logros de la ciencia y la técnica soviética* (Successes of Science and Soviet Technology) and, according to *Bohemia*, displayed "la vida, la técnica y la ciencia socialista" (socialist life, technology, and science).[10]

Existen documents the most recognizably insane people on Havana's streets. Like *Vostok*, which transforms the city's topography by exhibiting artists' memories of their country's relationship to the East, *Existen* foregrounds certain elements of a recent past that still haunt Havana, that are unforgettable within the discourse of the crazies. As a portrait of Havana, the twenty-five-minute film can be seen as a counterpoint to Fernando Pérez's (2003) *Suite Habana* wherein the actors living their lives articulate, through provocative silences, the dreams and disillusionments that compose Havana's revolutionary topography of social habits, dependencies, and aspirations. In *Existen* the camera focuses on a handful of insane men who are recognizable to habaneros precisely because they consistently situate themselves in the same public spaces. However, it is not the city's landscapes that are recalled in *Existen*, but rather it is the faces and words of those who inhabit it. Spectators merely get glimpses of the places that they occupy. Not only do the "characters" speak in *Existen*, their speeches are captioned below in the original Spanish, as if their disoriented argot were in need of translation. Besides having screened at a number of international festivals, *Existen* received the Coral Prize for the best experimental documentary by the Twenty-eighth International Festival of Latin America Cinema in Havana.

Thanks to the use of montage and a velocity of cuts reminiscent of a music video, spectators hardly can distinguish between the past and the recitation of it by the mentally ill in the present. What is especially interesting to me is the extent to which the globalizing present infringes upon how the Soviet past is remembered and represented and what the future consequences of this growing archive may be.

From the beginning of the documentary music, by the Cuban group Nacional Electrónica and the performer X Alfonso, is a central mechanism for exploring arrested sociopolitical development. Nacional Electrónica, composed of a diversity of styles, is influenced by German and British techno, but they make it clear in their publicity that their sound is " 'pobre,' rudimentario, sucio, de factura doméstica" ('poor,' rudimentary, dirty, homemade).[11] The documentary suggests that the insane are enslaved by the empowered discourse of so-called sanity, in line with the postmodern theory of Foucault, Deleuze, and Guattari, among many others. The most critical aspects of *Vostok*, for example, Lavastida's "Return to Colonialism," suggested that the Soviet and Cuban alliance placed Cubans in the roles of apes. In *Existen* the Soviets are the principal culprits of present-day Cuba's having been colonized and hijacked by numerous powers, but the words of the crazies themselves evidence that the United States' blockade and certain Cuban governmental policies are all complicit. It is as if the techno music leads into the very decapitation of a cartoon human figure. The captions below read: "¿Por qué perdemos la cabeza?" (Why do we lose our minds?).[12]

At this point spectators are directed to answers contained within a catalogue of distinct transnational relations. While *Vostok* puts a magnifying glass on the first part of the story, wherein the Cuban youth still has the potential of epitomizing the Soviet ideal, in *Existen* the Soviet ideal is already transformed into Cuban disfigurement. It is just this juxtaposition or expression of imposition that is the focus of many narratives of the last ten years, making the film's initial voiceover particularly illuminating:

Dadas las características ideológicas de la nación expositora debemos declarar
. . . que en manera alguna el hecho que el determinado estado en uso de su
perfecto derecho de ampliar su horizonte económico y comercial exponga ante
otro pueblo, sus productos, . . . no implica necesariamente que tengamos que
incorporarnos a esa ideología.

[Considering the ideological characteristics of the exhibiting nation, we must
declare that in no way does the fact that this state (enacting its given right of
expanding its economic and commercial horizons) exhibits its products for
another country necessarily imply that we have to become part of that ideology.] (Insausti 2005)

The statement leads spectators to wonder about the extent to which that claim
was validated or exceeded. Answers are to be found within the portraits of the
insane inhabitants themselves. The historical indentations of the Soviet legacy
left on individuals born after the 1960s, as were all of the film's "actors," are
immense, even if, or precisely because, as Jorge Luis Acanda (2000) has suggested of Cuba in the 1990s:

Desacralizamos a todos aquellos productos culturales abarcados por ese com-
plejo ideológico que podemos denominar como *lo soviético*, desde el realismo
socialista y los muñequitos rusos hasta la calidad de la tecnología *made in USSR*
y la pretendida omnisapiencia de los líderes del PCUS.

[We demystify all those cultural products covered up by this ideological complex that we can denominate as *the Soviet*, from socialist realism to Russian
cartoons to the quality of the technology *made in USSR* and the so-called
omnisapience of the PCUS leaders.]

The characteristic of *omnisapiencia* or "all-wisdom," most frequently used to
refer to God, is here applied to the Soviets, implying the extent to which
Soviets were an almost invisible force with superhuman power to determine.

How to convey that omnisapience, to re-create that Soviet-penetrated
world is not so obvious.[13] Victor Fowler-Calzada, a Cuban writer and li-
brarian, once conveyed to me that it was as if every discipline was approached
by and every structure of knowledge was known through the Soviet lens. One
of Fowler-Calzada's many anecdotes illustrating this omnisapience was that of
a colleague who, having studied the Soviet Bibliothecal-Bibliographic Classification (the BBK system), was proposing its adoption in Cuba just as the
Berlin Wall came down. Nikolái Kolésnikov's (1983) lengthy study quantifies
the extent of the influence of the Soviet Bloc on education; for example:

Bajo la dirección de los especialistas soviéticos en el período de 1961 a 1979, en los objetivos de la colaboración económica soviético-cubana fueron preparados 39.104 obreros calificados, técnicos y jefes de brigadas.

Una forma similar de preparación de los obreros y especialistas se realiza también en los objetivos de la colaboración económica de Cuba con otros países socialistas.

[Under the direction of the Soviet specialists between 1961 and 1979, adhering to the objectives of the Soviet-Cuban collaboration, 39,104 qualified workers, technicians, and heads of brigades were prepared.

A similar form of preparation of workers and specialists also are realized in the objectives of economic collaboration of Cuba with other socialist countries.] (Kolésnikov's 1983, 145)

My recent investigation of the Indexes of Serial Publications at the José Martí National Library and the short documentaries from the 1960s to the 1980s at the Cuban Film Institute (ICAIC) indicates the extent to which the Soviet Bloc culture, ideologies, sciences, and systems of framing increasingly penetrated the Cuban sphere—from special issues of journals on literature, the arts, and sciences dedicated to several countries in the Soviet Bloc, to different republics of the former Soviet Union, to cinematographic exposés on different realms of culture and society. Within the process of desacralization, it is as if *made in USSR* is deprived of its useful value and is in the process of becoming a relic. All that is derived from the Soviet Bloc is lumped together in Acanda's words and is on its way to becoming a brand.

A cut from the Soviet exhibition in Havana in 1960 introduces one of the madmen of Havana speaking about the Special Period—the period of immense deprivation caused by the disintegration of the Soviet Union, the empire that had sustained Cuba economically and ideologically throughout approximately three decades. As Antonio José Ponte indicates in his positive review of this film:

Y *Existen* podría entenderse como una exploración del nacionalismo en la locura. Y no es casual que *Existen* se inicie con imágenes de la gran exposición soviética celebrada en La Habana en 1960. Aquella exposición, muestrario de logros tecnológicos y científicos, procuraba un acercamiento entre ambas naciones. La voz del noticiero del cual provienen las imágenes advierte que lo expuesto allí no es forzosamente fruto de las virtudes de un régimen político tan alejado del cubano. Y, a juzgar por tal cita, parece tratarse de un caso de alienación. El país está en peligro de quedar fuera de sí, empeñado en destino ajeno, enajenado.

[And *Existen* could be understood as an exploration of nationalism in madness. And it's not a coincidence that *Existen* begins with images of the great Soviet exhibition celebrated in Havana in 1960. That exhibition of technological and scientific successes, sought a rapprochement of both nations. The voice of the newscast from which the images come warns that what is on display there is not forcefully the fruit of the virtues of a political regime that is so remote from the Cuban one. And, judging by that meeting, it seems that a case of alienation is being spoken about. The country is in danger of remaining outside of itself, given into a destiny that is not its own, driven crazy.] (Ponte 2006b)

Ponte's analysis of the degree that the historical events and normalized nationalistic discourse penetrate the psychotics' speech is especially fascinating upon considering a parallel within Ponte's short fiction. For instance, in *Corazón de skitalietz* (Ponte 1998) the condition of severely psychotic alienation needs to be expressed in the idiom of the previous provider—*skitalietz* being a Russian word for wanderer. The story takes the word from Dostoevsky's 1880 address on Pushkin in which he describes Pushkin as having discovered and traced that unlucky skitalietz in his own native soil. Having been abandoned by the Soviet Union, all the characters in Ponte's story live in the continual condition of being orphaned. Through the utilization of Russian to describe the contemporary Cuban situation, "Corazón de skitaliez" re-creates the disinherited nation's link to the Soviet Union.[14]

Within *Existen* an apparently thirty-something-year-old delirious man provides a possible solution for the Special Period, pontificating beside what for most insiders is very recognizable, the cafeteria La Pelota on Twenty-third street—one of the few cafeterias in Havana's El Vedado neighborhood that functions with national currency:

> Buscar todos los requisitos recaudables de dólares, hacer convenios con otros países menos con Rusia . . . hasta que Rusia no sea parte de la Unión Soviética otra vez y depende si nosotros no damos combustible a ellos . . . que sea por préstamo . . . creo que no podemos fallar más.

> [To look for the collectable requisites of dollars, to make agreements with other countries, except with Russia . . . until Russia is not part of the Soviet Union again and it depends if we don't give them fuel . . . if it's a loan . . . I believe that we can't fail again.] (Insausti 2005)

Hardly any effort has to be made to piece together the order of his madness since it keeps intact the collective sphere through the use of the first person plural. The subject is overly invested in the symbolic order, in Cuba's having distanced itself from the newly formed Russia, the effect of which he links to his life almost as intimately as the poor quality of the food at La Pelota.

The strategy of Insausti's critique relies, in part, on Angelica Salvador's brilliant editing, a montage-like technique that blurs distinct temporalities and on a careful selection of official declarations that allow spectators to measure the nation's progress and its discontents. As Ponte states:

> Resulta interesante comprobar cuánto pueblan esos monólogos los asuntos del país. Claro que Insausti, guionista y director, pudo elegir fragmentos que abundaran en lo mismo. Aunque, de ser así, queda en pie la coincidencia de tantos actores en idéntico tema.

> [It's interesting to examine the extent to which subjects related to the country inhabit these monologues. Of course, Insausti, screenwriter and director, could have selected fragments that dealt with the same thing. However, if that were the case, the coincidence of so many actors with identical themes still stands.] (Ponte 2006b)

Ponte's response to *Existen* elicits reflecting upon the documentary's similarities with an issue of the Benetton Group's (2002) *Colors* dedicated to life in mental institutions around the world and especially in Cuba. Both interweave strategies common to cutting edge photography, video, and marketing. *Existen*, financed by the Spanish Embassy in Cuba, the Spanish Agency of International Cooperation (AECI), El Ingenio, the Ludwig Foundation, and the ICAIC, mixes the speed of short music videos with the technique of montage to create a somewhat incongruent sensation. The combination leads to the question of whether the addition of the techno music ends up accommodating outside spectators or creates an uncanny feeling around the limits of the Cuban national sphere.

I could almost repeat what I said about a female representation of one of the insane in *Colors* for those representations in *Existen*: "the changes within her discourse extend to a game whose referents are outside of the mental institution, in the very nation: she confesses, then cries, her voice becomes infantile, she mentions something very powerful (exiting the country, she cries again, she affirms her nationality, and then—within the frame of categories constitutive of adversity—she seduces)" (Loss 2004, 88–89). Another intern within the Camagüey asylum portrayed in *Colors* declares: "Quise suicidarme dos veces, las dos veces con un Sputnik, una navaja rusa. . . . ¿Sabes cuál es mi planeta favorito? Plutón?" (I tried to commit suicide twice, both times with a Sputnik, a Russian knife. . . . You know which is my favorite planet? Pluto) (Benneton Group 2002, 10).[15] Soviet Sputnik razor blades, after Yuri Gagarin's Vostok flight in 1961, were uniquely packaged with CCCP letters and a space ship. The fact that they become an instrument of self-destruction for this insane Cuban intern speaks to the reproduction of social relationships in the form of the appearance of the Soviet. These days such razors are sometimes auctioned on Ebay or on other more specialized Internet sites such as Distribuciones Potemkin that, between 2006 and 2008, sold relics from Communist countries, into which Cuba, itself not yet a relic of Communism, is grouped. This is to say that the world's collectibles have slightly different functions within the Cuban asylum and in Havana's streets. The desacralization about which Acanda speaks betrays the continued mystification around the Soviet Bloc that even enters the delirium.

The rest of the speeches within *Existen* similarly imitate dominant revolutionary discourse. One of the witnesses, the film's subtitles indicate, went mad because he left Cuba. After revealing all the cities he came to know abroad, he states: "Todo eso es mío pero mi Cuba es mi Cuba" (All this is mine but my Cuba is my Cuba). Another madman declares: "Bueno quiero tener que querer a Cuba pero soy verdaderamente español" (Well, I want to have to love Cuba, but I am truly Spanish)—a statement suggestive of pervasive social politics in the 1990s. It alludes to the failure of "ideological affiliations" with "Our Soviet Brothers" and to Cubans' claiming filial ties with Spain and its autonomous regions in the prospect of acquiring dual citizenship and immigrating to Spain. A black man whom we are told went crazy after going to war in Angola delivers one of the most fragmented speeches concluding with "Y el de la bolchevique negra 'bing bang'" (And the one from the black Bolshevik "bing bang"). Finally, another declares: "En la Unión Soviética había una equivalencia del que ganaba poco o menos, ¿no? A nosotros lo que se nos bloqueó eso, porque, aquí todo el mundo iba en Lada a la playa. . . . Aquí 100 pesos eran 100 pesos, ¿era así o no es así?" (In the Soviet Union there was an equivalence of the one who earned a little or less, right? For us, that was blocked, because here everyone went to the beach in Ladas. . . . Here 100 pesos was 100 pesos. Was it like this or isn't it like this?). The interrogatives throughout the discourse suggest his desire to be understood and confirmed. He expresses indecisiveness about positionality—the responsibility for the blockade is left in the air. Is the equality "here" as equal as the Soviets'? In his words, the nation's recent past, which would coincide with his early adulthood, seems far away, but the past still needs the collective sphere to take hold of it and give it meaning.

The last madman on the screen speaks of linking Cuba to other lands:

Ya Cuba tiene un promedio de 375 mil "shopping" . . . hacen faltan unas 400,900 shopping más para que totalmente ya Cuba sea un capital total. ¿Me entiendes? . . . y que uniremos, unamos, esta tierra con otra tierra . . . que sea desconocida esta, unamos esta con la otra . . . y que sea un país grande como el Japón, como Norteamérica.

[Cuba already has an average of 375 thousand shopping centers—it needs about 400,900 more so that totally Cuba can be a total capital now. You understand me? . . . and so that we shall join, let's join, this land with another. . . . this one's unknown, let's join it with another . . . and make it a bigger country like Japan or North America.] (Insausti 2005)

Like the film's beginning, its conclusion suggests that the inability to cope with the capitalist system is a significant factor of the represented schizophrenia. The next statistic is then flashed on screen: "En el año 2000, hubo un 45% más de esquizofrénicos que en 1985." (In the year 2000, there were 45 percent more schizophrenics than in 1985.)

The parenthesis that was the fragmented representation of the insane on the streets is then closed with a sequence about the all-wise Soviet: the Soviet exhibition of 1960 and the discourse of expansion, once explained to Cubans through a discourse of fraternity and solidarity, returns. "Hay que romper fronteras que impiden conocerse y ayudarse a los hombres y . . . Cuba, aislada como isla, alza sus brazos . . . en cordial saludo para todo el que quiera venir a sus lares . . ." (It is necessary to break borders that prevent knowing each other and helping people and . . . Cuba, isolated as an island, extends its arms, in a cordial greeting, so that all who want to come to its lands . . .). In the frame's background, a poster announces "En la URSS crea potente industria de construccion tractors" (In the USSR a potent industry of tractor construction is created). Finally,

Y la admirable organización demostrada en esta exposición nos dicen, del adelanto que goza este pueblo, cosa que celebramos pero que mantenemos intacto nuestro sentido nacionalista informado del humanismo que tiene como filosofía, nuestra formidable revolución.

[And the admirable organization demonstrated in this exhibition talks to us about the advancement enjoyed by these people, a thing that we celebrate, but our informed nationalist sense of humanism that takes our formidable revolution as its philosophy must remain intact.] (Insausti 2005)

As did the Colors issue on madness, Existen inscribes itself within the language of the World Health Organization by presenting a discourse on solidarity and production that concealed inequalities and hid repression. Through its accelerated cuts, techno music, and editing, *Existen* represents a Havana plagued by schizophrenia. The film partakes in a fascinating mirroring: the World Health Organization's statistics evoke a scientific global discourse that is grounded in numbers and categories. In turn, within the film, it is as if they recall the madmen's obsessions with lists and numbers, the key to a nationalistic and heroic discourse. In a particularly transforming Cuban post–Special Period, representing the discourse of the insane in Havana becomes a useful recourse to reveal the experiences that reside within the nation's inhabitants.

The film is crucial for envisioning the collective memory of the presence of the Soviet Bloc within Cuba today; *Existen* conveys the sort of critique, for example, that was initially debated on the Internet over Pavón. A similar debate may appear on a wall momentarily within Havana's streets, but it may not remain so within *Vostok*. These insane inhabitants of Havana are contemporaries of many of the artists whose work is collected in *Vostok* and also of *Existen*'s director, Insausti, who was born in 1971 and, like them, came of age in the 1980s. It is through the recollections and critiques found in these new topographies that we come to understand a generation's affect on a transnational relationship that has been cast aside.

Notes

1. The Bolivarian Alternative for Latin America and the Caribbean (ALBA) is a treaty that was signed by Hugo Chávez and Fidel Castro in 2004 that embraced hemispheric social and economic welfare. Since then, several other Latin American and Caribbean countries have joined the alliance.

2. In February 2007 José Manuel Prieto and I organized the symposium "Cuba-USSR and the post-Soviet Experience" at the University of Connecticut and at the Cervantes Institute (NYC). See http://www.languages.uconn.edu/conferences/archived/cubaussr/ for details. In 2008 a group of intellectuals at the Centro Juan Marinello formed a permanent workshop entitled "Cuba y la URSS. Las revolución bolchevique, historia de la URSS y Cuba. Analisis Crítico Socialista Desde el Siglo XXI" (Cuba and the USSR: The Bolshevik Revolution, History of the USSR and Cuba. Twenty-first century critical socialist analysis). See http://www.cuba-urss.cult.cu/.

3. The phrase "Los hijos de Guillermo Tell" refers to the children of the Cuban Revolution; it was the name of a group exhibition of Cuban artists in 1991 in Caracas, which then traveled to Colombia, as well as the name of a compilation (2006) by the *trovador* Carlos Varela that contains several anthems of the 1990s, including "Guillermo Tell." *Perestroikos* refers to those Cubans, mainly young people, who were influenced by perestroika and glasnost and wished for the same phenomena in Cuba in the late 1980s

and early 1990s. The complex memorialization of the *muñequitos rusos*, sometimes misunderstood to be a form of monolithic nostalgia, has many points of comparison with the phenomenon of Ostalgie. To have a sense of the significance of the cartoons for this generation, see Ernesto René and Jorge E. Betancourt's documentary *9550* or Asori Soto's (2005) *Good bye, Lolek*. Aurora Jácome's blog, www.munequitosrusos.blogspot .com, is most exemplary of this phenomenon. Ernesto René also directed a video for the punk group Porno para Ricardo titled "Los músicos de Bremen" (The Bremen-town musicians) that I analyze in "Vintage Soviets in post-Cold War Cuba" (Loss 2003).

4. It is interesting that Yoani Sánchez, an acclaimed blogger based in Havana, recites by analogy the Soviet past in her call for change. Speaking of Fidel Castro's critique of Cuban youth, Yoani writes on her blog *Generación Y*: "The whole story of the fed-up youngster and the severe 'grandpa' recriminating him transported me to the years of the glasnost, and to the magazine *Novelties from Moscow*, where a young man warned the sixty-somethings that were stopping the changes 'You have all the power. We have all the time.' Of course, we have to color that phrase with the knowledge that even for Yuniesky or Yohandry the years pass, and they have every day less time" (Sánchez 2008, February 15). It is up to the so-called young people, who grew up with Soviet cartoons, caught the tail end of the "great Soviet," and lived through perestroika, to enact change. Relevant to understanding the function of temporal and technological lags, silences, and echoes is the Spanish language entry of the same date (February 15, 2008). Yoani states in her blog, "Las imágenes de la caída del muro de Berlín las vi once años después de los sucesos de aquel octubre de 1989" (I saw the images of the fall of the Berlin Wall eleven years after the events of that October 1989). Clearly, the moment resonates with Yoani's generation, a generation that she describes in the prologue to her blog as: "People like me, with names that start with or contain a 'Y.' Born in Cuba in the '70s and '80s, marked by schools in the countryside, Russian cartoons, illegal emigration and frustration. So I invite, especially, Yanisleidi, Yoandri, Yusimí, Yuniesky and others who carry their 'Y's' to read me and to write to me."

5. Frency Fernández and Victoria M. Gallardo Rubí received the Prize for Curatorship in 2007 from the Centro Provincial de Artes Plásticas y Diseño in Havana. For being an award-winning exhibition, it is somewhat surprising that *Vostok* is one of the few places that acknowledges its own blog (www.proyectovostok.blogspot.com).

6. See Kolésnikov (1983) for a detailed study on penetration of the USSR and the Soviet Bloc within Cuba's educational system.

7. See Campins's images at the blog for the *Vostok* exhibition at http://proyectovo stok.blogspot.com/, October 9, 2007.

8. Campins's work is also critical of other contemporary moments. His painting *Modern Democracy*, which implements a similar orange, red, and white color scheme, depicts some kind of personified hybrid object that, between an airplane, bus, and ship, possesses a sad-looking face. It does not appear as if the Soviets are the most guilty party in this visual narrative. See http://tromponmetabiotico.blogspot.com/2008/10/ alejandro-campins.html.

9. In an e-mail dated July 12, 2010, Marrero told me that those childlike scribbles

above Lenin were done by him around the age of five on a schoolbook about the October Revolution translated into Spanish.

10. It is the same exhibition that has more recently occupied a space of memorialization by the likes of Reina María Rodríguez and Jorge Miralles. Rodríguez's article "Nostalgia" will be published in Loss (forthcoming). Miralles's presentation was read at the symposium "Cuba-USSR and the post-Soviet Experience," on February 6, 2007.

11. "Nacional Electrónica," *Unsigned Entertainment*, July 21, 2008, http://www.unsigned.com/nacionalelectronica.

12. With respect to Insausti's reasoning for making the film, the director stated in an interview with Sandra del Valle Casals: "Sentía la curiosidad de descubrir cómo ve un loco los temas relacionados con la sociedad cubana, qué piensa una persona desequilibrada del bloqueo, de las relaciones Cuba-Estados Unidos; como otra manera de otorgarle también voz y voto a esa gente que uno ve todos los días en las esquinas de este país y de las que uno se ríe, ?cosa que al menos a mí me resulta medio alarmante" (Insausti 2006). I find it curious that the Soviets, the other pole in the Cold War, were not part of the initial conscious logic. We may speculate that the very discourse of the insane inspired the film's frame of the Soviet exhibition of 1960. One of the most fascinating songs of Nacional Electrónica is "¡Llegamos al futuro!" (We make it to the future). In the music video directed by Eduardo Benchoam, a character that looks as if he stepped out of Fritz Lang's *Metropolis* contemplates an issue of the journal *Sputnik* whose cover contains the headline "Gagarin: apertura de la era cósmica" (Gagarin: opening of the cosmic era) and a vinyl of Soviet music. From a little room, typical of today's Havana, the video's protagonist, a cosmonaut, launches into outer space.

13. Rafael Rojas's "Souvenirs de un Caribe soviético" (2008) provides an insightful account of the transformations between the 1960s and 1970s with regard to what and how Cubans read and interpreted Soviet literature and philosophical thought.

14. This is the thesis of Loss (2009).

15. It is possible to see some of the images from this issue minus the written text at the website for *Colors* magazine, www.colorsmagazine.com/issues/47.

11

Touring Havana in the Work of Ronaldo Menéndez

LAURA REDRUELLO

Translated by Robert Nasatir

The term *city* brings to mind other expressions like *urbs*, polis, and civitas from ancient Greek and Roman civilizations. For the great philosophers of Athens and Rome, the city represented the peak of cultural progress. Aristotle affirms in the first book of the *Politics* that the city was created principally to make mankind happy and truly fulfilled. While man began his development in the world of the family, he could only achieve maturity in the city. Cicero reasoned along similar lines. For the great orator, men left behind barbarity as they discovered the art of community life and created the first cities in which they learned civilization and cultivated the liberal arts. For both philosophers, man found a true sense of grandeur in the civitas or city. As much for the Greeks as for the Romans, the idea of the city brought a collective conscious-ness of unity in which particular interests were superseded by those of the community; in essence, it was viewed as a common project in which there existed a pact of mutual assistance. This consciousness encouraged them to develop a sense of belonging, which in turn encouraged them to improve their living conditions and, thus, helped them to reach a higher level of develop-ment. The ultimate goal of the polis was not just the survival of towns; rather, the polis also reflected the goals of human coexistence and human perfection. That is, the polis was conceived as a kind of community and, as any community, was inherently constituted in order to achieve some good (Orozco Orozco 2003).

Today, the city is conceived as a symbol. It references a collective representation that evokes the aspirations or the anxieties of man, aspirations and anxieties that are constantly changing and evolving. Along those lines, several contemporary Cuban writers have varied understandings of the polis. This chapter explores the work of one such author, Ronaldo Menéndez, and demonstrates how in his narratives the city moves away from the noble ideal it represented in its genesis and is transformed into a symbol of the decadence of man, finally becoming a space of human degradation. I move away from the Aristotelian conception of the city as a political community, and instead I emphasize its relational character as a model of intersubjective action constructed upon effects: the city as a community of ends and values, and the incontestable hope of loyalty and of reciprocity (González 1988, 13). Beginning with this understanding, I consider how in Menéndez's works the degradation of the city as the ideal space for communal living brings with it the end of the community as an example of the ideal type of social action.

I propose an itinerary through three Havanas and three types of communities represented in the works of this author. Each one appears in a different decade. The Havana of Menéndez's first stories is the city at the end of the 1980s, a polis that provides adequate space for debate, dialogue, and polemics. Nonetheless, this image of the city from which political ruptures are proposed will disappear in a posterior narrative, stepping aside for another kind of polis, the mercantile city of the 1990s, where the U.S. dollar becomes the only motivating force for the citizenry. The mercantile Havana also cannot endure and disappears, leaving behind Menéndez's last Havana and the last stop on this urban walking tour: the non-city, where the community is dehumanized, and its habitat approximates a Hobbesian state of nature rather than an Aristotelian polis.[1]

This tour begins with an exploration of the first Havana—impugning and nonconformist—clearly reflected in two of Menéndez's stories: "Tocata y fuga en cuatro movimientos y tres reposos" (Tocata and fugue in four movements and three reposes) and "La culpa" (guilt), both included in the book *Alguien se va lamiendo todo* (Someone goes around licking everything) by Ronaldo Menéndez and Ricardo Arrieta (1997a; 1997b). The book takes place in Havana during the 1980s. During those years, against the backdrop of the rectification process or "proceso de rectificación de errores," there arose in Cuba new artistic creations in response to the immobility of institutions that were either unable or uninterested in recognizing a new generation. They were years in which the visual arts boldly transformed into one of the most potent

examples of Cuban culture. There was an atmosphere of creativity, of searching, of polemics that blossomed into a regenerative movement headed by
young painters (Mosquera 2002, 153). Through this provocation, a new generation of artists tried to disrupt the established powers, bringing about nearly
daily actions in the street that emphasized questions relating to the revolution.
These groups based their approach on the need to remove the visual arts from
the galleries and take them to the streets. With this strategy in mind, they
covered walls and held performances in parks and plazas—ignoring authorities and institutions—with the intention of stimulating aesthetic, political,
and social reflection in the city community (Olivares 2002, 243).

In the first stories I analyze, the protagonists are youths who participate in
visual arts exhibitions, underscoring the interaction that new writers and visual artists maintained at the end of the 1980s. The action develops in a park in
Havana that acts as a zone of social construction where they negotiate identities
and power relations. One should note that in both stories it is not the city in
total that assumes the role of a questioning space; rather, this action remains
limited to determined public zones where youths gather periodically. The
parks, streets, or plazas become counterdiscursive spaces through iconoclastic
actions, out of tune with a system accustomed to order and organization.

"Tocata y fuga en cuatro movimientos y tres reposos" takes place in a park
at G and Twenty-third, where an art event is happening, brought about—we
are able to guess—by the group Arte y Derecho.[2] The protagonist of the story,
a young writer, walks through the exhibit that includes various works that will
be removed by the police at the end of the story. In the first installation, he
reads a sign that says, "reviva la revo" (revive the revo[lution]).[3] To the side he
sees a box with the inscription: "Este cuadro no ha podido concluirse por
problemas con los materiales, problemas con el transporte, problemas ad-
ministrativos, problemas del director, problemas de la secretaria del director,
etcétera, esperamos su contribución" (This work could not be finished due to
problems with materials, problems with transportation, administrative problems, the director's problems, the director's secretary's problems, etcetera, we
await your contribution) (Menéndez and Arrieta 1997b, 86). The second work
is a tedious drawing of Che Guevara that recalls his sphinx-like image on the
three peso note. High above, in red letters, reads: "justo a tu gusto" (just as
you like) (1997b, 86). The last work is a giant poster that states—also in red
letters—"amar al prójimo con más disciplina y calidad" (love your fellow man
with more discipline and quality) (1997b, 85) and below is the outline of a
machine gun like those used in military preparation classes.

The visual arts revolve completely around the national reality, although without relying on images of palm tree laden landscapes, peasants in typical sombreros, or exuberant mulatas. The artists are able to bring to the public space distorted symbols and icons of the revolution (Fornet 2007b, 100). The extinction of faith is demonstrated through humor. This irreverence represents the erosion and the lack of identification of a new group of social actors who no longer recognize themselves in the collective values and national interests (Bobes 2000, 196). Through the adulteration and ridicule of these symbols, the artists represent their disenchantment and question the revolutionary project with the political intention of reforming it. The city yields part of its space to critique and controversy and, above all, to breaking the homogenizing discourse of the revolution. If officially the city had been proposed as an exhibition space for patriotic busts and monuments that held up heroes as quasi-religious images, now a new generation seems to be coming forward in order to break the sacred national history. They represent a threat to the symbolic and moral order of the city on behalf of new cultural groups that are trying to influence the institutional order (Bobes 2000, 193). The park at G and Twenty-third acts as an island refuge that houses a counterdiscourse from which obsolete and sadly laughable attitudes and conceptions are satirized (Fornet 2007b, 100). The park is a public space where informal groups gather and, by acting in the cultural sphere, question the established system of values. Parks and plazas become the discursive settings in which these communicative codes are reexamined, the spaces where artists affirm an autonomous sensibility and reject totalitarian discourses, replacing them instead with an individual and inquisitive discourse (Bobes 2000, 197).

The appearance of these groups in the city seems to confirm the urgency of these first autonomous collective actions within the revolutionary society. It is a generation of rupture. The word, the art, the ideological burden are all there in search of change and showing a conflict of powers. The critique of cultural policy constitutes for them the first step in rejecting a symbolic universe with which they do not identify. This spirit of social criticism is what gives the collective an identity distinct from that of the urban masses:

> La cosa está bastante seria. Hay una pila de policías por todo el parque preguntando cosas sobre los montajes y pidiendo carnés de identidad a diestra y siniestra. El Peca les enseñó la autorización de U. J. C. provincial para la acción plástica, pero aun así no se están quietos. Algunos no intervienen en las pesquisas y transmiten por los walkies-talkies el contenido de los carteles. Es de lo más divertido. Carlos está discutiendo con otros dos que quieren desmontar los trabajos diciendo que eso es una payasada que no tiene nada de arte.

[The thing is pretty serious. There is a group of police officers going through the park asking questions about the works and wanting to see identification cards left and right. Peca showed his authorization for the show from the local Union of Young Communists but that did not satisfy them. Some police officers did not participate in the questioning and just described the posters into their walkie-talkies. It is very amusing. Carlos is discussing with two others who want to take down the works saying this is just foolishness that has nothing to do with art.] (Menéndez and Arrieta 1997b, 60)

In the story, the permission provided by the Union of Young Communists shows that this generation does not propose open confrontation with the institutions but rather collaboration, albeit under new conditions. In the same way that these spaces are within the city, the youths act within the system in order to establish a redefinition of the relation between individuals and the state, insisting upon their right to present their own proposal.

A similar scene occurs in the story "La culpa" (Menéndez and Arrieta 1997a). A few steps from the street, youths prepare "los carteles, el signo de la vida" (posters, the sign of life) (1997a, 99) while a new group of visual artists leaves for the Plaza del Canto. We never learn if the plaza really exists or if it is the same place where they are preparing the exhibit and only imagined as an open space. The Plaza del Canto is idyllic, nearly utopian, a place where citizens can shout their ideas freely without any sense of guilt. The street and the plaza are once again presented as spaces of exigency where, away from the hegemonic discourse, artists demonstrate their nonconformity in the public arena, appealing to the responses of occasional, unprepared spectators:

Que vas a poder imaginarte si nos hemos pasado la tarde dando vueltas en el cuarto para que las ideas entren por la ventana y revoloteen sobre la mesa de trabajo y se estrellen en mil letras rojas, que digan lo más aproximado a nuestra ansiedad, a esto de la lucha fatal por no querernos morder las uñas.

[You can imagine if we spent the afternoon turning around in a room waiting for ideas to come in through the window and whirl around on top of the work table, and smash into a thousand red letters, so they come closest to speaking our anxiety; that is what becomes of the fatal struggle from not wanting to break our nails.] (1997a, 99)

The youths consider the city to be the best environment from which to extract the materials they need for their works; they must take art to the streets, they shout. It is a spontaneous movement, without organization or even a program that has been connected with the syndicates, the assemblies, the student movement, or the press. The street transforms into the most daring tribune, a place to propose their own revolution:

> Dos pasos afuera está la calle y nosotros en ella dando saltos, *jump*, viva la libertad, se rompen las normas, la gente nos sigue como estaba previsto: primero curiosean, nos miran extraño, llego, se asombran cuando yo o Mastrapa o cualquiera le pasa una pancarta y se une a la causa empuñando una apología a la soberbia, una protesta a plena voz. . . . Esto es real, estamos haciendo la revolución, la revolución de los plásticos, es nuestra adaptación conceptual, una forma de agarrarnos.

> [The street is two steps outside and we are there, jumping, *jump*, long live liberty, break the rules, the people follow us like something they anticipated: first they are curious, look us over strangely, I arrive, they are frightened when I or Mastrapa or anyone hands them a placard and they join the cause grasping and apologizing proudly, protesting loudly. . . . This is real, we are making a revolution, a revolution of artists, it is our conceptual adaptation, a way of grabbing hold of each other.] (1997a, 102)

Again, the city is revealed as a space of negotiation, of representations in which the discrepancies of a sector of society, that is, of the disenchanted generation, are made manifest. It is a dynamic space that houses systems of differentiation, zones of visibility and of special exclusion, as well as conflict and tools of coercion and oppression. Most of all, it provides the opportunity of representation for subgroups that reflect the collective with their particular identities. Menéndez situates the group identity within the political community of the polis amidst the rise of a critical and polemic conscience characteristic of young artists at the end of the 1980s, artists who tried to establish connections with similar groups and extend their actions far beyond the artistic sphere (Bobes 2000, 203):

> En la Plaza del Canto no se oye una voz. O sí, hay cientos de voces desordenadas, gente terca que dice lo suyo sin remordimientos, como en una sesión pentecostal, o del espiritismo más refinado, o como en una revolución porque así le llamamos y creemos en ella.

> [In the Plaza del Canto you do not hear a voice. Or, yes, there are hundreds of voices mixed-up, stubborn people who say their piece without remorse, like a Pentecostal service or one by more refined spiritualists, or like in a revolution because that is how we call it and how we believe in it.] (Menéndez and Arrieta 1997a, 103)

Hundreds of "voces desordenadas" produce a rupture that fractures the unity of the revolutionary city. Each artistic creation has its own vision, every citizen has a voice, and each reader has his own criterion. Confrontation implies an advance; dialogue implies a necessity. One must startle the passivity of the community and its collective, monopolitical identity. The written word, or the visual artistic expression, becomes an arm capable of breaking the homogeneous discursiveness of the citizens. From the Plaza del Canto, artists ask questions and seek answers. It is a space for expression where a part of the community presents itself as an object of transformation seeking involvement in the public problems of the country, intending to reformulate the national project.

Nonetheless, alluding to the hard reality experienced at the beginning of the 1990s, Cecilia Bobes explains that at the beginning of the Special Period the majority of intellectuals and artists who headed the visual arts movement left Cuba. The lack of paper, painting materials, and other resources that caused the economic crisis were the impetus for their departure and the perfect excuse for the state to close down publications and galleries, and to prohibit the majority of performances (Bobes 2000, 212).

In Ronaldo Menéndez's later stories, situated well into the 1990s, the city also closes those places of representation associated with subaltern groups, transforming them into a mercantile space where the U.S. dollar and tourism mark the new rhythm of the polis. Dollarization and the need to survive economically in a reality where everything is in short supply, thanks to the collapse of European socialism and the end of the Soviet subsidy, act as the motivator in this decade. Money becomes the new protagonist of stories and novels; that is, getting or spending money becomes a vital project for Menéndez's characters (Whitfield 2003, 32).

The impulse to conquer public spaces and use them to explore new ideas and attitudes is substituted with another kind of search, the search for the dollar, where a generation of youths now demonstrates calculating behaviors and a desperate interest in economic survival, placing personal problems well ahead of those of the country. Honesty and idealism cease to be values. Prestige and social status are associated with privileged material consumption to such an extent that people are evaluated based upon their access to items: the most celebrated person is the one who gets the goods, without regard as to how (Bobes 2000, 242).

The Havana presented in the story "Una ciudad, un pájaro, una guagua" (One city, one bird, one bus) (Menéndez 1999), included in the book *El derecho al pataleo de los ahorcados* (The right to kick of the hanged), echoes this development. In Menéndez's story, the protagonist Humberto Travieso, a homosexual, intellectual, and Cuban émigré, returns to Havana for fifteen days in August of 1994. Travieso knows that he is dying of AIDS. On this trip, through an old friend, Humberto meets an unnamed youth enrolled in the Escuela Superior de Arte who agrees to help him buy some paintings by the Cuban painter Tomás Sánchez, and, at the same time, the unnamed youth acts as a guide for Humberto's reencounter with the city.

The thread of the story lies between Humberto, anxiously buying art in an effort to take back a small piece of Havana as a remembrance, and the narrator-guide and his colleagues who intend to sell him the paintings at any cost, clandestinely, in a city full of young artists. The guide helps his client, giving him entrée to a group of visual artists in Havana, now converted into a "mundo feroz y maravilloso, onírico, sicodélico, de mercantilismo incipiente, sórdido, bohemio y lúcido" (ferocious and marvelous world, dreamlike, psychedelic, of incipient mercantilism, sordid, bohemian, and lucid) (Menéndez 1999, 45). All see dollar signs on the visitor: "el dinero verde susurrando su presencia al ser contado de mano en mano" (the green money announcing his presence, ready to be counted from hand to hand) (1999, 45). The artists appear as hunters of tourists, of their dollars, and, finally, of Humberto. Attending an exposition with a new arrival was "como cargar con la lámpara de Aladino y exhibirla en el momento preciso" (like carrying Aladin's lamp and revealing it at the perfect moment), that is, "cada cual en su rincón de la ciudad deseaba tener un extranjero" (everybody in his corner of the city wanted to have a foreigner of his own) (1999, 50). The city's market economy alters the social relations produced in the polis. The young artists identify themselves with individual projects and material interests. This new mercantile city is characterized by the mediated character of sociability, the indirect nature of social relations, that is, social relations do not work effectively when they are direct; rather, relations succeed through mercantile mediation, exchanging products from diverse individuals, something the reader sees not only in the relationship between Humberto and his guide but also in the relationship between the guide and the other artists. This produces a way of relating and of socializing founded on mercantile logic that leads to a deepening fetishization, to the dominion of market and money, altogether contrary to the socialist sociability that presupposes an immediate, personal, and direct relation between citizens.

Each character's understanding is manipulated by self-interest and the need for survival. Competitiveness and individual success have destroyed the capacity for solidarity among citizens. Idealism has been substituted with picaresque commerce; slogans have been replaced with green money. The parks and streets, those urban islands from which artists once questioned the revolutionary project with exhibitions and performances, are now replaced by galleries and residences understood as spaces of pure commercialization, designed to attract curators and foreign visitors. Words are no longer exhibited openly on posters; paintings return to interior spaces. Art seeks a new interlocutor, one who is not a local citizen but, rather, a buyer. More than just economic incentives, one feels a sense of business in the community, competence and pride in knowledge of the products or services for sale. The polis becomes the stage where products are exhibited, a space for buying and selling, where everything is commercialized and where even Havana has a calculable worth. In other words, the city is just one more product to offer to visitors (Durán 2006, 79):

> Estaba muy claro: tenía que venderle La Habana: ciudad emblemática y añorada, con sus barrios, sus olores, sus peligros y tentaciones, sus encantos y desencantos. Su gente. O sea, todas las ciudades que hay en una, y que el artista paciente en el sanatorio de la ciudad real siempre está dispuesto a vender a bajo precio, sin otra alternativa.

> [It was very clear: he had to sell him Havana: emblematic and mourned city, with her barrios, her smells, her dangers and temptations, her spells and disenchantments. Her people. That is, all cities in one, which the patient artist in the city sanatorium is always willing to sell at a good price, without alternative.] (Menéndez 1999, 51)

Before, in Menéndez's first stories, we observed how the parks or plazas were alternative zones used to rupture the polis as a representative space of homogeneous values; now, the city unifies around the idea of exhibiting itself before foreigners. Humberto's guided visits to galleries coincide with his walks through Havana, a city that remains idealized in the mind of the stranger. Faced with Humberto's magical "Habana Inventada" (Invented Havana), which Emma Álvarez-Tabío Albo (2000, 317) describes as, "un sentimiento de congelación temporal y un inquietante anacronismo, recibe a quien se acerca a la huella de sus antiguas murallas" (a sense of being frozen in time and disquieting anachronism that receives anyone who approaches the remnants of her ancient walls), the story presents another Havana, that of the guide and the rest of the artists who accompany Humberto on his itinerary: "la Habana del derrumbe y el churre" (the collapsing, filthy Havana), which slowly merges with the magnified polis of the visitor.

At first Humberto rejects the decadence and disenchantment, confident in his own understanding of the city and its symbolic representations. This vision collides with that of the other characters in the story, all disillusioned artists, emissaries, and salespersons with their own experiences. Julián, one of the painters who accompany and help Humberto for a few hours, transforms the urban degradation of Havana into a money making proposition. In addition to its historic importance, the city reveals itself to Humberto as a repository of all that is forbidden, replete with hustlers who hang out around the Malecón "para cambiar billetes verdes por azules y mercancía anónima" (to change green bills for blue ones and anonymous commerce) (Menéndez 1999, 57). Little by little Humberto, practically unaware, incorporates the margins into his center and ends up enjoying a certain pleasure of marginality at the port "donde el ébano se mezcla con el ébano y la sombra con la sombra" (where ebony mixes with ebony and shadow with shadow) (1999, 57). Julián assures Humberto that his decadent Havana and Humberto's magical one unite, forming a whole that fascinates the foreigner.

In the same way that Humberto integrates the margins into his idyllic image of the city, the young painters incorporate the center into their works. They incorporate a necessary city magnified by the past into their disenchanted Havana, a city that is imaginary for them but real in terms of its commercial value:

> Ellos también sufren y pintan La Habana, incluso la inexistente, esa que levantaron en la República y que por falta de mantenimiento se ha ido desmoronando.

> [They also suffer and paint Havana, including the nonexistent city that they built up in the Republic and, from lack of maintenance, has fallen into disrepair.] (Menéndez 1999, 49)

The center and the margin engage in dialogue not only in painting but also in the exhibition spaces. The official galleries mark the starting point of the transactions that conclude in the decrepit tenements where the painters live. The center and the periphery collaborate in a dialogue, alternating the state model of distribution with the reality of economic necessity. Prior state-approved circuits of distribution, that is, museums and galleries, are now replaced by individual and private spaces like homes and tenements. The city becomes the perfect space for the development of a considerable black market:

> Cada vez que Julián consigue un galerista, comprador de plástica o alguien por el estilo, lo primero que hace es llevar al tipo a su aposento. El comprador admira las obras de Julián y al mismo tiempo contempla extasiado la miseria

que pulula en derredor como si se tratara de la sala autentica de una Bienal del Tercer Mundo; entonces pone cara de filántropo primer mundista (algo así como una virgen de Murillo) y decide comprar generosamente dos o tres obras muy por debajo de su precio justo.

[Every time Julián gets a gallery owner, art buyer, or someone stylish, the first thing he does is take him to his residence. The buyer admires Julián's works and at the same time ecstatically contemplates the misery all around him as if it were the actual room of a Third World Bienal; then he turns a philanthropic first world face (not unlike a virgin by Murillo) and generously decides to buy two or three paintings for far less than their actual worth.] (Menéndez 1999, 63)

The artist enters the process, taking on roles similar to those of the state in prior years: transportation, reproduction, storage, exhibition, or publicity. Humberto visits both official galleries and tenements. Julián and the unnamed narrator are aware that every space has its rules, and they know how to operate and distinguish perfectly what functions in one and what functions in the other, adapting their actions to what is permitted and approved in each. The legal and recognized logic mixes with the marginal and subterranean, and, while they remain distinct, they are simultaneous; both have the same range and can operate in the same public light (Bobes 2000, 227).

The story reorders the urban symbolism of the city where center and periphery unite to show a contemporary problem, that is, the goal of the utopian project has been replaced with the pragmatism of the dollar. Menéndez characterizes the community as mercantile, depoliticized, and fully competent. Unmoved by the ideal of constructing a better future for all, only material interests motivate the citizens. In their everyday reality individuals act based on their needs. The abandoned utopia has led to the proliferation of individualism, calculated actions, a focus on material well-being, and a preference for personal solutions to countrywide problems.

The dollar, and each person's ability to get it, underscores the inequality among citizens. Upon his return to the tenement, the full bags the guide carries—with the label Tiendas Cemex—separate and distinguish him from his neighbors and identify him as successful: the bags are full of products acquired after receiving his commission for selling the paintings. Material interest extends far beyond the artistic locales, invading the rest of the city. The guide identifies with the rest of the city community that "desde cada ventana, puerta, balcón interior, ángulo opaco, baño común o hueco, le caen como sanguijuelas" (from every window, door, interior balcony, dark corner, common bath or hole, fall to him like leeches) (Menéndez 1999, 55), and the guide is constantly afraid of competition, "el cubano es el lobo del cubano" (the Cuban is a wolf to other Cubans), he explains to Humberto (1999, 58). The central principle that configures the societal order is formed by mercantile logic. Politics, formerly the principal mechanism of integration and incorporation in society, no longer has any value or significance for this new citizenry. Humberto criticizes the government and thinks that any past time was better. At one point, Humberto and the guide encounter another citizen, also returning in August of 1994, who causes a police incident; the guide moves away, refusing to participate or offer an opinion. The guide keeps quiet. When it comes to political options, he chooses not to participate. Art returns to interior spaces, no longer a political arm but, rather, a means of material exchange.

The mercantile city, the city of the dollar and material competition, disappears completely, leaving barbarism in its wake in Menéndez's novel *Las bestias* (The beasts) (2006). Society has devolved into the Hobbesian state of nature where lives are solitary and miserable, closer to the condition of solitary beasts than of men. In *Las bestias* Menéndez explores the darkest corners of a few characters living permanently on the edge of disenchantment in a city that—despite constant winks to the reader that it is Havana, including blackouts and shortages—is never identified. It is a city with no history, no myths, no hope, and no dollars; a city that has lost its own name, where animal instinct seems to have replaced any trace of humanity.

In the tropical and unnamable city that provides the stage for this novel, there is no life, only survival, and it is that patent and sharp reality that sets the tone for the entire story. The protagonist of *Las bestias*, Claudio Cañizares, is a mediocre teacher at the Instituto who divides his time between the thesis he is preparing on symbolic representations of darkness and raising a pig in the bathtub of his house in order to combat the food shortage afflicting his country. Everything goes perfectly in his dull life until he overhears a telephone conversation between two people discussing their plans to kill him.

His presumed assassins are Bill and Jack or, as they are also identified, Benito Agramonte and Julio Miguel de Céspedes. Both are members of a secret society charged with eliminating carriers of the AIDS virus, including the teacher. However, it is Claudio Cañizares, helped by a writer and an arms dealer, who takes revenge against his attackers, incorporating the magnificent pig that waits in a deteriorated bathroom for his owner to feed him amid desperate howls.

Menéndez presents a city in the process of dehumanization where there is no living, only survival; a degraded life, lacking perspective and supposed ethics, moved not by sentiments but by needs of the flesh. The writer distances himself even farther from the concept of the city as a place that develops the fullness of human life and moves closer to the concept of the state of nature, a state of confrontation and abuse, with the absence of justice, without morality, where force is the only valid argument. It is, quite simply, an animal community.

Ronaldo Menéndez's novel describes a city torn apart, which the author compares to Beirut, "con calles orinadas y parques abolidos" (with streets full of urine and broken parks) and with a great port where "se despedazan barcos que ya no navegan" (they take apart boats that no longer sail) (Menéndez 2006, 82). The desolation reaches everything that exists, including the citizenry. It is a city on the verge of becoming a non-city or un-city or perhaps a city on the edge of death, where streets are no longer places for encounters, where groups gather, or where people find freedom and join a community. The streets of *Las bestias* shelter people who "amanece cansada" (awake tired), who wander like automatons without allowing themselves to see, transforming avenues into mute spaces, empty stages where one only glimpses "perros sin amos" (dogs without masters). The city feels static, as if the inexorable succession of time all around had never taken place. This void eclipses the history and memory of the city. The characters of *Las bestias* move and *andan* (walk) the city. Nonetheless, they never allude to the architecture or to the monuments and key spaces in the history of the city. Rather, they belong to a city with neither a past nor history. Urban memory—understood as the sum of spaces, buildings, and experiences and as the only tool that constructs the identity of a city—disappears, revealing a polis in the process of deconstruction that goes on diluting and disappearing in time. The city fades, changing into a non-place or, as one of the characters says, "en una oscura mancha en un luminoso día" (a dark spot on a bright day) (2006, 18).

In the city marked by desolation, silence becomes a fundamental element that takes control of both public and private spaces. Silence, not the lack of noise but, rather, as Cicero ("abstention from speaking") or Livy ("quietness, restfulness") interpreted it (Basulto 1974, 888). The two understandings could be applied to the city that Menéndez describes, a polis that begins each day with pig squeals from the bathtubs of houses. The animal noise, empty and hollow but also strident, is identified with the speech of the inhabitants, equally hollow and trivial. The absence of reflection, of questions and answers, defines the simple, basic dialogue between all the characters.

The inhabitants of *Las bestias* do not argue about ideas, values, or perceptions. Claudio lives a routine limited to the daily search for food for the pig he is raising. He barely relates or interacts with his companions. He has never asked himself why he lives the life he lives. The reasoning behind Claudio's marked racial prejudices remains unexplored. Claudio rejects everything black, but at no time does he ponder causes or ideas or, at the very least, share his phobia. Claudio "odia en silencio" (hates in silence) (Menéndez 2006, 47). In the same way, "odia a su país y a su barrio sin necesidad de establecer una causa tangible" (he hates his country and his barrio without the need for a tangible cause) (2006, 16). The animallike absence of reflection, of deliberation, and of reasonable options describes the personalities of all the characters. In the novel, José the neighborhood veterinarian personifies discursive control when he is given the responsibility of cutting the vocal cords of the pigs in order to achieve the silence the neighborhood desires. During the final confrontation between Claudio and one of the members of the secret society, José also manipulates Bill's vocal cords at the insistence of the teacher, as if Bill, too, were a pig. Like a censor, burdened with the instruments of his work, the physical operation becomes a means of dominating the discourse. José, by manipulating Bill's vocal cords, destroys language, leaving behind only enough volume for Bill to say what Claudio wants to hear. The rest is inaudible. Argument is a bother. Claudio does not argue, nor does he want to listen. The operation reduces Bill to the level of prelinguistic expression. The maimed cords can only produce wails and stammers.

Silence also controls written space. The most important is never mentioned: no one says *Cuba*. The narrator does not name a city. Is it Havana? When does the action take place? The names of many streets, hotels, and plazas are missing. And, most of all, politics are missing. *La palabra* (the word), too, is missing, that which aspired to take control of the streets in the first stories of Ronaldo Menéndez.

Since antiquity, the city has been considered the space of the word. Without it, according to Hobbes, there would have been as many republics, societies, or contracts among man as among lions, bears, or wolves (Le Bras-Chopard 2003, 91). Arendt also argues that to be political, to live in a polis, means that everything is communicated by means of words and persuasion and not by force and violence (Le Bras-Chopard 2003, 68). It is precisely force and violence that substitute for words and politics in *Las bestias*. Violence is the prepolitical act of self-liberation from the tensions of life. Access to the political is access to humanity and the nonpolitical insists on the animal character of noncitizens. Neither Claudio nor the rest of the characters proffer any reasons to obey or revolt. There is neither participation nor dilemma.

Apathy, desperation, and, perhaps, fear forces them to lose themselves as objects of transformation, leaving them with their preoccupations that are limited to distraction, recreation, distension, lust, and food.

In *Las bestias* initiatives proliferate in legitimate defense of a state of rights. All of the characters take justice into their own hands. All kill and, at times, fear for their lives. Claudio, at the moment he discovers the assassination plot, decides to buy a gun and resolve the threat by personally eliminating his would-be executioners. Jack and Bill liquidate any suspected AIDS carrier. One way or another, everyone tries to protect and get justice for himself. Man in the state of nature behaves like a wolf toward others. Beatriz Sarlo affirms that community attachments normally weaken when citizens cease to turn to the state for the security that, by definition, it is supposed to guarantee:

En la narración hobbesiana, los hombres entregan una parte de su soberanía, de su derecho natural, precisamente para evitar la guerra de todos contra todos. El Príncipe garantiza la paz; en esa garantía y en la entrega contractual que la hace posible, los hombres evitan la guerra de todos contra todos, la desconfianza extrema que origina violencia y pueden vivir como miembros de un cuerpo social.

[In the Hobbesian narration, men hand over a part of their independence, their natural right, to avoid a war where everyone is against each other. The Prince guarantees peace; through this guarantee, and the contractual exchange that makes it possible, men avoid all out war, the extreme distrust that generates violence, and are able to live as members of a social body.] (Sarlo 2002, 208)

The civil state appeals to humanity for the simple reason that it guarantees life, given that the first condition of being a human being is not being a cadaver.

Without any physical or moral stops, Claudio (who after eliminating Jack recognizes that he does not "tener ningún problema con eso" [have any problem with that]), the same as Bill or Jack, has the potential to kill his fellow men and the perpetual fear of being killed himself. None of the victims or potential victims in *Las bestias* turns to the law in search of security, yet again suggesting the state of nature where man is outside the law and where man lives a solitary, needy, arduous, animal, and brief life (Sarlo 2002, 209). The final pursuit between Bill and Claudio that transpires through the streets of the city alludes to the law of the jungle where two animals of different species never run together except when one pursues the other:

Mientras las babosas humanas arrastraban su anatomía blanca hacia la casa del Gordo, el mandril joven había retomado el hilote de su persecución y esta vez si estaba convencido de que el lince humano no lo sabía.

[While the human slugs dragged their white anatomy toward the Fat One's house, the young mandrill had taken back the thread of his pursuit and this time, if he was convinced by the human linx, he did not know it.] (Menéndez 2006, 77)

The pursuit ends when one of the two *presas* (preys) is left trapped in the claws of the other. It is perhaps at this point in the novel when the refined barbarian, the illustrious beast, demonstrates what kind of animal resides within him. A single-minded fury leads Claudio to lock Bill up with the pig. Claudio's irrational appetite has a bestial character. Upon condemning Bill to share the same space as the pig, he achieves the depersonalization of the individual of a species that Claudio considers inferior. Claudio locks Bill up with the pig, feeds him like the pig, and confronts him in a fight between equals. The closer Cañizares gets to achieving his objective, the deeper his immersion into vengeful and savage paranoia. Claudio, Bill, and the pig (that devours everything that is not his own body) end up in the same terrain of barbarity and bestiality, intermediate categories between human and animal in *Las bestias*, whose impulsiveness, irritability, absence of justice, and spirit provoke a mutation that integrates them into the complex animalistic landscape that constitutes the city community: mandrills, rhinoceros, gorillas, tyrannosaurus rexes crossed with chameleons, wolves masked as lynxes, human ticks, tapeworms, human lynxes, pavazos, human mandrills, magisterial ticks, bears, hogs, dead cows, deer, or swarms of insects are all names used to classify characters in this urban jungle. The line between man and animal is erased, dehumanizing the city to the point of changing it to an inhospitable space where racial conflicts are unavoidable and violence becomes the only possible form of interrelation in critical situations.

Las bestias is a story about the kind of animals humans can become given specific economic, social, and political circumstances. Indeed, while order does follow the state of nature, order can also descend into chaos, into an orgy of violence and humanity. *Las bestias* demonstrates a return to the beginning of a community where the deep personal dissatisfaction of its citizens leads the inhabitants to devour each other.

Ronaldo Menéndez's final city loses all the characteristics that have defined the polis since antiquity as the peak of civilization and cultural progress, converting it into a space where life once again becomes solitary, crude, brutal, and brief; where violence defines human relations, and concepts of virtue and justice no longer exist. It is a city that, slipping farther and farther away from its original conception, eventually comes to lose its very name. Despite allusions to Mesas Redondas, to protagonists drinking Patricruzado rum and walking down Obispo Street, to trafficking in the Jesús María neighborhood and smoking Popular cigarettes in El Gato Tuerto, the city is never identified as Havana. Our urban walking tour through the narrative of Ronaldo Menéndez ends in a city obscured and erased to the point of losing the language that names it. By losing its very name, the city loses itself, its original essence as the polis, and is feared lost forever.

The revolutionary project is also lost in much the same way; no one ever names the revolution that, like Havana throughout this narrative journey, also seems to move farther and farther away from its original meaning as a collective goal. The polis that Menéndez presents in his stories and novel betrays in its walls, buildings, and smells—as if it were yet another character—a "poetics of disenchantment," a disenchantment that begins with the end of the city as a privileged symbolic space, a place for the negotiation of political agendas, and continues little by little as the city devolves toward a state of barbarity, ultimately destroying the idea of the urban center as a space of achievements that allow for a hopeful vision of the future.

Notes

1. *State of nature* is the category that Thomas Hobbes presented in *The Leviathan* (1651) to indicate the hypothetical situation that precedes the constitution of the state.

2. Fidel Castro met with young Cubans in March 1988 in the Consejo Nacional de la Asociación Hermanos Saíz, alluding to an atmosphere of free expression that he saw as favorable. After the meeting, various groups appeared with the idea of bringing art to the streets. One of them was Arte y Derecho, which chose a central corner in Havana, the park located at G and Twenty-third, to do a series of weekly performances that always alluded to politics. Supported by the Asociación Hermanos Saíz and a few critics, the shows grew in intensity until the state police intervened. A visual testament of this movement is Ricardo Vega's documentary *G y 23*, which collects fragments of some performances and posterior reactions from the community.

3. *Translator's note*: The expression "reviva la revolución" has three meanings. I have opted for the primary meaning, that is, "revive" as in to bring back to life. Nonetheless, it can be translated as "live again" or "go for." Also, the prefix *re* can suggest emphasis, as well as haste and urgency.

PART III

CODA

12

La Habana: City and Archive

ANTONIO JOSÉ PONTE

Translated by Elisabeth Enenbach

The House of Memory

To speak of Havana, the Havana of today and the Havana of the future, allow me to stray a little farther. Far in time and space. To a night in Thessaly, in the center of Greece, approximately (because there is no exactness in the memory of the events to which I refer) around 500 BC. On this night a banquet is celebrated in the house of a certain noble of Thessaly named Scopas.

All of this news comes from a treatise by Cicero, *De oratore*. Cicero relates how Scopas, a noble and rich man, threw a banquet at his mansion and invited the poet Simonides, originally from the island Ceos, to sing praise to the host and his illustrious house before the invited guests. So, of course, Simonides of Ceos went to the banquet, began to sing what was agreed (in that day, poetry without music was unheard of), and his poem sang the praises of the noble Scopas.

At a certain point in the poem, however, Simonides seemed to forget the mission he had been given, stopped celebrating the host of the party, and dedicated himself to winning the favor of those who were higher up than the mortal (though noble) Scopas. According to Cicero, he sang the glorious deeds of Castor and Pollux, the children of Leda and Zeus, who had turned into a swan in order to mate with Leda. So, when it came time for him to be paid for his work, Simonides received only half of the agreed amount. He then had to ask for the monies that were missing, and his employer dismissed his demands with the following reasoning: since a good part of his poem had been dedicated to the Dioscuri, Castor and Pollux, then the Dioscuri, magnanimous descendants of Zeus, could pay him the rest.

Cicero relates that the fete followed its course, and we can assume that (although the author of *De oratore* does not parse out these details) once his act was finished and his payment received, the poet must have gone off to some corner, perhaps among the most favored servers, to devour the leftovers of the banquet, which they offered him. Then they came to inform him that someone was at the door looking for him. Two youths asked for him in the street, waiting for him to come out. Simonides must have thought that he was being presented, as if it had descended from heaven, another opportunity to sell his art. He left the banquet hall, went out to the street, found not a trace of the two youths whose presence had been announced, and, at that exact moment, the house of the noble Thessalian collapsed with all of the guests inside.

The roof of the banquet hall caved in on Scopas and his guests. No one managed to leave the party alive. It is easy to suspect that the two youths who called at the door and later disappeared were Castor and Pollux. Who knows how to appear and disappear better than the gods? Simonides must have taken a few indecisive steps in front of the house turned to ruins. Those steps of his are those of survival, steps of one who is learning to walk anew. His extended life was the compensation that was lacking from his payment, the courtesy that the Dioscuri paid him.

Perhaps these two did not decide the death of Scopas and his guests; perhaps those deaths had already been foretold by gods of greater magnitude, but it seems beyond doubt that the Dioscuri saved Simonides, he who had praised them, from the collapse. At least that was what Cicero believed. However, it was not to deal with the justice or injustice of the gods that Cicero brought the tale of Simonides at the house of Scopas into his story, since the events continue—and perhaps the best of this fable (if it is, indeed, a fable) comes next.

Once the rubble from the collapse had been cleared, and the cadavers separated from the debris, the families of those who had attended the banquet tried to procure funerary honors for their loved ones. However, they could not recognize them: they were that disfigured. Who was who, what was a fallen beam, and what was a person, only the sole survivor could say: Simonides of Ceos. And he whose services might have been rented to sing a panegyric had to go in and clear out the rubble. They gave him the task of remembering the position that each person had occupied as he sang his poem.

It had not even been twenty-four hours, and it seemed to be millennia since the party had taken place. Everything had happened in an instant: they told Simonides that someone was looking for him outside, he went out, the house came down, and now the dead were as unrecognizable as if all of those people had been buried for centuries, as if it were an archaeological excavation. Not even their own relatives were able to recognize the dead; it was as if they were countrymen from other places, foreigners in passing.

As he sang his poem, Simonides had done a visual sweep of the hall. He must have associated the faces that watched him (or didn't watch him, occupied with other business) with his verses. Due to this relationship between faces and words, between the deceased and the verses that had been recited, Marcus Tullius Cicero brought up the story of this episode of poetry and collapse. Because, starting with this forensic survey, Simonides de Ceos discovered—or invented—the art of memory, mnemonics. Thus, the Dioscuri were able to give him not only survival in exchange for his compliments but also a method, an art, to memorize long passages of words.

The memorization of a speech is, as one can understand, an indispensable ability for one who is paid to speak. Memorizing discourse is necessary for speechmaking (hence Cicero's interest in the episode). Simonides sang his poem before a circle of guests, those faces had been disfigured by the caving in of the roof, the house that brought them together disappeared, and the gods that were his salvation disappeared as well. But the poem? The memory of the poem, yes, remained. Those people would not come back, and, although they might reconstruct the mansion, it would no longer be that of the noble (if stingy) Scopas. As for the gods, who could guarantee anything? But the poem remained. The poem composed by the survivor Simonides could be recited among the ruins. Thus was founded (at least according to Cicero) the art of memorization.

In a wonderful book, *The Art of Memory*, the British scholar Frances A. Yates has chronicled the development (and disappearance) through the centuries of the art of memorization that originated with Simonides of Ceos. Summarizing quite briefly what this art consisted of during the time of the Greek poet (later it had very different developments), it can be said that it involves associating a building, real or imaginary, with the phrases that are to be committed to memory. As one can see, it has to do with relating two constructions: a building and a speech. It is a double architectural exercise, one of consummate engineering. Because if any building needed to be constructed with foundations that today remain hidden from sight, in the art of memorization invented (or discovered) and practiced by Simonides of Ceos, it was necessary to construct not only foundations but a whole edifice with a series of halls and patios, a building hidden from the sight of those who listened to a piece of oration or lengthy poem.

If one makes an imaginary room coincide with the phrase or verse being composed, then one would only have to go from one room to another, through all of those that make up a building, to have the whole text. Thus, the memory trained by this art retained an architectural blueprint, if you will, and a document. Or better stated, one plane in which walls and words were delineated, one that bound together architecture and language.

Understood thusly, any discourse contains a mentally constructed edifice, an invisible building. The poem that praised the nobility of Scopas and (more so) that of the Dioscuri no longer fit in the hall where it was being heard. As any survivor does, Simonides revisited the events of the entire evening. He did it right away; he was obliged to do so by the cries of those who were grieving. In articulating identities, cadaver by cadaver, he had to enter Scopas's house all over again.

His poetry would be marked definitively by the disaster. Simonides would take strength from the destruction; chaos would dictate a new compositional method to him. Henceforth, every time he attempted a poem, it was in that disappeared house that he recited it. It was in front of the faces, still recognizable and still not disfigured, of those guests. The collapsed mansion would accompany all of his poems. For him to create verses it seemed necessary to reenter Scopas's house again, face the visage of every one of the dead when the roof still rested on top of the walls.

Of course, as time went by, that environment would give way to less disgraced architectures. It is not difficult to assume that some of his later poems furnished different spaces. Simonides of Ceos's imagination must have moved to other buildings, and he created other places that underpinned his memorization.

We all have proof of how memorable places can be. We return, consciously or unconsciously, to places where we have already been or where we have never been. The most varied places appear in our dreams and our wakefulness (and I do not speak solely of the lucubrations of architects). The house of Scopas can adopt the most diverse forms. The invention of Simonides of Ceos, on the other hand, went beyond. He invented places to make himself believe that he had been in them. He invented the type of strange spaces that open up to us in our dreams. He built corners that would join certain words, he fixed words into those imaginary places, he raised the walls and roof within which a certain clause or a given verse would fit. A clause or a verse as fatal and as unavoidable as fate had been the night of Scopas's party.

If, as affirmed by Cicero and Yates, Simonides of Ceos is the inventor of mnemonics, it must be accepted that the house of Scopas is the house of memory. It is for this reason that I have begun this chapter by referring to it, going back to the episode where that building fell to achieve (thanks to the surviving poet) the phantasmagoric dignity of imaginary spaces. The relationship between the cave-in 2,500 years ago in Thessaly and the collapse of Havana today stands out immediately. Simonides's work in identifying the dead among the debris, I believe, has a great deal to do with the destiny of the archives of the most recent Cuban history. At some point, it will be up to us, just as with the ancient Greek poet, to confirm identities, to decide who was who.

And, whether it be about architecture or documents, about city or archive, I speak (as could be no less in the house of Scopas) about memory, about our memory.

False Urbanistic Memory

In Havana, in a short section of the Avenida del Puerto that goes from the Plaza de San Francisco de Assisi to the Muelle de Luz, just a few blocks, a strange collection of buildings has been thrown together in the last few years. The Office of the City Historian, responsible for any urban change within the limits of Old Havana, has been in charge of the planning of all of the construction projects listed here: a garden in homage to the memory of Lady Diana Frances Spencer (Princess Diana), another one opened in memory of Mother Teresa of Calcutta, a Greek Orthodox cathedral, a Rum Museum, and a Russian Orthodox cathedral.

I believe I am not mistaken if I tell you that habaneros had few opportunities to keep up with Lady Diana's life while she was alive. Her tensions with the British royal family, including the divorce, could not be included in TV newscasts and newspapers in Cuba. Even less so the humanitarian campaigns in which she was involved. Her changes in attire were only a topic of interest for the few favored people who received celebrity gossip magazines from abroad. The news of her death, on the other hand, was indeed published in Cuba, along with the people's reaction to it. Even so, it is hard to explain the presence of a garden dedicated to her memory in Havana.

It is a small space, fenced in like certain small parks in London, through which no one can walk. It cannot be crossed; one can enter and come out, one goes *to* it rather than *through* it. A horrible fountain, designed by the ceramicist Alfredo Sosabravo, was placed in the center; in coming upon it, looking around the whole little plaza, one might ask oneself why the heck such a park has been planned there. The same question applies when visiting, a few meters away, the garden dedicated to Mother Teresa.

The statue of this religious figure stands in the gardens of the Convent of St. Francis of Assisi, currently transformed into a concert hall. At the door of the hall dedicated to music one can hug (many tourists do) the bronze figure of the *Caballero de París* (Gentleman from Paris). The effigy of the city's most emblematic mentally ill man has more reason to be there than a far-off princess, as charitable or unlucky as she may have been. Or a religious mother, no matter how much piety may have driven her. The personal story of the *Caballero de París* is so interwoven with that of the streets and of an era that it makes sense to find him there again, standing still in bronze.

However, do not think that I am advocating for only having statues in Havana that are strictly local. I do not defend a narrow symbolism. But, what is the purpose of those two gardens to a nun and a princess who had nothing to do with the capital and with the country? I will say it soon, to proceed with the inventory of edifices: I see it as an exhibitionist extravagance that, in the middle of the anemia of the Cuban building industry, two memorials to such doubtful figures (in an area with such urgent residential needs) have been built.

One can affirm that they obey diplomatic gestures of the Office of the City Historian, necessary gestures in any administration. Perhaps some British delegation visited Havana, offered some necessary aid for the recovery of its historic area, and, in exchange, it might have received as a gesture of goodwill the founding of a park in the memory of Princess Diana. It could have happened. However, in such cases, there is usually a plaque to remind the public of the aid that was given. Thanks are usually given for monies with a privileged inscription, not with the excess of a park.

In defense of these two constructions, one can maintain that they celebrate (as with any monument) the sentimentality of an era. The Office of the City Historian, then, gives a history lesson to passing habaneros with those two gardens. One can even consider it a lesson that two figures so little related to the official ideology might receive homage there. Better Diana of Wales and Teresa of Calcutta than Tania the Guerrilla.[1] On the other hand, residential buildings could never be built in such a privileged area of the old city. The ground there, among plazas and old churches, must only exist for memorials.

I would have no objection to any of the above if not for the other extravagant pieces that I will discuss. (I do not include among them, of course, the opening of a museum about the history of rum where the Young Creators' House used to open its doors.)

A Greek Orthodox cathedral has also been built in the garden of the Convent of St. Francis of Assisi. It is a small temple. Rather, it is the mock-up of a bigger temple. The stone of its walls is extremely new, the gold inside shines in what little shadow can be had in sunny Havana. The cathedral has religious services and is open to tourists and anyone who is curious. In off hours religious hymns are played over the speakers. In a wall built during colonial times next to which this little temple is built, a plaque reads, "This cathedral is a gift of the Cuban people to the Greek Orthodox Church and Ecumenical Patriarch Bartholomew." Over this text, there is an image of a meeting between Fidel Castro (representing, once again, the whole Cuban people) and the Greek patriarch on a visit to the island.

There used to be a Greek Orthodox church in Havana before 1959. Anyone who has visited the headquarters of the Buendía Theater Company in Nuevo Vedado will have deciphered (if the darkness that reigns inside the walls, which are painted black, allows it), a plaque written in Greek letters. They will have been told that before it was a theater the place had been closed, empty. But there was once a Greek colony in Havana large enough to have its own church, and it was here.

What happened to that colony over the course of the years? Whatever may have been its fate, it would not have been necessary for some congregation member to call for building a new Greek church in Havana. As the plaque indicates, it has to do with very high-level political maneuverings. The Cuban head of state has given that church not to the Greek people but to the head of the Greek Church. It is a courtesy between people high up, and how much devotion might later come to be practiced between its walls matters little. The important thing (as we tend to say to forgive tiny gifts) is the gesture.

Once, in one of the round tables that occupy the afternoon spots on Cuban television, the city historian, Eusebio Leal Spengler, remembered (I think it was for Fidel Castro's birthday) the moment in which Castro had given him the key to his personal treasures. Thus he put at his own disposition a specialist who was able to evaluate them, the majority being gifts that foreign dignitaries and presidents had given him over the years. Fidel Castro gave Eusebio Leal Spengler (who praised the magnanimity of the head of the government for the cameras) the presents he had received on so many state visits. It must have been, surely, an impressive toy store. In the same way, the Ecumenical Patriarch Bartholomew, head of the Greek Orthodox Church, would count the little Havana church among his personal treasures.

The gift could not have done other than awaken envy and jealousy in the Russian Orthodox Church. Due to diplomatic pressure by this church, or due to new economic contracts signed with Russia, it was necessary to find a site for a cathedral to suit Muscovite taste. The place appeared after a collapse: the bar Los Marinos fell down; it had been, along with the rebuilt Two Brothers, the only place to drink to one's heart's content that remained there.

I can describe little of this new building because I only saw its foundations. I suppose it has already been opened or will be soon. I have looked for it in publications from Havana without finding any news about it. Although I did manage to find an image of what it would look like once it was finished, I saw the image hung by the builders on the barrier that hid the work from view, and I can assert that the church has or will have onion-domed towers. Let's imagine, if you will, a stunted version of St. Basil's Cathedral in Moscow. Once such a church is raised in front of the Muelle de Luz, it will also be a gift from the people of Cuba to a distant faith and an unknown patriarch.

That cathedral would have been more opportune in the era in which a considerable Russian colony inhabited the city, and not now, when there will be few of the faithful to visit it. But those were not Russians but Soviet men, people firm in their denial of God, scientifically atheist. Just as in the case of its Greek homologue, one does not have to seek a house of a certain alliance with a certain God under the onion domes. Its construction is no more than the seal of a pact between the Cuban government and the Russian government. A post-Communist pact between both states.

Gardens honoring a princess and a religious figure, churches of far-off faiths: perhaps this string of architectural presences that today seem strange to me may one day, once enough time has passed, achieve the quietude of habit. Then they will be (if that *then* arrives) familiar presences. The memory of Princess Diana will seem to many (above all to those who do not have previous memories of the place) indiscernible from that little corner of Havana. Perhaps the fountain that we find appalling today will be funny by then. Habit, as we know, is a teacher with abundant resources.

Nevertheless, although I have promised to talk about the Havana of the future, I prefer not to jump ahead, and remain stupefied by these occurrences. In the present, it is difficult to comprehend that the so-called Master Plan for the Overall Revitalization of Havana, run by the Office of the City Historian, can entertain such fantasies while the whole city is falling apart before everyone's eyes.

As in the case of the memorial gardens, one can object that those two cathedrals are doubtlessly a contribution to the imaginary of the city, that such particular towers augment the imagination of Havana and give testimony to the mutations of more recent Cuban history. They make the Cuban capital more ecumenical, after all: quite diverse credos pray in the city. Also, it would be fruitless to wait for all the residential problems to be covered to undertake building the requisite quota of symbolisms that are necessary in any capital. It would be unreasonable to demand such a thing: cathedrals have never waited for hunger to be alleviated. Although they are more like embassies than cathedrals. The Russian and Greek cathedrals built in Havana are embassy buildings.

They are not there to praise the familiar, since urbanism is not made merely from recurrences but also of necessary surprises. So it is irrelevant whether this or that church had never been there before. The recovery of the old city constitutes a creative act. It doesn't have to do with only the most faithful restorations; it is not simply archaeology. Old Havana must of course be understood as a living city. There are its inhabitants, and it is for them that new gardens and new temples are opened.

The previous reasons could be shared if there were not also, likewise covered under the so-called Master Plan for the Overall Revitalization of Havana, blunders in the treatment of the historic aspect of Havana. I will cite an example that is also quite recent. Approximately a year ago the Colegio Mayor San Jerónimo—the halls of which will shape future restorers, archaeologists, and diverse specialists involved with the historic renovation of Havana—was inaugurated on the block formed by the streets Obispo, Obrapía, Mercaderes, and San Ignacio. On the very same site, many centuries ago, was the first university house of the city, and until recently it was the location of the Ministry of Education. The building was a concrete and glass cube from the 1950s. It was an ugly modern building that came to substitute a more venerable building, but the decades that had passed since its construction—half a century— had softened the aggressiveness of that attack, and it could be said that it cohabited, for better or for worse, with its much older surroundings.

Confronted with the idea of opening a university inside that concrete cube, it became essential to make a temporal decision. The hulk from the '50s could be demolished and a colonial-style replica of the earlier university could be undertaken. Or that modern insertion of bad taste could be accepted with good humor, considering that it had half a century of existence to its credibility. Looked at this way, it was already legitimate. It had the legitimacy of that which had already been built, as one will be able to say in the future about the Orthodox cathedrals that are brand-new today. That building was also part of the city's past.

Pulled this way and that among options, those who planned the new school decided not to choose any of them. Or, one might say, they chose both, since they did not destroy the building they had on their hands but simply added a replica of the original university's bell tower. Concerned as they were with the successive histories of the site, any decision they took would have been partial and false. The modern architecture negated the colonial architecture and vice versa. It was more Solomonic (although even more false) to seek the intersection of those two eras. If the concrete walls were too out of place, it was better to sneak away with the scandal, to cover it with its surroundings. So the façade of the central mass was covered in mirrors and thus little was left of it, consumed by the reflection of nearby buildings.

A baroque portal was incrusted on one of these reflective façades, and they raised the tower that would hold the old university bell on the corner of O'Reilly and Mercaderes. Thus, an injury inflicted in the 1950s was substituted, half a century later, with a simulacrum. The bell tower was designed using old engravings and images, although it also followed the example of the Campanile de San Marco of the Venetian Hotel in Las Vegas. The work on the Colegio Mayor San Jerónimo was finished in time to celebrate Fidel Castro's eightieth birthday. The newspaper *Granma* named him the "promoter of the architectural transformation of this place."

To maintain any hope whatsoever regarding this architectural concoction, one must assume that the best students of the Colegio Mayor San Jerónimo will find excellent examples of what to avoid in the false tower and the mirrored box that houses their university. To nourish one's indignation, one has only to reason about what they have made there, destined (as if a joke) to house a center for historical restoration. Architects, urban planners, archaeologists, and historians have been known to preach there with the worst example. If the construction of various exoticisms on the Avenida del Puerto can be forgiven (the exotic immediately loses its rarity and manages to integrate itself into the urban fabric), what has been done with the historic aspect of the Colegio San Jerónimo is even more inexplicable.

This example says a lot about the philosophy with which the restoration of Old Havana is being undertaken. It is quite taken with fantastic exercises when it comes to the new (new cathedrals and new gardens) and exercises no less fantasy when intervening in historical buildings. It finds a robust building constructed half a century earlier and, in the name c̄ ... original building that no longer exists, creates a rushed result that does not correspond to any era whatsoever. It manages, at the same time, to create false colonialism and false republicanism. Appealing to historical truth, it adds a false tower to an intrusive mass until reaching sufficient size as to compete in unusualness with the onion-domed towers.

Imbued with the doctrine of a meticulously calculated urban plan, the group of specialists under the oversight of Eusebio Leal Spengler seems decided on the original folly and the historicizing folly. All of this occurs in a destroyed capital with extremely low indexes of construction, under an administration that is reluctant to deal with the material problems of the population and that only deals with the housing question quite sporadically (one has only to remember the birth, deaths, and resurrections of the Microbrigade system). It has done so lately and, according to official data (take into account how unreliable official Cuban statistics are), in the month of September 2008 the annual plan for construction was 40 percent behind schedule.

During this same time, Vice President Carlos Lage criticized the failure to accomplish what had been planned the previous year and alluded to the fraudulence of many recorded indexes. (One can only imagine the falseness of these statistics when it is enough to bring about the public complaint of a high-ranking official.) In the middle of such a panorama, the campaign to restore Old Havana remains notable. That such a campaign is dedicated to building false bell towers remains notable. However, the project of the Office of the City Historian is not only obligated to respond to the past but also to the present and future. All of the inhabitants of Old Havana fit into that present, as do the new cathedrals and gardens. Regarding these inhabitants, the doctrine consists of getting rid of as many of them as possible. To this end, two instructions are strictly observed within the municipal limits of the old city.

The first directive scrupulously quantifies the number of residents that move in and ensures that when a house changes hands in Old Havana, it will not bring in a larger family than the one that moved out. In this way, the border between Old Havana and Central Havana is not unlike the one that runs between the Dominican Republic and Haiti. The second directive, for its part, dictates that if the Office of the City Historian should be interested in a property, the inhabitants of said property must accept the offer to move that is extended to them. They will be sent to an apartment that might be in better condition than their former residence, but they will be unfavorably located, outside of the city in most cases. They are often obligated to live in Alamar.

The zealous application of this demographic policy contributes to the gradual emptying of the historic part. The city museum dedicated to international tourism needs these abandonment projects. Alamar, the largest bedroom community in Havana, takes in new sleepers as long as Old Havana remains cleared out. In the old city, galleries and museums acquire a nocturnal nonexistence, the majority of the bars close at midnight, and thus the city and the moon (as is the aspiration of any set of ruins) remain alone together.

The desert I have just described has come to be contradicted by a number of social works built in the municipality (some health centers, various schools). This desert that I am describing is being built, perhaps, with an eye to the future. One fine day we will know that the current measures being taken by the Office of the City Historian obeyed a determined calculation: that of reserving Old Havana for more prudent inhabitants than those that live there today. Understood thusly, what might happen to this area of the city with the return of the movement of realty, prohibited since 1959, is being achieved in advance. The ancient city, its beautiful buildings protected, can in the future be turned into a zone that is just as appealing as the historic centers of other world capitals.

Granted, it is difficult to believe that a cabinet immersed in the circumstances in which Cuba finds itself might have reached such a distant horizon with its calculations. Yet, we must agree that this same cabinet has managed to execute, in the last few decades, the only construction business that can take pride in its work in Havana.

Revolutionary Discourse on Ruins

The restoration of Old Havana represents the sole increase in construction in the capital in the last few years. For the most part, it consists of the renovation of preexisting buildings and barely includes new buildings; hence, it places its statistics under the rubric of "maintenance," among the labors that assure architectural funding. One might hope that, in the meantime, new edifices might be built, other areas might be urbanized, and Havana might grow.

But one visit to the City Model of Havana shatters these hopes. The model is found in a large hall built for it in Miramar. The publicity posters at the entrance promise "Past, Present, and Future," while little information about the future is given inside. A ramp spirals around the city in miniature, and theodolites through which one can look at Havana from above have been placed along the ramp. As visitors to the place, we have a privileged perspective. We reach the furthest rooftop that gets lost on the horizon; we see all of the historic eras of the city.

Havana, as it is known, has been a capital with few substitutions, characterized more by the addition of new spaces than by the reconstruction of preexisting spaces. Although its location has changed several times (historians assert that the current location is its third), the pieces that make up the city have moved little. One cannot speak of ancient temples that hold up new temples built atop them, as in other Latin American capitals, nor of old neighborhoods that have been leveled (think of Caracas, Bogotá, or Lima) to give rise to new buildings. Rather than insisting on the same point, Havana flees, running in every direction and starting with the fixed north of the seashore. As if it were spilling inland. The urge to capitalize has left definitive architectural shapes on the occupied terrain; it is difficult to return to them, since the principal interest runs toward new points, gives ambition to new horizons.

Thus Havana can show, thanks to a brief history that still allows it significant horizontal advances, a historic density that other capitals have lost by now. It has the paradox of being a city that is, at the same time, a recent and very ancient city. Recent, for the availability of space through which it could spill without overlapping other provincial areas. Very ancient, given the architectural continuum that can be found in it, where very little has been replaced —since, busy as its inhabitants have been in running to new settlements, it has not been necessary to reclaim the land on which the oldest buildings were built.

On the other hand, by the 1950s this type of reclaiming of the land had been thought about. The Sert Plan, commissioned from a U.S. architectural firm by the Cuban government, was then occupied with taking another look at the old city: it redesigned Old Havana and a few areas in Central Havana. Only a few colonial buildings were saved in this new plan. Between the Malecón and the streets of the city, skyscrapers would form a windbreak or curtain. The bay would have held an artificial little island. Wide highways would have crossed Old Havana, and there would have been plenty of parking lots.

Whether or not this plan would have been implemented, had the revolution of 1959 not triumphed, is fodder for a counterfactual history, a history where the imagination can ask what would have happened if certain changes of direction and certain choices had had different results. We can image a Havana reformulated according to the directives of the Sert Plan if we can imagine a Cuban history of the last half century without the political regime that took hold of Cuba in 1959. In another hypothesis, we can count on the opposition of Cuban architects to the realization of the Sert Plan. We could even imagine a Havana different from the one of today if we were able to imagine that the revolutionary triumph of 1959 had given the country a different administration, focused less on politics with the rest of the world and more on the administrative aspect, a regime more industrious and less imperialist, made up less of a state department than of a treasury department.

We could risk these and other counterfactual suppositions, but, despite the benefits of these imaginations (liberty is impossible without imagination) I do not have time here to elaborate upon them, so I will go over—with a theodolite—the model that reproduces the Cuban capital.

There is the past in abundance, since neither the Sert Plan nor any similar plan was ever implemented. There is the past with every piece intact, thanks to the urbanizing parsimony of the revolutionary regime, and the fact that this regime has had to content itself with the administrative buildings built by the previous administration—and has even utilized the symbolic center of the Civic Plaza to transform it into the Plaza of the Revolution. (Think, on the other hand, of the demolition of the Royal Palace of Berlin in 1950 to build the Marx-Engels Platz and the Palace of the Republic in its stead. Or of the streets and houses that disappeared in order to make way for the pachydermic palace of Ceaucescu in Bucharest.) If the constructive anemia of the Cuban regime can be judged as a disgrace, it can also be considered a fortunate sign.

The theodolite reaches both the past and present. There hasn't been a need for successive models, nor have transversal cuts in time been necessary. The city has suffered scarce superimpositions, as it has had little overcrowding. Spread out and simultaneous in all of its historical periods, Havana opens itself, in past and present, to a single glance. But, what does this same model, made for control and urban planning, tell us about the future?

Anyone who has been in an architect's study knows that, in general, models of buildings are in white. White or raw, they show the color of potential. They have yet to exist, and they are as if inside an eggshell. Anyone who has visited another architectural model of a city (New York has the largest in the world, and the Havana model boasts of following it in size) will have seen color on every piece: each reproduction has the same color as the real façade in the city. The Model of Havana, on the other hand, has opted for a solution between these two extremes: it is not entirely white, nor entirely in color.

If the colored option had been chosen, the question remains, what color would the builders have chosen for the façades of those buildings that haven't been painted for decades and decades? The color of time? The City Model of Havana has taken recourse to the colors of history. As such, everything built during the colonial era is brown; ochre marks the republican period; and ivory corresponds to the new revolutionary era.

The arrogance of the ochre and the paucity of ivory stand out immediately. The majority of the city is ochre (80 percent according to some, 88 percent according to others). If we understand the city as a speech, it would be abundant chatter, a conversation that goes on and on. The discourse of urban planning by the revolution is limited, for its part, to a comment here and there and (in the case of Alamar, Reparto Eléctrico, and Mulgoba) to a few marginal additions to the main discussion.

"The future?" we ask. Whoever laid out the pieces of this model reserved white for buildings that have yet to be built. The future has this color in common with monuments and cemeteries, and I will leave the conclusion about that equivalence to you. During a visit a couple of years ago, I found very few white pieces in the model. Some hotel was being built by the coast, toward the west. The future seemed quite improbable, as if those pieces belonged to a sleepy Monopoly player.

The ochre of six decades of the republic dominated the scarce ivory of half a century and, if one is to think that the future belongs to the revolutionary regime (and to think that this will persist in its disinclination for construction), very little hope remains for what is to come. "The future belongs entirely to socialism" can be read on the billboards of official propaganda, which can be translated, in terms of urban planning, as "the future belongs entirely to collapse."

The City Model of Havana is slow to reflect the destruction of buildings, as can be demonstrated in two or three examples. The miniaturized city avoids showing its cavity-filled mouth, and ruins don't show up in it. On the other hand, it also fails to show the only efforts at new construction in the city over the past few decades, the restoration of the historic area. This clearly indicates something that is often lost from sight: the impracticality of implementing that remedy outside the confines of the old part of the city. One could not aspire to an entire archaeology of the city, a city transformed into a museum, unless a fourth founding of Havana were attempted and—and, in the same way that Old Havana is now being emptied and Alamar repopulated—what is today known as Havana were left to the disposition of curious visitors and tourists, with habaneros taking refuge not in a bedroom community but a bedroom capital. Thus, the current Havana would become a new Old Panama, a new Pompeii, the Pompeii buried by the volcano of the revolution.

I also do not believe that the implementation of the plan of economic self-management, held by the Office of the City Historian in Old Havana, would be feasible in other municipalities of the city. In a recent issue of the magazine *Temas*, the architect Mario Coyula, a member of the Group for the Comprehensive Development of the Capital, points to the granting of economic autonomy to local governments as a solution, "increasing the authority of self-financed state corporate entities, in the manner of the Office of the Historian of Havana" (Coyula 2006).

Such a solution would assume, if the recipe practiced in the colonial area were to be followed, the influx of foreign tourism. It would assume the transformation of the entire capital into a theme park, and one must wonder what kind of tourist attraction Luyanó, for example, would be. A more or less happy formula (I am speaking of economic results rather than consequences) applied in the coastal city would be ineffective when applied inland to neighborhoods of lesser patrimonial value.

When we look at Havana, we see a paralyzed city, its most ancient buildings tended to, and the rest of it destitute. We might ask ourselves (and we will keep wondering) for what reason or reasons the administration that has governed Cuba for the last half century has allowed or provoked such a state of things. Touching on this point, different theories can be divided among those who understand that the decay of Cuban cities (of which Havana is the most extreme example) has been a conscious goal of such an administration, an objective achieved little by little, and those who maintain that everything has to do with sheer neglect, a simple apathy for internal affairs. Given these considerations, one can hold on to the theory of puritanical resentment against the city (Babylon as the Great Whore) or to the theory of shameful indifference. In my book *La fiesta vigilada* (and also in a documentary by Florian Borchmeyer in which I appear), I venture that there is a perfect correspondence between a destroyed Havana and an official discourse that has always dwelled on waiting for a U.S. military invasion and on its milder corollary, the U.S. economic embargo against Cuba. Seen as such, the city in ruins constitutes the best stage for such damning exercises. Havana is the simulacrum of an invaded city, the (actual-size) model on the campaign table of the state. Hence, Havana can show its collapsed buildings and its underpinnings in the same way that a victim shows the marks of a violent act to a court. Although the anticipated invasion will never arrive and although the Cuban administration seems capable of sorting out the barriers to commercial exchange with the United States, the decayed landscape of the Cuban capital is convenient for the administration. Such a landscape justifies the discourse of resistance exported by the revolutionary regime, and justifies its rhetoric of a besieged city.

And now, let us return to the relationship that Simonides of Ceos once established, in Greece in the year 500 BC, between discourse and collapse, between the speech (or poem) to be memorized and the imaginary building that housed its components. If, for Simonides, Scopas's ruined mansion served to return him to the poem, the official Cuban discourse legitimates itself by allowing the collapse of Havana. As in a macabre rewriting of the episode recounted by Marcus Tullius Cicero, Simonides manages in this case, through his speech, to make the roof of Scopas's house cave in. This is, in fact, one possible interpretation of the Greek episode, because it can be conjectured that if he had not mentioned the Dioscuri (and had not awoken the vengeful stinginess of Scopas), the destroyed mansion would have remained standing and the guests would have returned to their homes with the early light of the dawn.

Underground Havana and the Havana of the Future

We will stand before the ruins just as Simonides of Ceos did. In front of the ruins, inside of the ruins, are those who live in Havana. In light of the disaster, one fine day it will be necessary to forget about what needs to be rebuilt, what should disappear to make room for another mass, and what new city will need to be drawn. Unlike all of its previous history, the Cuban capital will have to undertake substitutions. It will be able to expand its city limits, as before, and to expand in new settlements—but it will also be obligated to take care of its old streets, its old buildings, and to take care of the debris. Therefore, the first stage of the Sert Plan or any such similar plan to level areas will have to be completed: neighborhoods will have to be cleared out, demolition will have to be done, not by choice (as would have happened in the 1950s, had the Sert Plan been executed) but by misfortune. It will be necessary to employ, for their planning and methodology, demolition artists, a title that Baron Hausmann once appropriated for the creation of the boulevards of Paris.

There would be one recurring problem to resolve: that sowed by the opening of the Colegio Mayor San Jerónimo. What to do with superimposed styles, how to manage the different elements present in the same space? In one of his novels, Joseph Conrad complained about the world in which we live, a world in which one cannot be in two places at the same time and in which two beings cannot be in the same place. For the Havana of the future, such a world will come to suffocate it with obligatory substitutions. It will be necessary to demarcate exactly what defines our heritage. This task is still pending, judging by the Office of the City Historian's tendency to reduce everything to colonialism. This task is also still pending, if we accept that a recently built Russian Orthodox cathedral might come to be part of the heritage that will need to be saved, even if in the future.

Here I warn of a danger to be avoided, that of believing that history will begin again at the same point where it left off, the danger of seeing the revolutionary period as an empty pause. Granted, the tiny amount of ivory to be seen in the Model of Havana would support such a belief. Nonetheless, we should take caution from the post-Communist examples of East Berlin and Moscow. In both capitals architectural legacies have been destroyed under ideological pretexts, as if it were necessary to destroy reminders, to get rid of suspicion.

The Palace of the Republic, built in the mid-1970s where the Royal Palace of Berlin had been located, has been torn down. For its construction, the Communist regime had leveled a monarchical palace that had dominated the center of Berlin since the fifteenth century. In its place it built a plaza (Marx-Engels Platz), and that multifunctional palace that included the Berlin House of Representatives and the largest cultural center of the country. It was there, in that building, that the members of the Parliament of East Germany voted to join the other Germany. The post-Communist administrations of Berlin, for their part, opted to bring it down. The German and international petitions against this decision did not manage to change things, nor did the recommendations of notable architects and urban planners. As the symbol of an unjust regime, as public discussion quickly came to maintain, it would have to disappear in the same way as the regime that glorified it.

For its part, what happened in Moscow reaches new heights of barbarity. Valuable examples of Russian constructivism have been lost in the last few years, and a society—the Moscow Architecture Preservation Society—has been created to take charge of denouncing such losses. According to the society's reports, since 1992 more than 400 historical buildings, from the sixteenth century to the Stalinist era, have been demolished in Moscow. Among them are the oldest wooden house in Moscow and classics of Stalinist architecture such as the Hotel Moksva and the Hotel Rossiya. (Just as in the case of the Communist palace in Berlin, this last hotel was constructed where there used to be a medieval area that dated back to the time of Ivan the Terrible.)

In the opinion of the Moscow Architecture Preservation Society, the bad principles that affect the patrimony of Russia are institutional indifference in the application of existing protection laws, urban-planning speculation (which makes it cheaper to demolish buildings and build new ones than to do restoration, and which favors façadism, or the emptying of historic buildings to maintain only their ancient façades), the lack of maintenance of historic architecture, and, finally, the lack of criteria in the restorations that are undertaken. These ills, for the most part, assume dark relationships between political power and the construction companies. These evils should be kept in mind for the future of Cuba.

However, when all is said and done, it is not in regard to the buildings that can be attributed to the current Cuban administration that these cautions should be kept in mind. Revolutionary Havana is related to very few (at least until now) symbolic buildings, and, even if threatened with punishment, the public pickaxe would attack those few walls. But, if in the city that can be swept with the gaze of a theodolite, there is very little ivory to be seen, there exists an extensive underground capital built during this last half century, which cannot be seen from the surface. I am not speaking of the subterranean galleries built here and there as air-raid shelters, nor of the underground tunnels that studied the possibility of building a Metro in Havana.

Just as one can speak of an underground economy through which goods stolen from state enterprises circulate, of an economy made up of secret channels through which appear those things that cannot otherwise be obtained, one can also speak of a secret, underground city, where the most unthinkable conversations have been relegated, along with letters that never arrived or never were sent to their destination and the most trivial observations about human behavior. I am referring to the city (or country, one could say without fear of exaggerating) that is made up of kilometers and kilometers of secret files. I am referring to the resources with which the Ministry of the Interior (the only ministry that exists in Cuba, as it is said) worked and still works: I refer to the extremely extensive library that would be established by putting together the books of all the records of the Committee for the Defense of the Revolution.

If it is certain that the Cuban revolutionary government has sufficiently washed its hands of the capital that it took over, if its works on the surface have been very few, this might be due (although it would be worth pointing to other causes) to its intense labor on this type of underground building. If it has seemed unconcerned with aqueducts, sewers, and the electric, telephone, and gas grids, using mostly the utilities it inherited, the same cannot be said of its works to channel secret surveillance, of its infiltration projects, of the creation of its parallel telephonic universe. As such, I correct what I said earlier about it being a political regime wholly concerned with international matters and apparently withdrawn from the actual government of its own people—because essentially it is obsessed with controlling its subjects, obsessed with making its own subjects watch each other until achieving, in this way, an even greater measure of destruction of the city: the destruction of civility. In short, it is a political regime that fosters distrust in the stability of its walls and nourishes distrust between neighbors; the roof might fall upon us just the same as our neighbor might.

On a page in his memoir, Heberto Padilla tells how José Lezama Lima was obligated to let in a policeman dressed as a civilian who had come to interrogate him. The policeman accused Lezama Lima of speaking badly of the revolutionary government, and, when Lezama Lima denied the accusation, he was faced with a recording where he could hear himself saying the sentence in question. I bring up this episode to show that unpublished secret recordings of José Lezama Lima exist (if they have not been lost).

In the same way, it is possible that an archive of Havana might hold recordings of other great figures, as well as of individuals who are less important but equally spied upon. There must also exist, if the Cuban secret police obeyed their Soviet and German masters, an immense library of reports, of faithfully transcribed conversations, of photocopies of correspondence, of confiscated papers and objects, of scrupulously balanced personal accounts. Remember that the posthumous books of Virgilio Piñera came from none other than the archive of State Security; these manuscripts were taken upon the death of the author and later sent, as the years passed, to the state publishers that published them.

We can wonder how much information must go, sooner or later, the way of those originals by Virgilio Piñera. In post-Communist Berlin (and more recently in Poland), they decided to open the files of the secret police. After the fall of Ceaucescu, Romania has been governed by a succession of officials of the Securitate, dedicated to making sure that nothing of what had been spied gets out. For its part, the post-Soviet administration of the secret archives of Moscow has debated between opening up and keeping things closed. For the Cuban case, there is yet another possibility: total destruction. It is possible that the same personnel who worked to build the secret Havana might be instructed to make all traces of the perverse city they founded disappear.

The conservation of those streets' worth of documents would doubtless constitute a valuable asset. We would recuperate, to cite one example floating in that ocean of evidence, the voice of José Lezama Lima speaking about a thousand topics without knowing that he was being recorded. We would also regain the first finished versions of *Otra vez el mar* by Reinaldo Areans (I am referring to the versions that were confiscated). More impersonally, that archive of voices and gestures would constitute precious documentation in terms of the history of daily life in Cuba in the second half of the twentieth century and the beginning of the twenty-first century.

You will assume that, as such, this is a cursed treasure, a poisoned gift. It would give abundant and resounding proof that among the customs of Cuban life in those decades were espionage, denouncements, informing, and, the worst of complicities and compulsions, the greatest contempt for liberty.

Understood in this way, it doesn't matter how much of this evidence might survive: the existence of that secret country, of that underground capital of snitchery, will stay with us (as it does now) in the future, be it tangible or intangible. The future of Havana will have to attend to not just the ruination of its buildings but also to the viciousness of humanity.

Havana has been paralyzed for fifty years, and we must face that paralysis and the ruin that it has brought about. It will be necessary to determine what can be removed, to save what ought to be conserved, and to decide new projects for the city. The magnitude of the disaster is such that we might speak of a fourth founding of the city. I say this without calling for the leveling anger of revolutions. It is not insane to venture that the Havana of the future will be very different from that of today, which has been held back for decades.

In exactly the same way, it will be essential to take into account what has happened among its inhabitants. Just as I imagine a Cuban public opinion geared toward the subject of the city, I would like to imagine a mature, coordinated discussion about the matter of the archives. It is useless to predict whether people will turn to the virtues of forgetfulness or to the wounds of remembering. I distinguish these two principal tasks when I think of Havana in the future: the reconstruction of the city and the reconstruction of the life of its citizens. When the time comes, we will be like Simonides of Ceos upon leaving the banquet. We will be standing before the city, that is, before its collapsed walls. We will have to deal with the remains of the disaster. We will have to work knee-deep in the debris, identifying the pieces.

Note

1. Haydée Tamara Bunke Bider (born in Buenos Aires in 1937 and died in Bolivia in 1967), the daughter of German parents, received her education in East Germany where she met Ernesto "Che" Guevara. She arrived in Cuba in 1961, received guerrilla training, entered the Bolivian guerrilla force of Guevara, and died in an ambush.

13

Bitter Daiquiris: A Crystal Chronicle

JOSÉ QUIROGA

Translated by Elisabeth Enenbach

One-Way Street

All trips to Havana are unfinished. One looks for a photo or loses the memory of one. A memory that didn't exist is erased, and another created that doesn't appear in any pictures. One recovers some insignificant detail—a little bottle of shampoo, a glass—and that detail is labeled with some new amnesia. Upon contact with the air of another time—that air, which you bring with you—the object remains, but that which is illustrated by the object dissolves.

For many years, one photo, many. Albums with patriotic monuments. Stamps. Havana was a whole mausoleum of patriots. Dates attached with pins to lives that were never led in its streets. A ranch in Viñales, the gesture of someone who looked at themselves in a mirror. Beyond these incidentals, nothing. Music records to remember those times. And on the cover of the records, again, the patriotic monuments: the column with the imperial eagle intact. Tidbits of exile. Little snacks with strawberry paste and cream cheese. Havana was always the time of an event never recovered, but more like invented. Another name for that time, another version of Proust. Or, as an ad for the Hard Rock Café in New York says, now it's time to remember what you never lived.

One always travels to Havana with the need—almost the desire—to try to make the trip a habit. One must forget the city, and that's why one must travel.

But the way there and the way back are more like two different kinds of leaving, not two different kinds of returning. Even when one returns, one is always leaving.

The story of a trip to Havana should be written in reverse: the chronicle of a trip toward forgetting. Habaneros, at the end of the day, erase the city constantly, every day. Aspiring to this kind of forgetfulness turns out to be the most genuine way of participating in that which is Cuban. I don't know if the word is *forget*, exactly, but it would be a synonym. In Havana, poems speak of other things, paintings show other realities. One looks for life behind the city's back or within it, deep within it. Too much so. Almost hidden: enclosures with cold, cold air-conditioning, well-presented canapés taken to a gathering where we also eat mangoes with our hands. That is also very Cuban: air-conditioning and mangoes.

This account is written with the tranquility lent by the taxonomy of my person so often repeated in Havana. I am a being who was born in that place, who left that place in this or that moment. Who lived in that country or the other. Who has or doesn't have, has lost or regained, or never had, the accent he should have had, never had, would have wanted to have. That whole set of parameters is a star placed on a piece of graph paper. The graph paper is enormous, and it spreads out, and it is Cuba. And somewhere on that graph paper, I don't care where, my point can be found. Going to Havana is like finding the paper, finding the point on the piece of paper, finding the repose that this amnesia can also invoke.

The Airport

But taxonomy begins from without, and much earlier. The graph paper was already in place—what's more, imposed—before leaving. The border is visible or invisible, according to how one chooses the form of departure (remember that there is no possible arrival—one is always leaving). A concrete signifier (an airport) or an abstract representation (a line in the ocean). Both have the same ambiguous effect: the dispossession of the citizen on the one hand, and on the other his or her exact positioning. Strictly speaking, there is not one border, nor two, but, rather, many.

The taxonomic delirium consumes us. So much uprooting, and still the need we all feel to locate ourselves in space. In the airport, habitual travelers can be distinguished from the curious and the nostalgic. Those, in turn, are different from those who live on the island but travel to see their families and return. Or from those who live elsewhere but have family in Cuba.

One line, two lines, paperwork at the Miami airport. Suitcases wrapped in plastic wrap, paying taxes at customs. Nostalgia has a price and there is no reason to pass from one world to another without that price being taken into account. One must traffic in nostalgia, make it profitable. Please fasten your seatbelts, observe the no smoking sign, and put your trays in the upright and locked position on the seat in front of you.

Figurative, abstract, or impressionist, the José Martí airport is not one but three. The historical terminal, through which those exiled in the 1960s and 1970s departed, is now reserved for air traffic within the island—that is the figurative. Flights from Havana to Cayo Coco, to Santiago, to Camagüey. The second terminal, completed not long ago, is an abstract work made for European, Canadian, and Latin American tourism. Boutiques, cafeterias, air-conditioning, no smoking signs, waxed floors. The third building is no-man's-land, between the figurative and the abstract: a type of shack devoted to flights between Havana and Miami, New York, or Los Angeles. All Van Gogh, late Matisse. Second-class people of indeterminate citizenship or nationality, who send the remittances that sustain the civic apparatus of second-class civilians (not that of those who are highest and certainly not that of the lowest) on the island.

In that shack a friend is selected for a thorough inspection of his luggage. Shirts, pants, underwear, fragrances, and shampoos. Then the photocopies, one by one. "This book, sir, about nineteenth-century architecture in Havana." "This essay, sir, about Virgilio Piñera." "About Virgilio Piñera, the homosexual," adds the official. "These magazines, these art catalogs, sir, are they art catalogs?" "Why are you bringing all of this material to Cuba?" "Are you some sort of messenger?" Nothing that was in the suitcase is impossible to get in Havana. The point is not that it is forbidden knowledge—it is simply the fact that knowledge must be controlled and managed and always must be for only a few. Books about marketing can be bought (in U.S. dollars) at La Moderna Poesía in Havana. (In Havana!) At the Mondadori bookstore, in the same place as the Instituto del Libro, you can pick up a book by Almudena Grandes for the beach. At literary talks in Havana, Reinaldo Arenas is spoken of, and pages by Cabrera Infante are discussed in great detail. Within the phantasmic realm of culture, books that were never published on the island can be quoted—books that, in a nutshell, came in some suitcase to be passed from hand to hand. Censorship is not what matters, it is access. What is sought at the border is more to put in an appearance. To remind the traveler— born in Cuba—that the island no longer belongs to him. The border is always the realm of the other, and Cuba is no longer yours. You gave it up when you left. You should accept your condition silently.

There Is No Silence in Havana

From eleven o'clock in the morning until dawn of the following day, there is no silence in Havana. In fact, there would be more noise if one did not have to repeat the same actions every day: going for water with a bucket, waiting in line for the *camello* (bus), dealing with the heat of June. Habaneros sit on the porches of their houses and shout to one another from the balconies. Dogs bark. The bitch of the block is in heat, pursued by all the stray dogs of Central Havana. Children throw rocks, mothers take the mortar and pestle out to the balcony to watch the ball game in the street. Deafeningly loud throughout the entire neighborhood is the *telenovela* at nine o'clock at night and the Friday movie. At Café París, silence is chased away with a radio program with commentary about the Cuban Adjustment Act. At El Rápido in Infanta, one afternoon when there is a blackout all over Central Havana the radio instructs citizens how to behave at a hotel. But at La Mina, at La Lluvia de Oro, in the cafes on Obispo Street—in Mercaderes, along the Avenida del Puerto, in the small shops and restaurants of Old Havana—the exorcism of silence has top priority. It is another plot, another policy, and it has its own internal logic.

Shooing away silence is part of a marketing ploy. It is not just the jukebox from the morning of one day to that of the next. It is the prefabricated but live segments. Sextets, trios playing romantic music. Drums and guitars, percussionists and *timbaleros*. Singers, bassists, electric pianos, maracas. Dance groups with kettledrums, voluntary workers dressed in the style of the nineteenth century. More than three days in Havana implies knowing the entire repertoire. At La Columnata Egipciana, a Cuban friend (a resident of the island, one must distinguish) calls it, before the ensemble begins to play: "They're going to play 'Yolanda.'" Indeed, the Pablo Milanés song is instantly recognizable at the first chord. "They're going to play 'Hasta siempre, comandante,'" the same friend says, and a *guaracha*, *bolero-son* version is played with a rhythmic refrain, harmony in three voices, and a twelve-string guitar. When the second coffee comes, he implores, "I hope they don't play 'Chan Chan.'" Too late. Not only "Chan Chan," but also "Dos Gardenias." The *Buena Vista Social Club*: a marketing phenomenon that deserves a separate commentary unto itself. The phenomenon is not just in Havana but also in Trinidad, in the cafe of a hotel in the Valle de Viñales, in Pinar del Río, in Matanzas.

Although this love for music is presented as a genetic predisposition among the Cuban people, there is no need to traffic in essentialisms. There is also no need to conclude, as if it were a bad lesson in cause and effect, that breaking out in song is a way to express what cannot be expressed in other ways: joy, pain, or even social criticism. That insistence upon not allowing even a minute of silence in a city that is about to fall apart says nothing about the Cuban people. Better yet, let's clarify: it says something about what someone thinks that the receptor of that signal wants. It is important for the tourist (or foreigner) not to sit down and write, not to sit and think, and not to observe. Better yet, it is important for the tourist (the foreigner) to observe only with music in the background. Imperative to cancel out the destruction of the city with the construction of the imaginary map of the possible city, just like it is more hygienic to insist upon the Cuban as a rumba dancer, than on the Cuban as the one who swears loyalty to the death, rigor in principles, work, and sacrifices. That official music is the mascara that crowns a made-up Havana. The slogans, either peeling or freshly painted, appeal to a different imaginary. Sacrifice, intransigence, perseverance. That imaginary excludes the Cuban *rumbero*; or if it includes him, it does so dialectically. In the backseat of a taxi, a resident Cuban in Aguada de Pasajeros takes a sip of bulk rum and tells me the well-known phrase, "Cubans love to party." It seems a state slogan by now, although I know very well that it is not. A friend who has come along with me has written a poem that encapsulates a bitter truth: "In Cuba, silence is bought." But there is no money capable of buying an instant of silence in a city that presents itself as the capital of rowdiness. Tropical dialectics: musical noise, silence of the painted slogans.

Impasto

Impasto: the dense application of pigment on fabric. Walking in Paris at sunset, Walter Benjamin says: "masses of golden-brown impasto that the demiurge had spread over the palette that is Paris" (Benjamin 1999, 351). These are the words of a believer: the impasto confuses his thinking, torments him, turns his thoughts into a disorderly kaleidoscope. The thick layer of paint brings Benjamin to the fragment.

Many have said it already: Havana needs a coat of paint. But after so much repetition I realize that the aestheticized decay is actually what's profitable. It seems to promise a certain nudity, like a body that reveals its layers in a desire for transparency. However, the effect lies. The peeling paint hides what makeup reveals. If Benjamin intuits fragmentation as the only possibility given by impasto, the peeling walls of Havana seek, rather, as Lezama Lima pointed out: *sucesivas, coordenadas* (successive events, coordinates). Continuities, following events, postrupture: revealing those successive breaks in time as a spectacle or show. To create the succession of those layers and not the violent break that the visible lack of paint represents. It is not surprising, in this respect, that an artist whom I visit in Havana is dedicated to collage. Everything seems to call for that way of appreciating reality. What is more, collage becomes almost a rite, as is all mimesis: an attempt to copy what is seen and perceived in the space of the canvas. A way of mimetizing oneself in one's surroundings, of understanding the syndrome of being uprooted, the lack of community between oneself and what surrounds us, revealing its continuity elsewhere.

The Cuban Revolution was always based on a principle of organicity: the creation of the organic intellectual, the organic relation between the country and city, the organic premise that runs throughout the work of Martí, and the organic relationship that exists among the fatherland, the nation, and the state. It was about creating a universe without tension, without fissures. Producing the surface of one unique terrain, which permitted a symbolic equation between the field of the signifier and the signified. While all of that organicity is ultimately subject to a deconstruction in which its own foundations may already contain the seeds of their own negation, the aim of the revolution always was and tried to be a plan without fissures of any type: the internal camp always worked with a principle of unanimity. Everything that was different was relegated elsewhere, to outside territory.

My own way of creating a collage. I confess to a friend who works in film that I don't want to write a chronicle of reality but a chronicle of *irreality*. However, the term is very hard for me to define. I realize that the only word I have to describe it is precisely that: *irreality*. I reiterate to my friend: I don't want to discover how Cubans (more specifically, habaneros) really live; I prefer to think about the different ways they imagine themselves living. No realism, the imaginary is what interests me. Not the yard in Central Havana, but the patio of the Hotel Sevilla. And not the history about the bar Floridita I find in a tourist guide, but the formula that allows a restaurant like La Maison to put on a fashion show going from table to table. It is not the reconstruction of the Havana of Ava Gardner, but the coexistence of the tourist circuit with the poetic ruins the tourist sees. Actually, I don't want to use the word *tourist*, but rather, *foreigner*.

My friend asks if I am seeking the unusual, and the word *unusual* (*insólito*) has a much clearer meaning that the word *irreality* lacks. I ask him to define a bit more his use of the term, but I clarify at the same time that I don't want to fall into the trap of moralizing, nor to get into sociology, anthropology: there are already too many travel books on the topic. He tells me about doctors who are taxi drivers, or stevedores who are transvestites. He mentions salaried restaurant workers who have engineering degrees from the Soviet Union or old heiresses of the musty Cuban aristocracy who now sell peanuts around the Malecón. I tell him no, that that seems too much like sociology, already getting into a cliché, a commonplace. It all smacks of an attempt to define the phenomenon and its meaning. "I am also interested in subjecting myself to experimentation," I tell him, "to force myself to write only in English in Havana for twenty-one days, to speak a language that isn't my own." It's all a performance for myself. I think that only from the viewpoint of that gesture can something I want to signify, but can't manage to articulate, be understood—without me having to explain it completely: a horizontal and vertical being out of step with things throughout the space of Cuba; the prerevolutionary sign of an elegant shoe store, where today screws and bras are sold; the insertion of various temporalities into one, like the layers of paint on an old Chevrolet; the Chevrolet itself and the Moskovitz; Cubans' joy, which is also a discipline demanded of them. The T-shirts of Che and 1950s Havana. Seeing or being seen in Havana is to lubricate oneself with the oil of a code that seeks to pass from one side to the other—to render foreignness invisible, to hide the transparency of an insistently marked border.

I attend a talk about Cuban poetry, given by a brilliant poet. I realize that José María Heredia gave Cuban poetry an image that is also a stance: the observer facing a phenomenon that manages to erase the distance between the observer and the observed. In this case, that of the foreigner who goes to Havana, the border never dissolves, but that separation is not necessarily agonizing. The pyramid and the waterfall remain on that side of the border. On this side, I with my Armani jeans, black T-shirt, and sneakers bought just for this occasion. Forget about romanticism.

Walter Benjamin, in his unfinished book, never tried to describe the city of Paris in the nineteenth century as it really was. Rather, he tried to define the dream that Paris had of itself. He attempted to reach this by digging deeper than the surface of the dream, at the same time remaining on the plane of the concrete. Marx and Freud. Dialectical materialism and the subconscious. Something like this should be done with Havana. The dream that its residents have of it, observed by the foreigner who is not a foreigner—diffused and disseminated in the face of the constant imposition of defining oneself.

Bourgeois Taste

"The cream color of the table cloth on which sparkled the perfection of the white porcelain, with edges of fired green, glowed and attained the tonal effect of a leaf resting in the center of the waning horn of the moon" (Lezama Lima

2000, 180). It is the little bell on the gate, the trunks that are difficult to close, so full are they with hatboxes. It is the collection of dolls at the bottom of a trunk, their eyes all open. Chatting in the living room in the afternoons. Transparent green chess pieces. English bonbons, bottles of rare liquor, trinkets. The clumsy toast made at a dinner party. The shop window, the arcade. It is the clinking of the fork on the wineglass. The soup tureen with plantain soup. The wicker baskets lined with a white linen napkin, the flowered water jugs on little wooden tables beside the four-post mahogany bed. The window blinds left open, the afternoon at the villa of a sugar plantation. It is the voluptuous black maid who brings water with lemon peel in a crystal glass on a small porcelain plate. It is a patio with malanga leaves, a bath prepared with aromatic flowers. It is, in short, a set of habits and customs in—one must be honest—terrible taste. Proust's legacy in Cuba is the nightmare that is the "MiHabana" area.

The MiHabana area takes delight in bad bourgeois taste essentialized as good Havanan bourgeois taste. Hence the abundant references to the possessive: "*Mi* Habana," "Havanan delirium," "Havana me," and so forth. One must repeat the name of the city as if it were an imaginary one, as if it actually did not exist. We must insist, with all this delirious tropicalia, on being seen as we wish to be seen through the eyes of the other. The possessive marks delirium, but it also shows the dispossession implied by the same: it is only possible to get into the MiHabana zone with dollars. It is a sanctuary of air-conditioned peace. It is a taste for the bourgeois, but the taste for the bourgeois that remained part of the good taste (that is bad taste) of your great-aunt's era. It is the bad taste that is the good taste of the bachelor uncle or of the elderly ladies that still sit on wicker chairs to get some fresh air, powdered and made up, with lace fans. It is the good taste, which is definitively bad taste, of little silver spoons.

This aesthetic has two central pieces: the store Mi Habana and the magazine *Opus Habana*. The first presents a tropics with a vague resemblance to the Raj—everything reminds one of a Britannicized Spain. The second wants to rescue the good taste of the republic, which is now turning into the bad taste of the late revolution: a baroque vocabulary without the scrolls, restored arches, antiquity turned into effect. Both are like a Carpentierian delirium but without the irony. As if they had placed a really fat Lezama in a shop window.

It's not that there wasn't bad taste before the revolution. In fact, Havana is where bad taste has always been taken for good taste, where a sense for taste implies a tacit acceptance of the eccentricity of the *taste* itself. Hence the open gestures of those overly ostentatious little palaces: the insistence of Orestes

Ferrara on building himself a castle or of Julio Lobo in building his collection of Napoleonic trinkets. But there is something different in these gestures now, which is neither a fiction nor something stuck in time. It smacks of a desperate fiction, a certain illusion of normality that one must create, even if the seams of that normality are showing. This is not a wealthy bourgeoisie, it doesn't build itself palaces, nor commission a monument from Picasso. It is like auctioning off a copy because the original is now completely beyond reach.

The defense of bourgeois taste can be found everywhere; it permeates all attitudes. Bourgeois space is an oasis in the middle of the struggle, a respite from the exhortations, a placid denouement for the downfall, a space created to get away from the photo of the son and the father, and from the plaza dedicated to the son and the father, with the statue of José Martí hugging his son.

In late Havana even the calls to the struggle have a bourgeois air. The construction of that plaza, across from the U.S. Interest Section, with those stylized banks of lights, as if they were palm trees. Although one must call it the José Martí Anti-Imperialist Tribune, it also has the scent of late taste, of the end of the game. Of many people applauding before going to pick up their remittances or before going to the Reparto Cubanacán to eat a succulent plate of *frijoles dormidos*.

Display

Meretsiana González Fuentes is the employee of the Department of Gastronomic Services who is in charge of changing every day the products displayed in the refrigerator and offered in the cafeteria of the Hotel Colina. The refrigerator is more like a simulacrum of a refrigerator, and the products shown likewise seem simulated.

Meretsiana wears a uniform of a black skirt and white shirt. She is getting on in years, although one wouldn't guess it. Behind the bar, she complains about where they have placed the press for heating ham and cheese sandwiches because bending over all day for the sandwiches has given her back pain.

The objects in the cooling case (it is not a refrigerator, but rather an apparatus that looks like one): one cheese sandwich; one ham and cheese sandwich; one can of Cristal beer; one can of Tropi-Cola; one bottle each of carbonated and noncarbonated Ciego Moreno mineral water; and one grilled chicken thigh displayed on a white plate covered with transparent paper.

La Moderna Poesía

There is no reason to point out that books are unaffordable for two-thirds of Cuban readers and for almost 99 percent of the writers who live in Cuba. To make that sort of review would be to fall into the trap of a poor, embittered discourse, sterilized and quarrelsome. The important thing is that Cuba remains without a publishing market to anchor it, without cultural *Vendredis*, without all-out book launches, and without high-class canapés; without shelves brimming with first or second editions, without employees who actually know about books rather than just operating the cash register; without fortuitous encounters, without bibliophiles, and even without a public. In an aseptic environment, one of technical quasi-efficiency in which one enters through one door and exits through another, and the security system preventing fortuitous theft is on display—stimulating the wish to do so in a different way (by means of electronic threat)—La Moderna Poesía remains open, imperishable, as Cuban as sun and palm trees, in the hot tropical afternoon.

Postscript

Books in the display cases: Raymond Moody's *Reunions: Visionary Encounters with Departed Beloved Ones* (by the author of *Life after Life*). Seneca, *De Vita Beata*; *El sexo en la edad madura* (Sex for seniors); *Como hacerse una auto-cura* (How-to home remedies); *Como utilizar tácticas militares para hacer dinero* (How to use military tactics to make money); *Diccionario de Marketing* (Marketing dictionary); *Técnicas de Fisicultura: Todo lo que hay que saber sobre el tema* (*Bodybuilding Techniques: Everything There Is to Know*); Cervantes, *Rinconete y Cortadillo*; Quevedo, *El buscón*; Moratín, *El sí de las niñas* (all Cátedra or Bruguera editions), between seven and twelve dollars. One copy of the cultural magazine *El caimán barbudo;* one copy of the daily newspaper *Granma* (in Spanish, English, and French); tour guides: *Havana, L'Havanne, Kuba*. Picture books of Che. T-shirts, postcards, key rings, stamps in the shape of tropical clouds, records, scissors, assorted color paper, glue, tape, cardboard boxes for filing papers.

The critical language calque of various issues of *La Gaceta de Cuba*.

Stagings, promotions, events that can be programmed. Workforce training, the dialogue with the purveyors of culture, the theater festival, the literary conferences with their token participants. The work of light technicians, stagehands, art critics. Set designers, selection committees. The panel that will judge the works, the typesetter, the costume designer. The work of writers from the provinces, some of such a high level.

The public responds to the performance, to the one-person show, to the poetry reading, to the afternoons in the house of poetry dedicated to the cultivation of the ten-line stanza in a lucid performance. A review of arts and cultural mechanisms, an ephemeral social gathering to recognize the new values. The labor of promotion, the aloof gesture, the very fact of elevating the quality, of considering oneself the victim of one's own artifice, of not being able to evade showing oneself, presented before the public attending the gallery, of pompous gestures.

Pan con timba

The peaceful oasis of La Columnata Egipciana. With its five enormous fans of white crosses hanging from a roof of turquoise blue rafters, and its interior patio decorated with malanga leaves in flowerpots and mud flowerbeds, its closed piano beside the door, and its red tiled floor. Its French-style tables with marble tops and wrought iron underneath, its wooden chairs, the enormous mirror on one side of the salon, its magazine rack without magazines, and the best coffee in Havana.

La Columnata Egipciana is a "house of infusions and elixirs, established 1835." It is open from Monday to Saturday, from nine in the morning until nine at night; and Sundays, from ten in the morning to ten at night. The menu emphasizes its "varieties of tea and coffee," "exotic tea," "malted milk," "criollo lemonade frappe," the not-to-be-missed, ineluctable *pan con timba* (bread with guava and cheese), and the "Columnata sandwich," perhaps the travelers' favorite. The menu also says, "The luxurious and elegant soda water called Columnata Egipciana has existed for a long time on Obispo Street, on the side near the corner with Mercaderes," and this appears copied out of the *Diario de la Habana* from June 1841. This is also mentioned on a plaque on the wall outside of the restaurant, which also informs us that Eça de Queiroz was among its illustrious visitors.

So much insistence upon authenticity might seem suspicious to many. But there is no reason to think badly of it when there is so much proof in its favor. In a guide for men seeking to meet Cuban men living on the island, it says that there is a "house of infusions" in Old Havana that attracts a more "effeminate," more "refined" clientele. Another person indicates to me that she herself saw the plaque being put into place and the removal of the debris. So it would seem that it is not a reconstruction but, rather, a reinvention. In tune with the times in which we live.

The *Jaba*

I go to meet a friend at his workplace so that we can go for coffee, a drink, to walk around Havana. Today he has gotten his *jaba* (plastic bag). The jaba is the boundary between the sacred and the profane, the boundary that marks the object and the being, represents the introduction of the world beyond Cuban territorial waters. It is difficult to speak of the jaba without talking about the person who receives it, and it is inconsistent with my most immediate objective, which consists of not making an anthropology of Cuba, which in turn consists of not making a survey of human things. Not the reality of Cuba, but its irreality.

To say it in *jitanjáfora* style: *la jaba de mi amigo abunda en jabones* (my friend's sack is full of soaps).[1] There is detergent, seven bars of scented soaps, and seven of soap for washing. There is toothpaste and, as a final sample, a disposable razor.

The price of the jaba is deducted at the end of the month for employees who work in the dollar zone, although the price of the bag is much less when purchased this way. The employee also has the right to more or less choose the content of the jaba, as long as the total amount doesn't exceed a certain stipulated sum. Not all jabas are alike, so the system is fed by what Marx called the "Asiatic mode of production," which mobilizes a large quantity of resources with the objective of doing a single thing. One employee reads the stipulated content, another writes the receipt, a third places the objects inside the bag, and a fourth hands it out.

The jaba's content renders something visible; and so, as if to underscore this, the bags are generally plastic but not transparent. The jaba forms part of a certain chronicle of the future, of some chronicle yet to be written.

A Ghost Haunts Obispo

Products that can be acquired at La Francia, at 452 Obispo Street: Stop Solar milk, Tropical, violet water. Fix Color hair dye. Nueva Imagen (Tropical) anti-lice lotion. Alicia enriched bioactive cream. Orquídea family shampoo. Fantasía talcum powder. Vitrario shampoo. A little black Nina Ricci bag on a mannequin wearing a black felt robe.

In the Napoleonic Museum

It is not just the Jaimanitas stone or the excellent stained-glass windows. It is not just the mahogany of the railing on the staircase and on the ceilings, but rather that all of this coexists with the imperial-style furniture, with the Sèvres crystal, with the portraits of Napoleon, Josephine, Pauline, Napoleon's in-laws, his brothers, the sables used by the army, the pistols used in Borodino, the standard-bearers, the clarinets of the musicians who announced the battles, the Sèvres porcelain, the *gueridon* with the portrait of Napoleon, his brothers, and their big marshal generals, the porcelain pitchers from the first and second empires, and finally, on the third floor, the enormous library of Cuban mahogany, with Julio Lobo's collection of books about Napoleon, which leads to a terrace made of Spanish tiles where Orestes Ferrara invariably practiced fencing, we imagine in the afternoon.

There are probably more interesting experiences in Havana, but few compare with a visit to the Napoleonic Museum, installed in the house of he who was the delegate Orestes Ferrara, and for the building of which the work on the construction of the National Capitol was stopped. The house is the work of the famous architects Govantes and Covarrubias, and was built expressly for Ferrara, who was not only a senator, but also a political man of the republic and a professor at the University of Havana. The collection is that of Julio Lobo, an important sugarocrat of the first republic whose descendants have returned to Cuba regularly to attend family-related activities.

The past is always visible to the extent that the present cannot be seen, and the first sensation produced by a visit to the museum is that of blindness. The past is observed in two superimposed layers, but the present of the visit remains outside of time. As if we were making a sweep through an Alejo Carpentier novel, the guide details every object, every imperial eagle, every statue, every dining-room suite: Napoleon's bed, with the covers he used, the paintings of Josephine, the painting of Paulina, the relatives who receive cushy jobs, military posts, commissions, kingdoms.

As a child, I had an album of stamps that showed scenes of Havana and of Cuba. Those stamps, as I remember, were collectable; the object was precisely to show children who had left, with or without their parents, the details of the Cuba that they had left behind. At some point on this visit, I realize that the guide knows Paris the same way that I knew Havana. She has worked in the museum for eleven years, giving guided tours. She knows every detail of every object: the mahogany chairs with claw-footed legs, the engravings that depict the obelisk, the Louvre, the Pantheon, Versailles. She points to Versailles and asks me, "Have you been there?" and I answer in the affirmative. She also shows me a picture of the Pantheon and asks the same thing, I tell her yes, and she answers, "It must be very impressive." An entire life, almost, dedicated to a place to which she has no possibility of visiting, getting to know an imperial family and a revolution that turned into an empire from the space of a republic that turned into a revolution before turning into something else, which we see now.

Glasses in Cuba

Everything is fragile, too fragile. Everything is a creation, for, from, and toward fragility. I order a mango smoothie in national currency at a stand full of people near Monte Street. One employee rings me up while another handles the blender. When he is finished mixing the drink, a third employee brings glasses on a green plastic tray and places them next to the man at the mixer, who proceeds to fill the glasses with the juice. The worker who rang me up is in charge of serving me the smoothie by hand in a glass cup.

All of Havana has its glassware. The friend who serves you coffee at the average house, the woman who gives you a glass of water, the girl at the *paladar* who brings you a beer, or the painter who serves you what she calls "iron nectar," a soft drink sold in bulk that looks like Ironbeer. All of them give you the drink in little porcelain cups that have been passed from generation to generation with the same broken handle, on little brass trays with an ad for a prerevolutionary beer, in glasses rescued from a hotel in Santa Clara when it still existed, in the 1940s, or in those glasses that can only be found outside of Cuba in retro shops and which appear in all of Almodóvar's films: little glasses of the '40s variety that surely were purchased with their own tray and were on display in the corner of the house reserved for the bar of the older set. They are glasses that evoke an afternoon at the country house or that ooze a long lost time from their pores.

Although it wouldn't do for us to talk about time here.

A life measured by little cups scrubbed by hand? The world of hand-washed glasses? The glass that recalls another glass you used to use in childhood? All of that. The fact that the man serves me the mango smoothie. That I drink it in the street, like everyone else. That it would never occur to me to take the glass with me (to steal it). That I drink the mango smoothie in the street, in that suffocating heat, with everyone out in that suffocating heat at three in the afternoon on Monte Street, and when I finish with the glass—the glass in which only the dregs of the mango smoothie remain—then, like everyone else, I put the glass back on a plastic tray next to the window of the man at the register, and then I go along my way. The glass remains, the moment has passed.

Roma

The levels, or rather the layers, that Fellini sketches out in Rome. His childhood memories and adolescence. The difficult entry into Rome on the highway, the rain pouring down, the travelers ensconced in their cars, everything culminating in that enormous traffic jam next to the Colosseum. The tourists and the hippies. That filming when his film crew joins the excavations being made for the Roman subway system, which have been stopped because they have suddenly found a wall, with an empty space searched behind the wall, and that space turns out to be a Roman house. They enter the house, observing its salons and galleries, and the frescoes on the wall, which are beginning to disappear from contact with the outside air. The brothels. The salons where the aristocracy is already somehow related to the church, which allows that lavish ecclesiastical fashion show. At the end, the camera again traces a path through the streets, full of guests, through the Trastevere neighborhood. It surprises Gore Vidal at an outside table and then finds and tries to follow Anna Magnani, who retires to her lodgings insisting without insisting on a secret, and pursues a group of bikers who offer one last spin around the fountains, monuments, and columns, before finally leaving and getting lost in the Roman night. We assume this is an urban motorway that allows the exit from the city, at this hour—almost dawn—without any traffic. The horizontality of the gesture, of the highway, in combination with the verticality of the urban layers that are shown, of the past that disappears upon contact with the present. The hybrid genre—between autobiographical narrative and documentary. Its divisions into clearly marked parts or sequences, not interrupted in between, but rather superimposed in a nonviolent fashion—everything appears lubricated by the voice and persona of the director, who avoids violence. As Gore Vidal says: everything has ended and begun so many times in Roma that we come here to await the end or the beginning of everything.

In this version of the allegory, Havana is Anna Magnani, too. There are no secrets in Havana. Everything is secret in Havana. As the rooms beneath the visible urban plan are revealed, their traces are erased. There was someone, but that someone is always subject to the loss of the same trace that he or she left. Entering is always difficult; the door is always open wider for the exit. Everything is subject to disappearing from one moment to the next. The best thing that can be done is to wait.

Here, in short, nothing has happened.

Note

1. A *jitanjáfora* is a poetic device that emphasizes sound over meaning.

Azotea (rooftop). The term refers to the flat rooftops of most buildings in Havana that increasingly have been put to use as alternate living spaces. Shacks on roofs, improvised with wood, or more elaborate "penthouses" accommodate growing families or newcomers to the city. Rooftops also can serve to breed pigeons and chickens and as spaces for informal gatherings, especially during the power outages of the 1990s, when people were looking to pass the time until fans went back on. As Emma Álvarez-Tabío Albo indicates in her chapter, from the rooftop one could also contemplate the spectacle of Havana in ruins.

Balsero **(rafter).** Under Cuban law it is illegal to leave the country without permission. While already before 1990 Cubans had fled the country by boat or raft, the number increased drastically with the economic crisis of the beginning of the 1990s and peaked during the so-called Cuban Rafters' Crisis in the summer of 1994. Between June and August 1994, several government-owned ferries and tugboats were hijacked by Cubans wanting to leave the country; not all made it to the United States. On August 5th riots broke out in Havana after the police prevented a ferry of would-be emigrants from leaving the port. They were ended with the help of paramilitary groups and, finally, by the personal appearance of Fidel Castro. A few days later, Castro withdrew Cuban coast guards, which led to the departure of about 30,000 rafters. The U.S. administration of Bill Clinton responded at first by sending those intercepted at sea to the Guantánamo naval base, from where, after some negotiation, they were finally admitted to the United States. Later, the "wet foot, dry foot" policy was created, allowing U.S. coastal guards to send Cubans intercepted on the sea back to Cuba, accepting for entry to the United States only those who had made it to its shores. The Cuban Rafters' Crisis also motivated the reactivation of a lottery, where all Cubans could apply to win one of 20,000 exit visas per year issued by the United States.

Barbacoa. Etymologically related to *bajareque*, a rudimentary type of construction used by the Siboney Indians, the term *barbacoa* originally referred to the arrangement of wood sticks over a hole in the earth to grill or barbecue meat. Today, it refers to the informal—and often illegal—constructions, mostly in old colonial buildings with high ceilings, where an additional mezzanine floor subdivides a room into an upper and a lower level, the upper level being reached usually through an extra staircase or a ladder. As Del Real and Scarpaci write, in Cuba barbacoas have been known to exist at least since 1914. In the 1990s this type of creative usage grew more common due to the increasing overpopulation of Havana and the impossibility of acquiring new property; it contributed to the collapse of buildings overburdened with additional weight. Barbacoas are not unique to Cuba and similar types of informal construction are known to exist in Mexico and Brazil.

Basic Secondary Schools of the Countryside (Escuelas Secundarias Básicas en el Campo, [ESBEC]). Toward the end of the 1960s these schools were devised to introduce young Cubans to study and agricultural labor alike and thus to "ruralize culture." Between 1968 and 1973 two hundred so-called ESBEC were built. Students generally spent at least three years in these full-time schools, returning to see their parents only on certain weekends. The ESBEC were often a relief for parents who in this way did not have to pay for the food and school uniforms of their children, but the system suffered later greatly from degrading living conditions.

Battle of Ideas (la Batalla de Ideas). This mobilization campaign was initiated after 1999 in response to the Elián González affair, to reaffirm the idea of socialism and demonstrate to the outside the continuing popular support for the revolution. It consisted of regular rallies, for which attendance was obligatory, media debates, and publications. It placed special emphasis on the participation of the young. The faces of the campaign were, besides Fidel Castro, a number of politicians of a younger generation, called by the journalist Jon Lee Anderson "the talibans." Around the U.S. Interest Section in Havana, a symbol associated with the battle of ideas was a statue put in place during the Elián González affair, showing José Martí with a child in his arms. (See also **Elián González affair**)

Bay of Pigs Invasion (Invasión de Bahía de Cochinos or Playa Girón). In order to avoid the consolidation of the new Castro regime, the CIA, with the backing of the administration of President Eisenhower, helped organize a group of Cuban exiles to invade the island and bring down the revolution. The invasion took place in April of 1961 but was brought down within three days by Castro's troupes. It turned into a fiasco for John F. Kennedy's early government and was followed by the Cuban Missile Crisis, after which Kennedy abandoned the idea of a future invasion of the island. (See also **Cuban Missile Crisis**)

Camello. After the Soviet Union stopped subsidizing the Cuban government, the public bus system in Havana was reduced in the 1990s by 80 percent, due to the sudden lack of gasoline and of replacement pieces. To remedy the problem, the Metrobus, a new type of mass transport called popularly the camello, was created. It consisted of a truck drawing a double-bus size, camel shaped wagon. Camellos were designed to transport about 220 passengers, but they became notorious for being overcrowded, dirty, and prone to sexual harassment. Little by little they were substituted for regular new buses and disappeared definitively in 2008.

City Model of Havana (Maqueta de La Habana). One of the first projects of the GDIC (see also **Group for the Integral Development of the Capital**). The model of Havana was built at a scale of 1:1000; it is more than 220 square meters large and one of the biggest city models worldwide. It was created originally as an instrument of urban planning and control. Its three colors indicate the main periods of construction in Havana, brown representing the colonial period, ochre the republican city, and marble the revolutionary city. The pavilion that houses the city model opened in 1995 to the public and has become an important tourist attraction.

Ciudad Universitaria José Antonio Echeverría (CUJAE). The construction of a new university campus for Havana was begun in 1961 and inaugurated officially in 1964 as the CUJAE, a complex of buildings that housed the Technical Schools of the University of Havana. In 1976, however, it was reorganized as an autonomous entity called the Instituto Superior Politécnico José Antonio Echeverría (ISPJAE). From then on, its focus lay on the training of professionals in architecture and engineering.

Communist Party of Cuba (PCC). The PCC was founded originally in 1925 by members of the Third International. It collaborated during the 1940s at times with Fulgencio Batista's government, but from 1954 to 1959 became a target of government suppression. In 1944 it had been renamed People's Socialist Party (PSP); this party merged in 1961 with Fidel Castro's Twenty-sixth of July Movement and Directorio to form the Organizaciones Integradas Revolucionarias (ORI). This party was purged and reconstituted into the Partido Unido de la Revolución Socialista (PURS), which in turn became the PCC in 1965. In the Constitution of 1976 the PCC was declared the only political party legally recognized in Cuba. Until recently, Fidel and Raúl Castro were respectively the first and the second secretaries of the party.

Cuban Film Institute (Instituto Cubano del Arte y la Industria Cinematográficos [ICAIC]). Founded in March of 1959 by Alfredo Guevara, the ICAIC is one of the most prestigious state organizations in Cuban contemporary culture. In the 1960s the ICAIC introduced Cuban audiences to the European film d'auteur and to Latin American movies, and invited many internationally known filmmakers to come to Cuba. It also generated an important movement in movie posters. Until the 1990s the ICAIC has produced all Cuban movies, making Cuban cinema into a trademark of experimental cinema in feature films, documentaries, and animated movies. The ICAIC also organizes annually the International Festival of New Latin American Cinema. After 1990 the ICAIC's efforts to offer a platform of debate and social criticism continued, even though it lost its monopoly on Cuban cinema, as movies have been increasingly filmed as coproductions or with the help of fellowships and grants from other countries.

Cuban Missile Crisis. One of the most dramatic episodes of the Cold War, this conflict involved Cuba, the United States, and the Soviet Union from October 14 to October 29, 1962. Also known as the October Crisis, the confrontation began when a North American spy plane discovered Soviet nuclear missiles on the island, of whose necessity Nikita Khrushchev had convinced the Cuban government only recently. After considering an invasion, John F. Kennedy discarded the plan and instead placed Cuba in "quarantine," prohibiting any ship from reaching the island or else threatening to intervene. After several tense days, during which Soviet ships hovered away from the zone, the Soviets and the United States arrived, without consulting with Cuban representatives, at the agreement that the USSR was going to withdraw its missiles from the island. The United States, in turn, declared it would not invade the island and also retrieved nuclear missiles it had stationed in Turkey.

Cuban Union of Artists and Writers (Unión de escritores y artistas cubanos [UNEAC]). Like the ICAIC a landmark cultural institution, founded in 1961, UNEAC was meant to support Cuban writers and artists financially, help them navigate administrative issues, and offer an intellectual forum of exchange. According to its declaration of principles, it also "rejects and combats any activity contrary to the principles of the Revolution." In the 1980s architects were integrated into the section of visual arts, which led to the inclusion and discussion of urban issues during several UNEAC congresses. In 1993 a decree law allowed writers to negotiate contracts with foreign publishers independently, which led to an increasing number of book publications outside the country.

Dollarization. On July 26, 1993, the use of the U.S. dollar was officially depenalized in Cuba and began to be used alongside the Cuban peso. As a consequence, Cubans continued to receive their salary in Cuban pesos but were now able to exchange them against U.S. dollars and to buy merchandise at U.S. dollar prices in supermarkets and other stores, formerly called *diplo-tiendas* and until then prohibited to most Cubans. The use of the dollar was discontinued in November 2004 in favor of the Cuban "convertible peso," which until today continues to coexist with the Cuban peso. During this decade a dual economy came into place that created new social and racial divides among Cubans receiving dollars through remittances or through their work in joint ventures and Cubans depending only on their Cuban peso salaries.

Elián González affair. One of the most controversial episodes in the recent relations between Cuba and the United States was that of the six-year-old Cuban boy Elián González, who arrived in the United States in November of 1999 by boat. The vessel, in which Elián and his mother were traveling together with twelve other passengers, had shipwrecked, and only Elián and two others had survived. The boy was reclaimed by relatives in Miami refusing to send him back to the father, who requested his return to Cuba. The debate was reported extensively in the media and polarized Cuban Americans and Cubans, who were reminded of traumatic family separations of the early 1960s. In June of 2000, Elián returned to Cuba in the company of his father after a court decision had been enforced by the police. (See also *balsero*)

Embargo. Economic relations between Cuba and the United States changed drastically when in the beginning of 1960 Cuba reached several commercial agreements with the USSR that guaranteed, among other things, a fixed rate of exported sugar in return for the import of raw oil. U.S. refineries on the island rejected buying Soviet oil, to which the Cuban government responded by nationalizing all foreign refineries. Consequently, the United States stopped importing Cuban sugar followed by the Cuban expropriation of all North American companies and properties in its territory. Finally, on October 19, 1960, President Eisenhower imposed a trade embargo that had turned into a total embargo at the arrival of John F. Kennedy to the White House. Diplomatic relations between both countries ceased to exist in the beginning of 1961, further motivating Cuba's alignment with the socialist bloc. In the 1990s the Law Torricelli (1992) and the Helms-Burton Act (1996) further tightened the embargo and made its revocation more difficult.

Free Farmer's Market (Mercado libre campesino [MLC]). In 1980 a decree allowed the expansion of the private business sector through so-called free farmer's markets. In those markets, agricultural workers were able to sell excess production directly to the consumer, determining the price and the quantity of products offered themselves. In 1986, however, Castro's government began a process of "rectification of errors," reacting to the restructuration of the Soviet Bloc. One of its measures was the closure of the MLCs. In the 1990s the MLCs were allowed to open again, as the government could not provide more goods to the population.

Frozen Zone (*zona congelada*). The term refers to an area of mostly elegant residential neighborhoods to the West of Havana that includes Miramar and parts of El Vedado and Nuevo Vedado. Houses that had been left behind by emigrating middle- and upper-class families were reassigned to embassies, officials, and to fellowship students. Until recently a special background check and permit were required to move to this area. In the 1990s new revitalization projects, hotels, offices for joint-venture enterprises, high-level retail stores, and the first shopping malls added further attraction to these areas, coveted now also by a newly wealthy class of Cubans. (See also **dollarization** and *maceta*)

Gray Period (*quinquenio gris*). It was the Cuban critic Ambrosio Fornet who coined the term *quinquenio gris* to refer to the repressive cultural climate that came to dominate Cuban society between 1971 and 1976. This period was symbolically demarcated by the Congress on Education and Culture, held in April 1971 where Fidel Castro denounced cultural imperialism, "pseudo-leftists," and bourgeois intellectuals. The congress was followed by shifts in the editorial committees of Cuban journals and publishing houses, and the demotion and transfer from Havana to other provinces of writers and officials considered ideologically deviant or undisciplined. Fornet considers, in allusion to the Cuban implementation in those years of the Soviet-style "five-year plans," that the period came to a close in 1976 with the new Cuban Constitution. Others, among them Mario Coyula, claim that it lasted much longer.

Greenbelt Plan (Plan del Cordón de La Habana). At the end of the 1960s this plan stipulated the development of the rural area surrounding the capital city and came to symbolize the attempts of the government to modernize agriculture in Cuba at large. Coffee and fruit were planted, and storage houses, animal farms, housing for farm workers, and cafeterias were created. Many residents of Havana were relocated and began to live in small rural communities in the outskirts, meant to offer an alternative to urban lifestyle more in tone with revolutionary ideas about the equal distribution of opportunities in the city and the countryside.

Group for the Integral Development of the Capital (GDIC). Founded in 1988, the GDIC is a team of specialists from various disciplines who promote the economic, social, and cultural development of Havana, the diffusion of a stronger communal conscience, and the bettering of the urban image. The GDIC has created, to this effect, the Pavilion of the City Model of Havana (see **City Model of Havana**). It also coordinates the Comprehensive Workshops for Neighborhood Change that ameliorate living conditions in the most neglected areas of the city. These workshops depend on the participation and solidarity of residents in individual neighborhoods to renovate dwellings and give impulses to local businesses and urban education.

Gusano **(worm).** Name given to the many Cubans leaving for exile in the early 1960s. Gusano came to stand as a pejorative term to refer to Cuban emigrants especially to Miami, associating them with lack of determination and with being "counterrevolutionaries." The word was used in later emigration waves during acts of repudiation organized to insult those who were leaving. This perception changed for the first time with the "dialogue" of 1978 and 1979, when a younger generation of Cuban exiles returned for the first time to the island to visit their families and friends there and brought presents and dollars. According to a popular saying, the "worms had turned into butterflies." This dialogue was interrupted by the Mariel exodus in 1980 (see also **Mariel exodus**). In the 1990s the term fell out of use, as the relations between the Cuban American community and their Cuban families and friends grew closer again.

Habagüanex. At the beginning of the 1990s Eusebio Leal Spengler, the city historian, founded Habagüanex, the only state company in Cuba with an independent financial budget. The company, which manages a network of restaurants, bars, hotels, and other tourist businesses in Old Havana, turned out to be financially successful, using its income to further renovate the historic center. It has also renovated or created schools, childcare centers and retirement homes to continue to make the center livable for a socially diverse population. The name is derived from a mythic indigenous chief who also inspired the naming of the city. (See also **Office of the City Historian**)

Jinetera **(street hustler).** While before the 1990s the term referred to a street vendor who dealt in black market goods, it has come to be used now with reference to a female or a male prostitute. Even though the revolutionary government had sweepingly eliminated prostitution in the 1960s, with the economic crisis of the 1990s the sudden need to provide for basic subsistence arose. The opening to international tourist markets in the 1990s produced a resurge in sex tourism. Jineteros and jineteras have in common with illegal taxi drivers, street musicians, self-taught painters, and the owners of illegal *paladares* (restaurants) the fact that they work outside official professional restrictions, motivated usually by dire economic constraints. (See **Special Period in Times of Peace**)

Lenin Vocational School. In one of his songs, the singer Silvio Rodríguez refers to the Lenin Vocational School as the "cradle of a new race." Indeed, the Lenin Vocational School was meant to produce a type of Cuban in the mold of Ernesto Che Guevara's new man. Created to orient students directly toward academic programs furthering the development of society, especially in the technical and natural sciences, the Lenin Vocational School opened in 1974 outside of Havana. Its population of pre-university students lives in an authentic city within a city that houses, next to classrooms and other school-related installations, dormitories, sports facilities, auditoriums, a museum, a library, a movie theater, and other recreational areas.

Maceta. The term refers to a new social actor in the Cuban public sphere, who has profited from the economic changes of the Special Period. Macetas are those newly wealthy Cubans who receive remittances, rent out rooms to tourists, own small restaurants, or sell merchandise informally. They often have developed a showy middle-class lifestyle.

Mariel exodus. In April 1980 a group of five Cubans crashed a bus into the Peruvian embassy and sought asylum. When the ambassador granted it to them against customary proceeding, Fidel Castro ordered the Cuban guard to stop protecting the embassy. In the following days 10,000 more Cubans flooded the embassy asking for asylum. An agreement was reached that everyone in the embassy and everyone else who wanted to leave the island could do so through the port of Mariel, the closest sea port to Havana, if someone came to take him or her. Between April and October of that year, the Cuban American community organized the rescue of 125,000 islanders, among them convicted criminals and even some mentally ill persons, of whom the Cuban government wanted to be rid of.

Master Plan for the Overall Revitalization of Old Havana. The Office of the City Historian, together with the Directorship of Cultural Patrimony created this plan in 1994 as a multidisciplinary project to examine the actual conditions of the municipality and design a series of measures to motivate the restoration and growth of the area. A group of specialists is in charge, but the plan also foresees the active participation of the residents. It follows four central themes: the protection of the cultural patrimony; the preservation of Old Havana as a residential zone; the better organization of the municipality's infrastructure; and the encouragement of local economic growth and self-financing.

Microbrigades. A project undertaken in the 1970s by the government to create, with the help of the population, new dwellings in the urban centers where they were most urgently needed. Materials were given out to the residents of future buildings so that they themselves could construct their own building with the help of a group of experts. These contingents of workers were called *microbrigadas*. The system of microbrigades was not particularly successful and fell into disuse in the 1980s, but it was revitalized after 1987 with the "social microbrigades."

National Art Schools (Escuelas de Arte Cubanacán). The five-building complex of the national art schools was created in 1962 on the terrain of the former Havana Country Club as a center for studying the performing arts (music, theater, plastic arts, ballet, and dance). Similar to the CUJAE, the National Art Schools incarnated the educational, cultural, and architectural ambitions of the new government. Three architects, the Cuban Ricardo Porro and the Italians Roberto Gottardi and Victorio Garatti, were contracted to build the schools. After four years, however, the government lost interest in the daring avant-garde constructions and ordered work on them to be stopped. The National Art Schools fell into ruin. They have received renewed attention in the last decades, especially after they were placed on

UNESCO's list of endangered monuments. Work on them has been taken up again, and as of 2009 three of the five art schools were finished and in use, the last two being still under construction.

"New man." One of the most influential concepts of Ernesto Che Guevara, articulated in his essay "Socialism and man in Cuba" (1965). For Guevara, a socialist state needed a new type of individual, a man of the future who would unite socialist values such as solidarity, interest in the greater good of all, commitment with the revolution and with the neighbor in a new, revolutionary conscience. On the practical level, the "new man" was conceived as an open-ended project. It was meant to strictly accompany the creation of the new society, and to "perpetuate, in daily life, a heroic attitude."

Office of the City Historian. Established in 1938 under the direction of Emilio Roig Leuchsenring, the Office of the City Historian began to assume a central role in the development of the capital fifty years later, in 1978, when Havana was declared a national monument. This new sense of national pride in the city was pushed even more when in 1982 the municipality of Old Havana and its fortresses were declared World Heritage Sites by UNESCO. As a result, the Office of the City Historian, with its current occupant Eusebio Leal Spengler, turned into a complex organization with a variety of architectural, economic, and cultural responsibilities. (See also **Habagüanex**)

Revolutionary Offensive. In the second part of the 1960s Cuba's economy was radically restructured. To accelerate the transition toward a communist system, the government organized a campaign against private initiatives, called the Revolutionary Offensive of 1968, which entailed the elimination of self-employment and the nationalization of about 50,000 small businesses. This created a quite unexpected deterioration in the process of distribution and availability of products and services.

Sert Plan. On the invitation of President Fulgencio Batista, Josep Lluís Sert together with a group of architects set to work at the end of the 1950s on a plan of urban development for the capital city. The Pilot Plan of Havana (1955–1958), better known as the Sert Plan, conceived the possibility to transform the capital into a modern city, with a special interest in the renovation of the historical center and the Malecón. A series of demolitions was to replace the colonial grid system with a new system of avenues; in the area of the Malecón, the Sert Plan proposed to build tall buildings and to add an artificial island with hotels, casinos, and commercial centers. The plan provoked polemic discussions among Cuban architects, and it was abandoned after 1959.

Solar **(tenement).** The word originally referred to a specific terrain designated for construction. With time, and the gradual degradation of dwellings, the term began to be used popularly to designate a building with a central patio, shared sanitary installations, and individually rented rooms. As Hamberg explains, a solar is similar to a *ciudadela*, both being smaller than a *cuartería*, housing sometimes more than sixty families. The Cuban solar can be compared to the Chilean *conventillo*, the Argentine *chorizo*, the Brazilian *cortiço*, or the Mexican *casa de vecindad*.

Special Period in Times of Peace. Euphemism used by Fidel Castro to name the period of economic crisis ushered in by the end of subsidized trade with the Soviet Union in 1990. Castro used the term first in a speech given in January 1990 to announce the lack of basic products, especially gasoline, for the functioning of the domestic economy. In order to counter the effects of the crisis, the government implemented a series of urgent measures reserved for times of war, such as blackout times for gas, water, and electricity in different areas of the island, and greater than before rationing of certain types of food. It also began to allow foreign investments, centered primarily on the reactivation of the tourist industry. Finally, in 1993 the use of the U.S. dollar was allowed on the island and continued in effect until 2004. The end of the Special Period is much less clear than its beginning. Although, today, Cubans on the island tend to refer to the Special Period in the past tense. (See also **dollarization**)

Tugurio **(slum).** Following Hamberg, tugurio is the generic Spanish name for a slum. It can be defined according to four categories used by the UN-Habitat commission: overpopulation, a group of dwellings insufficiently built, inadequate access to basic infrastructure, and unclear residential status. In the case of Havana, the *tugurization*, as Antonio José Ponte has called it, of parts of the city is related to the longtime neglect of old buildings and to the at times labyrinthine improvised additions that residents have made in order to create more living space. (See also **barbacoa**)

Union of Young Communists (UJC). Founded in 1962 the UJC is the youth organization of the Communist Party of Cuba. It has more than 500,000 members under the age of thirty and is dedicated to political education and the coordination of social and political activities. Its main publication is the journal *Juventud Rebelde*. (See also **Communist Party of Cuba**)

Urban Reform Law. In March of 1959 Law 35 decreed the reduction of rents by fifty percent, and in October of 1960 the Urban Reform Law stipulated that anyone who owned two or more buildings was only allowed to retain one building, leaving everything else to the state. These measures, together with the Agrarian Reform Law, motivated the departure of many whose belongings were confiscated by the authorities.

REFERENCES

Acanda, Jorge Luis. 2000. "Racapitular la Cuba de los 90." *La Gaceta de Cuba*, no. 3. July 21. http://biblioteca.filosofia.cu/php/export.php?format=htm&id=34&view=1.

Acosta, Dalia. 1998. "Cada vez es más difícil radicarse en La Habana." *InterPress Service*, June 10. http://domino.ips.org/ips%5Cesp.nsf/vwWebMainView/DB9EE2AF0888 B16180256A080046C442/?OpenDocument.

Agamben, Giorgio. 1999. *Potentialities: Collected Essays in Philosophy*. Edited and translated by Daniel Heller-Roazen. Stanford: Stanford University Press.

———. 2008. *La potencia del pensamiento*. Barcelona: Anagrama.

Alberto, Eliseo. 2005. *Esther en alguna parte*. Madrid: Espasa Calpe S.A.

———. 2008. *El retablo del Conde Eros*. Barcelona: El Aleph Editores.

Álvarez, Elena, and Jorge Mattar. 2004. *Política social y reformas estructurales: Cuba a principios del siglo XXI*. Mexico City: CEPAL-INE-PNUD.

Álvarez-Tabío Albo, Emma. 1989. *Vida, mansión y muerte de la burguesía cubana*. Havana: Letras cubanas.

———. 2000. *Invención de la Habana*. Barcelona: Casiopea.

———. 2001. "La ciudad en el aire." In *Cuba y el día después: Doce ensayistas nacidos con la revolución imaginan el futuro*, edited by Iván de la Nuez, 83–108. Barcelona: Mondadori.

Angotti, Tom. 2006. "Apocalyptic Anti-Urbanism: Mike Davis and His Planet of Slums." *International Journal of Urban and Regional Research* 30:951–67.

Appadurai, Arjun. 1996. *Modernity at Large: Cultural Dimensions of Modernity*. Minneapolis: University of Minnesota Press.

———. 2002. "Spectral Housing and Urban Cleansing: Notes on Millennial Mumbai." In *Cosmopolitanism,* edited by Carol Breckenridge, Sheldon Pollock, Homi Bhabha, and Dipesh Chakrabarty, 54–81. Durham: Duke University Press.

Arango, Arturo. 2001. *El libro de la realidad*. Barcelona: Tusquets.

Arenas, Reinaldo. 1991. *Viaje a La Habana*. Madrid: Mondadori.

Arquitectura. 1917. "Notas, Noticias y Comentarios." *Arquitectura* 1, no. 4 (October): 39.

———. 1919. "Ojeada Restrospectiva Sobre el Año 1918." *Arquitectura* 2, no. 7 (January): 11–12.

Arranz González, Héctor. 1998. "Algunas reflexiones acerca de la planificación local participativa a través de estudios de casos." In *Desarrollo Urbano: Proyectos y Experiencias de Trabajo*, edited by Roberto Dávalos Domínguez and Alain Basail Rodríguez. Havana: Universidad de La Habana.

Augé, Marc. 1995a. *Los "no lugares" espacios del anonimato: Una antropología de la sobremodernidad*. Barcelona: Gedisa.

———. 1995b. *Non-Places. An Introduction to Supermodernity*. London: Verso.

Auslander, Philip, ed. 2003. *Performance: Critical Concepts in Literary and Cultural Studies*. New York: Routledge.

Barthes, Roland. 1980. *Mitologías*. Mexico City: Siglo XXI.

Basulto, Hilda. 1974. "La fenomenología del silencio: Apuntes para una temática por investigar." *Revista Mexicana de Sociología* 36, no. 4 (October–December): 877–85.

Bauzá, Jorge. 1997. "Política Habitacional de Cuba." Paper presented at the Second Meeting of the Red Interamericana de Centros de Salud en la Vivienda. Havana.

Bedoya, Francisco. 2009. *La Habana desaparecida*. Edited by Emma Álvarez-Tabío Albo. Havana: Ediciones Boloña.

Benevolo, Leonardo. 1986. *Historia de la arquitectura moderna*. Barcelona: Gustavo Gili.

Benítez Pérez, María Elena. 1999. *Panorama sociodemográfico de la familia cubana*. Havana: Editorial de Ciencias Sociales.

———. 2002. *Cambios sociodemográficos de la familia cubana en la segunda mitad del siglo XX*. Havana: Centro de Estudios Demográficos (CEDEM). http://www.cedem.uh .cu/Catalogo-Biblioteca/document/PD/Cambios_sociodemograficos_de_la_fa milia_cubana.pdf.

Benjamin, Walter. 1999. "Paris Diary." In *Selected Writings (1927–1934)*, vol. 2: 337–55. Translated by Michael William Jennings. Cambridge: Harvard University Press.

Benneton Group. 2002. *Colors 47: Madness*. November 24.

Betancourt, Jorge E., and Ernesto René. 2006. *9550*. Producciones Por la izquierda.

Betancourt, Juan Carlos. Forthcoming. "Los hijos rebeldes de la revolución cubana: unas notas a la historia del sots art cubano." In *Caviar with Rum: Cuba-USSR and the Post-Soviet Experience*, edited by Jacqueline Loss. New York: Palgrave.

Bhabha, Homi. 1994. *The Location of Culture*. London: Routledge.

Bial, Henry, ed. 2004. *The Performance Studies Reader*. New York: Routledge.

Birkenmaier, Anke. 2009. "Art of the Pastiche: José Manuel Prieto's *Rex* and Cuban literature of the 1990s." *Revista de Estudios Hispánicos* 43: 123–47.

Blum, Martin. 2000. "Remaking the East German Past: *Ostalgie*, Identity, and Material Culture." *Journal of Popular Culture* 34, no. 3 (Winter): 229–54.

Bobes, Marilyn. 2005. *Fiebre de invierno*. San Juan: Isla Negra Editores.

Bobes, Velia Cecilia. 2000. *Los laberintos de la imaginación: Repertorio simbólico, identidades y actores del cambio social en Cuba*. Mexico City: El Colegio de México.

Boils, Guillermo. 1981. "La producción social del espacio en Cuba: 20 años de revolución urbana." *Revista Mexicana de Sociología* 43, no. 4 (October–December): 1487–501.

Bondil, Nathalie. 2008. "Cuba: Art and History from 1968 to Today." Edited by Montreal Museum of Fine Arts. Munich: Prestel.

Borchmeyer, Florian, director, and Matthias Hentschler, producer. 2006. *Habana: Arte nuevo de hacer Ruinas*. Berlin: Raros Media. 85 minutes.

Borofsky, Robert. 1987. *Making History: Pukapukan and Anthropological Construction of Knowledge*. Cambridge: Cambridge University Press.

Brenner, Philip, Marguerite Rose Jiménez, John M. Kirk, and William M. Leo Grande, eds. 2008. *A Contemporary Cuba Reader: Reinventing the Revolution*. Lanham, Boulder: Rowman and Littlefield.

Bruno, Giuliana. 2002. *Atlas of Emotion: Journeys in Art, Architecture, and Film*. New York: Verso.

Bueno, Juan Antonio. 2004. "Havana: Glorious Past, Ruinous Present, Boundless Future." *Florida International University Newsletter* 6 (August 18): 1–3.

Cáceres, Patricia. 2010. "Más facilidades para la reparación de viviendas y la agricultura." *Juventud Rebelde*. November 18. http://www.juventudrebelde.cu/cuba/2010–11–18/mas-facilidades-para-la-reparacion-de-viviendas-y-la-agricultura/.

Calvino, Italo. 1978. *Invisible Cities*. Translated by William Weaver. New York: Harvest Books; 1st Harvest/HBJ Ed edition.

Cámara, Madeline. 1991. "Adiós a los Ochenta: ajuste de cuentas con la joven literatura cubana." *Plural* (Mexico City) 228 (June): 66–72.

Carlson, Marvin. 2004. *Performance: A Critical Introduction*. New York: Routledge.

Carpentier, Alejo. 1970. *La ciudad de las columnas*. Barcelona: Editorial Lumen.

——. 1976. *Reasons of State*. Translated by Frances Partridge. New York: Knopf. Originally published as *El recurso del método* (Mexico: Siglo XXI, 1974).

——. 1979. *Los pasos perdidos*. Havana: Letras Cubanas, 1979.

——. 1990. *Explosion in a Cathedral*. Translated by John Sturrock. New York: Harper and Row. Originally published as *El siglo de las luces* (Barcelona: Seix Barral, 1979).

——. 1996. "El amor a la ciudad." In *El amor a la ciudad*, 63–68. Madrid: Alfaguara.

——. 1997. "Journey Back to the Source." Translated by Frances Partridge. In *Latin American Short Stories*, edited by Roberto González Echevarría, 221–33. New York: Oxford University Press. Originally published as "Viaje a la semilla," in *Guerra del tiempo* (Havana: Unión, 1963).

——. 2001. *The Chase*. Translated by Alfred MacAdam. Minneapolis: University of Minnesota Press. Originally published as *El acoso* (Buenos Aires: Losada, 1956).

Carrión, Miguel de. 1978. *Las impuras: Las honradas y Las impuras*. Havana: Arte y Literatura.

Carrobello, Caridad. 2006a. "Vivienda: Piedra sobre Piedra." *Bohemia*. 4 July. http://www.bohemia.cu/2006/07/04/encuba/vivienda1.html.

——. 2006b. " Vivienda: ¿Y, fuera de casa?" *Bohemia*. July 4. http://www.bohemia.cu/2006/07/04/encuba/vivienda2.html.

——. 2006c. "Vivienda: Pensar en Grande." *Bohemia*. July 4. http://www.bohemia.cu/2006/07/04/encuba/vivienda3.html.

Casal, Julián del. 1945a. "En el campo." In *Poesías completas*, edited by Mario Cabrera Saqui, 304–5. Havana: Publicaciones del Ministerio de Educación.

———. 1945b. "Nocturno." In *Poesías completas*, edited by Mario Cabrera Saqui, 98–100. Havana: Publicaciones del Ministerio de Educación.

———. 1945c. "Vespertino." In *Poesías completas*, edited by Mario Cabrera Saqui, 119. Havana: Publicaciones del Ministerio de Educación.

———. 1963. *Crónicas habaneras*. Havana: Universidad Central de Las Villas, Dirección de Publicaciones.

Case, Sue-Ellen, and Janelle Reinelt, eds. 1991. *The Performance of Power*. Iowa City: University of Iowa Press.

Castro, Fidel. 1960. *Dos discursos del Dr. Fidel Castro*. Havana: Department of Public Relations MINREX.

———. 1970. "Discurso pronunciado en la velada solemne en conmemoración del centenario del natalicio de Vladimir Ilich Lenin, efectuada en el teatro 'Chaplin,' el 22 de abril de 1970, 'año de los diez millones.' " http://www.cuba.cu/gobierno/discursos/1970/esp/f220470e.html.

———. 1976. *Discursos (1961–1976)*. Havana: Editorial de Ciencias Sociales.

———. 1995. "Discurso pronunciado en la Clausura del VI Congreso de la Federación de Mujeres Cubanas, efectuado en el Palacio de las Convenciones, Ciudad de La Habana, el 3 de marzo de 1995." In *Discursos e intervenciones del Comandante en Jefe Fidel Castro Ruz, Presidente del Consejo de Estado de la República de Cuba*. http://www.cuba.cu/gobierno/discursos/.

———. 2002. "Discurso pronunciado por el presidente Fidel Castro Ruz, en el acto de reinauguración de las 402 escuelas reparadas en la capital, el 29 de junio de 2002." *Granma*. July 1.

Castro, Raúl. 2008. "Discurso pronunciado en las conclusiones de la primera sesión ordinaria de la VII Legislatura de la Asamblea Nacional del Poder Popular, 11 de julio de 2008." *Granma*. July 13. http://granma.co.cu/2008/07/13/nacional/artic06.html.

CEDEM (Centro de Estudios Demográficos). 1996. *Resultados de la Encuesta Nacional de Migraciones Internas según Niveles de Sistema de Asentamientos: El Caso de Ciudad de La Habana*. Havana: CEDEM.

CEE-ONC (Comité Estatal de Estadísticas, Oficina Nacional de Censos). 1984. *Censo de población y viviendas. 1981. Provincia de Ciudad de La Habana. Vol. 3*. Havana: CEE.

Chinea, Madelín. 2003. "Ideas para un modelo de intervención en la vivienda de interés social." *Planificación Física* 1.

CIEM (Centro de Investigaciones de la Economía Mundial). 2000. *Investigación sobre Desarrollo Humano y equidad en Cuba 1999*. Havana: Caguayo S.A. www.undp.org.cu/idh99.shtml.

Ciucci, Giorgio. 1981. "The Invention of the Modern Movement." *Oppositions* 24 (Spring): 68–91.

Cluster, Dick, and Rafael Hernández. 2006. *History of Havana*. New York: Palgrave Macmillan.

Coipel Díaz, Manuel, and Ramón Collado Reyes. 2000. "Reflexiones sobre una experiencia de intervención comunitaria a escala de barrio." In *Ciudad y cambio social en los 90*, edited by Roberto Dávalos Domínguez and Aymara Hernández Morales. Havana: Universidad de La Habana.

Collado, Ramón, Smilet Mauri, and Manuel Coipel. 1998. "Revitalización urbana, desarrollo social y participación: La experiencia en el barrio San Isidro." In *Participación Social. Desarrollo Urbano y Comunitario*, edited by Aurora Vázquez Penelas and Roberto Dávalos Domínguez, 106–18. Havana: Universidad de La Habana.

Collado, Ramón, C. I. Robaina, Manuel Coipel, M. Menéndez, A. Arias, and A. Ventura. 1998. *San Isidro, la nueva imagen: proyecto social para la revitalización integral de un barrio habanero / San Isidro, the New Image: Social Project for the Total Revitalisation of a Havana Neighborhood*. Navarra, Spain: Ediciones Boloña.

Comisión de Asuntos Cubanos. 1935. *Problemas de la Nueva Cuba*. New York: Foreign Policy Association.

Connerton, Paul. 1989. *How Societies Remember*. Cambridge: Cambridge University Press.

Conquergood, Dwight. 1985. *Performing as a Moral Act: Ethical Dimensions of the Ethnography of Performance*. Cambridge: Harvard University Press.

Coyula, Mario. 1996. "The Neighborhood as Workshop." Latin American Perspectives 23, no. 4 (Fall): 90–103. Translated by John F. Uggen.

———. 1999. "Mis amores con La Habana." Interview with Camilo Venegas. *La Gaceta de Cuba* 2 (March–April 1999): 18–21.

———. 2006. "La ciudad del futuro o el futuro de la ciudad." *Temas* 48 (October–December): 49–55.

———. 2007. "La toma de la gran ciudad blanca." Talk given at the LASA conference, Montreal, 2007 (unpublished).

———. "La ciudad rampante: Cuando éramos jóvenes y hermosos." http//www.archivos dearquitectura.com.

Coyula, Mario, and Jill Hamberg. 2003. "Havana, Cuba." In *The Challenge of Slums: Case Studies for the Global Report on Human Settlements 2003*. London: University College London, Development Planning Unit. (CD-ROM and web). http://www.ucl.ac.uk/dpu-projects/Global_Report/pdfs/Havana.pdf.

———. 2004. "Understanding Slums: The Case of Havana, Cuba." Cambridge: David Rockefeller Center for Latin American Studies, Harvard. Working Paper No. 01/05–4. Reproduction of Coyula and Hamberg (2003). http://www.drclas.harvard.edu/files/The%20Case%20of%20Havana%20Cuba.pdf.

Coyula, Mario, Rosa Oliveras, and Milagros Cabrera. 1998. *Hacia un nuevo tipo de comunidad en La Habana: Los talleres de transformación integral del barrio*. Havana: Grupo para el Desarrollo Integral de la Capital.

Coyula, Miguel. 2009. "¿Un lugar donde vivir o un lugar para vivir?" *Temas* 58 (April–June 2009): 40–49.

CSVC (Centro de Salud en la Vivienda de Cuba). 2000. *Diagnóstico de Salud en la Vivienda*. www.cepis.ops-oms.org/bvsasv/e/diagnostico/cuba.pdf.

———. 2002. *Informe Bienal del Centro de Salud en la Vivienda de Cuba 2000–2002*. Paper prepared for the V Meeting of the Red Interamericana de Centros de Salud en la Vivienda. www.ensp.fiocruz.br/rbhs/Docs/cuba.doc.

Cuba, República de Cuba. Secretaría de Sanidad y Beneficiencia. Direccón de Sanidad. 1923. *Ordenanza Sanitarias para el Régimen de los Municipios de la Republica.* Decreto Presidencia no. 672, 6 de Julio. Havana: Imprenta Bouza y Ca.

Cuba. 1994. *La constitución cubana.* México D.F.: Fondo de Cultura Económica.

Dávalos, Roberto, Rene Cárdenas, Teresa Muñoz, and Josefina Vilariño. 2005. "El Barrio de Colón: una lectura desde la sociología." In *El Barrio de Colón: Rehabilitación Urbana y Desarrollo Comunitario en La Habana*, edited by Gina Rey, 57–74. Havana: Facultad de Arquitectura, Habana Ecopolis, and Grupo para el Desarrollo Integral de la Capital.

Davis, Mike. 2006. *Planet of Slums.* London: Verso.

De Certeau, Michel. 1984. *The Practice of Everyday Life.* Translated by Steven Rendell. Berkeley: University of California Press.

De Ferrari, Guillermina. 2003. "Aesthetics Under Siege: Dirty Realism and Pedro Juan Gutierréz's *Trilogía sucia de La Habana.*" *Arizona Journal of Hispanic Cultural Studies* 7:23–43.

De la Nuez, Iván. 1991. "Más acá del bien y del mal. El espejo cubano de la modernidad." *Plural* 228 (June): 21–32.

———. 2001. "El Hombre Nuevo ante el otro futuro." In *Cuba y el día después*, 9–22. Barcelona: Mondadori.

De las Cuevas Toraya, Juan. 2001. *500 años de Construccion en Cuba.* Madrid: Chavín.

Delgado, Manuel. 1999. *El animal público: Hacia una antropología de los espacios urbanos.* Barcelona: Anagrama.

del Real, Patricio, and Anna Cristina Pertierra. 2008. "Inventar: Recent Struggles and Inventions in Housing in Two Cuban Cities." *Buildings and Landscapes: Journal of the Vernacular Architecture Forum* 15 (Fall): 78–92.

Desnoes, Edmundo, and Tomás Gutiérrez Alea. 1990. *Memories of Underdevelopment. Continuity Script. Inconsolable Memories. Novel.* New Brunswick: Rutgers University Press.

Díaz, Duanel. 2003. *Mañach o la República.* La Habana: Letras Cubanas.

Díaz Gutiérrez, Joel. 2001. "Cayo Hueso: Un proceso de mejoramiento en un contexto urbano. Participación y protagonismo de los actores comunitarios." Paper presented at the Congress of the Latin American Studies Association (LASA), Washington, D.C.

Dilla, Haroldo. 2002. "Cuba: The Changing Scenarios of Governability." *boundary 2* 29, no. 3: 55–76.

Dopico, Ana Maria. 2002. "Picturing Havana: History, Vision, and the Scramble for Cuba." *Nepantla: Views from South* 3, no. 3: 451–94.

Duany, Andrés. 1998. "Prólogo: Sólo nos queda La Habana." In *La Habana. Arquitectura del siglo XX*, edited by Eduardo Luis Rodríguez with photography by Pepe Navarro, 9–11. Barcelona: Blume.

———. 1999. "Una ciudad con vista al mar." Interview with María Elena Martín in *La Gaceta de Cuba* 2 (March–April): 10–13.

Duchesne Winter, Juan. 2005. *Fugas incomunistas*. San Juan: Ediciones Vértigo.

Dufrenne, Mikel. 1973. *The Phenomenology of Aesthetic Experience*. Translated by Edward S. Casey. Northwestern University Studies in Phenomenology and Existential Philosophy. Evanston: Northwestern University Press.

Dunn, Carlos. N.d. "Old Havana: The Soul of a City." In "Havana and Its Landscapes," edited by Nicolás Quintana. Unpublished manuscript.

Durán, Diony. 2006. "¿Contar la Habana? Discurso, contradiscurso, transgresiones." In *Transgresiones cubanas: Cultura, literatura y lengua dentro y fuera de la isla*, edited by Gabriele Knauer, Elina Miranda, and Janett Reinstädler, 69–87. Madrid and Frankfurt: Iberoamericana; Vervuert.

Ellegiers, Sandra. 2006. "Una entrevista con el director de la pelicula *Arte Nuevo de Hacer Ruinas*." *El país*. October 18. http://foros.abc.es/cgilocal/forosabc/ultimat ebb.cgi?ubb=get_topic;f=14;t=004099.

Elsner, John. 1994. "From the Pyramids to Pausanias and Piglet: Monuments, Travel, and Writing." In *Art and Text in Ancient Greek Culture*, edited by Simon Goldhill and Robin Osborne, 224–54. Cambridge: Cambridge University Press.

Estrada, Alfredo José. 2007. *Havana: Autobiography of a City*. New York: Palgrave Macmillan.

Fagen, Richard. 1969. *The Transformation of Political Culture in Cuba*. Stanford: Stanford University Press.

Fagiuoli, Martino. 2003. *La Habana deco*. Bologna: CV export.

Fernandez, Ariel. 2000. "¿Poesía Urbana? o la Nueva Trova de los Noventa." *El Caimán Barbudo* 296:4–14.

Fernández, María de los Angeles. 1997. "Aprovechamiento económico de los desechos solidos domiciliarios en el barrio La Güinera, Cuba." In *¿Quiénes Hacen Ciudad? Ambiente Urbano y Participación Popular. Cuba, Puerto Rico, República Dominicana*, edited by Luis Eduardo Camacho. Cuenca, Ecuador: Ediciones SIAP.

Fernández Larrea, Ramón. 2002. "Carta a Yuri Gagarin." *Encuentro en la red* 279. January 14. http://arch.cubaencuentro.com/humor/2002/01/14/5351.html.

Fernández Nuñez, José Manuel. 1976. *La vivienda en Cuba*. Havana: Editorial Arte y Literatura.

Fernández Soriano, Armando, Haroldo Dilla Alfonso, and Margarita Castro Flores. 1999. "Movimientos comunitarios en Cuba: Un análisis comparativo." *Estudios Sociológicos de el Colegio de México* 17, no. 51: 857–84.

Forman, Murray. 2002. *The 'Hood Comes First: Race, Space, and Place in Rap and Hip-Hop*. Middletown, Conn.: Wesleyan University Press.

Fornet, Jorge. 2007a. "El camino de los cuestionamientos." Interview with Elizabeth Mirabal in *La Jiribilla* 6–10 (March). http://www.lajiribilla.cu/2007.

——. 2007b. *Los nuevos paradigmas. Prólogo narrativo al siglo XXI*. Havana: Letras cubanas.

Friedman, Jonathan. 1992. "The Past in the Future: History and the Politics of Identity." *American Anthropologist* 94, no. 4: 837–59.

Fuentes, Elvis, Yuneikis Villalonga, and Glexis Novoa. 2007. *Killing Time: An Exhibition of Cuban Artists from the 1980s to the Present*. New York: Exit Art Gallery.

Fuentes, Norberto. 1982. *Posición uno*. Havana: Unión.

Garaicoa, Carlos. 2000. *Carlos Garaicoa: La ruina, la utopia*. Edited by José Ignacio Roca. Bogotá: Banco de la República, Biblioteca Luis Angel Arango.

——. 2003. *Inside/Outside: Contemporary Cuban Art*. Edited by David Hart. Winston-Salem: Wake Forest University, Charlotte and Philip Hanes Art Gallery, in association with Edwin Wilson. Published in conjunction with the exhibition of the same name, shown at the Charlotte and Philip Hanes Art Gallery.

García Alfonso, Navil. 2007. "Planificación física cubana persigue desarrollo armónico de las urbes." *Granma*. August 16. http://www.granma.cu/espanol/2007/agosto/juev16/33Planificación.html.

García Fernández, Emilio, José Ramón Moreno García, A. Sánchez González, María Teresa Padrón Lotti and Eugenia Casanovas Molleda. 1998. *El malecón de La Habana: Un proceso de transformación y de cooperación*. Ciudad/City 3, no. 98. Navarra, Spain: Ediciones Boloña.

Garret, Daniel. 2001. "*Dirty Havana Trilogy*: A Novel in Stories." *Review of Contemporary Fiction* 21, no. 3 (Fall): 215–16.

Gazmuri Núñez, Patricia. 2004. *Reflexiones sobre algunas peculiaridades del crecimiento poblacional en relación con la familia y la demanda de viviendas*. Havana: Centro de Investigaciones Psicológicas y Sociológicas.

——. 2009. "Familia y Desarrollo urbano." *Temas* 58 (April–June): 58–64.

Goffman, Erving. 1959. *The Presentation of Self in Everyday Life*. Garden City: Doubleday.

Goldberger, Paul. 2001. "The Future of Cuban Cities." *Herencia Magazine* 7, no. 1 (Summer): 26–31.

González, Fuertes. 1988. *Psicología Comunitaria*. Madrid: Editorial Visor.

González, Reynaldo. 1988. "Entre la magia y la infinitud: Conversación inédita con el autor de *Paradiso*." In *Lezama Lima: El ingenuo culpable*, 111–52. Havana: Letras Cubanas.

González Cruz, Iván. 2000. *Diccionario. Vida y obra de José Lezama Lima*. Valencia: Generalitat Valenciana.

Gonzalez Gutierrez, Alfredo. 1997. "Economía y Sociedad: Los Retos del Modelo Económico." *Temas* 11:4–29.

González Rego, René. 2000. "Generalidades acerca de la problemática socioambiental de los barrios y focos insalubres en el municipio Playa." In *Ciudad y Cambio Social en los 90*, edited by Roberto Dávalos Domínguez and Aymara Hernández Morales. Havana: Universidad de La Habana.

González Rego, René Alejandro, Arturo Rúa de Cabo, and Berta Blanco Sánchez. 2000. "Una primera aproximación al análisis espacial de los problemas socioambientales en los barrios y focos insalubres en la Ciudad de La Habana." In *Desarrollo Local y Descentralización en el Contexto Urbano*, edited by Roberto Dávalos Domínguez. Havana: Universidad de La Habana.

Grillo, Rafael. 2007. "Vostok: la paradoja cubano-soviética." November 27. http://www.cubancontemporaryart.com.

Grogg, Patricia. 2007. "Luz de esperanza." InterPress Service. June 9. http://cubaala mano.net/sitio/client/report.php?id=649.

——. 2008. "Todo por un techo." InterPress Service. August. http://cubaalamano.net/ sitio/client/report.php?id=866.

——. 2010. "Central sindical cubana llama a unidad ante reducción de empleos." InterPress Service. September 13. http://cubaalamano.net/sitio/client/report.php ?id=1192.

Guerra, Lilliam. 2006. "Una buena foto es la mejor defensa de la Revolución: Imagen, producción de imagen y la imaginación revolucionaria de 1959." *Encuentro de la Cultura Cubana* (Madrid) 46 (Winter): 11–21.

Gugler, Joseph. 1981. "Un mínimo de urbanismo y un máximo de ruralismo: la experiencia cubana." *Revista Mexicana de Sociología* 43, no. 4 (October–December): 1465–86.

Guillén, Nicolás. 1979. "Tengo." In *Nueva antología mayor*, edited by Ángel Augier, 248–50. Havana: Letras Cubanas.

Gutiérrez, Pedro Juan. 1998. *Trilogía sucia de La Habana*. Barcelona: Anagrama.

——. 2001. *Dirty Havana Trilogy*. Translated by Natasha Wimmer. New York: Farrar, Straus and Giroux.

Haacke, Hans, and Pierre Bourdieu. 1995. *Free Exchange*. Cambridge: Polity Press in association with Blackwell.

Hamberg, Jill. 1994. "The Dynamics of Cuban Housing Policy." Ph.D. Dissertation. Columbia University.

——. 2001. "Revolutionary Cuba's Spatial Policies: Successes and Challenges." Working Paper in Planning No. 199. Ithaca: Cornell University.

Henken, Ted. 2008. *Cuba. A Global Studies Handbook*. Santa Barbara: ABC-CLIO.

Heredia Reyes, Carlos. 2008. "Programa de la vivienda en La Habana: máxima prioridad y seguimiento." Radiometropolitana.cu. March 13.

Highmore, Ben. 2005. *Cityscapes: Cultural Readings in the Material and Symbolic City*. New York: Palgrave Macmillan.

Holston, James. 1989. *The Modernist City: An Anthropological Critique of Brasília*. Chicago: University of Chicago Press.

Howe, Linda S. 2009. *Cuban Artists' Books and Prints / Libros Y Grabados De Artistas Cubanos: 1985–2008*. Edited by Wake Forest University, The Cuba Project. Winston-Salem, N.C.: J La' Verne Print Communications.

Insausti, Esteban García, director. 2005. *Existen*. Producciones Sincover.

Insausti, Esteban García. 2006. "Esteban Insausti: 'con el cine no se juega.'" Interview with Sandra del Valle Casals in *La ventana: portal informativo de la Casa de las Américas*. February 27. http://laventana.casa.cult.cu/modules.php?name=News& file=article&sid=3057.

InterPress Service. 1998. "Gobierno frena migración del interior hacia La Habana," InterPress Service. October 21. http://domino.ips.org/ips%5Cesp.nsf/vwWebMain View/7BD43BE4D29CFC5880256A0800497B1E/?OpenDocument.

——. 2007. "Capital rehabilita redes hidráulicas." *Cuba a la Mano* (InterPress Service). July 31. http://cubaalamano.net/sitio/client/brief.php?id=4405.

INV (Instituto Nacional de la Vivienda). 1990. *Control del Fondo de Viviendas*. 1990. INV.

———. 2000. *Boletín Estadístico Anual*. 2000. Havana: INV.

———. 2001a. *Boletín Estadístico Anual*. 2001. Havana: INV.

———. 2001b. *Informe Nacional Cuba. Istanbul + 5*. Havana: INV.

———. 2002. *Control del Fondo de Viviendas*. Havana: INV.

Iser, Wolfgang. 2000. *The Range of Interpretation*. New York: Columbia University Press.

Israel, Esteban. 2008. "Cuba aplaude buenas notas de UNESCO para su educación." *Reuters América Latina*. June 21. http://lta.reuters.com/article/domesticNews/id LTAN2141278120080621.

Jacome, Aurora. 2008. *Munequitos rusos . . . y otros*. July 21. http://munequitosrusos .blogspot.com/.

Juventud Rebelde. 2010. "Cuba con nueva división político-administrativa." *Juventud Rebelde*. August 1. http://www.juventudrebelde.cu/cuba/2010-08-01/cuba-con-nueva-division-politico-administrativa/.

Kämper, Andreas, and Reinhard Ulbrich. 1998. *Sandmännchen im Trabi-land*. Düsseldorf: Econ.

Kapcia, Antoni. 2005. *Havana. The Making of Cuban Culture*. Oxford: Berg.

Kimmelman, Michael. 2008. "In Spain, a Monumental Silence." *New York Times*. January 13.

Kolésnikov, Nikolái. 1983. *Cuba: Educación popular y preparación de los cuadros nacionales 1959–1982*. Moscow: Progreso.

Kostof, Spiro. 1999. *The City Shaped: Urban Patterns and Meanings through History*. 2nd ed. London: Thames and Hudson Ltd.

Lage Dávila, Carlos. 2008. "Discurso en la reunión de los presidentes municipales del Poder Popular." *Juventud Rebelde*. June 8. http://www.juventudrebelde.cu/cuba/2008-06-08/discurso-de-carlos-lage-davila-en-la-reunion-de-los-presidentes-municipales-del-poder-popular/.

Lasansky, Medina, and Brian McLaren, eds. 2004. *Architecture and Tourism: Perception, Performance, and Place*. New York: Oxford University Press.

Lavedan, Pierre. 1926. *Histoire de l'Urbanisme, Antiquité, Moyen Age*. Paris: H. Laurens.

Le Bras-Chopard, Armella. 2003. *El zoo de los filósofos*. Madrid: Ed Taurus.

Lee, Susana. 1997. "Migraciones incontroladas hacia la capital: Para que los esfuerzos del país no sean baldíos." *Granma*. May 13.

Lewis, Oscar, Ruth M. Lewis, and Susan M. Rigdon. 1978. *Neighbors: Living the Revolution. An Oral History of Contemporary Cuba*. Urbana: University of Illinois Press.

Lezama Lima, José. 1970a. "Homenaje a René Portocarrero." In *La cantidad hechizada*, 361–403. Havana: UNEAC.

———. 1970b. "Paralelos. La pintura y la poesía en Cuba (siglos XVIII y XIX)." In *La cantidad hechizada*, 145–87. Havana: UNEAC.

———. 1970c. "Preludio a las eras imaginarias." In *La cantidad hechizada*, 7–30. Havana: UNEAC.

———. 1988. "Julián del Casal." In *Confluencias*, 181–205. Havana: Letras Cubanas.

———. 1989. *Oppiano Licario*. Madrid: Cátedra.

———. 1991. *La Habana*. Madrid: Verbum.

———. 1999. "Oda a Julián del Casal." In *Poesía completa*, edited by César López, 474–80. Madrid: Alianza.

———. 2000. *Paradiso*. Translated by Gregory Rabassa. Normal, Ill.: Dalkey Archive Press. Originally published as *Paradiso* (Madrid: Colección Archivos, 1988).

Liggett, Helen, and David S. Perry. 1995. *Spatial Practices*. Thousand Oaks, Calif.: Sage.

Llanes, Llilian. 1993. *1898–1921, La transformación de La Habana a través de la arquitectura*. La Habana: Editorial Letras Cubanas.

Loomis, John. 1999. *Revolution of Forms: Cuba's Forgotten Art Schools*. New York: Princeton Architectural Press.

Loss, Jacqueline. 2003. "Vintage Soviets in post-Cold War Cuba." *Mandorla: Nueva Escritura de las Américas* 7:79–84.

———. 2004. "Portraitures of Institutionalization." *CR: The New Centennial Review* 4, no. 2: 77–101.

———. 2009. "*Skitalietz*: Traducciones y vestigios de un imperio caduco." In *La vigilia cubana. Sobre Antonio José Ponte*, edited by Teresa Basile, 95–109. Rosario, Argentina: Beatriz Viterbo.

———, ed. Forthcoming. *Caviar with Rum: Cuba-USSR and the Post-Soviet Experience*. New York: Palgrave.

Lowe, Setha. 1996. "Spatializing Culture: The Social Production and Social Construction of Public Space." *American Ethnologist* 23, no. 4: 861–79.

Lowenthal, David. 1985. *The Past Is a Foreign Country*. Cambridge: Cambridge University Press.

Maffesoli, Michel. 2005. *La transformación de lo político*. México D.F.: Herder.

Martín, Marianela, and Mayte María Jiménez. 2008. "Cuba edificará 50,000 viviendas en 2008." *Juventud Rebelde*. January 12.

Martín González, Marianella. 2010. "Más cerca de casa." *Juventud Rebelde*. May 8.

Martínez Hernández, Leticia. 2010. "Mucho más que una alternativa." *Granma*. September 24.

Mas, S. 2001. "Una obra que engrandece al ser humano." *Granma*. January 11.

Massey, Doreen. 1994. *Space, Place, and Gender*. Minneapolis: University of Minnesota Press.

———. 2005. *For Space*. Thousand Oaks, Calif.: Sage.

Mathéy, Kosta. 1989. "Recent Trends in Cuban Housing Policies and the Revival of the Microbrigade Movement." *Bulletin of Latin American Research* 8:67–81.

———. 1994. "Informal and Substandard Neighborhoods in Revolutionary Cuba." In *Phänomen Cuba: Alternative Wege in Architektur Stadtentwicklung und Ökologie*, edited by Kosta Mathéy. Karlsruhe, Germany: Fakultät für Architektur, Universität Karlsruhe.

———. 1997. "Self-Help Housing Strategies in Cuba: An Alternative to Conventional Wisdom?" In *Self-Help Housing, the Poor, and the State in the Caribbean*, edited by Robert B. Potter and Dennis Conway. Knoxville: University of Tennessee Press.

Matsuda, Matt K. 1996. *The Memory of the Modern*. New York: Oxford University Press.

Mayoral, María Julia. 2001. "El rescate de un sueño . . ." *Granma*. July 22.

———. 2008. "Sobre el tapete complejidades de la vivienda en Cuba." *Granma*. January 12.

McCoy, Terry, ed. 2003. *Cuba on the Verge: An Island in Transition*. Boston: Bulfinch Press.

McDowell, Linda. 1999. *Gender, Identity and Place: Understanding Feminist Geographies*. Minneapolis: University of Minnesota Press.

Meinig, D. W., ed. 1979. *The Interpretation of Ordinary Landscapes: Geographical Essays*. Oxford: Oxford University Press.

Menéndez, Ronaldo. 1999. "Una ciudad, un pájaro, una guagua . . ." In *El derecho al pataleo de los ahorcados*, 43–69. Madrid: Ediciones Lengua de Trapo.

———. 2006. *Las bestias*. Madrid: Ediciones Lengua de Trapo.

Menéndez, Ronaldo, and Ricardo Arrieta. 1997a. "Culpa." In *Alguien se va lamiendo todo*, 99–104. Havana: Ediciones Unión.

———. 1997b. "Tocata y fuga en cuatro movimientos y tres reposos." In *Alguien se va lamiendo todo*, 85–90. Havana: Ediciones Unión.

Mesías-González, Rosendo. 1995. "Las experiences facilitadoras de los procesos habitacionales augogestionables en Cuba (formalidad e informalidad)." *Revista INVI* 20, no. 25.

MINSAP (Ministerio de Salud Pública). 2000. *Anuario Estadístico*. MINSAP, Havana.

Montero Méndez, Hortensia. 2007. "A propósito de la exposición 'Puente para las rupturas: Pensar los 70.' " *La jiribilla: revista de cultura cubana*. April 28–May 4. http://lajiribilla.co.cu/2007/n312_04/mirada.html.

Montes Rodríguez, Norma. 2007. "La distribución espacial de la población en Cuba. Censos 1981 y 2002." *Revista Electrónica Zacatecana sobre Población y Sociedad*. Year 7. Third Era. 31 (September–December). http://sociales.reduaz.mx/.

Moore, Andrew. 2002. *Inside Havana*. San Francisco: Chronicle Books.

Mosquera, Gerardo. 1991. "Los hijos de Guillermo Tell." *Plural* 228 (June): 60–63.

———. 1996. "Carlos Garaicoa." *Poliester* (México) 5, no. 15 (Spring): 6.

———. 2002. "Renovación en los años ochenta." In *Déjame que te cuente. Antología de la crítica en los años 80*, edited by Margarita González, Tania Parson, and Jose Veigas, 153–62. Havana: Artecubano Ediciones.

Mumtaz, Babar. 2001. "Just as Slums Need Cities to Survive, So Do Cities Need Slums to Thrive." *UN-HABITAT Debate* 7, no. 3 (September).

Murray, Mary. 2008. "Cuba Braces for New Hurricane Season." June 19. http://worldblog.msnbc.msn.com/archive/2008/06/19/1156759.aspx.

Noval, Liborio. 2004. *Sólo detalles: La Habana, arquitectura, escultura*. Verdú, Spain: Greta.

Núñez Moreno, Lila. 2008. *La Vivienda en Cuba desde la Perspectiva de la Movilidad Social*. Cambridge: David Rockefeller Center for Latin American Studies, Harvard. Working paper No. 07/08–4. 2008. http://www.drclas.harvard.edu/files/Lilia%20 Nunez%20Moreno%20with%20cover_YR.pdf.

Olivares, José Pérez. 2002. "El pintor y la nube." In *Déjame que te cuente: Antología de la crítica en los años 80*, edited by Margarita González, Tania Parson, and Jose Veigas, 241–53. Havana: Artecubano Ediciones.

ONE (Oficina Nacional de Estadísticas). 2001. *Anuario Estadístico de Cuba 2000*. Havana: ONE.

———. 2005a. *Censo de Población y Viviendas: Cuba 2002. Informe Nacional*. Havana: ONE. http://www.one.cu.

———. 2005b. *Estudios y datos de la población cubana 2005: Cuba y sus territorios*. Havana: ONE. http://www.one.cu.

———. 2007a. *Anuario Demográfico 2006*. Havana: ONE. http://www.one.cu.

———. 2007b. *Anuario Estadístico 2006*. Havana: ONE. http://www.one.cu.

———. 2008. *Panorama Demográfico 2007*. Havana: ONE. http://www.one.cu.

ONE-OTECH (Oficina Nacional de Estadísticas—Oficina Territorial de Estadísticas Ciudad de La Habana). 1997. *Censo de Barrios y Focos Insalubres 1996*. Havana: ONE-OTECH.

Orozco Orozco, Pedro Ricardo. 2003. "Pensar la ciudad: un encuentro para construir." *Monografias.com*. http://www.monografias.com/trabajos14/cultura-ciudad/cultura-ciudad.shtml.

Orta, Yailin, and Dora Pérez. 2008. "Desarrollo territorial en Cuba ¿Cómo encontrar el equilibrio?" *Juventud Rebelde*. June 29.

Ortega Morales, Lourdes. 1996. "La Habana: Barrio de Atarés." In *Vivir en el "Centro," Viviendas de Inquilinato en Metrópolis Latinoamericanas*, edited by Hans Harms, Wiley Ludeña, and Peter Pfeiffer. Hamburg: Technical University Hamburg-Harburg.

OTE-CLH (Oficina Territorial de Estadísticas, Ciudad de La Habana). 1997. *Estudio Sobre la Migración en la Capital: Año 1996*. Havana: Oficina Territorial de Estadísticas, Ciudad de La Habana, Departamento Demografía y Censos.

Padrón Larrazábal, Roberto. 1975. *Manifiestos de Cuba*. Sevilla: Publicaciones de la Universidad de Sevilla.

Padrón Lotti, María Teresa. 1998. "Experiencia participativa en un proyecto de rehabilitación en Ciudad de La Habana." In *Desarrollo Urbano: Proyectos y Experiencias de Trabajo*, edited by Roberto Dávalos Domínguez and Alain Basail Rodríguez. Havana: Universidad de La Habana.

Padura, Leonardo. 2005. *La neblina del ayer*. Barcelona: Tusquets.

PAHO (Pan American Health Organization). 1999. "Country Health Data. Cuba." http://165.158.1.110/english/sha/prflcub.html.

Pardo Lazo, Orlando Luis. 2005. "Sweet Habana." In *Jóvenes autores cubanos*, edited by Alberto Virella, 43–56. Madrid: Editorial Verbum.

———. 2008. "Espero la noche para no soñarte, Revolución." *Fogonero emergente* (blog). April 4. http://jorgealbertoaguiar.blogspot.com/2008/04/espero-la-noche-para-no-soarte.html.

Pavlov, Yuri. 1994. *Soviet-Cuban Alliance: 1959–1991*. Miami: North South Center Press.

Paz, Senel. 2007. *En el cielo con diamantes*. Barcelona: Ediciones B.

PCC (Partido Comunista de Cuba). 2010. *Proyecto Lineamientos de la Política Económica y Social*. Havana: Prensa Latina. http://www.cubadebate.cu/wp-content/uploads/2010/11/proyecto-lineamientos-pcc.pdf.

PDHL (Programa de Desarrollo Humano Local—Cuba). 2000. "Caracterización y prioridades del Municipio de La Habana Vieja: Líneas Directrices para la III Fase del Programa de Desarrollo Humano Local." July.

Pereira, Manuel. 1980. *El ruso*. Havana: Unión.

Pérez, Dora, and Yailin Orta. 2008. "La Habana sumergida." *Juventud Rebelde*. August 4. http://www.juventudrebelde.cu/UserFiles/File/impreso/icuba-2008-08-03.pdf.

Pérez, Fernando, director. 2003. *Suite Habana*. Cameo Media and ICAIC. 80 minutes.

Pérez, Leafar. 2008a. "Tribus urbanas en la Habana. 1ª parte." *Cubanet*. December 16. http://www.cubanet.org/CNews/y08/dic08/16_C_1.html.

———. 2008b. "Tribus urbanas en la Habana. 2 parte." *Cubanet*. December 17. http://www.cubanet.org/CNews/y08/dic08/17_C_1.html.

Pérez, Louis A. 2001. *Winds of Change: Hurricanes and the Transformation of Nineteenth Century Cuba*. Chapel Hill: University of North Carolina Press.

Pérez Callejas, Leisa. 1997. "Transformación en la Güinera." In *Se Hace Camino al Andar: Experiencias Relevantes de los Talleres de Transformación Integral de Barrio*, edited by the Grupo para el Desarrollo Integral de la Capital. Havana: Grupo para el Desarrollo Integral de la Capital.

Pérez Firmat, Gustavo. 1999. "Con la lengua afuera." *Encuentro de la cultura cubana* 15 (Winter): 142–47.

Pérez Villanueva, Omar. 2002. "Ciudad de La Habana, desempeño económico y situación social." *Cuba Siglo XXI* (XVI). www.nodo50.org/cubasigloXXI/economia/villanueva1_310302.htm.

Pertierra, Anna Cristina. 2006. "Battles, Inventions and Acquisitions: The Struggle for Consumption in Urban Cuba." Ph.D. Thesis, University of London.

Peters, Philip. 2001. "Rescuing Old Havana." Arlington, Vir.: Lexington Institute. www.lexingtoninstitute.org/cuba/pdf/rescuingoldhavana.pdf.

Piñera, Virgilio. 1963. *Pequeñas maniobras*. Havana: Ediciones R.

———.1985. *Presiones y diamantes*. In *Pequeñas maniobras* y *Presiones y diamantes*, 215–334. Madrid: Alfaguara.

———. 1987a. "Hecatombe y alborada." In *Muecas para escribientes*, 286–96. Havana: Letras Cubanas.

———. 1987b. "Hosanna! Hosanna . . . ?" In *Muecas para escribientes*, 318–32. Havana: Letras Cubanas.

———. 1988. "Hell." In *Cold Tales*, translated by Mark Schafer and revised by Thomas Christensen, 117. Hygiene: Eridanos Press. Originally published as "El infierno," *Cuentos fríos* (Buenos Aires: Losada, 1956).

———. 1990. "Frío en caliente." In *Cuentos*, 259–78. Madrid: Alfaguara.

———. 1994. "*Terribilia meditans*." In *Poesía y crítica*, 170–74. Mexico: Consejo Nacional para la Cultura y las Artes.

Plan Maestro de Revitalización Integral de La Habana Vieja. 1996. "Datos del Censo de Población y Vivienda, Centro Histórico de La Habana. 1996." Unpublished manuscript.

PNC (Preparatory National Committee, Republic of Cuba). 1996. *Cuba's National Report. Habitat II.* Havana: n.p.

Podalsky, Laura. 2003. "Affecting Legacies: Historical Memory and Contemporary Structures of Feeling in *Madagascar* and *Amores Perros.*" *Screen* 44, no. 3 (Autumn): 277–94.

Polidori, Robert. 2001. *Havana.* Göttingen: Steidl.

Ponte, Antonio José. 1995. *Un seguidor de Montaigne mira La Habana.* Matanzas: Ediciones Vigía.

——. 1998. *Corazón de skitalietz.* Cienfuegos, Cuba: Reina del Mar.

——. 2000. *Cuentos de todas partes del imperio.* Angers: Deleatur.

——. 2001a. *Un seguidor de Montaigne mira la Habana/Las comidas profundas.* Madrid: Editorial Verbum.

——. 2001b. "La fiesta vigilada." In *Cuba y el día después*, edited by Iván de la Nuez, 23–37. Barcelona: Mondadori.

——. 2002. "A Knack for Making Ruins." In *Tales from the Cuban Empire*, 21–44. Translated by Cola Franzen. San Francisco: City Lights Books.

——. 2003. "What Am I Doing Here?" In *Cuba on the Verge: An Island in Transition*, edited by Terry McCoy, 14–16. Boston: Bulfinch Press.

——. 2005. *Un arte de hacer ruinas y otros cuentos.* Mexico City: Fondo de Cultura Económica.

——. 2006a. "Una catedral rusa para La Habana." *Encuentro en la red.* December 21. http://www.cubaencuentro.com/es/cuba/articulos/una-catedral-rusa-para-la-habana-28730.

——. 2006b. "*Existen*: ¿Nación es locura?" *Encuentro en la red.* April 18. http://www.cubaencuentro.com/es/cultura/articulos/existen-nacion-que-es-locura-15315.

——. 2007a. *La fiesta vigilada.* Barcelona: Anagrama.

——. 2007b. "La Habana está por inventarse." *El País.* January 21. http://www.elpais.com/articulo/opinion/Habana/inventarse/elpepiopi/20070121elpepiopi_4/Tes.

——. 2007c. "Respuesta a una respuesta de Argel Calcines." *La Habana Elegante, segunda época* (Summer). http://www.habanaelegante.com/Summer2007/Ronda.html.

Prieto, Abel. 1999. *El vuelo del gato.* La Habana: Letras Cubanas.

——. 2007. "A mitad de cien caminos, la voz breve." Interview with Elizabeth Mirabel Llorens and Carlos Velazco Fernández in *La juventud rebelde* (October 14). http://www.juventudrebelde.cu/cultura/2007–10–14/a-mitad-de-cien-caminos-la-voz-breve/. Edited by Walter Lippman and translated by Ana Portela as "Halfway of a Hundred Roads, a Brief Voice." http://www.walterlippmann.com/docs1614.html.

Quiroga, José. 2005. *Cuban Palimpsests.* Minneapolis: University of Minnesota Press.

Ramirez, Ronaldo. 2004. "State and Civil Society in the Barrios of Havana, Cuba: The Case of Pogolotti." Development Planning Unit. London: University College.

Reinelt, Janet, and Joseph Roach, eds. 2007. *Critical Theory and Performance.* Ann Arbor: University of Michigan Press.

Reinosa Espinosa, J. M., and Josefina Vilariño Delgado. 1998. "Las comunidades de tránsito: Una propuesta de estudio." In *Desarrollo Urbano: Proyectos y Experiencias de Trabajo*, edited by Roberto Dávalos Domínguez and Alain Basail Rodríguez. Havana: Universida de La Habana.

Relph, Edward C. 1976. *Place and Placelessness*. London: Pion Limited.

Rey, Gina, Lourdes Ortega, Orlando Cabello, and Mayckell Pagán. 2005. "Rehabilitación urbana integral del barrio de Colón en La Habana." In *El Barrio de Colón: Rehabilitación Urbana y Desarrollo Comunitario en La Habana*, edited by Gina Rey, 75–114. Havana: Facultad de Arquitectura, Habana Ecopolis, and Grupo para el Desarrollo Integral de la Capital.

Robainas Barcia, Ayleen. 1999. "Urban Strategies in Old Havana." Paper for the Advanced Training Program, Lund Institute of Technology, Lund, Sweden. http://www.lth.se/fileadmin/hdm/alumni/papers/ad1999/ad1999–05.pdf.

Rodríguez, Eduardo Luis. 1998. *La Habana. Arquitectura del siglo XX*. Barcelona: Art Blume.

———. 2000. *The Havana Guide: Modern Architecture, 1925–1965*. New York: Princeton Architectural Press.

Rodríguez, José Alejandro. 2008. "Más grave de lo que parece." *Juventud Rebelde*. April 30.

Rodríguez, Nestor. 2002. "Un arte de hacer ruinas: Entrevista con el escritor cubano Antonio José Ponte." *Revista Iberoamericana* 68, no. 198 (January–March): 179–86.

Rodríguez Abreu, Alina, director, and Nomar González Pastrana, producer. 2006. *Buscándote Havana*. Havana. 25 minutes. http://vimeo.com/976720.

Rodríguez Alomá, Patricia. 1996. *Viaje en la memoria: Apuntes para una acercamiento a la Habana Vieja. Ciudad/City* vol. 2/96. Navarra, Spain: Ediciones Boloña.

Rojas, Rafael. 2008. "Souvenirs de un Caribe soviético." *Encuentro de la Cultura Cubana* (Madrid) 48/49 (Spring/Summer): 18–33.

Rose, Tricia. 1994. *Black Noise: Rap Music and Black Culture in Contemporary America*. Hanover, N.H.: University Press of New England.

Ryan, Alan. 1997. *Reader's companion to Cuba*. San Diego: Harcourt Brace and Co.

Sainte-Beuve, Charles Augustin. 1996. *Retratos literarios*. México: Editorial Porrúa.

Sánchez, Yoani. 2008. *Generación Y* (blog). http://www.desdecuba.com/generaciony/.

Santa Cruz y Montalvo, María de las Mercedes, Countess of Merlín. 1974. *Viaje a La Habana*. Havana: Arte y Literatura.

Sarlo, Beatriz. 2002. "Violencia en las ciudades. Una reflexión sobre el caso argentino." In *Espacio urbano, violencia y comunicación en América Latina*, edited by Mabel Moraña, 205–14. Pittsburgh: Instituto Internacional de Literatura Iberoamericana.

Sassen, Saskia. 1998. "Whose City Is It? Globalization and the Formation of New Claims." International Metropolis Project. http://international.metropolis.net/events/goth/globalization.html.

Scarpaci, Joseph. 2000. "Winners and Losers in Restoring Old Havana." ASCE 10. http://lainc.utexas.edu/la/cb/cuba/asce/cuba10/scapaci.pdf.

Scarpaci, Joseph, and Armando Portela. 2009. *Cuban Landscapes: Heritage, Memory and Place*. New York: Guildford.

Scarpaci, Joseph, Roberto Segre, and Mario Coyula. 2002. *Havana: Two Faces of the Antillean Metropolis*. Chapel Hill: University of North Carolina Press.

Schechner, Richard. 2003. *Performance Theory*. London: Routledge.

Segre, Roberto. 1977. *Las estructuras ambientales en América Latina*. Mexico City: Siglo XXI.

——. 2003. "Medio siglo de arquitectura cubana (1953–2003): Variaciones sobre el tema del comunismo." *Café de las ciudades. Revista Digital*. http/www.cafedelasciudades .com.ar.

——. 2005. "Entrevista a Mario Coyula." *Café de las ciudades. Revista Digital*. http:// www.cafedelasciudades.com.ar.

Sert, José Luis. 1942. *Can Our Cities Survive? An ABC of Urban Problems, Their Analysis, Their Solutions*. Cambridge: Harvard University Press.

Shanks, Michael. 1996. *Classical Archaeology of Greece: Experiences of the Discipline*. London: Routledge.

Silva, Armando. 1992. *Imaginarios urbanos. Bogotá y Sao Paulo: Cultura y comunicación urbana en América Latina*. Bogotá: Tercer Mundo Ediciones.

Smorkaloff, Pamela María. 2003. *Cuba Reader: History, Culture, Politics*. Durham: Duke University Press.

Sopher, David. 1979. "The Landscape of Home." In *The Interpretation of Ordinary Landscapes*, edited by D. W. Meinig, 129–53. New York: Oxford University Press.

Soto, Asori. 2005. *Good Bye, Lolek*. Producciones Aguaje.

Spiegel, Jerry M., Mariano Bonet, Annalee Yassi, Robert Tate, Miriam Concepción, and Mayile Canizares. 2003. "Evaluating the Effectiveness of a Multi-component Intervention to Improve Health in an Inner City Havana Community." *International Journal of Occupational and Environmental Health* no. 2 (April–June 9): 118–27.

Tejera, Nivaria. 2002. *Espero la noche para soñarte, Revolución*. Miami: Ediciones Universal.

Terkenli, Theano, ed. 2006. *Landscapes of a New Cultural Economy of Space*. Netherlands: Springer.

Turner, F. J. 1920. *The Frontier in American History*. New York: Holt.

UN-Habitat. 2003. *The Challenge of the Slums: Global Report on Human Settlements 2003*. London: Earthscan Publications.

UNESCO and Oficina del Historiador de la Ciudad. 2006. *Una Experiencia Singular: Valoraciones sobre el Modelo de Gestión Integral de La Habana Vieja, Patrimonio de la Humanidad*. Havana: UNESCO La Habana and Plan Maestro (Oficina del Historiador del Ciudad).

Uriarte, Miren. 2002. *Cuba, Social Policy at a Crossroads: Maintaining Priorities, Transforming Practice*. Boston: Oxfam America.

——. 2008. "Rediscovering Lo Local: The Potential and the Limits of Local Development in Havana." In *The Changing Dynamic of Cuban Civil Society*, edited by Alexander I. Gray and Antoni Kapcia. Gainesville: University Press of Florida.

Valdés, Nelson P. 1997. "El Estado y la Transición en el Socialismo: Creando Nuevos Espacios en Cuba." *Temas* 9:101–11.

Vázquez Montalbán, Manuel. 1998. *Y Dios entró en La Habana*. Madrid: El País/Aguilar.

Vázquez Penelas, Aurora, and Minerva Cantero Zayas. 1998. "Rehabilitación habitacional y participación: Una visión desde Cayo Hueso." In *Desarrollo Urbano: Proyectos y Experiencias de Trabajo*, edited by Roberto Dávalos Domínguez and Alain Basail Rodríguez. Havana: Universidad de La Habana.

Vega Vega, Juan. 1986. *Comentarios a la Ley General de la Vivienda*. Havana: Editorial de Ciencias Sociales.

Vertov, Dziga. 1924. *On Kinopravda*. In *Kino-Eye: The Writings of Dziga Vertov*, edited by Annette Michelson and translated by Kevin O'Brien. Berkeley: University of California Press, 1995.

——. 1928. *The Man with the Movie Camera*. In *Kino-Eye: The Writings of Dziga Vertov*, edited by Annette Michelson and translated by Kevin O'Brien. Berkeley: University of California Press, 1995.

Vitier, Cintio. 1994. "La aventura de *Orígenes*." *La Gaceta de Cuba* 3:5.

WCED (World Commission on Environment and Development). 1987. *Our Common Future*. New York: Oxford University Press.

Weiss, Joaquín E. 1996. *La arquitectura colonial cubana: siglos XVI al XIX*. La Habana: Instituto Cubano del Libro.

Wenders, Wim, director and writer. 1999. *Buena Vista Social Club*. A Road Movies production in association with Kintop Pictures, ARTE, and ICAIC. Color, closed-captioned, Dolby color, Black & White, NTSC, 105 minutes.

Whitfield, Esther. 2002. "Autobiografía sucia: The Body Impolitic of *Trilogía sucia de La Habana*." *Revista de Estudios Hispánicos* 36, no. 2 (May): 329–51.

——. 2003. "Billetes buenos y falsos: El dinero en la reciente narrativa cubana." *Temas* 32 (January–March): 32–37.

——. 2008. *Cuban Currency: The Dollar and "Special Period" Fiction*. Minneapolis: University of Minnesota Press.

Wolfe, Lisa Reynolds. 2000. "Contesting the Global: Restoration and Neighborhood Identity in Old Havana." Paper delivered at the meeting of the Latin American Studies Association.

Woods, Shadrach. 1964. "Urban Environment: The Search for System." In *World Architecture* I, edited by John Donat, 150–55. London: Studio Vista.

Yassi, Annalee, Pedro Mas, Mariano Bonet, Robert B. Tate, Niurys Fernández, Jerry Spiegel, and Mayilee Pérez. 1999. "Applying an Ecosystem Approach to the Determinants of Health in Centro Habana." *Ecosystem Health* 5 (1): 3–19.

Zambrano, María. 1951. "Una metáfora de la esperanza: las ruinas." *Lyceum* 7, no. 26 (May): 9–11.

——. 1955. *El hombre y lo divino*. Mexico: Fondo de Cultura Económica.

Žižek, Slavoj. 2007. "The Dreams of Others." *In These Times*. May 18. http://www.inthesetimes.com/article/3183/.

EMMA ÁLVAREZ-TABÍO ALBO is an architect and the author of *Vida, mansión y muerte de la burguesía cubana* (Letras Cubanas, 1989) and *Invención de La Habana* (Casiopea, 2000).

ERIC FELIPE-BARKIN is a graduate of Brown University and Columbia University's Writing Division. He is the winner of a Weston Award and works as a translator, editor, filmmaker, and visual artist. He is from Palm Beach County, Florida.

ANKE BIRKENMAIER is assistant professor of Latin American and Caribbean literature at Indiana University, Bloomington. She is co-editor of *Cuba: un siglo de literatura* (Colibrí, 2004) and the author of *Alejo Carpentier y la cultura del surrealismo en América Latina* (Iberoamericana-Vervuert, 2006), which received the Latin American Studies Association's Premio Iberoamericano.

VELIA CECILIA BOBES is a Cuban sociologist residing in Mexico. She is a research professor at FLACSO and a specialist of Cuban topics. She is the author of *Los laberintos de la imaginación: Repertorio simbólico, identidades y actores del cambio social en Cuba* (El Colegio de México, 2000) and *La nación inconclusa: (Re)constituciones de la ciudadanía y el cambio social en Cuba* (Flacso México, 2007).

MARIO COYULA-COWLEY is an architect, urban designer, and critic. He is a Profesor de Mérito (university professor) at the Higher Polytechnic Institute José A. Echeverría (CUJAE) and has received numerous prizes, among them the National Prize of Architecture (2001) and the Habitat Prize (2004). In 2010 he was elected Académico de Mérito at the Cuban Academy of Sciences. He also is the former director of the School of Architecture, of the Architecture and Urban Planning Department, of the Group for Integral Development, and first president of Havana's Landmarks Commission. His coauthored *Havana: Two Faces of the Antillean Metropolis*, received the Choice prize in 1998 for relevant academic books in the United States.

PATRICIO DEL REAL is a Ph.D. candidate in architectural history and theory at GSAPP at Columbia University. His dissertation focuses on the construction of a Latin American imaginary through modern architecture during the early years of the Cold War. His second area of research engages contemporary vernacular practices, focusing on Havana, where he has also participated in the construction of informal structures. He has taught architecture since 1991 in the United States and Latin America. He was previously the director of the Clemson University Architecture Center in Barcelona.

ELISABETH ENENBACH has a master of arts in Latin American literature from Yale University. She is an editor and translator in New York City.

SUJATHA FERNANDES is an assistant professor of sociology at Queens College and the Graduate Center of the City University of New York. She is the author of *Cuba Represent! Cuban Arts, State Power, and the Making of New Revolutionary Cultures* (Duke University Press, 2006) and the book *Who Can Stop the Drums? Urban Social Movements in Chávez's Venezuela* (Duke, 2010).

JILL HAMBERG is an urban planner who teaches at Empire State College of the State University of New York (SUNY). She has written extensively about housing and urban planning in Cuba.

CECELIA LAWLESS is a senior lecturer in the Department of Romance Studies at Cornell University. She has published various articles on architectural manifestations in Latin American cinema and the book *Making Home in Havana* (2004).

JACQUELINE LOSS, an associate professor of Latin American literary and cultural studies at the University of Connecticut, is the author of *Cosmopolitanisms and Latin America: Against the Destiny of Place* (Palgrave, 2005) and the coeditor of *New Short Fiction from Cuba* (Northwestern, 2007). She is completing a book entitled "Dreaming in Russian: The Politics of Memory in Post-Soviet Cuban Culture."

ORLANDO LUIS PARDO LAZO is a writer, photographer, and blogger whose books include *Collage Karaoke* (Letras Cubanas, 2001), *Empezar de cero* (Extramuros, 2001), *Ipatrías* (Unicornio, 2005), *Mi nombre es William Saroyan* (Abril, 2006), and *Boring Home* (digitally domestic, 2009). He is editor of the online journals *The Revolution Evening Post* and *Lunes de Post Revolución* and of the photo-blog *Boring Home Utopics*. He lives in Havana.

ANTONIO JOSÉ PONTE is a poet, essayist, and narrator. He has published, among other titles, *Las comidas profundas* (Deleatur: Angers, 1997); *Asiento en las ruinas* (Sevilla: Renacimiento, 2005); *In the Cold of the Malecón and Other Stories* (City Lights Books, 2000); *Cuentos de todas partes del Imperio* (Deleatur, 2000); *Un seguidor de Montaigne mira La Habana/Las comidas profundas* (Verbum, 2001); *Contrabando de sombras* (Mondadori, 2002); *El libro perdido de los origenistas* (Renacimiento, 2004); *Un arte de hacer ruinas y otros cuentos* (Fondo de Cultura Económica, 2005); *La fiesta vigilada* (Anagrama, 2007); and *Villa Marista en plata. Arte, política, nuevas tecnologías* (Colibrí, 2010).

NICOLÁS QUINTANA (1925–2011) was an architect and, until 2010, professor at the School of Architecture at Florida International University. As a member of the International Congress for Modern Architecture (CIAM) in the 1950s he collaborated closely with the great modern masters of architecture: Le Corbusier, Sert, Gropius, and Rogers. Besides his fifty-four years of practice in Cuba, Venezuela, Puerto Rico, and the United States, he published essays and articles specializing in visual arts, architecture, and urbanism. He was a recipient of numerous national and international awards and recognitions.

JOSÉ QUIROGA is professor of Spanish and comparative literature at Emory University. He is the author of *Cuban Palimpsests* and *Tropics of Desire*, and his collection "The Havana Reader," co-edited with Francisco Morán, is forthcoming from Duke University Press.

LAURA REDRUELLO is an assistant professor at Manhattan College. She received her Ph.D. in Hispanic literature from Vanderbilt University. Her primary research interests are Cuban fiction and essay, film studies, and popular music.

RAFAEL ROJAS is a Cuban historian and essayist, and a professor of history at the Centro de Investigación y Docencia Económicas (CIDE) in Mexico City. He is the author of several books on intellectual history and politics in Cuba, Mexico, and Latin America, among them *Tumbas sin sosiego: Revolución, disidencia y exilio del intelectual cubano* (2006, Premio Anagrama), *Essays in Cuban Intellectual History* (2008), *El estante vacío* (2009), and *Las repúblicas del aire: Utopía y desencanto en la Revolución de Hispanoamérica* (2009, Premio Internacional de Ensayo Isabel Polanco).

JOSEPH L. SCARPACI is an independent scholar and adjunct professor of marketing at Virginia Tech in Blacksbury. He is the coauthor of *Cuban Landscapes: Heritage, Memory, and Place* (Guilford Press 2009), author of *Plazas and Barrios: Heritage Tourism in the Latin American Centro Histórico* (University of Arizona Press, 2005), and coauthor of *Havana: Two Faces of the Antillean Metropolis* (University of North Carolina Press, 2002).

ESTHER WHITFIELD is associate professor of comparative literature at Brown University. She is the author of *Cuban Currency: The Dollar and "Special Period" Fiction*; editor of a critical edition of Antonio José Ponte's *Un arte de hacer ruinas y otros cuentos*; and coeditor, with Jacqueline Loss, of *New Short Fiction from Cuba*.

Note: "f" indicates figure

Anke Birkenmaier is assistant professor
of Spanish, Indiana University.

Esther Whitfield is associate professor of
comparative literature, Brown University.

....

Library of Congress Cataloging-in-Publication Data
Havana beyond the ruins : cultural mappings
after 1989 / Anke Birkenmaier and
Esther Whitfield, editors.
p. cm.
Includes bibliographical references and index.
ISBN 978-0-8223-5052-1 (cloth : alk. paper)
ISBN 978-0-8223-5070-5 (pbk. : alk. paper)
1. Havana (Cuba)—Intellectual life. 2. Havana
(Cuba)—Civilization. 3. Post-communism—
Cuba. 4. City planning—Cuba—Havana.
I. Birkenmaier, Anke. II. Whitfield, Esther
Katheryn.
F1799.H35H383 2011
972.91'23—dc22
2011006307